JOURNAL FOR THE STUDY OF THE NEW TESTAMENT SUPPLEMENT SERIES
152

Executive Editor
Stanley E. Porter

Sheffield Academic Press

Conflict in the Miracle Stories

A Socio-Exegetical Study of Matthew 8 and 9

Evert-Jan Vledder

Journal for the Study of the New Testament
Supplement Series 152

Copyright © 1997 Sheffield Academic Press

Published by Sheffield Academic Press Ltd
Mansion House
19 Kingfield Road
Sheffield S11 9AS
England

Printed on acid-free paper in Great Britain
by Bookcraft Ltd
Midsomer Norton, Bath

British Library Cataloguing in Publication Data

A catalogue record for this book is available
from the British Library

ISBN 1-85075-699-6

CONTENTS

ACKNOWLEDGMENTS

Financial assistance from the following organizations is hereby acknowledged: *Stichting: Het Scholten–Cordes Fonds*, Aert Nesstraat 45, 3000 AM Rotterdam, The Netherlands; *Stichting 'Aanpakken'*, Jachtlaan 128, 7313 ED Apeldoorn, The Netherlands and *Stichting Zonneweelde*, Van Heenvlietlaan 416 IV, 1083 CS Amsterdam, The Netherlands. Opinions expressed in this study, or conclusions drawn, are those of the author and not necessarily those of these organizations.

ABBREVIATIONS

ATR	*Anglican Theological Review*
AusBR	*Australian Biblical Review*
BAGD	W. Bauer, W.F. Arndt, F.W. Gingrich and F.W. Danker, *Greek-English Lexicon of the New Testament*
BEvT	*Beiträge zur Evangelischen Theology*
BiLiSe	Bible and Literature Series
BJRL	*Bulletin of the John Rylands Library of Manchester*
BJS	*Brown Judaic Studies*
Br J Social	*British Journal of Sociology*
BTB	*Biblical Theology Bulletin*
BU	Biblische Untersuchungen
CBQ	*Catholic Biblical Quarterly*
EvT	*Evangelische Theologie*
ExpTim	*Expository Times*
FRLANT	Forschungen zur Religion und Literatur des Alten und Neuen Testaments
HNT	Handbuch zum Neuen Testament
HSRC	Human Science Research Council
HTKNT	Herders theologischer Kommentar zum Neuen Testament
HTR	*Harvard Theological Review*
HTS	*Hervormde Teologiese Studies*
HTS Suppl	*Hervormde Teologiese Studies*, Supplement
HUCA	*Hebrew Union College Annual*
Int	*Interpretation*
JAAR	*Journal of the American Academy of Religion*
JBL	*Journal of Biblical Literature*
J Confl Res	*Journal of Conflict Resolution*
JETS	*Journal of the Evangelical Theology Society*
JRH	*Journal of Religious History*
JSJ	*Journal for the Study of Judaism in the Persian, Hellenistic and Roman Period*
JSNT	*Journal for the Study of the New Testament*
JSNTSup	*Journal for the Study of the New Testament*, Supplement Series
JTS	*Journal of Theological Studies*
LV	*Lumen Vitae*
LWF.D	*Lutheran World Federation Documentation*

Neot	*Neotestamentica*
NTD	Das Neue Testament Deutsch
NovT	*Novum Testamentum*
NTS	*New Testament Studies*
RNT	Regensburger Neues Testament
SBL	Society of Biblical Literature
SBLDS	SBL Dissertation Series
SBLSP	SBL Seminar Papers
SBS	Stuttgarter Bibelstudien
Social Forc	*Social Forces*
ThEv(SA)	*Theologica Evangelica: Pretoria*
THKNT	Theologischer Handkommentar zum Neuen Testament
TQ	*Theological Quarterly*
TS	*Theological Studies*
TynBul	*Tyndale Bulletin*
UBS	United Bible Societies
WdF	Wege der Forschung
ZNW	*Zeitschrift für die neutestamentliche Wissenschaft*
ZTK	*Zeitschrift für Theologie und Kirche*

INTRODUCTION

> In all times the discussion about the miracle problem presents itself anew,
> and therefore was never laid to rest.[1]

Through the ages there has always been a great fascination with the
wonderful and the miraculous. Whether concerning the miracles of
Jesus, or miracles in their broadest sense, it has always remained a fas-
cinating topic in both popular and academic discussion.[2] The interest in
miracles over the ages is clearly illustrated in the historical study of
Brown.[3] He has done a comprehensive survey of the way miracles were
perceived through the centuries.[4] I personally share this age-old and
lively interest and wish to contribute to the discussion. More specifically I wish to contribute to the discusson on the miracle stories in
Matthew 8 and 9 because of its neglected character (see Chapter 1
below).[5]

1. A. Suhl, 'Einleitung', in A. Suhl (ed.), *Der Wunderbegriff im Neuen Testament* (WdF, CCXCV; Darmstadt: Wissenschaftliche Buchgesellschaft, 1980), p. 1.
2. See for example the short and popular article of S. Freyne, 'Query: Did Jesus
Really Work Miracles?', *The Furrow* 26.5 (1975), pp. 283-86; the popular works of
D.J. Smit, 'Die Prediking van die Wonderverhale in die Evangelies', in C.W.
Burger, B.A. Müller and D.J. Smit (eds.), *Riglyne vir prediking oor die gelykenisse
en wonderverhale* (Woord teen die Lig, II/2; Kaapstad: NG Kerk-Uitgewers, 1987),
pp. 201-24 and K. McCaslin, *What the Bible Says about Miracles* (What the Bible
Says Series; Joplin: College Press, 1988), and the thorough academic works of H.
Van der Loos, *The Miracles of Jesus* (Leiden: Brill, 1968); Suhl, *Der Wunderbegriff
im Neuen Testament*; C. Brown, *Miracles and the Critical Mind* (Grand Rapids:
Eerdmans, 1984) and A. Van de Beek, *Wonderen en Wonderverhalen* (Nijkerk:
Callenbach, 1991)—to name but a few.
3. Brown, *Miracles and the Critical Mind*.
4. Cf. W.L. Craig, 'Colin Brown, Miracles and the Critical Mind: A Review
Article', *JETS* 27.4 (1984), pp. 473-85 (473) and E.J. Vledder, ''n Kritiese evaluasie
van Colin Brown se studie: "Miracles and the Critical Mind"', *HTS* 42.2 (1986),
pp. 327-38 (327).
5. See U. Luz, *Das Evangelium nach Matthäus. II. (Mt 8-17)* (EKK, I/2;
Zürich: Benzinger, Verlag 1990), p. 147.

In essence this book will be a socio-exegetical study. It cannot be said better than in the words of Elliott:

> The method is *sociological* in that it involves the employment of the perspectives, presuppositions, modes of analysis, comparative models, theories and research of the discipline of sociology [conflict theory]. It is *exegetical* in that it focuses centrally upon a biblical document [Matthew 8 and 9; his emphasis].[6]

The general aim of this socio-exegetical study is the analysis and the interpretation of conflict in the text of Matthew 8 and 9 and, more particularly, the conflict between Jesus (and the Matthean community) and the Jewish leaders.

There is no doubt that conflict in the Gospel of Matthew has been investigated before (see Chapter 1). The implied reader is constantly made aware of the tension in the text. The emphasis here, however, will be more on the *dynamics* of conflict. How does conflict 'work' and why are people in conflict? I intend to use conflict theory, to develope this theory (see Chapter 3) on a relatively high level of abstraction. My aim thus is to offer a systematic way of organizing the information on conflict in order to focus attention on the social structures and their processes. Furthermore I intend to provide the necessary interpretive framework and theoretical jargon to investigate the conflict. The basic question is: 'Why is there conflict between Jesus and the leaders?'

As a model, I have put forward five basic statements:

(1)   All conflicts are essentially conflicts of class/group *interests.* All human activities are driven by the drive to maximize one's own interests.

(2)   Closely related to the above is the urge to *survive.*

(3)   In basically all societies/groups there are those who in terms of *power and authority* are in positions of either domination or subordination.

(4)   Conflict almost always brings about *change.*

(5)   Conflict is *always present as a never ending spiral.*

The thesis is that, according to Matthew, Jesus was in conflict with the Jewish leaders because of their opposing interests. The leaders acted on

6.   J.H. Elliott, *A Home for the Homeless: A Social-scientific Criticism of I Peter: Its Situation and Strategy* (Minneapolis: Fortress Press, 1990), p. 8.

behalf of the Roman rulers as retainers, and therefore ignored the interests of the marginalized. Jesus (and the Matthean community) acted on behalf of the marginalized, the lowest classes of society. The community challenged the authority of the Jewish leaders because it was in the process of leaving Judaism and departing from the sphere of authority of the leaders. This was perceived by them as a threat to their position. Furthermore, the community challenged the dormant values of the leaders to forgive and to act mercifully, that is, to act in the interests of the marginalized (which the leaders did not do). The conflict is resolved in an negative way in Mt. 9.34 by the epithet that Jesus was possessed by the devil (by implication this also applies to the community). At the same time the conflict has the potential to go further and challenge the leaders of the community themselves to act in the interests of the marginalized, which I call: 'to become voluntarily marginalized'.

I am aware of the fact that any model unavoidably both obscures *and* reveals. Any model helps us focus on specific aspects and leads to the downplay (or neglect) of others.[7] We only know a part of the actuality when using a model. It specifies only those aspects of the situation on which it focuses. Alternative aspects are often left out of account.[8] Or, as Carney says: 'One cannot consider other issue areas or other viewpoints once within the framework of his model's terms of reference.'[9] My attention is selective and limited, although I have attempted to be methodical and structured in thought—and I am conscious of my viewpoint!—I hope to be stimulating and relevant. Rohrbaugh says that each time a text is read by a new reader, the field of reference tends to shift and multiply because each new reader fills in the text in a unique way.[10] This is often called 'recontextualization'. This refers to the multiple ways different readers may 'complete' a text as a result of reading it from a different social location. This book is thus an own attempt at such a 'recontextualization'.

To achieve the above aim, this book is arranged in five chapters: Chapter 1 will be a short accounting of social-scientific criticism,

7. Cf. J. Powell, 'Social Theory as Exegetical Tool', *Foundations & Facets Forum* 5.4 (1989), pp. 27-40 (28).

8. Cf. T.F. Carney, *The Shape of the Past: Models and Antiquity* (Lawrence: Coronado Press, 1975), p. 12.

9. Carney, *The Shape of the Past*, p. 34.

10. R.L. Rohrbaugh, 'Social Science and Literary Criticism: What is at Stake?', *HTS* 49.1 and 2 (1993), pp. 221-33 (229).

conflict theory and the use of the model as template and heuristic tool. Furthermore, different scholars will be investigated in terms of their views on the marginalized and their use and explication (or not) of conflict. The aim of this chapter is to account for the epistemological and methodological assumptions, and an attempt will be made to account for the specific contribution I wish to make with regard to Matthew 8 and 9.

In Chapter 2, conflict theory is set against structural functionalism. The latter is unable to explain conflict and coercion in society sufficiently, whereas conflict theory does. An own synthesis is developed, predominantly from the theories of L.A. Coser and R. Dahrendorf. The above-mentioned five statements are derived from this particular chapter.

In between the high level of abstraction on a macro-level (conflict theory; Chapter 2) and the text to be interpreted on a micro-level (Matthew 8 and 9; Chapter 4), Chapter 3 is placed to act on a 'meso-level' and to bring these two poles together. In Chapter 3 the social location of the Matthean community is investigated in terms of the so-called *intra* and *extra muros* debate, that is, was the community still part of Judaism or were they totally on their own? In any case, the community is still related to formative Judaism. It will be argued that they were not on their own yet, but were in a process of parting from Judaism.

The implications of Chapters 2 and 3 are applied to the text of Matthew 8 and 9. Chapter 4 is the exegetical part of the study. Emphasis is placed on the plot as it unfolds in terms of time and causality. Background information and insights from other commentaries are utilized to further highlight the conflict.

All the loose ends are tied up in Chapter 5. The findings of the study are implemented in terms of the five statements: interests, survival, power and authority, change, and the never-ending potentiality of conflict.

Chapter 1

CONFLICT IN THE MIRACLE STORIES INADEQUATELY EXPLAINED

In recent years the miracle stories of the Gospel of Matthew have rather been a step-child of the research.[1]

Introduction

Miracles and miracle stories have been investigated in the past from a number of different approaches.[2] They can be approached from a *form critical* perspective;[3] a *Religionsgeschichtliche*-perspective;[4] the

1. U. Luz, 'Wundergeschichten von Mt 8-9', in G.F. Hawthorne and O. Betz (eds.), *Tradition and Interpretation in the New Testament: Essays in Honor of E. Earle Ellis for His 60th Birthday* (Grand Rapids: Eerdmans, 1987), pp. 149-65 (147).

2. See E.J. Vledder, 'Conflict in the Miracle Stories in Matthew 8 and 9: A Sociological and Exegetical Study' (DD dissertation; Pretoria: University of Pretoria, 1994), pp. 5-12.

3. See R. Bultmann, *Die Geschichte der synoptischen Tradition* (FRLANT, 29; Göttingen: Vandenhoeck & Ruprecht, 7th edn, 1967); M. Dibelius, *Die Formgeschichte des Evangeliums* (Tübingen: Mohr, 6th edn, 1971); G. Theissen, *Urchristliche Wundergeschichten: Ein Beitrag zur formgeschichtlichen Erforschung der synoptischen Evangelien* (StNT, 8; Gütersloh: Gütersloher Verlaghaus, 1974); H.D. Betz, 'The Early Christian Miracle Story: Some Observations on the Form Critical Problem', *Semeia* 11 (1978), pp. 69-81; R.W. Funk, 'The Form of the New Testament Healing Miracle Story', *Semeia* 12 (1978), pp. 57-96.

4. See the works of H. Köster, 'One Jesus and Four Primitive Gospels', *HTR* 61 (1968), pp. 203-47; H. Köster, 'Grundtypen und Kriterien frühchristlicher Glaubensbekenntnisse', in H. Köster and J.M. Robinson (eds.), *Entwicklungslinien durch die Welt des frühen Christentums* (Tübingen: Mohr, 1971); P.J. Achtemeier, 'Gospel Miracle Tradition and the Divine Man', *Int* 26 (1972), pp. 174-97; D.L. Tiede, *The Charismatic Figure as Miracle Worker* (SBLDS, 1; Missoula, MT: Scholars Press, 1972); G. Petzke, 'Historizität und Bedeutsamkeit von Wunderberichten: Möglichkeiten und Grenzen des religionsgeschichtliche Vergleichs', in H.D. Betz and L. Schotroff (eds.), *Neues Testament und christliche Existenz:*

perspective of *Redaktionsgeschichte*;[5] or from the narrative viewpoint.[6] One could furthermore try to determine the historicity of the miracles (*wie es eigentlich gewesen ist*),[7] or attempt to answer the question of the probability/possibility of the miracles, depending on what one defines as a miracle.[8]

However, I have not opted for any of these approaches. Not that they are of no value; it is simply that the 'newer' social-scientific approach with regard to the miracle stories has not yet been explored to its full potential, especially in as far as conflict theory is concerned (see below for more detail on this). Therefore, I have chosen the social-scientific method.

Festschrift für H Braun (Tübingen: Mohr, 1973), pp. 347-85; J.M. Hull, *Hellenistic Magic and the Synoptic Tradition* (London: SCM, 1974); C.H. Holladay, *Theios Anér in Hellenistic Judaism: A Critique of the Use of this Category in New Testament Christology* (SBLDS, 40; Missoula, MT: Scholars Press, 1977); Betz, 'The Early Christian Miracle Story', pp. 69-81; M. Smith, *Jesus the Magician* (London: Gollancz, 1978); P.H. Menoud, 'Die Bedeutung des Wunders nach dem Neuen Testament', in A. Suhl (ed.), *Der Wunderbegriff im Neuen Testament* (WdF, CCXCV; Darmstadt: Wissenschaftliche Buchgesellschaft, 1980), pp. 279-99; H.C. Kee, *Miracles in the Early Christian World: A Study in Socio-historical Method* (New Haven: Yale University Press, 1983).

5.   See the works of H.J. Held, 'Matthew as Interpreter of the Miracle Stories', in G. Bornkamm, G. Barth and H.J. Held (eds.), *Tradition and Interpretation in Matthew* (trans. P. Scott; London: SCM, 1963), pp. 165-299 (165-211); A. Suhl, 'Die Wunder Jesu: Ereignis und Überlieferung', in Suhl, *Der Wunderbegriff im Neuen Testament*, pp. 464-509.

6.   See S.M. Praeder, 'Miracle Stories in Christian Antiquity: Some Narrative Elements', *Foundation & Facets Forum* 2.4 (1986), pp. 43-54; J. Engelbrecht, 'Trends in Miracle Research', *Neot* 22 (1988), pp. 139-61 (153).

7.   See the works of Kee, *Miracles in the Early Christian World*, pp. 1-41; E.J. Vledder, 'Die rol van "historisiteit" in die kommunikasie van die wondervertelling: Evaluasie van twee eksegetiese benaderinge', *HTS* 40.2 (1984), pp. 71-119 (84).

8.   See J.M. Court, 'The Philosophy of the Synoptic Miracles', *JTS* 23.1 (1972), pp. 1-15 (2); M. Bastin, 'Jesus Worked Miracles: Texts from Matthew 8', *LV* 39.2 (1984), pp. 131-39 (132); Brown, *Miracles and the Critical Mind*, p. 7; J. Engelbrecht, 'Wonders in die Nuwe Testament', *ThEv(SA)* 17.3 (1984), pp. 4-11 (5); Engelbrecht, 'Trends in Miracle Research', p. 140; Vledder, 'Die rol van "historisiteit" in die kommunikasie van die wondervertelling', p. 79. See also Bultmann's own peculiar way of dealing with the problem of the historicity/possibility of the miracles: R. Bultmann, 'Zur Frage des Wunders', in R. Bultmann, *Glauben und Verstehen* (4 vols.; Tübingen: Mohr, 1958), I, pp. 215-28.

Epistemological and Methodological Orientation

The aim of this section is to place my work within the sphere of the so-called social-scientific approach.

The Social-Scientific Approach

There exists a perception that the *Formgeschichte* (and historical criticism as a whole) has failed to lay bare the *Sitz-im-Leben* of New Testament texts. However, in the last two decades there has been a renewed interest in the so-called social sciences.[9] It is not that historical criticism has been totally abandoned and is now regarded as worthless. The social-scientific approach, as Elliott puts it: '... is an *expansion*, not a replacement, of the conventional historical-critical method. It *complements* the other subdisciplines of the exegetical enterprise.'[10] Of course, sociological data have previously been taken into account, but a sociological (social-scientific) approach attempts to do more. Says Elliott:

> Social data have been used often merely to 'round out the picture', illustrating or clarifying literary or theological conclusions already formulated. What is needed is a procedure for appropriating and applying sociological models and concepts which at each stage of exegetical analysis could aid our understanding and interpretation of the interrelation of literary, theological and sociological aspects and dimensions of composition.[11]

Malina also, in choosing between a social-scientific and historical-critical method, states, 'In sum, social science methods can offer biblical interpretation adequate sophistication in determining and articulating the social systems behind the texts under investigation.'[12] This is also

---

9. Cf. R. Scroggs, 'The Sociological Interpretation of the New Testament: The Present State of Research', in N.K. Gottwald (ed.), *The Bible and Liberation: Political and Social Hermeneutics* (Maryknoll: Orbis Books, 1983), pp. 337-56 (339); Kee, *Miracles in the Early Christian World*, p. 290; P. Van Staden and A.G. Van Aarde, 'Social Description or Social-scientific Interpretation? A Survey of Modern Scholarship', *HTS* 47.1 (1991), pp. 55-87 (56); S.J. Joubert, ''n Verruimende invalshoek tot die verlede? Die sosiaal-wetenskaplike benadering tot die Nuwe Testament', *HTS* 47.1 (1991), pp. 39-54 (40).

10. Elliott, *A Home for the Homeless*, p. xix.

11. Elliott, *A Home for the Homeless*, p. 3.

12. B. Malina, 'The Social Sciences and Biblical Interpretation', in Gottwald (ed.), *The Bible and Liberation*, pp. 11-25 (21).

true of the miracle stories, and thus I also wish to take the social sciences
as my starting point, because the full potential with regard to the miracle stories of Jesus has not yet been explored. In fact, the question of
the sociological function of the miracle stories in the New Testament
has long been neglected in favour of an historical-critical approach.[13]

But, even within the broader field of the *social-scientific* criticism,
choices have to be made. There seems to be broad consensus that there
exist two fundamentally different points of departure within this
method, which are easily confused.[14] An overall distinction is made
between *socio-historical* (or *social description*), and *social-scientific
analysis*.

Social Description. The socio-historical or *social descriptive approach*
(hereafter called the latter), provides us with the broad background to
the New Testament period and the early church. Its focus is description rather than analysis.[15] Van Staden explains this approach as follows: 'A social description *accumulates* data that it regards as relevant
in order to contribute to the historical understanding of the background of the New Testament texts or text segments... When needed,
pieces of the amassed information are fitted together like a jigsaw
puzzle.'[16] A good example of a social description of the miracles as

13.   Cf. Engelbrecht, 'Trends in Miracle Research', p. 150.
14.   Cf. Scroggs, 'The Sociological Interpretation of the New Testament', p. 341;
Malina, 'The Social Sciences and Biblical Interpretation', p. 11; W.R. Domeris,
'Social Scientific Study of Early Christian Churches: New Paradigms and Old
Questions', in J. Mouton, A.G. Van Aarde and W.S. Vorster (eds.), *Paradigms and
Progress in Theology* (HSRC Studies in Research Methodology, 5; Pretoria: HSRC,
1988), pp. 378-93 (379); J. Botha, 'Socio-historiese en sosiologiese interpretasie
van die Nuwe Testament', *Koers* 54.4 (1989), pp. 480-508 (485); C. Osiek, 'The
New Handmaid: The Bible and the Social Sciences', *TS* 50 (1989), pp. 260-78 (269);
P. Van Staden, *Compassion—The Essence of Life: A Social-scientific Study of the
Religious Symbolic Universe Reflected in the Ideology/Theology of Luke* (HTS
Suppl., 4, Pretoria: Tydskrifafdeling van die Nederduitsch Hervormde Kerk, 1991),
p. 32; Van Staden and Van Aarde, 'Social Description or Social-scientific Interpretation?' pp. 56-60.
15.   Cf. Domeris, 'Social Scientific Study of Early Christian Churches', pp. 379-
80; see also Botha, 'Socio-historiese en Sosiologiese Interpretasie van die Nuwe
Testament', p. 485.
16.   Van Staden, *Compassion—The Essence of Life*, p. 32.

such, is to be found in the works of Kee.[17] Another scholar who deals with the sociological functions of the miracles is Gerd Theissen.[18] But since his work has some implications for this study, it will be dealt with separately in the part on 'Conflict as phenomenon, studied in relation to the Gospel of Matthew' (see below).

The social description method is highly compatible and useful to my study, and I will make use of some of the results 'filling in the gaps' or 'rounding out the picture'. However, I will not use this approach as a point of departure and method of research, for it does not appropriately address the *dynamics* of the social conflict that is present in Matthew 8 and 9. I will, in fact, use the perspective of *social-scientific criticism* instead.

Social-Scientific Criticism. The 'sociological approach/analysis' refers to the implementation of methods of analysis and research based on epistemologies relevant to the social sciences. It '. . . abstracts data in the sense of unearthing, *making explicit* what is buried and implicit in the narrative discourse' (my emphasis).[19] To a certain extent, this approach builds on the data of the historian, but much more emphasis is placed on the underlying *dynamics* of the societies, and questions asked are: What type of interactions took place and what kind of conflicts emerged? By understanding these dynamics, we are able to grasp the relations within the texts and perhaps also the texts themselves.[20]

But when one enters the field of the so-called *social-scientific criticism*, a few more choices have to be made. Scroggs distinguishes the following fields: Typologies, cognitive dissonance, role analysis, sociology of knowledge and Marxist interpretation.[21] Domeris extends this list to include the use of normative dissonance, legitimation of power struggles, cultural anthropology, and Mary Douglas's group/grid model.[22]

17.   Kee, *Miracles in the Early Christian Worl; idem, Medicine, Miracle & Magic in New Testament Times* (Cambridge: Cambridge University Press, 1986).

18.   Theissen, *Urchristliche Wundergeschichten*, pp. 229-61.

19.   Van Staden, *Compassion—The Essence of Life*, p. 33.

20.   Cf. Scroggs, 'The Sociological Interpretation of the New Testament', p. 337; see also Botha, 'Socio-historiese en sosiologiese interpretasie van die Nuwe Testament', p. 485.

21.   Scroggs, 'The Sociological Interpretation of the New Testament', pp. 344-56.

22.   Domeris, 'Social Scientific Study of Early Christian Churches', p. 383; see

Also Elliott,[23] with Malina, includes sociology, anthropology, economics, sociolinguistics and semiotics all as related subdisciplines in the field of the social sciences. But, to me, the most comprehensive and systematized (and standardized) overview of the social sciences in relation to the New Testament, comes from Van Staden. He states,

> Even the names given to the exegetical subdiscipline devoted to this branch of exegesis—Sociology of the New Testament—is a misnomer, since it promotes terminological confusion by using as umbrella term a word that has become associated with a specific discipline in the field of the social sciences, namely sociology. This exegetical subdiscipline does not make use of sociology alone, but of other disciplines in the field of the social sciences as well, namely anthropology and psychology.[24]

also Botha, 'Socio-historiese en Sosiologiese Interpretasie van die Nuwe Testament', p. 495.

23. Elliott, *A Home for the Homeless*, p. xix.

24. Van Staden, *Compassion—The Essence of Life*, p. 112; see also Van Staden, *Compassion—The Essence of Life*, pp.113-14 for more on the subdivisions. A psychological investigation into the miracle stories of the New Testament is done by Scheffler (E.H. Scheffler, 'Jesus from a Psychological Perspective', *Neot* 29.2 [1995], pp. 299-312). Den Heyer mentions the work of E. Drewermann, *Tiefenpsychologie und Exegese* in this regard (C.J. den Heyer, *Opniew: Wie is Jezus? Balans van 150 jaar onderzoek naar Jezus* [Zoetermeer: Meinema, 1996], pp. 170, 174 n. 35).

Pilch has done (cultural) anthropological studies on the miracles and the health care systems in Matthew and Luke (J.J. Pilch, 'The Health Care System in Matthew: A Social Science Analysis', *BTB* 16.3 [1986], pp. 102-106; Understanding Biblical Healing: Selecting the Appropriate Model', *BTB* 18.2 [1988], pp. 60-66; 'Reading Matthew Anthropologically: Healing in Cultural Perspective', *Listening* 24 [1989], pp. 278-89; 'Sickness and Healing in Luke–Acts', in J.N. Neyrey [ed.], *The Social World of Luke–Acts: Models for Interpretation* [Peabody, MA: Hendrickson, 1991], pp. 181-210; 'Insights and Models for Understanding the Healing Activity of the Historical Jesus', in E.H. Lovering [ed.], *SBL: Seminar Papers 1993* [Atlanta: Scholars Press, 1993], pp. 154-77; See also Joubert, ''n Verruimende invalshoek tot die verlede?', p. 47). The health care system and consequently also the miracles are not to be viewed from our modern bio-medical models (as opposed to the study of Hengel & Hengel [R. Hengel and M. Hengel, 'Die Heilung Jesu und Medizinisches Denken', in Suhl [ed.], *Der Wunderbegriff im Neuen Testament*, pp. 338-73). Rather they have to be viewed as part of the total wellbeing of the person, and the sick are seen as culturally appropriate wellbeings. They have to be interpreted in terms of the three symbolic corporate zones: (1) heart/eyes, (2) mouth/ears, and (3) hands/feet (cf. Pilch, 'Reading Matthew Anthropologically', p. 283).

For my part, I wish to do a *social-scientific* study, taking the models from the subdiscipline of sociology.[25]

But, once 'inside' sociology, still another choice has to be made. At a high level of abstraction, there are three different main theoretical perspectives within the social sciences which one might use to understand social interaction. They are called *structural functionalism*,[26] the *conflict/coercion theory*[27] and *symbolic interactionism*.[28] My choice is to focus on conflict theory in more detail as an appropriate model to investigate the existing conflict in the text. More attention will be given to structural functionalism in comparison with the conflict model in Chapter 3 below.

25.   I am aware of the criticism of S.J. Joubert, 'Much Ado about Nothing? In Discussion with the Study of Evert-Jan Vledder: "Conflict in the Miracle Stories in Matthew 8 and 9: A Sociological and Exegetical Study"', *HTS* 51.1 (1995), pp. 245-53 (248) that a more nuanced use of social-scientific terminology should be made. However, I take this 'unnuanced' stand, because it illustrates my point of departure as being not at all from the so-called social anthropology, but from *sociology* as such. I do not wish to dive too deep into methodological matters.

26.   Cf. M. Haralambos, *Sociology: Themes and Perspectives* (Slough: University Tutorial Press, 1980), pp. 9-19, 521-59; C. Osiek, 'The New Handmaid, p. 272; Van Staden, *Compassion—The Essence of life*, p. 114-43; Joubert, '"n Verruimende Invalshoek tot die Verlede?', p. 48. At the basis of structural functionalism is the view that a society is constantly in equilibrium, that is, in good balance. Society is viewed as cohesive and integrated through consensus on meaning, values and norms. The society is held together by means of core values (cf. Malina, 'The Social Sciences and Biblical Interpretation', p. 16; see also Haralambos, *Sociology*, p. 9).

27.   Conflict models explain social systems in terms of various groups which are in constant conflict with each other in order to maximize their own interests and goals (cf. Malina, 'The Social Sciences and Biblical Interpretation', p. 17; see also Joubert, '"n Verruimende invalshoek tot die verlede?', p. 48. Note that Haralambos [Haralambos, *Sociology*, pp. 12 and 534] calls conflict theory 'Marxism'. But this is not entirely correct. Conflict theory to a certain extent is based on the insights of Marx, but is not entirely the same as 'Marxism' [see Chapter 2 for more on conflict theory]).

28.   Symbolic interactionism focuses on systems of symbols that consist of persons, things and events, which have unique reality because of their perceived symbolic meaning. 'It supposes that human individual and group behaviour is organized around the symbolic meaning and expectations that are attached to objects that are socially valued' (Malina, 'The Social Sciences and Biblical Interpretation', p. 18; see also Van Staden, *Compassion—The Essence of Life*, p. 132).

A Model

How to Use a Model

Since the introduction of social-scientific criticism some two decades ago, there have always been objections, most of which are quite well known by now. The critique against social-scientific criticism as a whole, is valid also in respect of conflict theory, which, as indicated previously, forms part of this approach. Some objections have to a large extent been overcome in the course of time, but a few stubborn (and legitimate) ones still remain, and require specific attention. Therefore, the aim of this section will be to account for the way in which conflict theory will be used as a *model*, in an attempt to overcome some of the strong reservations about social-scientific criticism, and conflict theory in particular.

In an early article on the sociological approach, originally published in 1980, Scroggs indicated a few problems confronting sociological analysis.[29] Since then, many have built and elaborated on this.[30] The first difficulty was that of *methodology*. The second objection was the *problem of the data*. A third objection to the social-scientific approach was the *problem of reductionism*.[31] But these early objections to the social-scientific approach, which are still being raised, can to my mind now be laid to rest. This is so, especially if one weighs the advantages and contributions of the method against its disadvantages, and if one sees the steady flow of literature on the subject produced over the last two decades.[32] One can assume that it is already a strongly vested

29. Scroggs, 'The Sociological Interpretation of the New Testament', p. 339.

30. Cf. Malina, 'The Social Sciences and Biblical Interpretation', pp, 19-21; O.G. Harris, 'The Social World of Early Christianity', *Lexington Theological Quarterly* 19.3 (1984), pp. 102-14 (112); C. Rowland, 'Reading the New Testament Sociologically: An Introduction', *Theology* 88 (1985), pp. 358-64 (362); Osiek, 'The New Handmaid', p. 276; *idem*, 'The Social Sciences and the Second Testament: Problems and Challenges', *BTB* 22.2 (1992), pp. 89-95 (89); see also Vledder, 'Conflict in the Miracle Stories in Matthew 8 and 9', pp. 18-19.

31. Cf. Scroggs, 'The Sociological Interpretation of the New Testament', p. 340; Malina, 'The Social Sciences and Biblical Interpretation', p. 19; Harris, 'The Social World of Early Christianity', p. 112; Rowland, 'Reading the New Testament Sociologically', p. 362; Osiek, 'The New Handmaid', p. 276, 'The Social Sciences and the Second Testament', p. 89.

32. See the review article of Joubert, ''n Verruimende invalshoek tot die Verlede?', pp. 39-54.

approach, already accepted as an important complement to other approaches, such as historical criticism.[33] As for the advantages, one can agree with Osiek that social-scientific criticism makes an important contribution to the interpretive venture.[34]

There are, however, two other major pitfalls to account for: the charge of *ethnocentrism* and more specifically that of *anachronism*. Judge calls these charges the *sociological fallacy*.[35] The problem of anachronism (and ethnocentrism) evolves from the fact that there is a historical distance between the subject and the object. There is no possibility for live observation, while the original focus of sociology was the observance of life cultures.[36] Is it really valid to apply models, composed by modern people (often for modern societies) on ancient cultures? Is it valid to transfer data from contemporary cultures (Western or non-Western) to ancient Mediterranean cultures? This applies in particular to conflict theory in the way it will be used in this study, for one of the major contributors to this theory, namely Dahrendorf,[37] postulated the theory of conflict to be applied to modern industrial societies. Is it possible to apply this modern conflict theory to a pre-industrial society or a pre-industrial text like Matthew 8 and 9? If so, what do we have to take into account?

With regard to the charge of anachronism, the aim should be to account for the *use* of conflict theory as a *model* in order to try to argue and demonstrate the commensurability of this theory to the data.[38] The applicability of modern conflict theory to an ancient text, needs to be demonstrated and not assumed and therefore we need to account for the way in which models are used.[39] Not only the use of the model

---

33.   Cf. Elliott, *A Home for the Homeless*, p. xix.

34.   Osiek, 'The New Handmaid', p. 277.

35.   E.A. Judge, 'The Social Identity of the First Christians: A Question of Method in Religious History', *JRH* 11 (1980), pp. 201-17 (206); see also P.F. Craffert, 'More on Models and Muddles in Social-scientific Interpretation of the New Testament: The *Sociological Fallacy* Reconsidered', *Neot* 26.1 (1992), pp. 217-39 (217); Rohrbaugh, 'Social Science and Literary Criticism, p. 227.

36.   Cf. Osiek, 'The New Handmaid', p. 275.

37.   R. Dahrendorf, *Class and Class Conflict in Industrial Society* (Stanford: Stanford University Press, 1959).

38.   Cf. Craffert, 'More on Models and Muddles in Social-scientific Interpretation of the New Testament', p. 229.

39.   Cf. J. Powell, 'Social Theory as Exegetical Tool', p. 35, in his critique

but also the 'level of abstraction' on which the model is used, must be accounted for.[40] This will not eliminate anachronism for even the explicit and conscious use of models, as Craffert has correctly indicated, '. . . does not necessarily prevent anachronism or ethnocentric interpretation, since the way models function is determined by preferences which are not implicit in the model themselves'.[41] It could, however, contribute to the narrowing of the historical gap, or limit (not eliminate[42]) the charge of anachronism.

A Model as Heuristic Tool

It is hard to imagine any interpretation without the use of a theory or model. Quite a large amount of literature on what models are, and why they are needed, has emerged.[43] With regard to what a model is, most of these writings are based on the thorough work of Carney.[44]

There is no doubt that one *needs* models to understand reality. Says Rohrbaugh: 'Human perception is selective, limited, culture-bound and prone to be unaware that it is any or all of the above. The cognitive maps with which we select, sort and categorize complex data interpose themselves between events and our interpretation of them whether we like it or not.'[45] Reality comes to us as a complex configuration of data which should be controlled. We need to sort, select, categorize, compare, generalize and synthesize the detail (and sometimes the chaos) of

against R.A. Horsley, *Jesus and the Spiral of Violence: Popular Jewish Resistance in Roman Palestine* (San Francisco: Harper & Row, 1987), p. 85.

40. Cf. Osiek, 'The Social Sciences and the Second Testament', p 90.

41. Craffert, 'More on Models and Muddles in Social-scientific Interpretation of the New Testament', p. 226.

42. See Vledder, 'Conflict in the Miracle Stories in Matthew 8 and 9', pp. 21-22.

43. See Carney, *The Shape of the Past*; Scroggs, 'The Sociological Interpretation of the New Testament'; Malina, 'The Social Sciences and Biblical Interpretation'; J.H. Elliott, 'Social-scientific Criticism of the New Testament: More on Methods and Models', *Semeia* 35 (1986), pp. 1-33; R.L. Rohrbaugh, 'Models and Muddles: Discussions of the Social Facets Seminar', *Foundations & Facets Forum* 3.2 (1987), pp. 23-33; Powell, 'Social Theory as Exegetical Tool'; Osiek, 'The New Handmaid'; *idem* 'The Social Sciences and the Second Testament'; B. Holmberg, *Sociology and the New Testament: An Appraisal* (Minneapolis: Fortress Press, 1990); Van Staden, *Compassion—The Essence of Life*; Craffert, 'More on Models and Muddles in Social-scientific Interpretation of the New Testament'.

44. Carney, *The Shape of the Past*.

45. Rohrbaugh, 'Models and Muddles', p 23.

reality in order to be able to understand and control it. Otherwise, the data (and reality) is likely to control us.[46] Models are needed '. . . to enable us to cope with a complex configuration of data by screening out those which are too big or too small to be appropriately considered and by focusing on a specific aspect or level therein. . . As a model is necessarily so selective, it can be an approximation to reality.'[47] In order to handle this complex reality and the associated data, we tend to 'chunk' or abstract similarities and, as Malina says: '. . . thus reduce the number of items being dealt with.'[48] It seems that human beings cannot make sense of their experiences and their world without making models of it and without thinking in terms of abstract representations of it. By models we establish the meaning of what we want to see.[49] As Carney says: 'Models save us from mental or decision overload.'[50]

What, then is a model? It is a filtering process, it is the presentation of an organizational framework.[51] A model is defined thus: 'A model presents us with a general framework or generalization of complex social data, simplified into a scheme or pattern, in order to understand. It acts as a workhorse, tool or speculative instrument to transform theories into research operations.'[52] But, how is a model used? In particular, an explanation must be given for the way in which the model (for example, conflict theory) will be used in this study. The sharp distinction Carney makes between a *theory* and a *model* will not be made.[53] The theory of conflict will be used *as a model,* that is a

---

46.   Cf. Carney, *The Shape of the Past*, p. 5; see also Malina, 'The Social Sciences and Biblical Interpretation', p. 14; Craffert, 'More on Models and Muddles in Social-scientific Interpretation of the New Testament', p. 225.

47.   Carney, *The Shape of the Past*, pp. 8-9.

48.   Malina, 'The Social Sciences and Biblical Interpretation', p. 14; see also Carney, *The Shape of the Past*, p. 9.

49.   Cf. Malina, 'The Social Sciences and Biblical Interpretation', p. 14; Elliott, 'Social-scientific Criticism of the New Testament', p. 5.

50.   Carney, *The Shape of the Past*, p. 19.

51.   Carney, *The Shape of the Past*, pp. 3-4.

52.   Derived from the works of Carney, *The Shape of the Past*, pp. 7, 9, 11; Malina, 'The Social Sciences and Biblical Interpretation', p. 14; Elliott, 'Social-scientific Criticism of the New Testament', pp. 4, 6; Osiek, 'The New Handmaid', p. 271; Holmberg, *Sociology and the New Testament*, pp. 13-14.

53.   Carney, *The Shape of the Past*, pp. 7-8; see also Elliott, 'Social-scientific Criticism of the New Testament', p. 3; Holmberg, *Sociology and the New Testament*, p. 14; Van Staden, *Compassion—The Essence of Life*, p. 154.

'theory in operation'. Thus the terms 'theory' and 'model' will be interrelated and interchangeable. However, the conflict theory/model will be used to evaluate the text of Matthew 8 and 9 in a certain way. It will be used as a sort of 'mould' or 'template' which will be placed like a frame over the text. The model indeed will be used in a way which Holmberg calls a 'deductive one'; that is, we start with a sociological theory (conflict theory) and then apply it to the data (that is, Matthew 8 and 9).[54] It will indeed be used as a 'fact-finding instrument'. The theory of conflict will be used to serve as an heuristic device for investigating, organizing and explaining the social data from the text and their meanings.

Although Holmberg does not himself prefer this approach, he does, however, acknowledge that a 'specified sociological hypothesis', which conflict theory is, '. . . can be very useful *as an heuristic guideline, indicating what kind of phenomena the researcher should look for*' (my emphasis).[55] In using the model (conflict theory) as an *heuristic tool*, new questions emerge, and new evidence previously neglected, might come to light.[56] In using the model for its heuristic value, I hope that it will serve to illuminate the unique phenomenon of the conflict I intend to study.

In the 'deductive use' of the model I propose, I do not at all *assume* commensurability without criticism. In the words of Craffert on the deductive use of models: '*Commensurability* between the phenomena of the model and the evidence *is assumed*. . . and consequently the aim of interpretation resembles that of the natural sciences, namely to explain by means of a law-like model' (my emphasis).[57] I hope to fill the 'historical gap' through the secondary use of different historical studies in the chapter on *The Social Location of the Matthean Community* (see Chapter 3). However, commensurability is not *assumed* at all. In this regard, the level of abstraction of this study should be taken into consideration. Generally speaking, one can accept the remark by Rohrbaugh: 'The higher the level of abstraction, the more specific

54.   Holmberg, *Sociology and the New Testament*, p. 73; see also Craffert, 'More on Models and Muddles in Social-scientific Interpretation of the New Testament', p. 231.

55.   Holmberg, *Sociology and the New Testament*, p. 73.

56.   Holmberg, *Sociology and the New Testament*, p. 15.

57.   Craffert, 'More on Models and Muddles in Social-scientific Interpretation of the New Testament', p. 231.

details of a historical situation tend to lose their focus. The lower the level of abstraction, the more important such particularities become.'[58] A high level of abstraction is almost like taking a photograph with a wide-angle lens. A low level of abstraction could be compared with taking the same picture with a telephoto lens. Rohrbaugh says,

> The point. . . is that models can and do operate as different levels of abstraction and that the higher the level, the more *generalized* the details in focus. Questions (and/or conclusions) appropriate to a given level of abstraction may well be warranted at the same time that conclusions appropriate to a level that is lower or higher may not. . . The proper question *is whether the conclusions drawn from the use of the model match the level of abstraction at which the model is drawn* (my emphasis).[59]

Underestimated Conflict

There is little doubt that the Sermon on the Mount (Matthew 5–7) and the miracle stories (Matthew 8–9) are linked. This is shown by the compositional frame created by the summaries in Mt. 4.23 and 9.35.[60] Because the words of these two summaries are virtually the same, 4.23 acts as an introduction and 9.35 as a 'rounding up' or summary of the whole unit. Between these two verses the themes διδάσκειν and κηρύσσειν refer to the words and teachings of Jesus in the Sermon on the Mount, and the term θεραπεύειν refers to the acts of Jesus in the miracle stories in chs. 8 and 9. This frame around the material makes the Sermon on the Mount and the miracle stories stand out very prominently in the Gospel of Matthew. In this study I will concentrate on the latter, the part less exhaustively studied by theological research.

58. Rohrbaugh, 'Models and Muddles', p. 25; see also Osiek, 'The New Handmaid', p. 270; Craffert, 'More on Models and Muddles in Social-scientific Interpretation of the New Testament', p. 226.

59. Rohrbaugh, 'Models and Muddles', p. 28.

60. Cf. W. Grundmann, *Das Evangelium nach Matthäus* (ThHK, I; Berlin: Evangelische Verlagsanstalt, 2nd edn, 1971), p. 110; W.G. Thompson, 'Reflections on the Composition of Mt 8:1-9:34', *CBQ* 33 (1971), pp. 365-88 (366); C. Burger, 'Jesu Taten nach Matthäus 8 und 9', *ZTK* 70 (1973), pp. 272-87 (273, 281); U. Luz, *Das Evangelium nach Matthäus*. I. *(Mt 1-7)* (EKK, I/1; Zürich: Benzinger Verlag, 1985), pp. 21, 24; D.J. Harrington, *The Gospel of Matthew* (Sacra Pagina, 1; Collegeville, MN: Liturgical Press, 1991), p. 5; D.C. Duling and N. Perrin, *The New Testament: Proclamation and Parenesis, Myth and History* (Fort Worth: Harcourt Brace, 3rd edn, 1994), p. 341.

A short note on the use of the term 'miracle stories' is necessary. Gnilka calls these two chapters the 'Wunderzyklus'.[61] But, since there also exists non-miracle material in Matthew 8 and 9, the term 'Wunder-zyklus' is too static and misleading. I would, however, in this study prefer to use the term 'miracle stories' in Matthew 8 and 9, which also includes the non-miracle material, namely the summaries, callings and redactional explanations.[62] Therefore, the term 'miracle stories', leaves open the possibility that the miracles are embedded in narratives that could include more material than just 'miracles'. It does, however, indicate that the emphasis is placed on the stories about miracles, put together into one narrative whole.

Although 'conflict' plays an important role in the miracle stories (as in the whole Gospel),[63] the conflict between Jesus and the Jewish leaders has, up to now, been insufficiently analysed in the research on the narrative of Matthew 8 and 9. Some progress has indeed been made to indicate that conflict has a function in these two chapters, especially in relation to the community of Matthew. However, where this conflict does feature, it is inappropriately explained in terms of the conflict theory I have chosen. In this regard I take up the challenge to investigate the *particular nature* of the conflict in Matthew 8 and 9.[64]

Furthermore, one has to see how (if at all) the so-called 'marginal-ized' are dealt with in previous research on these two chapters. Because the miracle stories in Matthew 8 and 9 are so prominent (see above), the question arises as to what the function(s) of this unit is (are). Do these two chapters feature as narratives with christological, or ecclesi-ological ends in the same way as Schweizer suggests as being a feature

61.　J. Gnilka, *Das Matthäusevangelium*. I. *Kommentar zu Kap. 1,1–13,58.* (HThK; Freiburg: Herder, 1986), p. 348.

62.　See Burger, 'Jesu Taten nach Matthäus 8 und 9', p. 276 and J.P. Louw, 'The Structure of Mt 8:1-9:35', *Neot* 11 (1977), pp. 91-97 (91); see also W.D. Davies and D.C. Allison, *A Critical and Exegetical Commentary on the Gospel according to Saint Matthew*. I. *Introduction and Commentary on Matthew I–VII* (Edinburgh: T. & T. Clark, 1988), p. 67; H.J.B. Combrink, 'Dissipelskap as die doen van God se wil in die wêreld', in J.H Roberts *et al.*, *Teologie in konteks* (Halfway House: Orion, 1991), pp. 1-31 (6-7).

63.　Cf. R. Hummel, *Die Auseinandersetzung zwischen Kirche und Judentum im Matthäusevangelium* (BEvTH, 33; Munich: Chr. Kaiser Verlag, 1966), p. 9.

64.　See P.F. Craffert, Review of *Teologie in konteks* (Halfway House: Orion) by J.H. Roberts, W.S. Vorster, J.N. Vorster and J.G. Van der Watt (eds.), in *Religion & Theology* 1.1 (1994), pp. 105-108 (108).

of the Gospel of Matthew in general?[65] Do they function as *demonstration material to illustrate* Jesus' *christologically* authoritive position, that is to give legitimacy to his office and position as the incarnated messiah? Or do they have an *ecclesiological function*, describing something of the Matthean church-community, and if so how does conflict feature in this regard? A single answer could not be found among the scholars. Therefore, in order to determine a lacuna in the research, and to give some structure to the selection of some of the scholars, they have been divided into three groups: (1) scholars who see the miracle stories as having a christological function; (2) those who regard these two chapters as having a more ecclesiological function, also in terms of the Gospel as a whole; (3) those who deal particularly with *conflict* with regard to the miracle stories and the Gospel of Matthew as such.[66] What the first group have in common is that they take the *miracle stories as an entity on its own*, out of the context of the Gospel as a whole, and place it under one or more (christological) themes. The second group have in common the fact that the stories form part of the *ideological (or theological) perspective* of the whole Gospel. The focus of the third group is self-evident. In this last section a few scholars who tried to focus on conflict from a sociological perspective have been selected.[67]

---

65. E. Schweizer, *The Good News according to Matthew* (trans. D.E. Green; Atlanta: John Knox, 1974), pp. 13-15.

66. This division must not be seen as being too rigid, for (as will be seen later on), the first two groups have much in common. It must only be seen as an aid to better understanding of the different representatives.

67. In Chapter 3 more attention will be paid to scholars in the third group such as: D.A. Carson, 'The Jewish Leaders in Matthew's Gospel: A Reappraisal', *JETS* 25.2 (1982), pp. 161-74; A.J. Saldarini, *Pharisees, Scribes and Sadducees in Palestinian Society: A Sociological Approach* (Wilmington, DE: Michael Glazier, 1988); *idem*, 'Political and Social Roles of the Pharisees and the Scribes in Galilee', in D.L. Lull (ed.), *SBL: Seminar Papers 1988* (Atlanta: Scholars Press, 1988), pp. 200-209; *idem*, 'The Social Class of the Pharisees in Mark', in J. Neusner *et al.*, *The Social World of Formative Christianity and Judaism: Essays in Tribute to Howard Clark Kee* (Philadelphia: Fortress Press, 1988), pp. 69-77; K. Pantle-Schieber, 'Anmerkungen zur Auseinanderzetzung von ἐκκλησία und Judentum im Matthäusevangelium', *ZNW* 80 (1989), pp. 145-62; J.A. Overman, 'Who Were the First Urban Christians? Urbanization in Galilee in the First Century', in Lull, *SBL: Seminar Papers 1988*, pp. 160-68; *idem, Matthew's Gospel and Formative Judaism: The Social World of the Matthean Community* (Minneapolis: Fortress Press, 1990); J.D.G. Dunn, 'Pharisees, Sinners and Jesus', in Neusner *et al.*, *The Social World of Formative Christianity and Judaism*, pp. 264-89; *idem, The Parting*

I have taken the works that specifically deal with Matthew 8 and 9 as an entity, although not much has been published in this regard.[68] There is already scope therefore to apply the social sciences and conflict theory in particular to Matthew 8 and 9.

The Christological Function(s) of the Miracle Stories in Matthew 8 and 9

The miracle stories are viewed as illustrative material for Jesus' christological position and authority as the messiah. Furthermore, the stories

of the Ways: Between Christianity and Judaism and their Significance for the Character of Christianity (London: SCM, 1991); J.D. Kingsbury, 'Conclusion: Analysis of a Conversation', in D.L. Balch (ed.), *Social History of the Matthean Community: Cross-disciplinary Approaches* (Minneapolis: Fortress Press, 1991), pp. 259-69; A.F. Segal, 'Matthew's Jewish Voice', in Balch, *Social History of the Matthean Community*, pp. 3-37; R. Stark, 'Antioch as the Social Situation for Matthew's Gospel', in Balch, *Social History of the Matthean Community,* pp. 189-210; L.M. White, 'Crisis Management and Boundary Maintenance: The Social Location of the Matthean Community', in Balch, *Social History of the Matthean Community*, pp. 212-47; G.N. Stanton, 'The Communities of Matthew', *Int* 46.4 (1992), pp. 379-91; D.C. Duling, 'Matthew and Marginality', in E.H. Lovering (ed.), *SBL: Seminar Papers 1993* (Atlanta: Scholars Press, 1993), pp. 642-71. They all in some way or another contributed to the description of the community of Matthew in conflict with the Jewish leaders.

68. See the works of Thompson, 'Reflections on the Composition of Mt 8:1–9:34'; Burger, 'Jesu Taten nach Matthäus 8 und 9'; Louw, 'The Structure of Mt 8:1–9:35'; J.D. Kingsbury, 'Observations on the "Miracle Chapter" of Matthew 8–9', *CBQ* 40 (1978), pp. 559-73; J. Moiser, 'The Structure of Matthew 8–9: A Suggestion', *ZNW* 76 (1985), pp. 117-18; Gnilka, *Das Matthäusevangelium*; U. Luz, 'Wundergeschichten von Mt 8–9', pp. 149-65; E.P. Sanders and M. Davies, *Studying the Synoptic Gospels* (London: SCM, 1989).

I also obtained the unpublished works of D. Dormeyer, 'Analyse von Matthäus 8 und 9' (unpublished SNTS paper, 1991); B.C. Lategan, 'Reading Matthew 8 and 9: A Response to Detlev Dormeyer' (unpublished SNTS paper, 1991) and J.W. Voelz, 'Response to Detlev Dormeyer: Analysis of Matthew 8 and 9' (unpublished SNTS paper, 1991) on Matthew 8 and 9. Much work has been done in the field of research on the gospel of Matthew as a whole Gospel. Discourse-analysis, the immanent-syntactic aspects of the text, literary and narrative criticism, structuralism, the language, pragmatic and rhetorical aspects of the parables and the Beatitudes, a contextual reading of the text, the theology and ethics of Matthew and the African context, all, according to Combrink, have received attention in the South African research (H.J.B. Combrink, 'Resente Matteusnavorsing in Suid-Afrika', *HTS* 50.1 and 2 (1994), pp.169-93 [173-90]).

could be placed under a number of different themes to illustrate different aspects of Jesus' office and ministry. Conflict as such, conflict between Jesus and the Jewish leaders or conflict in relation to the Matthean community hardly ever features in this research. Under the above heading the works of H.J. Held,[69] W. Grundmann,[70] B. Gerhardsson[71] and J. Gnilka[72] will be discussed in brief.

H.J. Held. Held primarily intended to explain the evangelist's intentions in retelling the individual miracle stories.[73] By way of comparison between Matthew and the other two synoptic Gospels (and Mark in particular), Held concludes that the abridgements (and extensions) of Matthew's sources were to serve the interests of his own interpretation.[74] In an extended discussion on the miracle stories (which includes more than the two miracle chapters of the Gospel), Held puts forward the view that the collection of the miraculous deeds of Jesus has a christological function.[75] By this Held means that together with the Sermon on the Mount, the double office of Christ—his teaching and his healing activity—is portrayed.[76] Jesus is presented not only as the messiah of the word (Sermon on the Mount), but also as the messiah of the deed (by his miracles).

But the miracle collection does not only have a christological function; it also serves to highlight the themes of faith and discipleship. Matthew re-interpreted his sources in such a way that these three themes in particular come to the fore.

The theme of 'Christology' is reflected, for example, in Mt. 8.2-4; 8.14-15; 8.16-17; 8.28-34; 9.2-8. Held believes that, for instance in 8.28-34 (the expulsion of the demons of Gadara), the story is abbreviated in this way so that all the attention falls on Jesus himself.[77] There is a complete absence of the concluding section present in Mk 5.18-20:

69.   Held, 'Matthew as Interpreter of the Miracle Stories', pp. 165-68.
70.   Grundmann, *Das Evangelium nach Matthäus.*
71.   B. Gerhardsson, *The Mighty Acts of Jesus According to Matthew.* (trans. R. Dewsnap; Lund: Gleerup, 1979).
72.   Gnilka, *Das Matthäusevangelium.*
73.   Cf. Held, 'Matthew as Interpreter of the Miracle Stories', p. 165.
74.   Cf. Held, 'Matthew as Interpreter of the Miracle Stories', p. 167.
75.   Held, 'Matthew as Interpreter of the Miracle Stories', p. 246-47; see also Gnilka, *Das Matthäusevangelium,* p. 349.
76.   Held, 'Matthew as Interpreter of the Miracle Stories', p. 246.
77.   Held, 'Matthew as Interpreter of the Miracle Stories', p. 172.

> As Jesus was getting into the boat, the man who had been demon pos-
> sessed begged to go with him. Jesus did not let him, but said, 'Go home
> to your family and tell them how much the Lord has done for you, and
> how he has mercy on you'. So the man went away and began to tell in the
> Decapolis how much Jesus had done for him. And all the people were
> amazed.

In Matthew there is no mention of the healing itself. No interest is
attached to the person healed, nor to his wish to follow Jesus. The christological interpretation in Matthew's pericope is seen in particular in
the cry of the two possessed men (Mt. 8.29): τί ἡμῖν καὶ σοί, υἱὲ τοῦ
θεοῦ; and ἦλθες ὧδε πρὸ καιροῦ βασανίσαι ἡμᾶς; Matthew does
not wish to depict the demons as trying to exercise counter-magic.
Instead, by putting a christological statement (*Son of God*) into their
mouths, Jesus has come to deliver the demons to the judgment of tor-
ture before the 'time', before the final irruption of the rule of God.
Matthew abridges the Markan narrative in order to concentrate almost
exclusively on the christological element.[78]

Two other themes are highlighted by the miracle stories, namely faith
and discipleship.[79] But, since they have no direct relevance for this
study, no purpose is served by discussing them here.

Held emphasizes the christological function of Jesus as the messiah
of the deed. However, the challenge (conflict) between Jesus and the
Pharisees is understated. Also, the notions of the help Jesus presents to
the marginalized and the consequences of Jesus' authority in connection
with the conflict with the Jewish leaders, have to be developed to their
full potential.

W. Grundmann. Similar to Klostermann,[80] Grundmann divides the
whole of Mt. 4.23–9.35 into two main parts under the headings: *The
Works of Christ Jesus Through the Word: Sermon on the Mount 4,23–
7,29* and *The Works of Christ Jesus Through the Deed: The Deeds of
his Compassion 8,1–9,34.*[81] In this way, Grundmann links the Sermon

---

78.   Cf. Held, 'Matthew as Interpreter of the Miracle Stories', p. 172-75.
79.   See Held, 'Matthew as Interpreter of the Miracle Stories', p. 178, 200.
80.   E. Klostermann, *Das Matthäusevangelium* (HNT 4; Tübingen: Mohr, 2nd
edn, 1927), p. 72. See also Burger, 'Jesu Taten nach Matthäus 8 und 9', p. 273;
A. Sand, *Das Evangelium nach Matthäus: Übergesetzt und erklärt* (RNT;
Regensburg: Pustet, 1986), p. 173 and Harrington, *The Gospel of Matthew*, p. 115.
81.   Grundmann, *Das Evangelium nach Matthäus*, pp. 110-11, 245-46.

on the Mount and the miracle stories in the sense that both are viewed as the deeds (*Taten*) of Jesus. The difference is that the former are Jesus' deeds through his words and the latter the deeds of Jesus through his actions. This indicates that Grundmann sees the collection of 8.1–9.34 also as christologically determined.

Matthew portrays ten miracles that correspond with the ten miracles of Moses, which feature prominently in the history of Israel. Thus, both the Sermon on the Mount and the collection of miracles have a common christological purpose. As Grundmann says: 'The eschatological prophet, promised by Moses, has appeared (Deut.18,15.18)'.[82]

Furthermore, Grundmann correctly takes the view that Matthew presented Jesus as the messiah in word and deed. However, he sees a peculiarity of the word in the radicalness of the demands made upon the listeners and a peculiarity of the deed in the radicalness of his mercy.[83] As he views it:

> Turning to sinners, ill people, outcasts and the humiliated is nothing more than Jesus' fulfilling of the way he understands the commandment to love your neighbour, and in doing this, he liberates people to fulfil the commandment in imitation of him. Jesus expects nothing more than what is already there.[84]

Further on Grundmann states,

> The word of Jesus as a demand encourages people, who through God's mercy as they see it in Jesus' actions, are free to have faith, to show complete merciful love, which takes the other person's rights seriously.[85]

This could all be true and even quite convincing, but Grundmann still does not give an answer as to *why* Jesus' words and deeds were 'peculiar and radical'. Chapter 2 of this study, the chapter on conflict theory, and Chapter 3 on the social location of Matthew, might help in answering this.

B. Gerhardsson. Like Held and Grundmann, Gerhardsson also concentrates on the christological function of the miracle stories, although he does not explicitly state it. He depicts Matthew as describing the messiah

82. Grundmann, *Das Evangelium nach Matthäus* (2nd edn), p. 246.
83. Cf. Grundmann, *Das Evangelium nach Matthäus* (3rd edn), p. 281.
84. Grundmann, *Das Evangelium nach Matthäus* (3rd edn), p. 282.
85. Grundmann, *Das Evangelium nach Matthäus* (3rd edn), p. 283.

in terms of his ἐξουσία.[86] This, together with the fact that he admits
that he heavily relied on the work of Held, leads me to place him in
this section.[87]

One of the purposes of all the so-called summarizing accounts in the
Gospel (Mt. 4.23; 4.24-25; 8.16; 9.35; 14.13-14; 14.35-36; 15.29-31;
19.1-2; 21.14), is to show that Jesus himself teaches and heals with an
authority which in some way is one with himself.[88] Jesus' task is to
teach and heal and this he does in a miraculous manner. 'Jesus acts as
the *healer of Israel*, the one who heals the wounds of Israel. In the pericope of his individual healing miracles we are given a closer insight
into his secrets: his incomparable *exousia* and the way in which he
exercises it.'[89]

The pericopes on Jesus' miracles are divided into two main groups,
each with its own particular theme: (1) 'The pericopes of Jesus' therapeutic miracles in individual cases',[90] and (2) 'The pericopes of Jesus'
non-therapeutic miracles'.[91]

The principle theme of the therapeutic miracles (Mt. 8.1-4; 8.5-13;
8.28-34; 9.1-8; 9.18-26; 9.20-22; 9.27-31; 9.32-34; 12.9-14; 12.22-32;
15.21-28; 17.14-20; 20.29-34) is the *exousia* of Jesus and the faith of
the people. The main interest of the evangelist is to focus on the relationship between Jesus and the supplicants. He wants to show the *exousia*
of Jesus and the faith of the supplicants, and what happens when the
two meet.

According to Gerhardsson, Matthew saw Jesus as a divine figure; he
was the messiah, the son of the living God who had incomparable
exousia.[92]

In Chapter 4 of his book, Gerhardsson proceeds to deal with the so-
called 'non-therapeutic miracles' (Mt. 8.23-27; 14.13-21; 14.22-33;
14.28-31; 15.29-39; 21.18-22; 17.(24-) 25b-27).[93] The main theme of

    86.   Cf. Gerhardsson, *The Mighty Acts of Jesus according to Matthew*, pp. 19,
36-37.
    87.   See Gerhardsson, *The Mighty Acts of Jesus according to Matthew*, p. 7.
    88.   Cf. Gerhardsson, *The Mighty Acts of Jesus according to Matthew*, pp. 20-
21, 37.
    89.   Gerhardsson, *The Mighty Acts of Jesus according to Matthew*, p. 37.
    90.   Cf. Gerhardsson, *The Mighty Acts of Jesus according to Matthew*, p. 38.
    91.   Cf. Gerhardsson, *The Mighty Acts of Jesus according to Matthew*, p. 52.
    92.   Cf. Gerhardsson, *The Mighty Acts of Jesus according to Matthew*, p. 45.
    93.   Gerhardsson, *The Mighty Acts of Jesus according to Matthew*, p. 52.

this group of miracles is the *exousia* of Jesus and the disciples.[94] 'Jesus reveals his *exousia* to his disciples on his own initiative, and in an unexpected and surprising manner.'[95] Jesus is shown as having power over wind and waves. A new side of his *exousia* is revealed: it is greater and richer than his disciples had believed.

The chapter on *Material Concerning Resistance and Controversies* is somewhat disappointing, because it only touches very briefly on the issue of conflict.[96] As his point of departure, Gerhardsson assumes (quite vaguely) that the total picture in the Gospel of Matthew presupposes the conception that official Israel has definitively rejected Jesus. But he doubts whether the adversaries' polemics (from Mt. 13.54-58 and 11.20-24) can give any intimation of how they interpreted his wondrous acts.[97] Furthermore, the reaction of the Pharisees on the exorcisms in Mt. 9.34 is simple and clear but negative through and through: 'Jesus' exorcisms have a satanic background. He stands in the service of Satan, works through his power, and strengthens his reign.'[98] By this he 'spiritualized' the conflict. The conflict is taken out of real life environment (conflict) and placed in a spiritualized context of a conflict between God and Satan. Of course it can be viewed in this way, but we must not forget that even 'spiritualized conflict' is a reflection of a real conflict. The 'real life conflict' is transferred to a higher level, a symbolic universe, which should act as legitimation of the real conflict.[99] This real conflict still has to be described, and this will be done in Chapters 3 and 4 below.

Gerhardsson does indicate that forgiveness, which is strongly demonstrated by the controversy on the forgiveness of sins in Mt. 9.1-8, has a very important place in the Gospel of Matthew, but does not sufficiently show how and why this actually leads to conflict with Jesus' adversaries.[100] Although this was not his intention, it still highlights the gap to be filled. This leads Gerhardsson to a disputable conclusion:

94.   For a discussion of each individual pericope, see Gerhardsson, *The Mighty Acts of Jesus according to Matthew*, pp. 52-60.

95.   Gerhardsson, *The Mighty Acts of Jesus according to Matthew*, p. 60.

96.   Gerhardsson, *The Mighty Acts of Jesus according to Matthew*, p. 68.

97.   Cf. Gerhardsson, *The Mighty Acts of Jesus according to Matthew*, p. 72.

98.   Gerhardsson, *The Mighty Acts of Jesus according to Matthew*, p. 74.

99.   See Van Staden, *Compassion—The Essence of Life*, pp. 93-101 for a discussion of the so-called symbolic universe.

100.   Gerhardsson, *The Mighty Acts of Jesus according to Matthew*, pp. 75-77.

> I must repeat one point which as far as I can see is of great importance: *the adversaries only play a small, casual role in the texts on Jesus' miracles.* Confining ourselves to Matthew, we can observe that they are not even mentioned in the summaries nor in the narratives of the non-therapeutic miracles (his emphasis).[101]

It is not true that the adversaries are not mentioned in the non-therapeutic miracles.[102] Even more seriously, can Gerhardsson really not see that the adversaries do play a more than small and casual role in Jesus' miracles. He simply neglects and underestimates the controversies present in the miracle stories in an otherwise well-reasoned study.

Gerhardsson fully develops the mighty acts of Jesus to indicate that he behaves with incomparable *exousia* as the healer of Israel. No doubt, he clearly explained Jesus' christological function in terms of this *exousia*. But, *exousia*, or *authority* also features strongly in conflict theory. Gerhardsson, however, failed to link the *exousia* of Jesus to the *controversy* with his opponents. Indeed, although this was never his intention, I intend to examine this important point.

J. Gnilka. Although Gnilka does not see that the so-called miracle cycle can have one general theme, he nevertheless presents one. The conclusion Gnilka comes to is:

> At the end, the miracle cycle emphasises the merciful help the Son of David offers to his people Israel... The variety of concerns in the miracle cycle adds to the overall view that the Son of God and Son of David, Jesus, who turns to his people in mercy, can be encountered in faith and in the preparedness of his followers to imitate him. (my emphasis)[103]

It seems from this extract that Gnilka does perceive the miracles as having one particular (christological) theme: to portray Jesus, the messiah (Son of David), as the merciful helper of Israel. This might be true, but it does not bring us closer to finding an explanation for the emerging conflict in the two miracle chapters of Matthew's Gospel.

---

101. Gerhardsson, *The Mighty Acts of Jesus according to Matthew*, p. 79.

102. See Mt. 17.24-26; cf. A.G. Van Aarde, 'A Silver Coin in the Mouth of a Fish (Matthew 17:24-27): A Miracle of Nature, Ecology, Economy and Politics of Holiness', *Neot* 27.1 (1993), pp. 1-25 (14-20).

103. Gnilka, *Das Matthäusevangelium*, pp. 350-51.

The Ecclesiological Function of the Miracle Stories
The works of W.G. Thompson,[104] C. Burger,[105] J.D. Kingsbury[106] and U. Luz [107] will be discussed.[108] They all in one way or another emphasize this ecclesiological function, although some shortcomings will also be stressed in order to indicate the contribution I wish to make in this present study.

W.G. Thompson. The conclusion Thompson comes to, is:

> Finally. . . the double reaction to the cure of the blind and dumb demoniac with the following debate (12.22-37) builds on the conclusion to the miracle-section (9.32-34). The obvious connections reveal that Matthew selected, arranged and composed his version of Jesus' miracles (8.1–9.34) *to demonstrate that the greater part of Galilee...did not become his disciples because they failed to recognize in his activity that he was the promised messiah* (my emphasis).[109]

At first sight there seems to be little difference between the point of view of Thompson and the scholars as presented in the previous section. He also divided the material according to themes. The difference lies in that Thompson also uses the miracle stories as demonstrative material, but not as pointing *backwards* to the Sermon on the Mount, but *forwards* to the forthcoming conflict between Jesus and the Pharisees, which eventually leads to Jesus' crucifixion. Although he does not develop it in detail, he at least acknowledges that conflict (opposition) is an *emerging element*. He says: 'Now, however, their harsh accusation that Jesus casts out demons by the prince of demons sets the tone for future confrontations in which they become increasingly hostile (e.g., 12.14).'[110] This opens up the possibility of viewing the conflict in the broader context of the community of Matthew.

---

104. Thompson, 'Reflections on the Composition of Mt 8:1-9:34'.
105. Burger, 'Jesu Taten nach Matthäus 8 und 9'.
106. Kingsbury, 'Observations on the 'Miracle Chapter' of Matthew 8–9', pp. 559-73.
107. Luz, 'Wundergeschichten von Mt 8–9' and *Das Evangelium nach Matthäus*.
108. See also Hummel, *Die Auseinandersetzung zwischen Kirche und Judentum im Matthäusevangelium*, p. 54.
109. Thompson, 'Reflections on the Composition of Mt. 8:1-9:34', p. 387.
110. Thompson, Reflections on the Composition of Mt. 8:1–9:34', p. 386.

C. Burger. Burger challenges the widely accepted view that the miracles have a christological meaning.[111] Chapters 8 and 9 of the Gospel
of Matthew, can no longer be seen as a collection of miracles demonstrating christological function.[112] The thesis he proposes is that the
two chapters are too complex to be regarded as just a simple collection. The chapters comprise not only miracle stories but also dialogues
and explanations. He says: 'And various pericopes have been revised
in such a way as *to betray a strong ecclesiastical interest in the Gospel*
as well as a Christological one' (my emphasis).[113]

The conclusion Burger comes to is:

> To begin with, Matthew describes Jesus turning to the people with no
> rights and the outcasts of society, then he deals with Jesus' followers,
> and then he talks about the new situation in the community and then
> closes with a series of scenes in which believers are promised new life,
> new sight and new speech. The general theme of this composition is the
> church of Jesus Christ. Matthew portrays the public appearance of Jesus
> in such a way as to reflect what will be the nature and tasks of the
> church.[114]

The evangelist legitimized the reality of the church. He transferred his
understanding of the church back into the life of Jesus. Chapter 8 and
9 of his Gospel present the ἱερὶὸς λόγος of the church or, in Burger's
own words: 'The founding myth of the Christian church'.[115]

Burger correctly sees Jesus as the merciful helper, turning to those
in the Jewish community with limited or no rights, but his thesis also
takes the focus away from the exclusive christological point of view
and places the miracle stories in the broader (ecclesiological) context
of the opposition between the church and the Jewish community. Burger
says,

---

111. See Klostermann, *Das Matthäusevangelium*, p. 72; J. Schniewind, *Das
Evangelium nach Matthäus: Übergesetzt und erklärt* (NTD, 1, vol. 2; Göttingen:
Vandenhoeck & Ruprecht, 11th edn, 1964), p. 36; Grundmann, *Das Evangelium nach
Matthäus*, p. 111; W. Marxsen, *Einleitung in das Neue Testament: Eine Einführung
in ihre Probleme* (Gütersloh: Gütersloher Verlaghaus, 1964), p. 130; Hummel, *Die
Auseinandersetzung zwischen Kirche und Judentum im Matthäusevangelium*, p. 139;
Held, 'Matthew as Interpreter of the Miracle Stories', p. 246.

112. Cf. Burger, 'Jesu Taten nach Matthäus 8 und 9', pp. 275-76; See also
pp. 276-83 for the six arguments he uses to substantiate his view.

113. Burger, 'Jesu Taten nach Matthäus 8 und 9', p. 283.

114. Burger, 'Jesu Taten nach Matthäus 8 und 9', p. 287.

115. Burger, 'Jesu Taten nach Matthäus 8 und 9', p. 287.

> The common theme of the sequence of disputes is the ceding of the Christian community from the umbrella of Judaism. The forgiveness of sins, table fellowship and freedom from Jewish customs are typical of the new church (my emphasis). [116]

This is a step forwards. It implies that conflict is present, which means that now at least it is recognized. Yet much work needs to be done to explain this 'ceding of the Christian community' in terms of conflict theory. This make it necessary to be more specific about the community of Matthew, which I intend to be in Chapter 3.

J.D. Kingsbury. To Kingsbury, Matthew 8 and 9 have a twofold function: a christological and paradigmatic function. It is on account of this second function, that is, the *paradigmatic* function, that Kingsbury is placed here. He says: 'Chaps. 8–9 function not only as a major part of the gospel-story Matthew narrates, *but also as a form of theological address directed to the members of his community*'(my emphasis).[117] The miracle stories are paradigmatic in the sense that they could reveal something of the real life conflict of the community.

The two chapters also function as a form of theological address directed to the members of his community. Says Kingsbury: 'In passages such as 8:18-22 and 9:1-17, Matthew employs words of Jesus and stories of his deeds in order to tell fellow Christians of the cost and commitment of discipleship *and of matters that distinguish them from contemporary Judaism*' (my emphasis).[118] Kingsbury is of the opinion that Matthew, in his editing of the miracle stories, placed emphasis on the personal encounter between Jesus and the supplicant(s), concentrating as much or more on the dialogue than on the miraculous deed.[119] In this encounter, Jesus stands out as a figure of exalted station and divine authority. 'They, in need, call upon him as "kyrie" ("Lord"), i.e., as one who wields divine power... He for his part mercifully hears their appeal for help or healing and... he "saves" them... or "heals" them... '.[120] In their encounter with Jesus, the supplicants were described as persons of faith who desired and reached out for help of God.

---

116. Burger, 'Jesu Taten nach Matthäus 8 und 9', p. 286.

117. Kingsbury, 'Observations on the "Miracle Chapter" of Matthew 8–9', p. 568.

118. Kingsbury, 'Observations on the "Miracle Chapter" of Matthew 8–9', p. 568.

119. Kingsbury, 'Observations on the "Miracle Chapter" of Matthew 8–9', p. 570.

120. Kingsbury, 'Observations on the "Miracle Chapter" of Matthew 8–9', p. 570. See also p. 570 for textual substantiation of his statements.

By way of summary, Kingsbury says that christologically these two chapters presented Jesus as the messiah, the son of God.[121] Paradigmatically they make clear to Matthew's community the cost and commitment of discipleship. Paraenetically, they invite these Christians to approach the exalted son of God and to offer to him their petition for help in the sure knowledge that he desires to hear them and will aid them in time of trial and need.

Kingsbury, as indicated above, again falls back on the christological function of the miracle stories. Nevertheless, he does emphasize that there is emerging conflict (see below) but nowhere indicates why there is persecution of the community and thus *why* there is conflict. Where he does refer to conflict, he (as Gerhardsson[122]) spiritualizes it as an eschatological conflict between Jesus and Satan: 'As a present reality in Jesus, Son of God, the Kingdom of Heaven *has entered into eschatological conflict with the kingdom of Satan* (8:29; 12:25-28; cf. also 9:34). *The miracle-stories reflect this conflict . . .*'(my emphasis).[123] By this he leaves open the question as to why there was such severe tension between Jesus and Judaism.

In his later works Kingsbury[124] does deal with the conflict between Jesus and the leaders of Israel, but here also, there are still deficiencies. The later work of Kingsbury could have been dealt with separately from his 1978 work reflected in this section, because in his 1978 work he under-estimated conflict as such. In his later works he deals more prominently with conflict. But because these works are by the same author, and there is progress in his thoughts, we have to give him the credit for that in this section. He notably introduces us to the aspect of conflict in the whole of Matthew. Kingsbury states,

> In the development of the plot in the respective Gospels, the Jewish leaders play a more significant role than the disciples. The reason is *that the element of conflict is of the essence of the Gospel-plot*, and at the human level

---

121. Kingsbury, 'Observations on the "Miracle Chapter" of Matthew 8–9', pp. 572-73.

122. Gerhardsson, *The Mighty Acts of Jesus according to Matthew*, p. 74.

123. Kingsbury, 'Observations on the "Miracle Chapter" of Matthew 8–9', p. 571.

124. J.D. Kingsbury, 'The Developing Conflict between Jesus and the Jewish Leaders in Matthew's Gospel: A Literary-critical Study', *CBQ* 49 (1987), pp. 57-73; *idem, Matthew as Story* (Philadelphia: Fortress Press, 2nd rev. edn, 1988); 'The Plot of Matthew's Story', *Int* 46.4 (1992), pp. 347-56.

it is particularly with the Jewish leaders that Jesus became embroiled in moral struggle (my emphasis).[125]

According to Kingsbury, the second part of the Gospel (4.17–16.20), can be divided into two sections, namely 4.17–11.1 and 11.2–16.20.[126] To Kingsbury, the conflict in 4.17–11.1 *still remains preparatory to the real conflict to come* in 11.2–16.20.[127] In the first section (4.17–11.1), Jesus discharges his ministry of teaching, preaching, and healing to Israel. In the second section (11.2–16.20), Israel responds by rejecting Jesus, which in turn calls for Jesus' repudiation in 11.6, 16-24 and 13.57. But Kingsbury's view that the conflict in 4.17–11.1 is 'preparatory,' and more specifically that the emerging conflict in chapter 9 is still preliminary to the more intense conflict to come, is not convincing. I would like to challenge the arguments Kingsbury uses to support his view: conflict does not need to become mortal first to be intense or real (as we shall see later in the discussion on the definition of conflict).[128] The fact that the conflict in ch. 9 is not yet 'to the death' does not imply that it is not intense.

Turning to the third part of his analysis of Matthew's story (16.21–28.20), Kingsbury says: 'As is apparent, Jesus' conflict with the Jewish leaders is likewise integral to the leitmotif of this part of the story.'[129] Here the conflict described is mortal in nature, with the final clash and resolution of the conflict in dramatic detail in the passion narratives in chs. 26–28. Jesus reduces all the leaders to silence (22.46) and the only option left to them in order to resolve the conflict was to put him to death (26.2-5). Ironically, it is by putting him to death, and later by the resurrection, that God vindicates Jesus in his conflict with the leaders (28.6, 18-20).[130]

125. Kingsbury, 'The Developing Conflict between Jesus and the Jewish Leaders in Matthew's Gospel', p. 57.

126. Kingsbury, 'The Developing Conflict between Jesus and the Jewish Leaders in Matthew's Gospel', pp. 66-67.

127. Kingsbury, 'The Developing Conflict between Jesus and the Jewish Leaders in Matthew's Gospel', p. 66.

128. Kingsbury, 'The Developing Conflict between Jesus and the Jewish Leaders in Matthew's Gospel', pp. 67-68.

129. Kingsbury, 'The Developing Conflict between Jesus and the Jewish Leaders in Matthew's Gospel', p. 70.

130. Kingsbury, 'The Developing Conflict between Jesus and the Jewish Leaders in Matthew's Gospel', p. 73.

It is obvious, up to this point, that conflict forms an integral part of Matthew's Gospel. In fact, Kingsbury has indicated (however, not in detail concerning chs. 8 and 9), that conflict forms a strong leitmotif in the Gospel. But although Kingsbury clearly indicates the development of conflict, as it unfolds in the plot of the narrative of Matthew as a whole, nowhere does he give an explanation or an answer to the important question: 'Why is Jesus in constant conflict with the Jewish leaders?' It cannot be doubted that conflict is intertwined in the story of Jesus, but the question 'why' remains open. In order to help answer this basic question, we will have to turn to 'conflict theory'.

U. Luz.[131] The whole narrative, to Luz is directed to 9.33b-34: 'The crowd was amazed and said, "Nothing like this has ever been seen in Israel". But the Pharisees said, "It is by the prince of demons that he drives out demons".' It is the different reaction of the crowd and the Pharisees.[132] At the end of the miracle cycle of Matthew 8–9, there was a split (division) in Israel: the negative reaction of the Pharisees, who were to Matthew the strongest representatives of the Jewish leaders, is contrasted with the neutral-positive reaction of the crowd. 'In the macrotext of the gospel, the miracle stories in chapters 8–9 have the function of causing the split in Israel. They constitute the exposition of the conflict *that will break out later... They prepare for the split in Israel*' (my emphasis).[133]

The conflict Luz talks about is seen clearly as culminating in the last great conflict of the passion-narratives. But the question can be raised: what about the previous conflicts? Are they also to be seen as 'preliminary' to the great conflict, as Kingsbury suggests?[134] This is a view already challenged (see above).

There is yet another outcome of ch. 8-9, which has consequences for the Gospel as a whole: in 9.36 Jesus sees the crowd as sheep not having a shepherd (*hirtenlosen*) and takes pity on them. From 9.36, we know

131. See U. Luz, 'Wundergeschichten von Mt 8-9', pp. 149-65; U. Luz, *Das Evangelium nach Matthäus*. II. *(Mt 8–17)* (EKK, I/2; Zürich: Benzinger Verlag, 1990), pp. 64-68.

132. Luz, *Das Evangelium nach Matthäus* II, p. 65.

133. Luz, 'Wundergeschichten von Mt 8–9', p. 153; Luz here builds his thesis on an earlier assumption, as reflected in the first part of his commentary on Matthew (see Luz, *Das Evangelium nach Matthäus* I).

134. Kingsbury, 'The Developing Conflict between Jesus and the Jewish Leaders in Matthew's Gospel', pp. 66-67.

they were without a pastor (shepherd). The Pharisees, in contrast to the crowd, rejected Jesus, and through this they were no longer their pastors. In this situation, the disciples are commanded to harvest the crop (*Ernte*)—the shepherdless people. Towards the beginning of the miracle cycle, a new situation with regard to the disciples emerged. At the beginning of the Sermon on the Mount, they were, together with the crowd, *listeners* to the Gospel; in the miracle cycle, they were Jesus' partners and after chs. 8 and 9 they became the leaders themselves. He says,

> In fact, the theme of 'discipleship' in chapters 8-9 is not just one theme among many, rather the whole narrative of Matthew 8-9 revolves around discipleship. . . As an answer to these merciful acts of Jesus the community (*Gemeinde*) comes into existence. . . But also as a result of these healings, the conflicts develop which lead to the divisions in Israel. . . [135]

Thus, through the miracles of the messiah, a community (*Gemeinde*) came into existence in Israel.

But, why is it that Matthew placed the miracles together in one section? To answer this question, Luz says that Matthew has a deep structure (*Tiefenstruktur*) through which he communicates with his readers.[136] Matthew wants to comfort, strengthen, encourage, admonish and make demands on the reader at this level. To do this, Matthew tells about the founding history of his church, not only telling the history (*Geschichte*) of Jesus, but also that of the community who follow him. This community had its origins in Israel, departed from Israel, was persecuted by Israel, separated from Israel and finally turned its mission to the Gentiles (see also Chapter 4 below). They experienced the history of Jesus as their own basic history and also as the continuation of God deeds before and after Easter.[137]

Luz continues, '*As well as the indirect significance they have as the beginning of the community's own history, Jesus' miracles also have a direct significance*' (his emphasis).[138] Jesus' deeds in the past serve as 'transparencies' (reflections) of the community in the present. The transparencies function on different levels. The miracles of Jesus could relate to happenings that the community are still able to experience.

---

135. Luz, 'Wundergeschichten von Mt 8–9', p. 155.

136. Luz, 'Wundergeschichten von Mt 8–9', p. 156.

137. Cf. Luz, 'Wundergeschichten von Mt 8–9', pp. 156-57; *Das Evangelium nach Matthäus 2*, p. 66.

138. Luz, 'Wundergeschichten von Mt 8–9', p. 158.

For instance, Mt. 10.1, 8 indicates that the healings are constitutive by his command to the disciples. Also, when the faith of the healed or the 'little faith' of the disciples is referred to, the faith of Matthew's congregation is implicit. The same is true for the forgiving of sin. 'Blindness' and 'seeing' are meant metaphorically as well: 'The physical healing of the blind is, so to speak, only the core or physical expression of what happens to everyone who meets Jesus: they become seeing'.[139] The word ἀκολουθέω denotes to be underway obeying, and being with Jesus Christ. 'Elements of liturgical language like the kyrie address used in prayer, also help to clarify the miracle stories'.[140] The raising of the daughter of the ruler is the precursor to the forthcoming raising of the dead.

We must acknowledge that Luz, in both his aforementioned article and in the summary of his commentary on the two chapters, has given the most comprehensive view on Matthew 8 and 9 thus far, and therefore we cannot lightly pass him by. He does not place too much emphasis on the christological function of the miracle stories (except for the last remark quoted above) and in the interests of our investigation we have to acknowledge that he rightly observes conflict to be already present in these two chapters.

But a criticism of Luz is that although he seems, like Kingsbury (see above),[141] to acknowledge some conflict, he sees the *real* conflict as culminating in the passion narratives (at the end of the Gospel). Even where he does deal with conflict in Matthew 8 and 9, it evolves only at the *end* of the so-called miracle cycle, in the reaction of the Pharisees in 9.34.[142] This seems to contradict his own view that 9.2-8, involves conflict with the scribes. Furthermore, I accept the possibility of a split between Jesus and Israel (congregation and the Jews), but not his view that the separation between the Matthean community and Israel was *already complete* and this highlights the need for a chapter on the social location of Matthew. But, *why* was there such a split? This remains the important question (as we will also see in the following section). It would seem obvious that there was conflict because Jesus acted out of mercy and forgave sinners, that is the weak and the helpless. Yet, why

139. Luz, 'Wundergeschichten von Mt 8–9', p. 158.
140. Luz, 'Wundergeschichten von Mt 8–9', p. 159.
141. Kingsbury, 'The Developing Conflict between Jesus and the Jewish Leaders in Matthew's Gospel', pp. 66-67.
142. Cf. Luz, 'Wundergeschichten von Mt 8–9', p. 153.

should he be in conflict with the Jewish leaders at all, when it seems as if he (Jesus) had such 'noble motives'?

Conflict as Phenomenon, Studied in Relation to the Gospel of Matthew
As has already been indicated, much mention is made of the existing conflict between Jesus and the Jewish leaders, not only in Matthew 8 and 9, but also in the Gospel as a whole.[143]

There are a number of scholars (apart from Kingsbury and Luz) who stress conflict in the broader context of the Gospel or miracle stories. We will try to determine whether they explained the conflict satisfactorily. In this section the works of G. Theissen,[144] D. Patte,[145] B.J. Malina,[146] B.J. Malina and J.H. Neyrey,[147] A.J. Saldarini[148] and G.N. Stanton[149] will be reviewed. With the exception of Patte, these scholars view the miracle stories and the conflict from a sociological perspective, which explains why I have chosen them.[150]

143. See Luz, *Das Evangelium nach Matthäus 2*, p. 63.

144. Theissen, *Urchristliche Wundergeschichten*.

145. D. Patte, *The Gospel according to Matthew: A Structural Commentary on Matthew's Faith* (Philadelphia: Fortress Press, 1987).

146. B.J. Malina, 'A Conflict Approach to Mark 7', *Foundations & Facets Forum* 4.3 (1988), pp. 3-30.

147. B.J. Malina and J.H. Neyrey, *Calling Jesus Names: The Social Value of Labels in Matthew* (Sonoma, CA: Polebridge Press, 1988).

148. A.J. Saldarini, 'The Gospel of Matthew and Jewish–Christian Conflict', in Balch (ed.), *Social History of the Matthean Community*, pp. 38-61.

149. G.N. Stanton, *A Gospel for a New People: Studies in Matthew* (Edinburgh: T. & T. Clark, 1992).

150. This, of course, is only a selection from the many scholars (Hummel, *Die Auseinandersetzung zwischen Kirche und Judentum im Matthäusevangelium*; D.R.A. Hare, *The Theme of Jewish Persecution of Christians in the Gospel according to St Matthew* [Cambridge: Cambridge University Press, 1967]; Saldarini, *Pharisees, Scribes and Sadducees in Palestinian Society*; *idem*, 'Political and Social Roles of the Pharisees and the Scribes in Galilee'; *idem*, 'The Social Class of the Pharisees in Mark'; Pantle-Schieber, 'Anmerkungen zur Auseinanderzetzung von ἐκκλησία und Judentum im Matthäusevangelium'; Overman, *Matthew's Gospel and Formative Judaism*; Dunn, *The Parting of the Ways*; Kingsbury, 'Conclusion'; Segal, 'Matthew's Jewish Voice'; Stark, 'Antioch as the Social Situation for Matthew's Gospel'; White, 'Crisis Management and Boundary Maintenance'; Stanton, 'The Communities of Matthew'; and Duling, 'Matthew and Marginality'), who all in some way or other contributed to the description of the community of Matthew in conflict with the Jewish leaders, and should be considered. However, they will be dealt with more specifically in Chapter 3 in relation to the community of Matthew.

G. Theissen. The miracle stories, to Theissen, have a social function.[151] What is of particular importance is his thesis that the belief in miracles (*Wunderglauben*), the miracle-worker (*Wundercharismatiker*) or charismatic miracles (*Wundercharisma*), have a *legitimating and motivating function* in social conflict.[152] The miracle-worker operates in the open. He seeks new forms of social integration and articulates a new social identity. Through this he inevitably comes into conflict with his environment (*Umwelt*), whereas the magician avoids such conflict.[153] After presenting a few examples Theissen goes on to say:

> In political resistance movements it is obvious that charismatic miracles have a function in social conflict. That is also true for every miracle worker who stands not so much for political change as for a comprehensive doctrine of salvation or a new religious way of thinking. *Almost all of them are in conflict or tension with their environment.* . . There are fundamental reasons for rejecting miracle workers: they are religious reformers, stand for new ways of thinking and acting. They pose alternatives to current lifestyles. *This can only lead to conflict.* . . Jesus (will be) was crucified. . . The social function of the charismatic miracle lies in its legitimizing and motivating power in social conflicts of various kinds (my emphasis).[154]

To Theissen most of the miracle stories are directed at the lower layers of the society.[155] He says: '. . . the miracle stories can be understood as the mode of expression of the lower classes'.[156] Both the exorcisms and the healings benefit those who are isolated, and this rehabilitates the supplicants back into society.

The miracle stories also include socio-cultural factors but go beyond the socio-cultural lines (*Grenzen*).[157] They also articulate the consciousness of these lines. The gentile in Mt. 8-9 comes across as having a low self-esteem.

Thus, the miracle stories have a legitimating and motivating function in social conflict. In early christianity, says Theissen:

151. Theissen, *Urchristliche Wundergeschichten*, p. 229.
152. Cf. Theissen, *Urchristliche Wundergeschichten*, pp. 241, 244, 255.
153. Cf. Theissen, *Urchristliche Wundergeschichten*, p. 240.
154. Theissen, *Urchristliche Wundergeschichten*, p. 241.
155. Theissen, *Urchristliche Wundergeschichten*, pp. 247-51.
156. Theissen, *Urchristliche Wundergeschichten*, p. 247.
157. Cf. Theissen, *Urchristliche Wundergeschichten*, pp. 251-55.

... the conflict of a new way of understanding healing is limited by three
social factors in the existing ways of life: by the opposition of town and
country, which is not a decisive factor here, the class differences and the
tensions between different cultures and national groups.[158]

It is clear that Theissen unambiguously linked the miracle stories to
social conflict, a view which I share. Theissen, however, was speaking
in very general terms. In this study, I intend to elaborate on this, placing
particular emphasis on Matthew 8 and 9.

D. Patte. Patte emphasizes the existence of opposition in the text, but
does not link it to the conflict in the community. This is why he is not
placed in the section above.

In the introduction to his commentary, Patte states that he particularly wants to focus on Matthew's faith.[159] By faith he means *'Believing is holding to a system of convictions, or, better, it is being held by
a system of convictions'* (his emphasis).[160] Matthew's function as a
religious text is to communicate a faith to the reader, either to strength-
en the faith of the reader, or to transmit a new kind of faith.[161] There
are many kinds of oppositions, both *implicit* and *explicit* in the text.
Patte concentrates more on *explicit* opposition, which is more fully
expressed in the text, thus giving a direct view of the author's convic-
tion.[162] With regard to this *explicit* opposition, Patte further distinguishes two other types of opposition. On the one hand there are the
semantic oppositions, i.e. '. . . that is oppositions that specify the conno-
tations in terms of which a situation, a personage, a phrase, or a word
needs to be understood'.[163] On the other hand, and of more importance to our study, there are the so-called *narrative oppositions*, that
is, oppositions of action. He says that in a story, narrative oppositions
are what makes the story progress. 'For instance, without the misdeed
of a villain, there would be no need for counteraction of a hero who
attempts to undo the villain's misdeed. Thus, without this opposition
of actions there would be no story.'[164] With this Patte stresses the

158. Theissen, *Urchristliche Wundergeschichten*, p. 255.
159. Patte, *The Gospel according to Matthew*, p. 1.
160. Patte, *The Gospel according to Matthew*, p. 4.
161. Cf. Patte, *The Gospel according to Matthew*, p. 5.
162. Patte, *The Gospel according to Matthew*, pp. 6-7.
163. Patte, *The Gospel according to Matthew*, p. 7.
164. Patte, *The Gospel according to Matthew*, p. 7.

importance of opposition (or conflict) in the progress of a narrative. He says: '... it appears *that narrative oppositions directly reflect the author's faith*' (his emphasis).[165] The fact that the oppositions in the narrative reflect the faith of the author is certainly true of the miracle stories, where there is undoubtably opposition between Jesus and the leaders. He does indicate (correctly) the different aspects of the author's faith as they come to the fore in the three different groups of miracle stories by means of the different narrative oppositions in the text.[166]

What is said about Gerhardsson above, is also true of Patte, for he also lays strong emphasis on the *authority* of Jesus, although without linking it to the conflict with his adversaries. Regarding the miracle stories, the fact that he concentrates on *authority* does makes his work very useful, but the link with conflict theory still has to be made.

We have to note the emphasis Patte placed on the oppositions (conflict) in the text to show the faith of the author. In Chapter 4 I will make considerably more use of his insights. However, although Patte laid the correct emphasis on the opposition in the *text*, this still has to be related to the community of Matthew.

B.J. Malina. An attempt to bring the conflict in the Gospel(s) and 'conflict theory' together, is made by Malina. In a paper which he called 'A Conflict Approach to Mark 7', Malina analyses the text from a 'conflict theory' point of view.[167] He says, 'Conflict theory is one of a number of social science theories that are to explain how and why human beings interact the way they do.'[168] It will, however, be argued that although Malina's approach does explain 'how human beings interact', the question 'why' they interact in a conflicting way still remains to be answered.

In his conflict approach, Malina assumes that people are motivated to act *in terms of their own interests*, which normally impinge on the interests of others.[169] Apart from Boissevain,[170] whom he quotes, he

---

165. Patte, *The Gospel according to Matthew*, p. 7.

166. See Patte, *The Gospel according to Matthew*, pp. 112, 114, 116, 119, 122, 124-29, 131.

167. Malina, 'A Conflict Approach to Mark 7', pp. 3-30.

168. Malina, 'A Conflict Approach to Mark 7', p. 3; see also Malina and Neyrey, *Calling Jesus Names*, p. xii.

169. Malina, 'A Conflict Approach to Mark 7', p. 9.

170. J. Boissevain, *Friends of Friends: Networks, Manipulators, and Coalitions* (New York: St Martin Press, 1974), pp. 231-32.

might also find support from Lenski[171] and Collins,[172] who see the nature of mankind as one of maximizing its own satisfaction. Although Malina makes an important point, his view needs to be elaborated upon. Furthermore, according to Malina, conflict is always rooted in grievance. This view is deduced from Turner,[173] who in turn adopted it from the conflict theories of Dahrendorf[174] and Coser.[175] But this view also needs to be elaborated upon because the question asked here is whether there is not *more* to conflict than that it is rooted in 'grievance' alone (see the discussion on the causes of conflict below). That conflict is based on self-interest and grievance is an important and correct insight, but Malina does not sufficiently develop this in his study. To take the criticism one step further: the conflict approach of Malina is based on a model for a disputing process, taken from Nader and Todd.[176] Following this model, disputes have three stages: the grievance or pre-conflict stage, the conflict stage and finally the dispute stage.

The model of Malina is a useful tool to understand the process and the development of conflict (or disputes), but it does not sufficiently answer *how and why* conflict emerges, or where it originates from. The category 'grievance' or 'pre-conflict', might be of help, but we still need to turn to 'conflict theory' in broader terms in order to find a firmer base from which to explain conflict.[177] The basis of Malina's theory is regarded as being too narrow.

B.J. Malina and J.H. Neyrey. Malina and Neyrey, in their book *Calling Jesus Names: The Social Values of Labels in Matthew*, also deal with conflict, but this time in the Gospel of Matthew, using a so-called

171. G.E. Lenski, *Power and Privilege: A Theory of Social Stratification* (New York: McGraw–Hill, 1966), pp. 25-32.

172. R. Collins, *Conflict Sociology: Towards an Explanatory Science* (New York: Academic Press, 1975), p. 60.

173. J.H. Turner, *The Structure of Sociological Theory* (Homewood: Dorsey, rev. edn, 1978).

174. Dahrendorf, *Class and Class Conflict.*

175. L.A. Coser, *The Functions of Conflict* (Glencoe: Free Press, 1956). See Malina, 'A Conflict approach to Mark 7', p. 10.

176. Malina, 'A Conflict Approach to Mark 7', p. 10. See L. Nader and H.F. Todd (eds.), *The Disputing Process: Law in Ten Societies* (New York: Columbia University Press, 1978), pp. 14-15.

177. Malina, 'A Conflict Approach to Mark 7', p. 10; see also Nader and Todd, *The Disputing Process*, p. 14.

'conflict approach'. In this book it is even more apparent that conflict
is taken as the point of departure. They say: '. . . our approach will be
one of conflict analysis, since *conflict* is the stuff of this Gospel'.[178]
But it immediately strikes one that Malina and Neyrey make no mention of the conflict in Matthew 8 and 9 in their brief overview of conflict in the Gospel:

> From start to finish, the whole gospel is one extended account of Jesus'
> conflict, from the genealogy in chapter 1 that legitimates Jesus' familial
> standing as one of honour, to Herod's quest for the life of the child in
> chapter 2, to the battle between Jesus and Satan in chapter 4, to Jesus'
> fight with the Pharisees in chapter 12, eventually to his confrontation with
> the Chief Priests in chapter 21–27.[179]

They view ch. 12 specifically as the major conflict scene, and chs 8–9
as only providing scant evidence of Jesus' conflict with the Pharisees.[180]
Like Kingsbury and Luz (see above), they also view conflict in ch. 9
as intending to prepare the reader for future conflict. But their argument fails for the same reasons as those of Kingsbury (see above); the
conflict could be viewed as much more intense and lively in ch. 8 and 9
than the way in which Malina and Neyrey presented it.[181]

In their book, it is much more apparent 'how' conflict proceeds, than
in the above-mentioned paper of Malina. But the question 'why' here
also remains open. That Jesus was effectively cast out as 'witch', and
that Jesus was effectively labelled as deviant is indeed explained in
much detail. But why Jesus was accused of witchcraft, and why Jesus
was thus labelled still needs to be answered. Malina and Neyrey effectively analyzed the very important *expressions* of conflict (witchcraft
accusations and deviance), in fact, they explicitly state, 'Conflict can
be expressed and monitored in the ways people hurl harmful epithets,
derogatory names and negative labels against outsiders, as well as in
the ways they affix honourable titles, laudatory names and positive
labels on acclaimed insiders.'[182] But they do not present a sufficient
explanation of the basis of that conflict. Deviance and witchcraft accusations are part of a process of conflict, they *build* on existing conflict
but they do not form the *basis* for conflict.

178. Malina and Neyrey, *Calling Jesus Names*, p. ix.
179. Malina and Neyrey, *Calling Jesus Names*, p. ix.
180. Cf. Malina and Neyrey, *Calling Jesus Names*, p. 58.
181. Malina and Neyrey, *Calling Jesus Names*, pp. 58-59.
182. Malina and Neyrey, *Calling Jesus Names*, p. 35.

A.J. Saldarini. In an article called: 'The Gospel of Matthew and Jewish–Christian Conflict', Saldarini, like Malina and Neyrey, approached the conflict in the Gospel from a labelling and deviance theory. The community of Matthew was a deviant Jewish group. They had been labelled deviant by the authorities. They were a minority group, still regarding themselves as Jewish. They had recently withdrawn or been expelled from the Jewish assembly and Matthew had a fading hope of succeeding in making his programme the norm for the whole of Israel. The community was a Christian–Jewish group. Matthew regarded himself as the true interpreter of the Torah; he is faithful to God's will as revealed by Jesus as the messiah and seeks to promote his interpretation of Judaism over that of the Jewish leaders.[183]

As far as deviance in the Gospel of Matthew is concerned, Saldarini says, 'The Gospel of Matthew and the community behind it are Jewish in that they accept all the fundamental commitments of first-century Judaism, but argue about their interpretation, actualization, and relative importance.'[184] Matthew's Jewish community is a deviant one because it modifies the interpretation or actualization of the law so that it is in conflict with other Jewish groups. Matthew is deviant, as Saldarini sees it, not because of disagreement with normative Judaism, but because he recommends a more fundamental reorientation of the tradition than other Jewish movements.[185]

Saldarini views the Matthean community as a deviant association.[186] To achieve legitimacy, Matthew uses all the sources of Jewish teaching and authority. He constructs an alternative community myth, centred on Jesus, to create a foundation for his community. 'The disputes with the Jewish community leadership and the changed customs in the Matthean community have led Matthew's community to form its own assembly and to compete with the other Jewish assemblies for members.'[187] This is how it became deviant. Says Saldarini:

183. Cf. Saldarini, 'The Gospel of Matthew and Jewish–Christian Conflict', pp. 38-41.

184. Saldarini, 'The Gospel of Matthew and Jewish–Christian Conflict', p. 48.

185. Saldarini, 'The Gospel of Matthew and Jewish–Christian Conflict', pp. 49-50.

186. Saldarini, 'The Gospel of Matthew and Jewish–Christian Conflict', pp. 54-60.

187. Saldarini, 'The Gospel of Matthew and Jewish–Christian Conflict', p. 54.

At any rate, Matthew's community engages in many of the functions of a deviant association. It recruits members, is developing a coherent world-view and belief system, articulating an ideology and rhetoric to sustain its behaviour, and devaluing outside contact and norms. The formation of such a voluntary association requires adjustment to a new situation, the need to assign new community functions and status rankings, and the creation of new community goals.[188]

Of the four different types of deviant groups, Matthew's community seems to be an *alienative–expressive* group (that is, as both seeking societal change and focusing on the needs of their own members).[189] It offers its adherents a new Christian–Jewish world as an alternative to the conventional Jewish one. Because of the conflict, the members of the community find a new core identity as being believers in Jesus (see also the section on the identity of the Matthean community in Chapter 3 below).

As part of his conclusion, Saldarini says, 'Matthew's community or its successors were engulfed by their deviant role and adopted their deviance as a "master status", that is, as the set of values and characteristics that defined and controlled all other aspects of their lives.'[190]

I have to admit that Saldarini's work provides some very useful information, and in Chapter 4 I will make much use of his insights. But, for the same reasons as pertaining to the work of Malina and Neyrey, I will not use his work as starting point for the study of the conflict between Jesus and the Jewish leaders in Matthew 8 and 9, for this work also fails to explain properly the *dynamics* of conflict. One can still ask this important question: Why, apart from forming a new (deviant) association, is there deviance at all? Is there not something even *more* basic to deviance and conflict (and I am not losing sight of the fact that these concepts are all related)? I think there is, and this is expounded further in Chapter 3.

G.N. Stanton. As part of the fourth chapter in his book entitled, 'Matthew's Gospel and the Damascus document in Sociological Perspective of his book', Stanton sheds some light on the Gospel from what he

---

188. Saldarini, 'The Gospel of Matthew and Jewish–Christian Conflict', p. 55.

189. Saldarini, 'The Gospel of Matthew and Jewish–Christian Conflict', pp. 56-57.

190. Saldarini, 'The Gospel of Matthew and Jewish–Christian Conflict', p. 60.

calls a 'social conflict theory'.[191] He draws on the studies of Lewis Coser, as we will later also attempt to do and especially on three of Coser's observations about conflict: (1) *close relationship: intense conflict*; (2) *social conflict, boundaries, and dissent*; (3) *group cohesion and centralized control*. However, and this is quite surprising and disappointing, Stanton does not really contribute to the agonizing question as to *why* there was conflict. He does acknowledge that sociological models (and thus conflict theory), can give rise to fresh insights and questions.[192] This is exactly what I will attempt to do in my presentation of conflict theory below.[193]

Conclusion

The model/theory I will be using, will indeed be applied at a *high* level of abstraction, and therefore, is a generalized theory. Although developed for an industrial society, it will be applied to the text that was formulated in an ancient agrarian society. The use of a general theory accounts for the lack of peculiarities as far as the particular social environment of the Gospel of Matthew is concerned, because it is used more on a cross-cultural level. The conclusions drawn will be quite general, in line with the level of abstraction. The commensurability of the conflict theory is not assumed beforehand, but because of the high level of abstraction, it is legitimate to use this general (modern) model (theory). Later and in more detail it will be argued that, generally speaking, even ancient agrarian societies, even *more* than industrial ones, were highly stratified. Therefore the commensurability of the conflict theory to the ancient text and society can well be argued. Conflict theory is quite flexible, because of the ever present potential of stratification in any society so that it is quite *transcended to particular cultures* (in the words Osiek).[194]

In the section on the christological function of the miracle stories, we have seen that the conflict between Jesus and the Jewish leaders hardly features at all in the works of Held, Grundmann, Gerhardsson and Gnilka. Held understates the conflict and the miracle stories in their relation to the marginalized. Grundmann gives no explanation at all as

191. Stanton, *A Gospel for a New People*, pp. 85-107.
192. Cf. Stanton, *A Gospel for a New People*, p. 107.
193. Stanton, *A Gospel for a New People*, p. 98.
194. Osiek, 'The Social Sciences and the Second Testament', p. 90.

to why he viewed Jesus' acts as 'peculiar' and 'radical'. Gerhardsson does not link the important aspect of authority to conflict. Patte, as we saw in the third section, stresses Jesus' authority, but does not link it to the conflict.[195] Indeed, this was not their intention, but it now is necessary to do exactly this in a chapter on conflict. Furthermore, Gerhardsson in fact underemphasizes the conflict between Jesus and the adversaries in the miracle stories and Gnilka does not explain the emerging conflict either. They all, however, to their credit, high-lighted the christological function of Jesus as it prevailed in the miracle stories.

The section on the ecclesiological functions of the miracle stories starts with the work of Thompson. Although he is still closer to the section on their christological functions, Thompson highlights the emerging conflict between Jesus and the Jewish leaders. Burger takes this a step further. The miracle stories legitimate the reality of the church as a community turning to the helpless. He moves away from a christological explanation of the miracle stories, and places the empha-sis on the ecclesiological function. This is a step forward. Burger is followed by Kingsbury in that he also sees the miracles as having a

---

195. The same is true of the work of Sanders and Davies, *Studying the Synoptic Gospels*, pp. 163-65 (see also A. Sand, *Das Gesetz und die Propheten: Unter-suchungen zur Theologie des Evangelium nach Matthäus* [BU, 11; Regensburg: Pustet, 1986], p. 174). They also stress the miracles as *authenticating* Jesus, not only as the unique metaphysical son of God, but also as God's spokesman. Also Hare sees the miracle stories as manifestations and demonstrations of Jesus' divine power, having *authority* as the messiah (D.R.A. Hare, *Matthew* [Interp: A Bible commentary for teaching and preaching; Louisville: John Knox, 1993], p. 87). Garland also indicates that there are three themes in Mt. 8.2–9.35 (his own division): (1) The motive of matchless power and authority of Jesus; (2) the motive of disci-pleship; (3) the response to Jesus' power and authority, in which the rift between the scribes, the Pharisees and Jesus appears in 9.2-17 and is taken up again in 9.32-34 (D.E. Garland, *Reading Matthew: A Literary and Theological Commentary on the First Gospel* [Reading the New Testament Series; New York: Crossroad, 1993], pp. 91-99). Thus, although still dwelling on the Christology, Garland indicates the emerging conflict, also in as far as the *community* is concerned. He says, 'His [Jesus'] rejection of the Pharisee's holiness paradigm will lead to bitter conflict. The consistent reference in Matthew to "their synagogues" (9.35; 10.17; 12.9; 13.54; see also 6.2, 5; 23.6, 34) and once to "their cities" (11.1) hints of his own community's alienation from those who have disowned Jesus. Matthew's perspective is decidedly defensive: it is them versus us' (Garland, *Reading Matthew*, p. 108). The technical-ities of this community still have to be worked out.

paradigmatic function in the community, but he again falls back to the christological function, and spiritualizes the conflict as one between God and Satan. However, in his later works, although he does emphasize the conflict in Matthew, he underemphasizes its emergence in Matthew 8 and 9. Luz also stresses the tension then and the split between the church and Israel. The Gospel is a 'transparency' (reflection) of the community. There is tension that culminates in the passion narratives. Although this is true, it does not mean that there is less tension in the miracle stories. Like Burger, Luz also sees the miracle stories as 'Gemeinde grundlegende Geschichte'. He, however, like Kingsbury, still underemphasizes the tension, in that he sees the emerging conflict only in the negative reaction of the Pharisees in 9.34. Conflict, as we have seen in the section on the ecclesiological function, is definitely an emerging element in the miracle stories. Furthermore, the miracle stories and the conflict therein, are correctly placed in the broader context of the community, creating the need for a section on the social location of the text. However, as previously stated, no scholar, to my mind, has yet touched on the vital question of *why* there was tension. This makes a section on conflict theory necessary.

The link between the social function and the miracle stories has been correctly made by Theissen. The stories have a *legitimating and motivating* function in social conflict. Emphasis is also placed on the *lower layers* of the society in that they benefitted from the miracles. This view will be followed in the present study but further elaborated upon, so indicating the more precise function of social conflict as it prevails in the miracle stories. Patte correctly recognised the opposition in the text as being connected to the underprivileged in society, but the link with the community of Matthew had been lost. Furthermore, Malina's, Malina and Neyrey's, Saldarini's and Stanton's contributions in using a conflict approach as a means of interpreting the text and, more specifically, the conflict in the Gospels, need to be acknowledged, but also need to be elaborated upon in order to answer the basic question: 'Why is there conflict between Jesus and the Jewish leaders?' Malina's conflict approach is a useful tool in understanding the process of conflict. But as a tool for explaining the basic cause of conflict, it is too flimsy. As for the works of Malina and Neyrey and Saldarini, no sufficient basis is presented for explaining the *dynamics* of conflict. Stanton's work is useful for the insights he took over from Coser, but we have to develop this in greater detail to explain the intense conflict between Jesus and the Pharisees.

In conclusion then, conflict hardly features at all in the section on the christological functions of the miracle stories. The representatives of what I called the ecclesiological function of the miracles, acknowledge that conflict features in these two chapters, especially in relation to the community of Matthew. But, as the representatives of those who explicitly acknowledge conflict imply, conflict is still inadequately dealt with. It is either spiritualized as eschatological conflict with Satan,[196] viewed as 'preliminary' to the 'real' conflict to come at the end of the passion narrative of the Gospel, or acute in the text, but detached from the community of Matthew. Furthermore, nowhere is the real cause(s) for the underlying conflict addressed. Either the basis for the explanation is too narrow, or the process of conflict is explained in terms of deviance. However, the real cause(s) is not fully explained. Although regularly stressed, the real consequences of Jesus' culture and ideology breaking, conflicting and merciful acts, are not followed up. By giving too little attention to the dynamics of the conflict in the text, its full potential is not only reduced, but also the *real interests* of Jesus, being those of the underprivileged and suppressed, are understated (with the exception of the work of Theissen). The acuteness of the conflict needs to be stressed in order to understand its dynamics in the Gospel of Matthew. Therefore I turn to *conflict theory* as such in the chapter to follow.

---

196. Powell comes to a similar conclusion: 'In short, the conflict between Jesus and the religious leaders which is so important to Matthew's narrative *can be identified as a derivative of the basic opposition between God and Satan*' (my emphasis; M.A. Powell, 'The Plot and Subplots of Matthew's Gospel', *NTS* 38 [1992], pp. 187-204 [202]; see also W.F. Albright and C.S. Mann, *Matthew* [AB; Garden City, NY: Doubleday, 1971], p. 79; Harrington, *The Gospel of Matthew*, p. 134).

Chapter 2

CONFLICT THEORY

Human beings are sociable but conflict-prone animals.[1]

Structural Functionalism or Conflict Theory?

In the previous chapter it was argued that the challenge is to explain the conflict between Jesus and the Jewish leaders from a conflict theory point of view. This is necessary in order to explain the conflict for what it basically comes down to, namely a conflict of interests. In reviewing the research carried out so far, it is clear that there is room for an extended study on the conflict in Matthew 8 and 9, and this challenge is now taken up.

Before 'conflict theory' is presented, it is necessary to view it against the background of 'structural functionalism' although it is not the intention to describe 'structural functionalism' in detail here.[2] It will be presented only as a sociological theory to which 'conflict theory' belongs.

One of the basic assumptions of structural functionalism is that society is in a constant equilibrium. The whole of society strives for order, stability, harmony, and balance. All elements in and of society strive towards the maintenance of that society.[3] According to Angell, 'the essence of this theory is that a community or society forms a system of action, each of which has one or more functions to perform, all the

---

1. Collins, *Conflict Sociology: Towards an Explanatory Science*, p. 59.

2. See R. Dahrendorf, *Homo Sociologicus* (London: Routledge & Kegan Paul, 1968), p. 55 n. 46; Turner, *The Structure of Sociological Theory*, p. 19; Van Staden, *Compassion—The Essence of Life*, p. 114; R.A. Wallace and A. Wolf, *Contemporary Sociological Theory: Continuing the Classical Tradition* (Englewood Cliffs, NJ: Prentice–Hall, 3rd edn, 1991), p. 30.

3. Cf. Van Staden and Van Aarde, 'Social Description or Social-scientific Interpretation?', p. 72.

parts being integrated into the ongoing system by virtue of some consensus'.[4] Malina, shares Angell's view:

> *Structural functionalism* studies society as: (1) an enduring system of
> groups (2) composed of statuses and roles (3) supported by values and
> connected sanctions (4) which values and sanctions operate to maintain
> the system in equilibrium. Thus life is described in terms of norms, hence
> as interactions which are morally sanctioned, reciprocal exchange of rights
> and obligations. Focus of attention is on enduring corporate groups, with
> analysis requiring nothing more than ascribed roles and statuses. Here a
> human being is a member of groups and institutional complexes passively
> obedient to their norms and pressures.[5]

But one of the greatest problems of structural functionalism is that it neglects too easily the existence of conflict and inconsistency in society. Says Angell: 'This way of looking at a society tends to make conflict appear as deviant or abnormal, since the central concern is the successful integration of the various parts into a smooth-running whole.'[6] Everything that has to do with conflict, aggression, disorder, violence or coercion could easily be viewed as negative and therefore neglected or underemphasized.

When conflict threatens or causes injury, larger collectives or systems, it is easily regarded as disruptive and considered to be harmful and evil.[7] But such a negative evaluation of conflict need not be necessary. Conflict can and has been valued as positive as well.[8] Kriesberg

---

4.   R.C. Angell, 'The Sociology of Human Conflict', in E.B. McNeil (ed.), *The Nature of Human Conflict* (Englewood Cliffs, NJ: Prentice–Hall, 1965), pp. 91-115 (104).

5.   B.J. Malina, 'Normative Dissonance and Christian Origins', *Semeia* 35 (1986), pp. 35-59 (40-41).

6.   Angell, 'The Sociology of Human Conflict', p. 104.

7.   Cf. L. Kriesberg, *The Sociology of Social Conflicts* (Englewood Cliffs, NJ: Prentice–Hall, 1973), pp. 2-3. Such a negative evaluation of conflict is given for example by Blau and Schwartz, who want to give an explanation for conflict but nevertheless value it negative as: 'Not all social relations are positive and involve integrative social bonds. Some are *negative* and find expression in discordant social interactions. There is animosity and conflict as well as love and friendship. . . In this last chapter. . . we turn briefly to an analysis of *negative social interaction and conflict'* (P.M. Blau and J.H. Schwartz, *Crosscutting Social Circles: Testing a Macrostructural Theory of Intergroup Relations* [Orlando: Academic Press, 1984], p. 173 [my emphasis]).

8.   See G. Simmel, 'Conflict as Sociation', in L.A. Coser and B. Rosenberg (eds.), *Social Theory: A Book of Readings* (New York: Macmillan, 1957), p. 194.

even calls conflict 'exciting'.[9] It can be seen as part of an ongoing reality and even as necessary for change in society. Strong, even vigorous criticism against structural functionalism comes from one of the classical conflict theorists, Ralf Dahrendorf, who chooses to employ a model that emphasizes the so-called 'ugly face' of society.[10] But it is exactly because of this choice that Dahrendorf sharply criticises structural functionalism (also called 'consensus theory' or 'integration theory'). This critique almost contradicts his positive evaluation of functionalism, as seen below. However, he is against the claim of generality of the structural functionalist theory and especially wants to abandon the utopian image of structural functionalism.[11]

The criticism Dahrendorf has of the structural functionalism is directed against the use of the analogy of society as a (biological) organism.[12]

> But by contrast with the structure of other objects of knowledge, especially of organisms with which they are frequently compared, social structures have one important peculiarity. They are not as such 'given', they cannot in principle be analyzed independent of their historical context, but they are themselves subject to continuous change.[13]

The entire structural arrangement of a society can change, whereas in an organism the functions of the different organs like the heart or the liver do not change. However, for instance, the function and functional importance of religious or economical institutions in society '. . . not only can change but are subject to a continuous process of change in all known societies'.[14] He proceeds, 'Anatomy and physiology have heuristic value and scientific validity even without a social psychology of relations between organisms'.[15] All social structures, however, already

9. Kriesberg, *The Sociology of Social Conflicts*, p. 2.
10. R. Dahrendorf's strong critique can be found in two of his articles: 'Out of Utopia', in R. Dahrendorf, *Essays in the Theory of Society* (London: Routledge & Kegan Paul, 1968), pp. 107-28; this article was originally published in 1958, and 'In Praise of Thrasymachus', in Dahrendorf, *Essays in the Theory of Society*, pp. 129-50. Less vigorous is his critique in his work *Class and Class Conflict*.
11. Cf. R. Dahrendorf, 'Towards a Theory of Social Conflict', *J Confl Res* 2.2 (1958), pp. 170-83 (175); see also Turner, *The Structure of Sociological Theory*, p. 143.
12. Cf. Dahrendorf, *Class and Class Conflict*, pp. 120-23.
13. Dahrendorf, *Class and Class Conflict*, pp. 120-21.
14. Dahrendorf, *Class and Class Conflict*, p. 121.
15. Dahrendorf, *Class and Class Conflict*, p. 121.

carry within themselves the seeds of other structures that lie beyond
their (fictitious) borderlines. 'They reach... beyond themselves; at
any given point in time they either are no longer or not yet what they
appear to be. Process and change are their very nature...'[16]

But change does not have to be imposed onto a society from the outside (as sometimes is the case with an organism). 'For this is the most
difficult problem of analysis of structural change: by contrast to organic structures, the "dynamically variable elements" which influence
the construction of social structures do not necessarily originate outside the "system" but may be generated by the structure itself.'[17] In any
social structure, there are certain elements or forces that are at the
same time both their constituent parts *and* the impulses operating towards their supersedence and change.

Structural functionalism (according to Dahrendorf) has failed to
explain sufficiently this reality of change that lies inside the structure
of society itself, because it does not account for the peculiar character
of *social* as opposed to *organic* structures. It fails to see that certain elements inside society could determine not only stability, but *also* the
kind and degree of change.[18] Dahrendorf equates the structural functionalist theory with what he calls 'utopia', from which all change is
absent. It is here where his strongest critique lies.[19] 'Utopian societies',
as Dahrendorf presents them, display five features. Firstly, they do
not grow out of familiar reality, following realistic patterns of development. 'For most [utopian] authors, utopias have but a nebulous past
and no future; they are suddenly there, and there to stay, suspended in
mid-time or rather somewhere beyond the ordinary notion of time.'[20]
A second feature is that utopias seem to be societies of uniformity.
There exists a universal consensus on prevailing values and institutional arrangements.[21] And, because of this 'universal consensus', the
third feature is that there is an absence of structurally generated
conflict. Conflict over values is impossible and unnecessary: 'Utopias
are perfect... and consequently there is nothing to quarrel about.
Strikes and revolutions are... conspicuously absent... Social harmony

---

16.   Dahrendorf, *Class and Class Conflict*, p. 121.
17.   Dahrendorf, *Class and Class Conflict*, p. 123.
18.   Cf. Dahrendorf, *Class and Class Conflict*, p. 123.
19.   Dahrendorf, 'Out of Utopia', p. 107.
20.   Dahrendorf, 'Out of Utopia', p. 108.
21.   Dahrendorf, 'Out of Utopia', p. 108.

seems to be one of the factors adduced to account for utopian stability.'[22] This does not mean that there are no disrupters of the unity. But, in utopian societies, they are the 'outsiders'. They are not the products of the social structure, they are the deviants and pathological cases infected with some unique disease. The fourth feature is that all activities sustain society: 'All processes... follow recurrent patterns and occur within, and as part of, the design of the whole. Not only do they not upset the status quo; they affirm and sustain it, and it is for this reason that most utopians allow them to happen at all.'[23]

The final feature is that a utopian society would be isolated from all communities. 'Utopias are monolithic and homogeneous communities, suspended not only in time but also in space, shut off from the outside world.'[24]

But the question remains: Can we actually encounter all these features in *real* societies? Is a society ever without history? Can there be a society with universal consensus? Is there ever a society without conflict? Can the status quo only be sustained? Can a society be isolated at all?

> It is obvious that such societies do not exist—just as it is obvious that every known society changes its values and institutions continuously. Change may be rapid or gradual, violent or regulated, comprehensive or piecemeal, *but it is never entirely absent where human beings create organizations to live together* (my emphasis).[25]

From this last remark, it is obvious that Dahrendorf values change and also conflict positively. For, according to Dahrendorf, the creative force of change is social conflict.[26] It is not the *presence* of conflict which is abnormal, '... but the *absence* of conflict is surprising and

22.   Dahrendorf, 'Out of Utopia', p. 109.
23.   Dahrendorf, 'Out of Utopia', p. 110.
24.   Dahrendorf, 'Out of Utopia', p. 110.
25.   Dahrendorf, 'Out of Utopia', p. 111.
26.   Dahrendorf, 'Out of Utopia', p. 127. See also Dahrendorf, 'Towards a Theory of Social Conflict', p. 176; E.H. Pfuhl, *The Deviance Process* (New York: Van Nostran, 1980), p. 95.
      Note that Boskoff views it the other way round: Conflict is not the creative force of change, but conflict is seen as the consequence of change (A. Boskoff, *The Mosaic of Sociological Theory* [New York: Crowell, 1972], p. 80). I, however, content myself with the theory of Dahrendorf. Furthermore, as will be argued below, conflict always prevails as a spiral: once there is conflict, there is change, when there is change, there is again conflict because of the new changes.

abnormal' (my emphasis).[27] By this he abandons the utopian image of structural functionalism. It is seen as unrealistic and naive, even absurd, for we live in a world of uncertainty.[28] We do not know all the answers. We do not know what the ideal society looks like. Because there is no certainty, constraint is to assure some liveable minimum of coherence. Because we do not know all the answers, there has to be continuous conflict over values and policies. Because of uncertainty, there is always change and development.[29] Nowhere does Dahrendorf pretend that conflict is pleasant. It might, indeed, even be experienced on an emotional level as stressful and disruptive. Dahrendorf never pretends that conflict is the paradigm or norm to live by. What he does is to present conflict as part and parcel of a reality that needs to be explained. Dahrendorf is against the claims of 'utopian' structural functionalists, who claim that their theory is the most general or even the only possible model. He wants to replace this view with a more useful and more realistic approach.[30] Conflict is thus not seen as 'evil'. It reminds us of our being human, living in history:

> Antagonisms and conflicts appear no longer as forces looking for a solution, but they themselves become the meaning of human *history*: societies remain human societies in so far as they reconcile their disagreements and keep their conflicts alive (my emphasis).[31]

27.   Dahrendorf, 'Out of Utopia', p. 127.

28.   Cf. Dahrendorf, 'In Praise of Thrasymachus', p. 139.

29.   Cf. Dahrendorf, 'Out of Utopia', p. 128; see also R. Dahrendorf, *Gesellschaft und Freiheit* (Munich: Piper, 1965), p. 129.

30.   Cf. Dahrendorf, 'Out of Utopia', p. 113.

31.   Dahrendorf, *Gesellschaft und Freiheit*, p. 130. It has to be acknowledged that he does accept a role for structural functionalism, he does not abandon it totally. He never nihilates structural functionalism as 'false'. Dahrendorf calls integration and values versus coercion and interests, the 'two faces of society' (Dahrendorf, *Class and Class Conflict*, p. 159; see also 'Towards a Theory of Social Conflict', pp. 174-75; Angell, 'The Sociology of Human Conflict', p. 13; L. Layendecker, 'Conflict-sociologie', in L. Rademaker and H. Bergman [eds.], *Sociologische stromingen* [Het Spectrum, 1977], p. 70; Turner, *The Structure of Sociological Theory*, p. 143). To Dahrendorf neither of these models are *exclusively* valid or applicable (Dahrendorf, 'Towards a Theory of Social Conflict', p. 174; *idem, Class and Class Conflict*, p. 163). They are rather viewed as being *complementary*. To Dahrendorf, choosing between the two theories is a matter related to the explanation of specific problems. It is a matter of emphasis rather than fundamental difference (Dahrendorf, *Class and Class Conflict*, pp. 163-64).

The answer to the initial question: 'Why use conflict theory to explain Matthew 8 and 9?' could be as follows: conflict is so obviously present in the whole of the Gospel, including chs. 8 and 9, as was shown in Chapter 1 that it cannot be ignored and has to be explained properly, which has not been the case so far. Furthermore, because conflict is valued positively, even meaningfully as *part and parcel* of human reality and society—thus also of New Testament and Matthean society—I turn to conflict theory as a highly appropriate sociological model to explain the dynamics, conditions, causes and consequences of conflict in Matthew 8 and 9.[32]

A Theory of Conflict

To choose one specific model of conflict theory is difficult, if not impossible, for *one unitary specific* conflict model does not exist. In fact, it would be inconsistent with the basic approach of conflict theory in broader terms to speak of *a single* conflict model. Against the background of the consensus–conflict debate, it would be inconsistent, and even unnecessary, to speak of 'consensus' among conflict theorists. Layendecker states that because of the multitude of approaches, the question arises whether we can talk of *one* specific conflict paradigm.[33] Accepting that multiple perspectives exist, the question arises as to which model to choose, or what tradition to follow? Layendecker proposes two steps: firstly, to create some orderly structure amongst the different perspectives and secondly, to analyze the different perspectives as testable hypotheses.[34] This approach will not be followed here, since, as Layendecker correctly observes, there is a risk that different 'orders' of both ordering (or structuring) and analyzing, would not coincide with one another.[35] This could be effectively illustrated by the efforts to create some order by Turner,[36] Collins,[37] and Wallace and Wolf.[38] I will, furthermore, not follow Layendecker's second step,

32. See also Elliott, 'Social-scientific Criticism of the New Testament, p. 25.
33. Layendecker, 'Conflictsociologie', p. 86.
34. Layendecker, 'Conflictsociologie', p. 87.
35. Layendecker, 'Conflictsociologie', p. 87.
36. Turner, *The Structure of Sociological Theory.*
37. R. Collins, *Three Sociological Traditions* (New York: Oxford University Press, 1985).
38. Wallace and Wolf, *Contemporary Sociological Theory.* See the work of

since I am not really interested in 'analyzing' or evaluating the different perspectives. A third way will be followed, namely an attempt to synthesize the different models of conflict theory, in order to create my own theory.[39]

Because there is no 'unitary, standard' theory of conflict, my own analysis of the theories of (predominantly) Coser and Dahrendorf will be presented. This will not be the first effort towards a synthesis. Turner mentions the work of Pierre van den Berghe, *Dialectic and functionalism: Towards a theoretical synthesis*, as one of the most influential attempts at synthesis.[40] Even the work of Turner himself, although he denies it, is an example of a synthesis. Perhaps a remark of Valkenburgh is a good starting point for my own synthesis: 'The line Marx-Dahrendorf thus brings us to the problem of the origin and *causes* of conflicts; the line Simmel-Coser leads us to the *functions*, the *consequences* (or results) of conflicts for mankind and society' (my emphasis).[41] Furthermore, the three problems, stated by Turner, present us with the basic questions to deal with in a conflict theory: 'In sum then, these three problems—the definition of conflict, the units of conflict, and the confusion over the causes and functions—present a challenge to conflict theory.'[42] This is a challenge which will be taken up. The last question of Turner will be dealt with as two separate questions, which means that the questions can be put as follows:

(1) What is the definition of conflict?
(2) What are the causes of conflict?
(3) What are the units of conflict?
(4) What are the functions of conflict?

Vledder for a thourough analysis of each of these orders/models (Vledder, 'Conflict in the Miracle Stories in Matthew 8 and 9, pp. 90-95).

39. In their efforts to rationalize the different perspectives on conflict, Turner, Collins and Wallace & Wolf not only present it in different orders, but also group the theorists differently. However, according to the scholars, no matter in which group they are placed, Dahrendorf and Coser are the two prominent and leading theorists in the field of conflict theory (see Vledder, 'Conflict in the Miracle Stories in Matthew 8 and 9', pp. 90-95; see also Boskoff, *The Mosaic of Sociological Theory*, p. 83).

40. Turner, *The Structure of Sociological Theory*, p. 243.

41. P. Valkenburgh, *Anatomie van het conflict: Een model theoretische benadering* (Alphen aan de Rijn: Samson, 1969), p. 7.

42. Turner, *The Structure of Sociological Theory*, p. 187.

A Definition of Conflict

We have already seen above that conflict is viewed positively by Dahrendorf as an inevitable and pervasive part of society. There is (dialectically speaking) not only harmony, but also disharmony. People are in constant interaction with each other and this (dialectically) creates both consensus and conflict. But conflict is not only inevitable, it is also necessary to create change in society. We have already seen that conflict is viewed as the creative force that leads to change.[43] Conflict is a dynamic impulse that keeps society alive, prevents boredom or, to say it in Coser's words: '... conflict... prevents the ossification of the social system by exerting pressure for innovation and creativity... A social system... is in need for conflict if only to renew its energies and revitalize its creative forces.'[44] To Dahrendorf it is clear that a theory of consensus cannot explain, or even describe the phenomena of social conflict. 'For this purpose, one needs a model that takes the diametrically opposite position on all the four points above.'[45] These then, are the essential elements of the conflict theory:

(1) Every society is at every point subject to processes of change; social change is ubiquitous.
(2) Every society displays at every point dissensus and conflict; social conflict is ubiquitous.
(3) Every element in a society renders a contribution to its disintegration and change.
(4) Every society is based on the coercion of some of its members by others.[46]

Conflict theory poses a few basic questions. How can we rationalize and understand the existence of power? How can we identify the limits of power? How can we rationalize clashes of interests and conflict of groups? How can we explain those sweeping social changes that we call

---

43. Dahrendorf, *Gesellschaft und Freiheit*, p. 125. See also 'Out of Utopia', p. 127.

44. L.A. Coser, 'Social Conflict and the Theory of Social Change', *BrJ Social* 8 (1957), pp. 197-207 (197).

45. Dahrendorf, 'Towards a Theory of Social Conflict', p. 174.

46. Dahrendorf, *Class and Class Conflict*, p. 162; see also 'Towards a Theory of Social Conflict', p. 174 and *Gesellschaft und Freiheit*, p. 210.

revolutions, as well as the lesser, almost imperceptible changes that occur in our lives every day? In short, why is there conflict at all?

With these basic assumptions and questions on conflict theory in mind, we now can turn to the definition of conflict.

It is not easy to define conflict. The question indeed is: what is, and what is not, conflict? How far should we stretch the concept 'conflict'? Can terms like hostility, war, competition, antagonism, tension, contradiction, quarrels, disagreements, inconsistencies, controversy, violence, opposition, revolution, dispute, to name but a few, all be put under the umbrella of 'conflict'? Is it correct to follow Mack and Snyder (cited by Fink) in saying: 'Obviously, "conflict" is for the most part a rubber concept, being stretched and moulded for the purpose at hand. In its broadest sense it seems to cover everything from war to choices between ice-cream sodas or sundaes?'[47] Can 'conflict' thus be stretched to include seemingly ridiculous quarrels, which is the problem Mack and Snyder have with too broad a definition?[48] Should 'conflict' include only *overt* action between two parties? Or, should it involve *covert tensions*? Or, should 'conflict' involve *competition* between two parties striving for mutually exclusive, or even the same goals? Or, is conflict only antagonisms involving *overt violence or efforts to injure* one another? What is clear is that there is no consensus regarding the definition of conflict.[49]

Both Fink and Bieder reduce the debate on the definition of conflict to two basic issues: whether the definition should be narrow, to include only conflict that leads to overt struggle, that is, what Fink calls an 'action-centred' definition, or broad, to include latent antagonism, that is, where opposition exists although no overt antagonistic interactions are visible.[50] This is what Fink calls a 'motive-

47.   C.F. Fink, 'Some Conceptual Difficulties in the Theory of Social Conflict', *J Confl Res* 12.1 (1968), pp. 412-60 (431); see also Turner, *The Structure of Sociological Theory*, p. 180.

48.   R. Mack and R.C. Snyder, 'The Analysis of Social Conflict: Towards an Overview and Synthesis', *J Confl Res* 1.2 (1957), pp. 212-48 (212-13); see also Fink, 'Some Conceptual Difficulties in the Theory of Social Conflict', pp. 431-32.

49.   Cf. Fink, 'Some Conceptual Difficulties in the Theory of Social Conflict', p. 431; see also Turner, *The Structure of Sociological Theory*, p. 180; K. Bieder, 'Determinanten der interpersonellen Konfliktbewältigung' (PhD dissertation; Hamburg: Universität Hamburg, 1988), p. 58.

50.   Fink, 'Some Conceptual Difficulties in the Theory of Social Conflict',

centred' definition.[51] Fink presents a considerable list of protagonists of this narrow view, with Mack and Snyder, and Coser in the forefront.[52] As prime representatives of the broader view, Fink, Turner and Bieder all present Dahrendorf's view.[53] Fink and Bieder, after all, also opt for a broader conflict definition. The narrow and broad views are but the extremes. Kriesberg can be regarded as a representative of an in-between viewpoint.[54] In this study we will opt for a broad definition of conflict along with Bieder.[55]

What the supporters of a narrow definition view to be conflict, *only* visible action or struggles, and what Kriesberg views as a means to an end, persuasion, reward and coercion, can all be included in the concept 'conflict'.[56] A definition of conflict could then be:

> Conflict is the permanent presence of antagonism (conscious or unconscious), opposition and incompatibility between two or more persons or groups. This antagonism, opposition and incompatibility lies on the level of interests, goals, values and expectations,[57] and may or may not escalate to the point of violent coercion.[58]

p. 438; see also Bieder, 'Determinanten der interpersonellen Konfliktbewältigung', pp. 5-8.

51.   Fink, 'Some Conceptual Difficulties in the Theory of Social Conflict', p. 438.

52.   Fink, 'Some Conceptual Difficulties in the Theory of Social Conflict', p. 432; see Coser, *The Functions of Conflict*, p. 37, L.A. Coser, 'Conflict: Social Aspects', in D.L. Sills (ed.), *International Encyclopedia of the Social Sciences* (New York: Macmillan and Free Press, 1968), III, pp. 232-36 (232).

53.   Dahrendorf, *Class and Class Conflict*, p. 135; see Fink, 'Some Conceptual Difficulties in the Theory of Social Conflict', pp. 432-33; Turner, *The Structure of Sociological Theory*, p. 181; Bieder, 'Determinanten der interpersonellen Konfliktbewältigung', p. 58.

54.   Kriesberg, *The Sociology of Social Conflicts*, pp. 17-21.

55.   See Vledder, 'Conflict in the Miracle Stories in Matthew 8 and 9', pp. 99-106.

56.   Cf. Mack and Snyder, 'The Analysis of Social Conflict', p. 217; Kriesberg, *The Sociology of Social Conflicts*, p. 17.

57.   The notion of 'scarcity of goods' is certainly implied by these four concepts. I, however, deal with 'scarcity of goods' as part of the *causes* of conflict. Therefore it is not taken up explicitly in a definition of conflict. In the next section I will go into these four concepts in more detail.

58.   See also Fink, 'Some Conceptual Difficulties in the Theory of Social Conflict', p. 456; Dahrendorf, *Class and Class Conflict*, p. 135; Bieder, 'Determinanten der interpersonellen Konfliktbewältigung', pp. 7, 69-70.

What are the Causes of Conflict? Why is There Conflict?

A matter closely related to the definition of conflict is the question of its cause(s). In fact, arguing from a broader perspective, the question of the causes of conflict is related to the definition of conflict in such a way, that it is perceived as part and parcel of conflict itself. This differs from the way Nader and Todd, see it.[59] They perceive 'grievance' as the first phase (and cause) of a 'disputing process' and 'conflict' as the second phase. The question is whether the cause(s) of conflict can be reduced to one or more basic principle(s), or whether it is more a question of a complex interplay of different factors. What is/are the basic cause(s) of conflict? Should we, as Nader and Todd, reduce the cause of conflict to 'grievance'?[60] A person or group feels wronged and injured? Or is inequality the ultimate source of conflict?[61] Can scarcity of resources and the control over them be valid causes for conflict? Such scarce resources can be material goods: food, housing, land and income, or non-material: values, status, power, domination over territory, honour, pride and prestige.[62] Is the materialization of self-interests of individuals or groups the basic cause of conflict?[63] Are the categories that Bieder presents, that is, incompatible interests, goals, values and expectations, the grounds for conflict?[64] Unfortunately Bieder does not elaborate on how these elements relate to each other and whether they are causes for conflict or merely manifestations of conflict.[65] From her definition of conflict, the latter is deduced to be the case.[66] Also from the following citation it is clear that she sees interests, goals, values and

59.   Nader and Todd, *The Disputing Process*, pp. 14-15; see also Malina, 'A Conflict Approach to Mark 7', p. 10.

60.   Nader and Todd, *The Disputing Process*, pp. 14-15.

61.   Cf. R. Dahrendorf, 'On the Origins of Inequality Among Men', in *idem*, *Essays in the Theory of Society*, pp. 151-78; Turner, *The Structure of Sociological Theory*, p. 185.

62.   Cf. Coser, 'Conflict', pp. 233; Nader and Todd, *The Disputing Process*, p. 19; J. Galtung, 'International Development in Human Perspective', p. 307. See below in a specific section on *Scarcity of Resources*.

63.   Cf. Collins, *Conflict Sociology*, p. 60; J. Rex, *Social Conflict: A Conceptual and Theoretical Analysis* (London: Longman, 1981), p. 7; Malina, 'A Conflict Approach to Mark 7', p. 9.

64.   Bieder, 'Determinanten der interpersonellen Konfliktbewältigung', p. 68.

65.   Bieder, 'Determinanten der interpersonellen Konfliktbewältigung', p. 68.

66.   Bieder, 'Determinanten der interpersonellen Konfliktbewältigung', pp. 7, 69-70.

expectations as levels on which conflict manifests itself rather than as its causes:

> Incompatibility of interests, goals, values and expectations *is not something that comes out of the blue, rather it is something that results from the rights, ideas and requirements of the actors.* Whether incompatibilities of interests are a given and are obvious from the outside, depends to a large extent on the actors, for they behave in a way that produces incompatibilities, that is, incompatibilities result from them (my emphasis).[67]

To Bieder then, the categories of incompatible interests, goals, values and expectations are seen as the result of the claims, ideals and desires of the actors involved.[68] Yet the question regarding the relation between these elements remains open. Nevertheless, these four categories remain useful as points of departure to systemize the discussion on the causes of conflict as these concepts are frequently used by the distinguished conflict theorists. The above-mentioned questions do not bring us closer to a single principle cause of conflict. What it does show us is the complexity of the matter. What Bieder fails to do, namely to give content to, and to indicate in what relation the elements—interests, goals, values and expectations—stand to each other, I will attempt to do.

Incompatible Interests. In the discussion on interests, a number of closely related issues will be dealt with, namely survival, the pursuit of own interests, inequality, scarcity of resources, control over resources, power and the distribution of power, authority, privilege, status and prestige.[69] In order to give substance to the concept of 'incompatible interests' as a basic cause of conflict as such, I will turn to the works of Dahrendorf [70] and Lenski.[71] For the related issues, that is, inequality and scarcity, and so on (see above), I will primarily make use of the insights of Dahrendorf,[72] Coser [73] and Nader and Todd.[74]

---

67. Bieder, 'Determinanten der interpersonellen Konfliktbewältigung', p. 70.
68. Bieder, 'Determinanten der interpersonellen Konfliktbewältigung', p. 68.
69. See also R.J. Fisher, 'Needs Theory, Social Identity and an Eclectic Model of Conflict', in Burton, *Conflict*, pp. 89-112 (103).
70. Dahrendorf, *Class and Class Conflict.*
71. Lenski, *Power and Privilege.*
72. Dahrendorf, 'In Praise of Thrasymachus'.
73. Coser, 'Conflict'.
74. Nader and Todd, *The Disputing Process.*

On the issue of authority I will use the works of Dahrendorf[75] and again the work of Lenski.[76] These issues, however, are so closely intertwined that it is difficult to keep them apart, especially in the way they are used by the different authors.

Common to the above-mentioned authors, is the basic assumption that (generally speaking) a human being acts in such a way in order to further pursue his or her own interests. Therefore, this pursuing of own interests is the most important cause of conflict, especially when these interests clash or are *incompatible* with those of another. This phenomenon involves both individuals and groups, for individual interests can be shared by a large group as common interests. Dahrendorf uses the term 'interests' in the context of 'class interests', terms which he adopted from Karl Marx.[77] Dahrendorf relies heavily on Marx on this issue (as I, of course, in turn do on Dahrendorf).[78] Classes do not exist in isolation. They exist in *relation* to other classes, to which they are opposed. The relation lies in the conflicting interests between different classes. It is important to see that the concept of 'class' here, as in the thoughts of Dahrendorf, is rather a *relational*, than a gradational concept.[79] In due course in this study I will indeed make some gradational distinctions between the different classes in agrarian societies (see below). The emphasis is on the qualitative positions in a society. Basic to this is, for instance, not how much money a person has which classifies him or her in relation to others, but, rather the person's position as that enables him or her to acquire the money. 'Position is the key.'[80] It is a matter of mutually defining relations in which one party is in control.[81] It is not a matter of the static description of the strata of society (although it is related to that), but, to provide an explanation for both the source of inequality and the dynamics by which it thrives.

75.   Dahrendorf, 'Towards a Theory of Social Conflict'; *idem, Class and Class Conflict; idem, Gesellschaft und Freiheit; idem,* 'Out of Utopia'.

76.   Lenski, *Power and Privilege.*

77.   Dahrendorf, *Class and Class Conflict,* p. 14.

78.   Dahrendorf, *Class and Class Conflict,* pp. 14-16.

79.   Dahrendorf, *Class and Class Conflict,* pp. 136, 138; see also R.L. Rohrbaugh, 'Methodological Considerations in the Debate Over The Social Class Status of Early Christians', *JAAR* 52.3 (1984), pp. 519-46 (529, 531).

80.   Rohrbaugh, 'Methodological Considerations', p. 531.

81.   Cf. Dahrendorf, *Class and Class Conflict,* p. 136; Rohrbaugh 'Methodological Considerations', p. 531.

There are various types of relational views, as Wright and Rohrbaugh put forward.[82] These can be market, production, technical division of labour, authority and exploitation. Of interest to this study is the so-called *authoritative relations* by which classes are defined. Authoritative relations of dominance/subordination have been experienced in almost all societies everywhere.[83] By *domination* we understand the possession of authority, that is the right to issue authoritative commands. By *subordination* or *subjection* we understand the exclusion from authority, that is the duty to obey authoritative commands.[84] Rohrbaugh continues, 'The term "social class" can be broadly defined a "power group", charting any and all power relationships and therefore pointing to groups which participate in or are excluded from the exercise of power.'[85]

Classes are formed by individuals (and groups) who are engaged in a common struggle with other classes. '*The force that effects class formation is class interests*' (my emphasis).[86] Class interests are not merely the random personal interests of one person or even many persons. The shared interests exist in the mutual dependence of the individuals among whom, for example, labour is divided.[87] Members of one class have contradicting interests with other classes. This occurs as soon as they are confronted by other classes.

Class interests can be expressed in various ways. The immediate interest of, for instance, the 'proletariat' is wages and that of the 'bourgeoisie' is profit. 'This means that two particular interests are increasingly articulated: the conservative interests of the ruling class, and the revolutionary interests of the oppressed class.'[88]

Misled by the revolutionary tradition of the eighteenth century, says Dahrendorf, Marx made the mistake of believing that the only way in which social conflicts could produce structural changes, was by

82. E.O. Wright, *Class Structure and Income Determination* (New York: Academic Press, 1979), p. 5 and Rohrbaugh, 'Methodological Considerations', p. 532.

83. Rohrbaugh, 'Methodological Considerations', p. 534.

84. Cf. Dahrendorf, *Class and Class Conflict*, p. 237.

85. Rohrbaugh, 'Methodological Considerations', p. 534; see also Lenski, *Power and Privilege*, p. 75.

86. Dahrendorf, *Class and Class Conflict*, p. 14.

87. Cf. Marx, interpreted by Dahrendorf, *Class and Class Conflict*, p. 14.

88. Dahrendorf, *Class and Class Conflict*, p. 15.

revolutionary upheavals.[89] 'But despite such errors he [Marx] did discover the formative force of conflicting social groups or classes.'[90] Dahrendorf supports two aspects of Marx's analysis. Firstly, that conflicts that effect change can be traced back to the pattern of social structure itself. Conflicts are necessary offshoots of the structure of any society, especially a capitalist society. Dahrendorf disagrees with Marx's assumption that property relations are the structural origin of conflict, but nevertheless acknowledges his analytical achievement in tracing in the structure of a given society the seeds of its super-sedure.[91] The idea of a society that produces in its very structure the antagonisms that lead to its modification appears an appropriate model for the analysis of change in general.

Secondly and even more significantly, Dahrendorf supports Marx's view that in any given situation *one* particular conflict is always dominant.[92] Any theory of conflict operates with a 'two-class model'. 'There are but two contending parties—this is implied in the very concept of conflict.' He proceeds,

> There may be coalitions, of course, as there may be conflicts internal to either of the contenders, and there may be groups that are not drawn into a given dispute; but from the point of view of a given clash of interests, there are never more than two positions that struggle for domination. . . If social conflicts effect change, and if they are generated by social structure, then it is reasonable to assume that of the two interests involved in any one conflict, one will be pressing for change, the other one for the *status quo*. This assumption, again, is based on logic as much as on empirical observations. In every conflict, one party attacks and another defends. The defending party wants to retain and secure its position, while the attacking party has to fight in order to improve its own condition.[93]

It is clear that Dahrendorf defines 'interests' in terms of 'class interests'. Class interests become the force that *forms* the classes. The classes have different 'interests', that is there are different desires or motivational forces for either retaining the status quo or changing the social structures. It is in the interest of one class to defend, and in the other's,

89. Dahrendorf, *Class and Class Conflict*, p. 125.
90. Dahrendorf, *Class and Class Conflict*, p. 125.
91. Dahrendorf, *Class and Class Conflict*, pp. 125-26.
92. Dahrendorf, *Class and Class Conflict*, p. 126.
93. Dahrendorf, *Class and Class Conflict*, p. 126; see also *idem, The Modern Social Conflict: An Essay on the Politics of Liberty* (London: Weidenfeld & Nicolson, 1988), p. 28.

to attack. The value of Dahrendorf's analysis, along with Marx's, is to clearly indicate that there are, in fact, only two contending parties in a particular conflict. This seems quite obvious but it needs to be stressed again. Nevertheless, Dahrendorf fails to explain clearly what is meant by 'interests'. In fact, he even acknowledges his own limitation: 'Once again, it is clear that these statements [quoted above] remain on a high level of formality. *They imply no relevance to the substance or the origin of conflicting interests'* (my emphasis).[94] To explain 'interests' in terms of 'attacking' or 'defending', or in terms of 'changing' or 'retaining' the social structure, says more about the *means* by which 'interests' are pursued, than about 'interests' themselves. This is indeed correct in order to explain the *relationships* between the different classes. Furthermore, to define 'interests' only in terms of 'class interests', raises the question as to whether conflicting interests really have no other manifestation than in 'classes', which after all is a category more frequently used in relation to more industrialized societies. Can 'interests' then only refer to 'class interests'? To answer this question, and to give a clearer indication of what 'interests' are, I turn to Lenski.[95]

To understand how Lenski deals with 'interests', we have to know how he views the nature of human beings. The first postulate of his general theory is the '... simple assertion *that man is a social being obliged by nature to live with others as members of society'* (his emphasis).[96] Not only is social life essential for survival, it is also necessary for the maximum satisfaction of human needs and desires. 'Through cooperative activity men can satisfy many needs and desires which could never be met otherwise and can satisfy most other needs much more efficiently, that is, with greater return for less effort or other investment.'[97]

The *second postulate* more or less coincides with the view of Dahrendorf, who seeks to abandon all utopian views of human nature. Lenski also undermines the romantic view on the 'natural goodness of

---

94. Dahrendorf, *Class and Class Conflict*, p. 126.

95. Lenski, *Power and Privilege*; see also *idem*, 'A Theory of Inequality', in R. Collins (ed.), *Three Sociological Traditions: Selected Readings* (New York: Oxford University Press, 1985), pp. 89-116.

96. Lenski, *Power and Privilege*, p. 25.

97. Lenski, *Power and Privilege*, p. 26.

humankind'.[98] From a very young age, humankind tends to be a self-centred creature who nevertheless is a social being and has to take others into account. This does not mean that he or she is any less motivated to maximize his or her own satisfactions. It means rather that he or she has learned that the attainment of his or her own goals is inextricably linked with the interests of others. For example, a boy who acquires a taste for football soon finds that he can satisfy his taste only by co-operating with others who share his enthusiasm.[99] To maximize self-interests, individuals are forced to work (or play) together. Lenski takes over Sumner's 'coined' phrase 'antagonistic cooperation' as a source of conflict, although it may sound paradoxical and ironical.[100] If humankind were a solitary species, each living apart, conflict would be less. But, because people join forces, 'the opportunity and motivation for conflict are increased.'[101]

Lenski reasons that even self-sacrificial, morally highly commendable activities involve a strong element of self-seeking.[102] Even noble activities of self-sacrifice have to be seen in a broader context: 'Seen in context, such actions appear as part of a mutually beneficial system of exchanged favours.'[103] These actions are seldom taken on behalf of strangers or outsiders. He argues that another questionable form of self-sacrifice is the practice of *noblesse oblige*. Charity, alms giving and public service yield no obvious returns. But, he says,

> Again, however, the element of self interests intrudes. For the very wealthy, philanthropy costs relatively little but usually yields substantial dividends. It is one of the few trustworthy routes to honour and prestige. . . This is not to say that all charitable actions are prompted by self-interest but only that the element of self-interest is not incompatible with philanthropy.[104]

He does not intend to say that unselfish deeds and altruistic love are impossible or never happen. In fact, he reasons that altruism or unselfish love remains extremely important from both the psychological and moral standpoints and human existence would be much poorer and

98. Lenski, *Power and Privilege*, p. 26.
99. Lenski, *Power and Privilege*, p. 27.
100. Lenski, *Power and Privilege*, p. 27.
101. Lenski, *Power and Privilege*, p. 28.
102. Lenski, *Power and Privilege*, p. 28.
103. Lenski, *Power and Privilege*, p. 28.
104. Lenski, *Power and Privilege*, p. 28.

harsher if it were absent.[105] But, as Lenski argues, this pattern of response has only a limited development. Altruistic actions are most likely to occur in minor events of daily life where little is really at stake. Many people desire to be generous and kind, but find it impossible when there is much at stake. Thus, altruism and unselfish love, says Lenski: 'Is not, however, a major determinant of the distribution of power and privilege'.[106] He concludes,

> Thus, when one surveys the human scene, one is forced to conclude that when men are confronted with important decisions where they are obliged to choose between their own, or their group's, interests and the interests of others, they nearly always choose the former—though often seeking to hide this fact from themselves and others (his emphasis).[107]

The third postulate pertains to the objects for which humankind strives. 'Some, such as the air we breathe, are readily available to all, but most are not. *Most are in short supply*—that is, the demand for them exceeds the available supply' (his emphasis).[108] A normal feature of the world of nature is that there is a limited supply of food and resources, resulting in the fact that large numbers of creatures die before the end of their natural lifespan, whilst others live close to the margin of subsistence. But humankind, to some extent, has freed itself from the difficulties of nature and learned to increase its food supply and to control reproduction. Lenski says,

> Yet while man enjoys certain advantages when compared with other living things, he also suffers from certain disadvantages. Unlike various plants and animals, *man has an insatiable appetite for goods and services*. No matter how much he reproduces and consumes, he always desires more. This is true chiefly because the goods and services he consumes have a *status value as well as a utilitarian value. . . The very nature of status* striving makes it inevitable that the demand will exceed the supply: those of lower status constantly strive to equal those of higher status and those of higher status always seek to preserve the difference. Given these conditions, satiation is impossible no matter how much man increases production or restricts population increase (his emphasis).[109]

105. Cf. Lenski, *Power and Privilege*, p. 30.
106. Lenski, *Power and Privilege*, p. 30.
107. Lenski, *Power and Privilege*, p. 30.
108. Lenski, *Power and Privilege*, p. 31.
109. Lenski, *Power and Privilege*, p. 31.

He concludes that it follows logically that a struggle for rewards will be present in every human society.[110]

The nature of society is subsequently described by Lenski, but I have already dealt with it in the discussion on social structuralism and/or conflict theory, in relation to Dahrendorf's views (see above).[111] I will proceed by presenting Lenski's viewpoint on the relation between 'social interests' and 'individual interests', which will bring us closer to an understanding of the concept of 'interests'. Building on the following statement: '. . . we must learn to think of distributive systems as reflecting simultaneously system needs and unit needs, with each often subverting the other',[112] he says that 'conservative theorists' (a term he uses as an equivalent for the 'structural functionalist' view) wrongly deny that there is a basic conflict between the interests of the group and the interests of the individual, 'asserting that what is good for the society is good for the individual, and vice versa'.[113] There is surely a link between the destinies of an individual and his or her society but there is no simple one-to-one relationship between them. To Lenski it is impossible for the interests of society to be compatible with the interests of *all* its members, if the interests of these members are themselves incompatible to any appreciable degree. He says,

> . . . the most that is possible is that the interests of society are consistent with the interests of *some* of its members. . . There is good reason to believe that in many societies throughout history the interests of only a small minority of the members were significantly identified with the interests of the total society.[114]

Lenski admits that he uses the terms 'social interests' and 'individual interests' without stating what they are, as if their meanings are quite obvious.[115] Under the two headings: 'Individual Interests: Their nature', and: 'Social interests: Their nature', he gives substance to these concepts.[116]

Individual Interests. The majority of humankind regard *survival* as the

110. Lenski, *Power and Privilege*, pp. 31-32.
111. Lenski, *Power and Privilege*, pp. 32-34.
112. Lenski, *Power and Privilege*, p. 34.
113. Lenski, *Power and Privilege*, p. 35.
114. Lenski, *Power and Privilege*, p. 35.
115. Lenski, *Power and Privilege*, p. 36.
116. Lenski, *Power and Privilege*, pp. 36-41 and 41-42 respectively.

highest priority. The implications of the fact that most people strive for survival are that it firstly *causes might or force to be the most effective deterrent and also the supreme sanction in human affairs.* 'It is no coincidence that violence is the last court of appeal in human conflict.'[117] Furthermore '. . . anything which facilitates survival is also valued highly. Practically, this means that food and other goods and services which provide *sustenance* are highly valued, especially since they are normally in short supply.'[118] After survival, *health* and *status or prestige follow.* For the sake of health, people are prepared to pay dearly and freely admit it. But, says Lenski, with status or prestige it is different. Few people will admit that they value status highly, but from their actions, the concern for status becomes evident. 'Fear for the loss of status, or honour, is one of the few motives that can make men lay down their lives on the field of battle.'[119] This is certainly true in an 'agrarian society', or more specifically in the first-century Mediterranean world in which honour and shame were regarded as pivotal values.[120] *Self-respect* is another facet of status. 'Where self-respect is destroyed, motivation is undermined.'[121] Other interests are creature comfort, salvation and affection, and some instrumental values.[122]

117. Lenski, *Power and Privilege*, p. 37; see also P. Sites, 'Needs as Analogues of Emotions', in Burton, *Conflict*, pp. 7-33 (11).

118. Lenski, *Power and Privilege*, p. 37.

119. Lenski, *Power and Privilege*, p. 37.

120. Cf. B.J. Malina, *The New Testament World: Insights from Cultural Anthropology* (London: SCM, 1981), pp. 25-50; D.C. Duling, 'Matthew's Plurisignificant "Son of David" in Social-science Perspective: Kinship, Kingship, Magic, and Miracle', *BTB* 22.3 (1992), pp. 99-116 (108); A.G. Van Aarde, 'Aspekte van die sosiale stratifikasie van die ontwikkelde agrariese samelewing in die eerste-eeuse Palistina', *HTS* 49.3 (1993), pp. 515-45 (535-36).

121. Lenski, *Power and Privilege*, p. 38.

122. Another basic goal, although it does not compare with survival, health and status, is *creature comfort.* But the difference between people's concern for status and for comfort is difficult to ascertain, with the result that comfort is easily overestimated (cf. Lenski, *Power and Privilege*, p. 38.). Lenski indeed is very scant on this issue. Comfort is not to be seen as a major driving force behind human behaviour, although it can contribute to conflict (Lenski, *Power and Privilege*, p. 38).

Salvation in the next world (Lenski's own terms) and *affection* in this world are two other widely shared goals. Salvation is available, like the air we breathe, to all who seek it. It is to be found in most of the major religions of the world. Affection, however, is not so readily available. It really is disappointing that Lenski does not

In turning to the discussion on *social interests*, Lenski starts off by saying that 'social interests' are difficult to define because human societies are such imperfect systems.[123] Their members frequently work at cross-purposes with one another and the actions of the whole are often harmful to the parts. Nevertheless, Lenski defines the goals (interests) of a given society as:

> ... *those ends towards which the more or less coordinated efforts of the whole are directed—without regard to the harm they may do to many individual members, even the majority*. This means, in effect, that in those societies controlled by a dominant class which has the power to determine the direction of the coordinated efforts of the society, the goals of the society are the goals of this class (his emphasis).[124]

This approach helps clarify the relation between social and individual interests. It explains why the interests of the individual need not necessarily be the same as those of the society. They could be the same, but this largely depends on the nature of the society and the individual's position in it.

The co-ordinated actions of societies are directed largely towards one or the other of two basic interests (goals). Firstly, '.. they are directed towards *the maintenance of the political status quo within the group*. Since perfect stability or equilibrium is impossible, this goal might better be described as *the minimization of the rate of internal political change* (his emphasis).'[125] The second basic goal of societies, Lenski describes as: '... *the maximization of production and the resources on which production depends*. Sometimes this has been sought by efforts to promote technological advance; more often it has been through war and conquest' (his emphasis).[126] Depending on the kind of

---

give us more information on the aspect of salvation and affection, and more specifically the relationship between the two (cf. Lenski, *Power and Privilege*, pp. 38-39).

   The above-mentioned interests are valued in their own right (Lenski also calls interests 'goals'; see the discussion on 'goals' below). The goals that follow, however, are sought for their *instrumental* value. They facilitate the attainment of the goals already mentioned. The classic example is *money* as a medium of exchange. As such it can serve equally well for men with very different goals (cf. Lenski, *Power and Privilege*, p. 39).

   123. Lenski, *Power and Privilege*, p. 41.
   124. Lenski, *Power and Privilege*, p. 41.
   125. Lenski, *Power and Privilege*, p. 42.
   126. Lenski, *Power and Privilege*, p. 42.

society, either one the other of the above goals receives priority. He says,

> In general it appears that *the goal of maximizing production has priority in relatively unstratified societies and that the goal of minimizing political change has priority in societies in which power and privilege are monopolized by a few*. In societies in which neither of these conditions exist, the two goals seem to be given roughly equal priority (his emphasis).[127]

In conclusion, Lenski suggests *that societies, like individuals, are basically self-seeking units*. In fact, the history of intersocietal relations suggests that the self-seeking element in societies is, if anything, more pronounced than in individuals.[128]

I now return to the initial question of what 'interests' are. With what does Lenski present us? Like Dahrendorf, he also takes the notion of *self-interests*, whether in a society or in an individual, as the *basic force* which brings humankind into motion. *Self-interest* is viewed as the basis of all human activities and therefore it is also viewed *as the basic cause of conflict*. For its own benefit, mankind co-operates with others, even therefore making co-operation or consensus a possible deductive (deduced from the principle of self-interests) cause of conflict. In fact, even consensus could be forced upon someone else.

Lenski is much clearer on the matter of interests than Dahrendorf. This is, in fact, the great value of Lenski's work. He gives content to the concepts 'individual' and 'social interests'. Individual interests, by way of summary, are described as the desire or striving for survival, health, status and prestige, comfort, salvation and affection, and a few instrumental values (like money). Social interests are described as striving for the minimization of the rate of internal political change and the maximization of production by one dominant group. Social interests are furthermore interpreted as the *interests of the dominant group in a society*.

Closely related to the issue of the pursuit of one's own interests, but nevertheless distinguished from it, are the issues of inequality and scarcity, which in turn are related to the *control* over scarce resources and the desire for *power, privilege and prestige (status)*.

A few remarks have to be made on *inequality*. To Dahrendorf it is clear that what remains a 'stubborn' and remarkable fact is that people

---

127. Lenski, *Power and Privilege*, p. 42.
128. Lenski, *Power and Privilege*, p. 42.

are unequally placed.[129] Society not only has crude forms of gradu-
ations such as property and income, prestige and power, but is also
characterized by a multitude of differences of rank that can be subtle
and yet penetrating. This existing inequality, whether crude or subtle,
can and does cause conflict among people. 'Throughout our society,
social inequality *is still turning men against men*' (my emphasis).[130]
This does not mean to say that there could or should not be a *striving*
towards some form of equality. It merely describes inequality as an
empirical fact.[131] To Dahrendorf, inequality becomes the dynamic
impulse that serves to keep social structures alive. He says, 'Inequality
always implies the gain of one group at the expense of others; thus
every system of stratification *generates protest against* its principles
and bears the seeds of its own suppression' (my emphasis).[132] Because
inequality and social stratification exist, it remains likely that society is
intrinsically explosive. Dahrendorf presents an exhaustive work on the
origin of inequality among men.[133] Suffice it to say that as long as there
is inequality between individuals or groups (and indeed there always
will be), there will always be a cause for conflict, since everyone, in
his or her own interest, will strive to gain advantage over the other
and better his or her own position.

Scarcity of resources can be another cause of conflict closely related
to own interests. Scarcity of resources can be viewed broadly as Coser
sees it: 'Conflict may break out over the distribution of a great variety
of scarce *values* and *goods*, such as income, status, power, dominion
over territory, or ecological position' (my emphasis),[134] or as Nader
and Todd present it: 'Scarce resources have generally been defined in
material terms (e.g., land, money, control over women [sic]). But
...*non-material* resources may also be considered scarce: honour,
pride, prestige, valour' (my emphasis).[135] Because, as we have seen

129. Dahrendorf, 'On the Origins of Inequality among Men', p. 151.

130. Dahrendorf, 'On the Origins of Inequality among Men', p. 151.

131. See also M. Honecker, *Das Recht des Menschen: Einführung in die evangelische Sozialethik* (Gütersloh: Gütersloher Verlagshaus, 1978), p. 180 and W. Huber
and H.E. Tödt, *Menschenrechte: Perspektiven einer menschlichen Welt* (Munich:
Chr Kaiser Verlag, 1988), p. 91.

132. Dahrendorf, 'On the Origins of Inequality among Men', p. 177.

133. Dahrendorf, 'On the Origins of Inequality among Men', pp. 151-78.

134. Coser, 'Conflict', p. 233.

135. Nader and Todd, *The Disputing Process*, p. 19; see also Dahrendorf, *Class*

before, mankind needs to survive (see above), and because mankind has an insatiable appetite for goods and services (see above), the desire for the above-mentioned scarce resources will always remain strong. It could also lead to conflicting desires to *control* these resources.

Surpluses were not a feature of agrarian society, since farmers only produced enough for themselves. Therefore the elite groups forced the farmers to produce more by means of heavy taxation. Taxes on crops were often between 30 and 70 per cent. This contributed to severe crises on Palestinian soil. In first-century Mediterranean society things of value were always scarce. In particular, this was true of honour and prestige, and their symbols. Very few had the privilege of having a position with status. Not only was honour a limited good, there were also other aspects that functioned as symbols of honour. These included money, power and position, all of them means by which manipulation could take place. The peasant community was impoverished by heavy taxation, but its members were also in strong competition with each other in order to gain the few resources available. It is for this reason that agrarian society is often referred to as an 'agonic' (strongly competitive) society.[136]

Since control over scarce resources and power are interconnected, Dahrendorf and Lenski place great emphasis on power and its unequal distribution.[137] To get a clearer picture of 'power and authority', we once again turn to Dahrendorf.

In dealing with *power and authority*, Dahrendorf places 'coercion theory' in opposition to 'integration theory'.[138] He says that it is not voluntary co-operation or general consensus that makes social organizations cohere, but enforced constraint. This means that in every social organization some have the right to exercise control over others in order to ensure effective coercion. There is a *differential distribution of power and authority*. When people live together, says Dahrendorf '. . . there always are positions whose occupants have powers of

---

and Class Conflict, p. 209; Galtung, 'International Development in Human Perspective', p. 307.

136. Cf. Van Aarde, 'Aspekte van die sosiale stratifikasie van die ontwikkelde agrariese samelewing in die eerste-eeuse Palistina', p. 530.

137. See also Nader and Todd, *The Disputing Process*, p. 19.

138. Dahrendorf, *Class and Class Conflict*, p. 165; see also the work of F.O. Van Gennep, *De terugkeer van de verloren vader: Een theologisch essay over vaderschap en macht in cultuur en christendom* (Baarn: Ten Have, 1989), p. 389-415.

command in certain contexts. . . and there are other positions whose occupants are subjected to such commands'.[139] The *differential distribution of power and authority* is the determining factor of social conflicts. He says, 'The structural origin of such group conflicts must be sought in the arrangement of social roles endowed with expectations of *domination or subjection*' (my emphasis).[140] Dahrendorf makes a distinction between 'power' and 'authority'. This distinction he adopted from Max Weber:

> Power is the 'probability that one actor within a social relationship will be in a position to carry out his own will despite resistance, regardless of the basis on which this probability rests'; whereas authority (*Herrschaft*) is the 'probability that a command with a given specific content will be obeyed by a given group of persons'.[141]

The important difference between power and authority is that power is related to the personality of individuals whereas authority is always associated with social positions or roles. 'Power is merely a factual relation, authority is a legitimate relation of domination and subjection. In this sense, authority can be described as legitimate power.'[142]

Dahrendorf prefers authority because it alone is part of the social structure. Whenever authority is exercised, group conflicts are likely to arise in all societies and under all historical conditions. Authority consists of the following five elements:

> (1) Authority relations are always relations of super- and subordination. (2) Where there are authority relations, the superordinate element is socially expected to control, by orders and commands, warnings and prohibitions, the behaviour of the subordinate element. (3) Such expectations attach to relatively permanent social positions rather than to the character of the individuals; they are in this sense legitimate. (4) By virtue of this fact, they always involve specification of the persons subject to control and of the spheres within which control is permissible. Authority, as distinct from power, is never a relation of generalized control over others.

139. Dahrendorf, 'Towards a Theory of Social Conflict', p. 176.

140. Dahrendorf, *Class and Class Conflict*, p. 165; see also Rohrbaugh, 'Methodological Considerations', p. 531.

141. Dahrendorf, *Class and Class Conflict*, p. 166; see also *idem*, 'Towards a Theory of Social Conflict', p. 176, *idem, Gesellschaft und Freiheit*, p. 214.

142. Dahrendorf, *Class and Class Conflict*, p. 166; see also Van Gennep, *De terugkeer van de verloren vader*, p. 393.

(5) Authority being a *legitimate relation*, noncompliance with authoritative commands can be sanctioned; it is indeed one of the functions of the legal system. . . to support the effective exercise of *legitimate authority* (my emphasis).[143]

Dahrendorf's view is confirmed by a remark of Van Gennep: 'In general the term "authority" sounds much more favourable than "power", because it is closely linked to the "right", the competence to do particular things or to say particular words.'[144] With his definition of authority in mind, Dahrendorf holds the view that in every group, which he calls 'imperatively co-ordinated associations' (see below on 'the units of conflict'), whether the state, a church, an enterprise, a political party, a trade union, or a chess club, two aggregates can be distinguished: those that have only general ('civil') basic rights and those that have rights of authority over the former.[145] To him (as a point of critique to Marx), *authority,* rather than property or even status, is a universal element of social structure (or society). Authority is a more general and significant relation. 'Authority relations exist wherever there are people whose actions are subject to legitimate and sanctioned prescriptions that originate outside them but within social structure.'[146] That is why he sees conflict as based on authority 'under all historical conditions.'[147] He says that there is a clear dichotomy in authority relations: every position in an 'imperatively co-ordinated association', can be recognized as belonging to either one who dominates (participating in the exercise of authority) or one who is dominated (subjected to, but excluded from the exercise of authority.[148]

The conclusion Dahrendorf comes to is: '(1) The distribution of authority in associations is the ultimate 'cause' of the formation of conflict groups, and (2), being dichotomous, it is, in any given association, the cause of the formation of two, and only two, conflict groups.'[149] The first statement, he takes as a logical assumption. The second statement implies that some have authority and others do not;

143. Dahrendorf, *Class and Class Conflict*, pp. 166-67, 237.

144. Van Gennep, *De terugkeer van de verloren vader*, p. 394.

145. Dahrendorf, *Class and Class Conflict*, pp. 167-68.

146. Dahrendorf, *Class and Class Conflict*, p. 168.

147. Dahrendorf, *Class and Class Conflict*, p. 166.

148. Cf. Dahrendorf, 'Towards a Theory of Social Conflict', p. 177 and *Class and Class Conflict*, p. 167.

149. Dahrendorf, *Class and Class Conflict*, pp. 172-73.

authority implies both domination and subjection, and therefore two distinct sets of persons.

The link between Dahrendorf's notion of 'class-interests' (see above) and that of authority, is obvious: those in control, those who exercise authority, have an interest in maintaining the status quo in society in order to remain in positions of authority. But those who are in a subordinate position strive for change to gain authority, and therefore they are in constant conflict with each other. Dahrendorf, I suppose, is correct in thinking that as soon as groups are in conflict with each other, it involves their own interests and prevails on the level of 'who takes control over whom', or who attacks and who defends, or who wants to keep at the status quo and who desires change.

Goals. For social conflict to develop from potential to *manifest* conflict, three criteria are necessary, namely (1) the groups must be conscious of themselves as a group (identity), (2) they must be dissatisfied with their condition and (3) '... they must think that they can reduce their dissatisfaction by the *other* group acting or being different; that is, they must have aims which involve the other group yielding what it would not otherwise yield' (I will, however, concentrate no further on this third aspect).[150] Kriesberg formulates the question as: 'Who we are, what we have to complain about, and who is to blame for it?'[151] These questions are all related to each other and help determine each other.

Identity is understood to be the sense of knowledge a person or group has about its own character, its boundaries and who is included and who is excluded from the group. This identity depends on a number of factors. Says Kriesberg: 'A prerequisite for a sense of common identity is communication among the members of the category.'[152] If communication is hindered, it is less likely that a sense of communality or collective identity will develop. Furthermore, homogeneity of the members, says Kriesberg 'facilitates communication and the growth of a sense of solidarity and common fate'.[153] The clearer the boundaries, the more likely it is that a group will develop a sense of common fate.

150. Kriesberg, *The Sociology of Social Conflicts*, p. 61.
151. Kriesberg, *The Sociology of Social Conflicts*, p. 63.
152. Kriesberg, *The Sociology of Social Conflicts*, p. 64.
153. Kriesberg, *The Sociology of Social Conflicts*, p. 66.

A sense of grievance ensues when the members of a group have less than they would like and think it possible to have more. But what are the sources of the sense of grievance? Kriesberg gives three factors that stimulate grievance: deprivation, rank disequilibrium and change in attainments and expectations.[154] Only the latter is relevant to this study.

A major source of grievance is *the changes in attainment and expectations* of which Kriesberg says, 'Dissatisfaction arises as people have a decreasing proportion of what they feel they should and could have.'[155] If what has been attained falls below what is expected (fig. 1), and when the rate of what is attained decreases, compared to what is expected (fig. 2), and when expectations rise compared to attainments that remain constant (fig. 3), there is a widening of the gap or a discrepancy between the two and it is likely for grievance to increase. Kriesberg gives three figures to illustrate this point:[156]

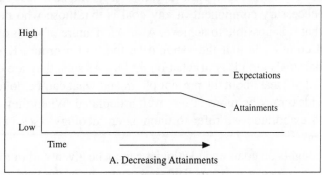

Figure 1

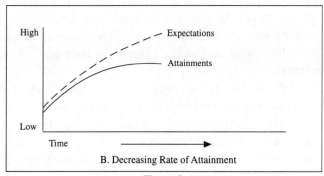

Figure 2

154. Kriesberg, *The Sociology of Social Conflicts*, pp. 68-81.
155. Kriesberg, *The Sociology of Social Conflicts*, p. 76.
156. Kriesberg, *The Sociology of Social Conflicts*, p. 77.

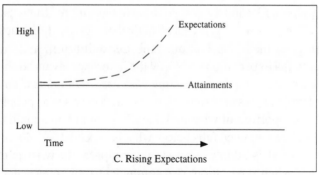

Figure 3

Kriesberg continues: 'For a social conflict to emerge, groups must be-lieve that they *hold incompatible goals*' (my emphasis).[157] Further-more, a necessary component of any goal is that those who desire it, believe that it is possible to achieve. A second feature of goals as cause of social conflict, is that they should be those of a group. Kriesberg argues that goals are ideas of what might be. 'As such they are embed-ded in a set of ideas about the present plight and what can be done about it. These ideas may be more or less well articulated. When they are ex-plicit and elaborated we refer to them as an ideology' (see below on ideologies).[158]

Any thoughts on goals and ideologies cannot be given without reflect-ing on the *leaders of a group*. The spokespersons or the leaders play a primary role in formulating the aims of the group. They articulate the interests of the group. In elaborating goals, the leaders promulgate beliefs about the past, present and future.[159] They increase the sense of grievance or discontent and at the same time hold out a better and attainable future.

The role of the leaders is also dealt with by Coser.[160] He, however, places more emphasis on what he calls the 'intellectuals'. He says that conflicts are likely to be more intense according to the degree to which the contenders are collectively oriented. Their struggle is then waged for the sake of supra-individual ends. Ideological struggles transcend individual ones and allow participants a 'good conscience' about the

157. Kriesberg, *The Sociology of Social Conflicts*, p. 81.
158. Kriesberg, *The Sociology of Social Conflicts*, p. 82.
159. Kriesberg, *The Sociology of Social Conflicts*, p. 85.
160. Coser, 'Conflict', p. 234.

struggle. But this phenomenon highlights the importance of intellectuals (and the leaders), who develop the ideologies of society. Says Coser:

> Intellectuals who transform conflicts of interests into conflicts of ideas help provide public justification of conflicts and hence to make them more intense. Conflicts may involve the pursuit of personal interests by private individuals or they may arise from the pursuit of the interests of various types of collectivities. Intellectuals, when they function as 'ideologists', tend to strip such conflicts of their merely personal or merely interested aspects and to transform them into struggles over eternal truths.[161]

The *nature and direction* of the goals are strongly shaped by the grievance underlying it. If economic deprivation is experienced, then efforts will usually be directed at improving those conditions.[162]

What then is the relation between 'interests' and 'goals'? We saw that Lenski made no differentiation between the two. In fact, he used the terms as synonymous concepts.[163] This indicates that the terms are closely related to the degree that both goals and interests can be seen as part of the general concept of 'interests'. Nevertheless, there are some differences in nuance. Where interests lie at the basis of mankind's actions and form the motivating force, goals are the more visible expression of these interests. De Jager and Mok see goals as the solidification of interests.[164] Out of self-interest mankind seeks identity, experiences grievance and formulates specific goals to improve his situation. Self-interest (or interests as such) is the motivating force that creates goals in the interests of the individual or the group. Therefore, in relation to goals, interests come first and stand as the foundation of goals.

Values. The terms values, ideologies, and norms, are all interrelated. Different concepts are often used when dealing with 'values' and it is necessary to give some clarification of the use of the concepts of 'values', 'ideologies' and 'norms'.

A set of *values* provides a group (or individual) with broad social definitions of what is good, right or preferred. Or, when used in the context of conflict, values present the *rightness* of the claims and beliefs

---

161. Coser, 'Conflict', p. 234.

162. Cf. Kriesberg, *The Sociology of Social Conflicts*, p. 86.

163. See Lenski, *Power and Privilege*, p. 36.

164. H. De Jager and A.L. Mok, *Grondbeginselen der sociologie: Gezichtspunten en begrippen* (Leiden: Kroese, 1983), p. 128.

(a belief is that which is thought to be true[165]) for which one will even be prepared to go into confrontation with others. De Jager and Mok (1983: 412) define values as: '. . . collective proposals within a society or group about what is right, proper and therefore (for the general good) to be pursued'.[166]

In every society there exists a variety of values and often there is disagreement on how to interpret the most important ones, such as equality and morality. But despite these variations, Benkin sees the link between values and ideologies as:

> . . . every society's social structure—the interrelationships of family, the state, the church, the economy, the mass media, and so forth—must, in order for the society to survive, *rest on a relatively coherent and consistent set of values and their rationalizations, that is, on an ideology* (emphasis mine).[167]

A set of values that legitimizes a society or a system of legitimation that characterizes a particular society is called its *ideology*. De Jager and Mok also define ideology in terms of legitimation. They see ideology as: '. . . an entire set of views and convictions that gives meaning to the endeavour of a group and at the same time *justifies* it, and that is beyond any doubt for its supporters' (my emphasis).[168]

Norms are values translated into behaviour; that is what people should and should not do. Says Benkin: 'Norms are shared standards of behaviour rooted in values and [they are] enforceable.'[169]

In conflict theory these sharp distinctions between the terms are not always made and they are even in some cases used synonymously. Values, ideologies and norms play a more important role in functional structuralism than in conflict theory. What is important to realize, is that these terms are all translated as *interests*. Consistent with conflict theory, we will take the same position.

Ideologies and norms, according to Dahrendorf, are all part of a process of forming interest groups and it forms part of what he calls the

---

165. Cf. R.L. Benkin, *Sociology: A Way of Seeing* (Belmont: Wadsworth, 1981), p. 69.

166. De Jager and Mok, *Grondbeginselen der sociologie*, p. 412.

167. Benkin, *Sociology*, p. 70.

168. De Jager and Mok, *Grondbeginselen der sociologie*, p. 400; see also P. Van Staden, *Compassion—The Essence of Life*, p. 86.

169. Benkin, *Sociology*, p. 71.

'technical conditions of organization'.[170] Taken from Malinowski, he says that there are six important features for interest groups: '. . . such groups require a charter, a personnel, certain norms, a material instrumentarium, certain regular activities, and an "objective" function'.[171] Two of these are of considerable importance for this study, namely charter and personnel.

Dahrendorf defines the *charter* of an organization (again in Malinowski's terms) as: '. . . the system of values for the pursuit of which human beings organize'.[172] He says that in the particular case of conflict groups, these values consist of what he had earlier called 'manifest interests'. *Manifest interests*, as opposed to *latent interests*, are 'conscious goals'; they are 'psychological realities'. They describe the fact that the emotion, will, and desire of a person are directed towards some goal.[173] He proceeds,

> The specific substance of manifest interests can be determined only in the context of given social conditions; but they always constitute a formulation of the issues of structurally generated group conflicts of the type in question. In this sense, manifest interests are the *program of organized groups*. . . While latent interests are, in a psychological sense, 'nonexistent', manifest interests *are always realities in the heads of the occupants of positions of domination or subjection in association* (my emphasis).[174]

Manifest interests are articulated and formulated programmes. Furthermore Dahrendorf states,

> The articulation and codification of such interests is again a process that presupposes certain conditions. Either there must be a person or circle of persons who take on them the task of articulation and codification, or, alternatively, *an 'ideology'*, a system of ideas, must be available which in a given case is capable of serving as a program or charter of groups (my emphasis).[175]

But, ideologies as articulated and codified manifest interests, are to Dahrendorf, but a technical condition of organization. He says, *'Ideologies do not create conflict groups or cause conflict groups to emerge.*

170. Dahrendorf, *Class and Class Conflict*, pp. 184-86.
171. Dahrendorf, *Class and Class Conflict*, p. 185.
172. Dahrendorf, *Class and Class Conflict*, p. 185.
173. Cf. Dahrendorf, *Class and Class Conflict*, p. 178.
174. Dahrendorf, *Class and Class Conflict*, pp. 178-79.
175. Dahrendorf, *Class and Class Conflict*, p. 186.

Yet they are indispensable *obstetricians* of conflict groups' (his emphasis).[176] Political conditions—together with social conditions of organization—are also needed in the forming of interests groups but we will not elaborate on this. Suffice it to say that to Dahrendorf, ideologies and values serve as 'articulated manifest interests', and thus they can only in an indirect sense act as a cause of conflict.

Coser is even clearer on this point. To him values (and ideologies) *intensify* conflict. Coser devotes a whole chapter to 'Ideology and conflict'.[177] Objectified struggles that transcend personal struggles are likely to be more radical and merciless than conflicts over immediate personal issues.[178] He continues,

> The consciousness of speaking of a super-individual 'right' or system of values reinforces each party's intransigence, mobilizing energies that would not be available for mere personal interests or goals. He [Simmel] bases this assertion on two arguments: (1) that individuals entering into a super-individual conflict act as *representatives* of groups or ideas; and (2) they are imbued with a sense of *respectability* and self-righteousness since they are not acting for 'selfish' reasons.[179]

I proceed to elaborate on Dahrendorf's concept of *personnel*. If personal interests can be transformed to impersonal values with a sort of 'objective' quality, conflict can be pursued with a 'good conscience' because it is collectively approved. Collective orientation and approval add to the 'respectability' of a conflict. 'The "respectability" of a conflict may be held to depend on whether individual success orientation *is approved in the normative system*' (my emphasis).[180] Coser regards Marx's interpretation of class struggle as a good example: the struggle has to be 'depersonalized' by insisting on the impersonal character of the struggle.[181] The impersonal character of the struggle strengthens the group's (or individual's) interests. Struggle (or conflict) is thus intensified when depersonalized by ideologies or values that transcend the individual. Elsewhere, Coser states on the same issue: 'The *ideological end may justify the means* in the eyes of the participants and lead them to consider justifiable, in the public ideological contention, means

176. Dahrendorf, *Class and Class Conflict*, p. 186.
177. Coser, *The Functions of Conflict*, pp. 110-19.
178. Cf. Coser, *The Functions of Conflict*, p. 112.
179. Coser, *The Functions of Conflict*, p. 112.
180. Coser, *The Functions of Conflict*, p. 113.
181. Coser, *The Functions of Conflict*, p. 115.

that they might reject in private conflict' (my emphasis).[182]

To Coser this depersonalization of conflict, throws light on the role of the intellectuals in social issues.[183] Here he is clearer than Dahrendorf in discussing personnel and the leaders or founders of a group.[184] Intellectuals are of importance in transforming interest groups into ideological movements. *They transform conflicts of interests into conflicts of ideas or ideologies.* 'Intellectuals have contributed to the deepening and intensification of struggles by stripping them of personal motivations and transforming them into struggles over "eternal truths".'[185]

The role of the intellectuals, according to Lenski, is to create new ideologies to challenge and destroy the existing ones.[186] They are the opinion leaders with respect to important philosophical questions. But, they are easily seduced by systems of power and privilege to take a conservative position. In this way they prove to the common people the inevitability and the advantages of the status quo. But, not all intellectuals support the elites. Says Lenski:

> Sometimes, however, elites become careless, or certain intellectuals have refused to respond to their blandishments. By themselves, rebellious intellectuals are no threat to a political elite. They lack the numbers and resources necessary to bring about a successful revolution. However, working in conjunction with others, they can provide the catalytic agent, the counter-ideology which is necessary for every successful social revolution.[187]

Concerning power, those who have been able to seize it will do their best to keep it and remain in a position of authority. There is a variety of means available of which force is one. But, force is costly and in the long run inefficient. 'So long as it [a ruler] relies on force, much of the profit is consumed by the costs of coercion.'[188] In the long term, it is more advantageous to legitimize their rule by persuasion of an ideology (and laws). We could say, then, that values, ideologies and norms are normally created to suit the interests of the rulers. Usually the ruler's interests are maintained (and even coerced) by power and

---

182. Coser, 'Conflict', p. 234.

183. Coser, *The Functions of Conflict*, p. 116; *idem*, 'Conflict', p. 234.

184. Dahrendorf, *Class and Class Conflict*, p. 185.

185. Coser, *The Functions of Conflict*, p. 116; see also *idem*, 'Conflict', p. 234.

186. Lenski, *Power and Privilege*, pp. 70-71.

187. Lenski, *Power and Privilege*, p. 71.

188. Lenski, *Power and Privilege*, p. 51.

authority.[189] Of course, ideology does not only strengthen the position of the rulers, it makes them particularly vulnerable as well, for all ideologies incorporate the thesis that they exist to serve the 'common good'. But '... since no ideology can long survive if there is *no* substance to back up this claim, a ruler must make some delivery on the promises inherent in it'.[190]

The question remains whether values (or ideologies) can cause conflict or, in other words, whether two parties can be in confrontation with each other because they represent different sets of values or ideologies? This is of course possible; people do clash because of different ideologies. But, consistent to conflict theory, value differences will never be the basis for conflict; it will always be possible to reduce the conflict to differences in interests because value differences can almost always be translated back to differences in interests. Conflict of ideology is almost always an intensified conflict of interest, as we have seen above.

Values and ideologies suit the interests of those who uphold them. In the period of the so-called 'Cold War', the USA and the former USSR competed for world domination, prestige and power. These were their interests. But they legitimized their claims by using their different ideologies and presented *their* own view as 'superior' to the other. What was presented as a conflict of ideologies, capitalism versus communism, could in terms of conflict theory be seen instead as a conflict of interests. This probably lies behind a humorous Russian saying, cited by Lenski: 'Question: What is the difference between Capitalism and Communism? Answer: Under Capitalism man exploits man; under Communism it's the other way around!'[191] Interests are usually presented in terms of values. Two parties value power highly; therefore, in their own interest, they strive to gain the power. Their struggle can be intensified and legitimized by a set of values or an ideology. An ideology, as we have seen before, is seen as manifest interests that are the product of intellectual reflections on interests.

The difference between values and interests remains difficult to resolve clearly. De Jager and Mok distinguish between the two in terms

---

189. Cf. Lenski, *Power and Privilege*, pp. 50-54; Dahrendorf, 'Out of Utopia', p. 180 and 'In Praise of Thrasymachus', pp. 174-75.

190. Lenski, *Power and Privilege*, p. 181.

191. Lenski, *Power and Privilege*, p. 297.

of the verbs *being* and *having*.[192] For values one says: I want to *be* honest, courageous or loyal. In the case of interests one says: I want to *have* money, power or prestige. But again, consistent to conflict theory, one is never honest for no reason: because I want to have prestige, it suits my image to be honest.

Expectations. I can be brief with 'expectations', for it has already been discussed under the other categories, especially under 'goals'. We have seen above that Kriesberg views change in attainment and expectations as a major source of grievance.[193] Suffice it to say here that expectations are desires of what one thinks should be, both in the social conditions of the subject or in its relation to others. What is expected from social conditions or personalities, largely depends on the values of the subject, which, as we have indicated, are dependent on the interests of the individual or the group. If these expectations are not met, they could indirectly lead to conflict.

Preliminary Conclusion as to the Causes of Conflict. The real causes of any conflict depend, of course, on the particular conflict in question. Nevertheless, following Dahrendorf and Lenski as a 'rule of thumb', and on a high level of abstraction, almost all conflicts can be reduced to having a basic cause and that is the *strive/drive for the maximizing of own interests*.[194] Dahrendorf presented interests relationally in terms of class-interests, meaning that it is in the interests of the rulers to remain in power, to maintain a position of authority and to keep the status quo. But it is in the interests of the subordinates to seek change,

---

192. De Jager and Mok, *Grondbeginselen der sociologie*, p. 67.

193. Kriesberg, *The Sociology of Social Conflicts*, p. 76.

194. Although the maximizing of own interests is the determining factor for conflict to emerge, and although the laws of distribution (to Lenski) determine that there is a constant struggle for power, privilege and prestige in order to control the scarce resources as well as the surplus resources, we must not forget the first postulate of Lenski on the nature of humankind, namely that humankind is a social being. For the drive to maximize one's own interests must not be confused with individualism, egoism or, as Huber and Tödt call it, 'Anthropology of individuals without responsibilities' (Huber and Tödt, *Menschenrechte*, pp. 109-10). This indeed can easily happen if the first postulate is not kept in mind. If someone acts out of own interests to such an extent that he/she forgets that he/she is a social being as well, and that he/she sometimes has to co-operate with others to survive, he/she falls into egoism or individualism and this is viewed as counter-productive, or contra own interests.

for they too wish to gain power and authority. Dahrendorf correctly saw that in any *particular conflict* there are only two groups: those who attack and those who defend. There can be more than two interest groups in one society, but as soon as conflict emerges, it is only between two groups. Dahrendorf, however, does not present us with an adequate explanation of what interests are, except as 'defending' or 'attacking'. Lenski distinguishes between 'individual' and 'social' interests. He identifies a number of individual interests and ranks *survival* as the highest. After survival comes health, then status and prestige, comfort, salvation and affection and finally the instrumental interests like money, wealth and education. How these interests are ranked may differ from person to person or group to group.[195] But, to Lenski, they are all subordinate to survival. Survival, however, means more than just staying alive. To stay alive a human being has constant basic needs like food and housing. However, humankind has always been able to produce a surplus of goods, an advantage it has over nature. These basic requirements plus any surplus of goods produced, must remain available to all and therefore there is a constant struggle to control them. Furthermore, power and authority are always needed to control the scarce goods and services.

But, power and authority need not only be interpreted in terms of survival, as we have done above. Dahrendorf places the emphasis on authority, that is a sociological relationship of domination and subordination. Authority is legitimated power. Mankind (and especially the elites of the society) strives for the power and authority to be able to determine the distribution of surplus goods and resources in society. This causes inequality of power and authority in society, as well as an unequal distribution of scarce resources, and this in turn causes conflict. This brings us back to Dahrendorf's view: if there is a group with access to basic resources and surpluses, which also has the power, privilege and prestige, there will be a constant struggle between this group wanting to *keep* authority and those who want to *acquire* it.

We have seen Lenski's definition of 'social interests' as the ends towards which the co-ordinated efforts of the whole are directed. But these interests hardly ever represent those of the whole of society, rather as he indicated, they are the interests of the dominant group that present them as being those of the whole of society. Therefore, we

195. See Fisher, 'Needs Theory, Social Identity and an Eclectic Model of Conflict', p. 91; Galtung, 'International Development in Human Perspective', p. 309.

cannot really ever speak of 'social interests', only, as Dahrendorf does, of 'class' or group interests.

Almost all causes of conflict can be traced back to interests in some way or other. This is how reality presents itself to us. But, interests have to be defined. They can best be expressed in terms of group identity, which in turn finds expression in goals. But if goals are seldom reached, if expectations (expressed in terms of goals) are not met, if people feel deprived or misplaced with regard to their rank or experience, then there is cause for grievance and conflict.

Furthermore, interests are intensified and articulated in terms of the values of individuals or groups. Mostly this articulation and codification is done by intellectuals in the service of the rulers. To put it differently, interests are presented in the form of values or ideologies. Conflict caused by different interests therefore, can be broadly expressed in terms of ideologies, which appear to be incompatible because in fact they serve different interests.

I now turn to another vital question: What are the units of conflict or who is in conflict with whom?

What are the Units of Conflict? Who is in Conflict?
At first sight this question seems impossible to answer in general terms. We have to know the particular situation to identify who is in conflict with whom. To recognize whether they are individuals, groups, organizations, classes, nations or communities depends on the particular conflict in question. I have opted for a general theory to explain the units of conflict.

A general theory of conflict, in which the units are left vague, has the advantage of making the theory abstract and hence applicable to all social units from individuals to nation states.[196] Theoretical statements can be potentially more powerful for explaining conflict between all social units. But, as Turner proceeds,

> On the other hand, however, it is likely that the nature of the units influences the nature of the conflict among them. While conflict between individuals and nations may have certain common properties, and thus be subsumable under some general laws, there are also likely to be clear differences in conflict between such disparate units.[197]

196. Cf. Turner, *The Structure of Sociological Theory*, p. 183.
197. Turner, *The Structure of Sociological Theory*, p. 183.

In a general theory of conflict the units will remain vague and abstract. But, with this critique of Turner on Dahrendorf's (and Coser's) theories in mind, we nevertheless turn to Dahrendorf's views on the units of conflict. We are, in fact, searching for a general theory with basic trends by which all types of conflict could to a great extent be explained, including the conflict in the Matthean community and that between Jesus and the Pharisees. We therefore want to accentuate the other part of Turner's critique, or rather rephrase it: although the general theories are vague, they are highly perceptive (and commensurable as I have argued in Chapter 1).[198] Realizing the danger that a general theory can be 'enforced' on a particular conflict situation, we still do not want to throw out the baby with the bathwater. We need those 'basic laws' of conflict to understand the phenomenon of conflict. The variables of the situation involved will be dealt with as soon as the model is applied in the identification of the conflicting parties in the Matthean community. Furthermore, Malina, in describing the conflict in Mediterranean society in using terms like *the elites* (Roman imperial and aristocratic establishment, Greek magistrates, Judaean Sadducees or Galilean Herodians) and the *non-elites*, comes considerably closer, in any case, to the general principles of Dahrendorf's theory.[199]

Quasi-Group. As we have seen above, Dahrendorf postulated two distinctive, conflicting orientations of (latent) interests in any 'imperatively coordinated association'; those who dominate (have authority) and those who are subordinate (have no authority). He uses the term 'association' to imply the co-ordination (willingly or unwillingly by virtue of authority—thus 'imperatively') of organized aggregates in roles of domination and subjection.[200] 'The aggregates of incumbents with identical role interests are at best a potential group.'[201] In their position of domination or subordination they may have latent interests, but as yet are not necessarily organized into groups. They are at best, says Dahrendorf, a potential group with certain common latent interests which, following M. Ginsberg, he calls a *quasi-group*. Not all collectives or aggregates form groups. In Dahrendorf's terms groups are

---

198. Cf. Turner, *The Structure of Sociological Theory*, p. 184.
199. Malina, 'A Conflict Approach to Mark 7', p. 14.
200. Cf. Dahrendorf, *Class and Class Conflict*, p. 168.
201. Dahrendorf, *Class and Class Conflict*, p. 180.

masses of people in regular contact or communication, possessing a recognizable structure. A group needs a feeling of belonging (consciousness) and some organization (in order to interact on a regular basis).[202] Ginsberg (cited by Dahrendorf) says that there are aggregates or portions of the community which have no recognizable structure, but whose members have certain interests or modes of behaviour in common, which may at any time lead them to form themselves into definite groups.[203] To this category of quasi-groups belong such entities as social classes, which, without being groups, are the recruiting grounds for groups, and whose members have certain characteristic modes of behaviour in common. Dahrendorf uses the so-called 'peasant class' as an example: by virtue of their situation (being in a subordinate position), their conditions of existence, their way of life and their (latent) interests, they constitute a quasi-group rather than a class, for they have a common identity and interest, but lack the organization to regard themselves as a group. They remain the recruiting ground for those *interest groups* who are active amongst their ranks.[204]

Interest Groups. Interest groups, says Dahrendorf are groups in the strict sense of the sociological term.[205] They are the real agents of the group conflict. They have a structure, a form of organization, a programme or goal and a personnel of members. They are in regular contact or communication, although this is often secondary. The members have contact with each other by virtue of their membership or by way of their elected or appointed representatives.

How do quasi-groups and interest groups stand in relation to each other? To what extent are interest groups to be regarded as representative of the quasi-group behind them? Firstly, the interest group is always smaller than the quasi-group. Secondly, in social conflicts, the interest group functions as a unit of manifest interest, that can be explained in terms of latent role interests and their aggregation in the quasi-groups. To Dahrendorf the movement from quasi- to interest group under ideal conditions follows a certain process.[206] He says that in every 'imperatively coordinated association', two quasi-groups,

202. Cf. Benkin, *Sociology*, p. 151.
203. Dahrendorf, *Class and Class Conflict*, p. 180.
204. Cf. Dahrendorf, *Class and Class Conflict*, pp. 180, 182.
205. Dahrendorf, *Class and Class Conflict*, p. 180.
206. Dahrendorf, *Class and Class Conflict*, p. 183.

united by common latent interests, can be distinguished. Again Dahrendorf returns to an already known explanation: their orientation of interest is determined by possession of, or exclusion from, authority. He goes on to say that from these quasi-groups, interest groups are recruited, the articulated programmes of which defend or attack the legitimacy of existing authority structures. In this formation of interest groups, six features are of importance: a charter, personnel, certain norms, a material instrumentarium, certain regular activities and an objective function. We have, already dealt with a charter and personnel. Suffice it to say that in forming interest groups, the leaders and ideologies articulate those manifest interests emanating from the latent interests of the quasi-group, and therefore also represent a larger group than just the interest groups themselves.

Agrarian Society. Dahrendorf's theory is almost entirely based on industrial society. This might be seen as a limitation for the explanation of conflicts in other kinds of societies, and the conflict in the Matthean community to which we are eventually moving. However, many of his views can also be applied to the agrarian societies, in which the gap between those who rule (and have authority) and those who are subordinate (and have little or no authority) is much more apparent. If we assume that the Matthean community and, in fact, all first-century Mediterranean communities were typical advanced agrarian societies, the huge gap between rulers and subordinates also existed in these communities and also caused conflict.[207] There is good reason to assume that the first-century Mediterranean communities were typical agrarian societies, for Lenski regularly refers to the Roman empire of that time as a good example of such a society. Furthermore, Lenski and Lenski indicate that agrarian societies existed over a time span of more than 5000 years, beginning in about 3000 BCE and continuing, through to a

---

207. Cf. Saldarini, *Pharisees, Scribes and Sadducees in Palestinian Society*, pp. 20-27; J.D. Crossan, *The Historical Jesus: The Life of a Mediterranean Jewish Peasant* (San Francisco: HarperCollins, 1991), pp. 43-46; Duling, 'Matthew and Marginality', pp. 642-71 (650); Van Aarde, 'Aspekte van die sosiale stratifikasie van die ontwikkelde agrariese samelewing in die eerste-eeuse Palistina', p. 528; R.L. Rohrbaugh, 'The Social Location of the Markan Audience', *Int* 47.4 (1993), pp. 380-95 (383).

lesser extent, to the present day (notably the so-called Third World countries).[208]

A distinction is made between 'simple' and 'advanced' agrarian societies. 'Simple' agrarian societies went beyond the so-called horticultural societies because of significant advances in technology and production, especially in the field of agriculture (ploughs, weed control, harnessing of animals).[209] 'Advanced' agrarian societies were similar to simple ones, but more progressive in some areas, for example iron was increasingly used for ordinary everyday tools and implements. However advanced, these societies were constantly affected by famine, plagues, poor sanitary conditions, and high infant mortality rates. Regional and local economics were specialized. There was a stronger command economy in that it was dictated by the politically powerful and urban elite. This group was strengthened by taxation, growth in commerce, weakening kinships and the growth in expendable people. Exploitation of the peasants was the rule.[210]

One of the outstanding features of agrarian communities (or states) is that they were all *conquest states;* social groups (units) formed by the forcible subjugation of one group by another. Lenski says that few agrarian states ever came into being simply through the peaceful political evolution and expansion of a single people or through the voluntary federation or union of separate people. War was a chronic condition in all agrarian states and if struggles with foreign enemies were lacking, internal struggles often developed.[211] An example is to be found in the Roman empire:

> Of the seventy-nine Roman emperors from Augustus to Romulus Augustulus, no less than twenty-one were murdered, while six others were driven to suicide, four were forcibly deposed, and several others met uncertain ends at the hands of internal enemies.[212]

208. G.E. Lenski and J. Lenski, *Human Societies: Introduction to Macrosociology* (New York: McGraw–Hill, 1982), p. 88.

209. Cf. Lenski, *Power and Privilege,* p. 192; Duling, 'Matthew's Plurisignificant "Son of David" in Social-science Perspective', p. 100. Note that Lenski in his work *Power and Privilege* does not make a distinction between 'simple' and 'advanced' agrarian societies.

210. Duling, 'Matthew's Plurisignificant "Son of David" in Social-science Perspective', p. 101.

211. Lenski, *Power and Privilege,* p. 195.

212. Lenski, *Power and Privilege,* p. 197.

Another striking feature of agrarian societies is the *enormous inequality* that existed in those societies, especially between the ruler(s) and the common people.[213] The interests of the common people, in the event of wars between opposing factions of privileged classes, were hardly ever considered. The rulers regarded their subordinates as their 'property' with which they could do as they pleased. No distinctions were made between official duties or interests and private interests. Says Lenski:

> Guided by the proprietary theory of the state [according to which the state is a piece of property which its owner, that is the ruler, may use, within broad and somewhat ill-defined limits, for his own personal advantage], agrarian rulers saw nothing improper or immoral in the use of what we, not they, would call 'public office' for private gain.[214]

Supporting the *rulers* was the so-called small *governing class*. Also there was the so-called *retainer class*. Together with the *priestly class*, they formed the *upper classes* of society.[215] The *lower classes* included the so-called *merchant, peasant, artisan, unclean or degraded* and the

---

213. See above; see also the following works on the class system in agrarian empires who have all developed it from Lenski: Saldarini, 'Political and Social Roles of the Pharisees and the Scribes in Galilee', pp. 200-209 (200-202); *idem, Pharisees, Scribes and Sadducees in Palestinian Society*, pp. 39-45; D. Fiensy, *The Social History of Palestine in the Herodian Period: The Land is Mine* (Lewiston, NY: Edwin Mellen, 1991), p. 158; Duling, 'Matthew's Plurisignificant "Son of David" in Social-science Perspective', p. 101; *idem*, 'Matthew and Marginality', p. 651; Rohrbaugh, 'The Social Location of the Markan Audience', p. 383; Crossan, *The Historical Jesus*, pp. 43-46.

214. Lenski, *Power and Privilege*, p. 214.

215. Cf. Saldarini, *Pharisees, Scribes and Sadducees in Palestinian Society*, p. 313 and 'Political and Social Roles of the Pharisees and the Scribes in Galilee', p. 200. Note that Saldarini places the *merchants* under the upper classes (Saldarini, *Pharisees, Scribes and Sadducees in Palestinian Society*, p. 313; *idem*, 'Political and Social Roles of the Pharisees and the Scribes in Galilee', p. 200). However, as Saldarini himself has stated, they are difficult to place for they do not really fit into either the ruling or the lower classes (Saldarini, *Pharisees, Scribes and Sadducees in Palestinian Society*, p. 42). But, although they easily escaped any control by the governing classes, and supplied them with luxuries and essentials, I would rather place them with the lower classes because of the fact that, generally speaking, they had low prestige, no direct power and were recruited from the landless (cf. Saldarini, *Pharisees, Scribes and Sadducees in Palestinian Society*, pp. 42-43; see also Lenski, *Power and Privilege*, pp. 248-56.

expendable.[216] These classes are discussed in much more detail by Lenski and he also presents examples to support his statements.[217] These classes will be described in Chapter 3.

The possibility of upward mobility in these agrarian societies was slim (it did of course happen, especially when the wealth of an individual in some way or other increased). Downward mobility was more likely because of population growth and very few positions of privilege. Social stratification, therefore, was very apparent and conflict was an ever present possibility. This makes Dahrendorf's model also applicable to agrarian societies as far as authority is concerned (see Chapter 3 below on *Group boundaries and self-definition*, for the consequences of both Dahrendorf's and Lenski's views for the conflicting situation in the community of Matthew).

What are the Functions of Conflict? As we have already noted, the basic assumption of the conflict theory is that conflict is ubiquitous. Wherever there is life, there is conflict. Even as Dahrendorf asks, 'May we perhaps go so far to say that conflict is a condition necessary for life to be possible at all?'[218] This leads to a further assumption, also previously mentioned, that *conflict is the creative force of change in society.*[219] Conflict is an essential feature in any society in the process of development, not only for the maintenance of the status quo, as Coser sees it, *but also to bring about fundamental and structural,* as well as ideological changes.[220] Conflict is important, not only to foster the stability of a society, but, also to help abandon old systems and create new ones.

But, one of the main criticism of Dahrendorf is that he views conflict as the motivational force for change, but the question of what sort of change he has in mind, remains open. Turner is undoubtably correct when he says, 'Conflict is seen to emerge and cause change, but theories sometimes fail to specify what kind of conflict revealing what

216. Cf. Saldarini, *Pharisees, Scribes and Sadducees in Palestinian Society*, p. 312 and 'Political and Social Roles of the Pharisees and the Scribes in Galilee', p. 200.

217. Lenski, *Power and Privilege*, pp. 189-296.

218. Dahrendorf, *Class and Class Conflict*, p. 208.

219. Cf. Dahrendorf, 'Towards a Theory of Social Conflict', p. 178, *idem, Class and Class Conflict*, p. 208; *idem, Gesellschaft und Freiheit*, p. 125; *idem*, 'Out of Utopia', p. 127.

220. Coser, *The Functions of Conflict*, p. 80.

properties causes what alterations in what subsystems or systemic wholes.'[221] Turner asks, 'Is Dahrendorf seeking to explain conflict, or to assert an image of social organization as constantly in change?'[222] Indeed, Dahrendorf remains vague on what kind of changes are involved. It appears, as Turner also points out, that he concentrates more on severe and violent conflicts resulting in the redistribution of resources into new patterns of inequality, which in turn cause new waves of conflict and so on.[223] Conflict and change are never ending, but for what these changes involve, it seems, we will have to rely greatly on our own imagination, and of course, the particular conflict in focus. Turner is of the opinion that neither Dahrendorf (dialectical theory of conflict), nor Coser (conflict functionalism) really succeed in abandoning structural functionalism.[224] But as far as Dahrendorf's theory is concerned, this criticism rather supports his view of the 'two-facedness' of society. Conflict contributes both to the integration of social 'systems' *and* to the changing of them.[225]

A more detailed view on the functions of conflict, comes from L.A. Coser.[226] Despite the (justified) criticism by both Dahrendorf and Turner that Coser is only concerned with conflict in as far as it has a 'positive' function to re-establish unity and stability, his insights are most useful in the search for an answer as to what kinds of change conflict could bring about.[227] His view succeeds in doing what Dahrendorf failed to do, namely to give content to the concept of 'change'.

Coser assumes 16 propositions on the functions of conflict. Almost all of them are taken from the work of George Simmel, who also

---

221. Turner, *The Structure of Sociological Theory*, p. 186.

222. Turner, *The Structure of Sociological Theory*, p. 186.

223. Turner, *The Structure of Sociological Theory*, p. 185.

224. Turner, *The Structure of Sociological Theory*, p. 185. See also J.H. Turner, 'From Utopia to Where? A Strategy for Reformulating the Dahrendorf Conflict Model', *Social Forc* 52 (1973), pp. 236-44 (243) and 'A Strategy for the Reformulating of the Dialectical and Functional Theories of Conflict', p. 433.

225. See Dahrendorf, *Class and Class Conflict*, p. 157, 207.

226. Coser, *The Functions of Conflict*; *idem*, 'The Functions of Social Conflict', in L.A. Coser and B. Rosenberg (eds.), *Social Theory: A Book of Readings* (New York: Macmillan, 1957); see also G. Van Parys, 'Functies van het sociaal conflict: Een poging tot herformulering en actualisering van enkele proposities van L.A. Coser', *Tijdschrift voor Sociale Wetenschappen* 25.4 (1980), pp. 377-98.

227. Cf. Dahrendorf, *Class and Class Conflict*, p. 207; Turner, *The Structure of Sociological Theory*, p. 185.

views conflict as having a 'positive' function in society. We will not discuss all of Coser's propositions, only those that we consider to be of value for our prime focus: the conflict in the Matthean community, and in Matthew 8 and 9 in particular.

The Group-Binding Functions of Conflict. Only when challenged by another group does it become important to be conscious of one's identity. In terms of this view, conflict has a clarifying effect.[228] The distinction between ourselves, the we-group, or in-group, and everybody else, the other-groups, or out-groups, is established through conflict.[229] Coser states,

> Conflict serves to establish and maintain the identity and boundary lines of societies and groups.
>
> Conflict with other groups contributes to the establishment and reaffirmation of the identity of the group and maintains its boundaries against the surrounding social world.
>
> Patterned enmities and reciprocal antagonisms conserve social divisions and systems of stratification. Such patterned antagonisms prevent the gradual disappearance of boundaries between the sub-groups of a social system and they assign position to the various subsystems within a total system.[230]

However, according to the views of Dahrendorf, conflict can also lead to change. This encourages us to see that, depending on the force of the challenge, conflict can *also* lead to changes in boundaries and changes in identity, (and in extreme cases even the total breakdown of systems). Thus, conflict has adaptive consequences.[231] It is especially the aspect of *renegadism* that breaks through established boundaries (see below). This is particularly true of the Matthean community, in that they underwent a fundamental change of identity in relation to their next-door neighbours, the Jews, although they still considered themselves to be part of the Jewish world (see below in Chapter 3 on *Group boundaries and self-definition*).

Conflict has a group-preserving functions and has significance as a safety-valve. Conflict is not always dysfunctional with regard to relationships. By setting free pent-up feelings of hostility, conflict can

---

228. Cf. Boskoff, *The Mosaic of Sociological Theory*, p. 88.
229. Cf. Coser, *The Functions of Conflict*, p. 35.
230. Coser, *The Functions of Conflict*, p. 38; see also 'Conflict', p. 235.
231. Cf. Boskoff, *The Mosaic of Sociological Theory*, p. 89.

serve to maintain a relationship. It 'clears the air'. Social systems do provide specific institutions that serve to drain off hostile and aggressive sentiments.[232]

Conflict's Function to Intensify Relationships and Vice Versa. Although it may sound like a contradictory statement, every close social (as in a personal) relationship involves both converging and diverging elements. It involves both love and hatred. In fact, the closer the relationship, the more intense the conflict. Close relationships in which the participants are deeply involved and in which they engage their total personality, often create ambivalent feelings of affection and hostility. Marriage relationships serve as good examples of this fact. Coser says that the closer the relationship, the greater the affective investment, the greater also the tendency to suppress rather than to express hostile feelings.[233] Increased social interaction is often likely to bring about an increase of hostility as well as affection. Antagonism is often one of the elements in an intimate relationship.[234]

Arguing from this standpoint, in a close relationship, fear of intense disagreement or conflict often leads to the suppression of these hostile feelings. This leads to an accumulation of such feelings, which in turn is likely to further intensify the conflict once it does break out. Coser says that where total personalities are involved, there is a greater likelihood of nonrealistic elements, such as aggressive impulses, entering into realistic conflict situations.[235] Conflict, even if suppressed at first, will nevertheless occur and then it will be even more intense and passionate. As we will see later, this is particularly true of the relationship between the Jewish leaders and the Matthean community.

Coser continues to say that individuals who participate intensely in the life of such groups are concerned with the group's continuity.[236] Says Coser:

> If they witness the breaking away of one with whom they have shared cares and responsibilities of group life, they are likely to react in a more

232. Cf. Coser, *The Functions of Conflict*, p. 48.
233. Coser, *The Functions of Conflict*, p. 62.
234. Cf. Coser, *The Functions of Conflict*, p. 64.
235. Coser, *The Functions of Conflict*, p. 69.
236. Coser, *The Functions of Conflict*, p. 69.

violent way against such 'disloyalty' than less involved members. . .
Renegadism is perceived by a close group as a threat to its unity.[237]

Reactions towards the 'enemy from within', the renegade or heretic,
poses a threat to a group's values and interests, and its unity. Renegadism threatens to break down the boundary lines of the established
group:

> Therefore the group must fight the renegade with all its might since he
> threatens symbolically, if not in fact, its existence as an ongoing concern.
> In the religious sphere, for example, apostasy strikes at the very life of a
> church, hence the violence of denunciation of the apostate contained in the
> pronouncements of early Church fathers or in rabbinical statements from
> the time of the Maccabees onwards.[238]

To the group that the renegade has left, he appears as a symbol of
danger. The reaction to him/her (or the renegade group) is often more
hostile than against the apostate. A heretic is a more insidious danger
to the upholding of the group's central values and goals. He threatens
to split the group into factions that will have different views on the
means for implementing the goals of the group. The heretic will continue to compete for the loyalty of the members of his former group.
'Moreover, by professing to share the values of the group, the heretic
creates confusion and hence his actions are perceived as an attempt to
break down the boundaries.'[239] Conflict then, tends to be more passionate and intense if it arises out of a close relationship. As soon as
conflict evolves inside a group, one side often hates the other side more
intensely if it is felt to be a threat to the unity and identity of the group.
The greater the participation in the group and the greater the personal
involvement of the members, the more violent will be the reaction to
disloyalty.[240]

The Search for Enemies. Following Simmel, Coser says that groups in
conflict may actually 'attract' enemies in order to help maintain an
increased group cohesion.[241] A strange, but real, phenomenon is that,
with the disappearance of the original enemy, there emerges a search
for a new enemy. In this way, the group is able to continue engaging

237. Coser, *The Functions of Conflict*, p. 69.
238. Coser, *The Functions of Conflict*, pp. 69-70.
239. Coser, *The Functions of Conflict*, p. 71.
240. Coser, *The Functions of Conflict*, pp. 71-72.
241. Coser, *The Functions of Conflict*, p. 104.

in conflict, thereby maintaining a structure that it would be in danger of losing were there no longer an enemy.

Alongside the search for an 'outside enemy', is the search for an 'inside enemy', at the prospect of defeat or an unexpected increase in external danger.[242] If a group experiences the increased strength of the adversary, or a defeat of some sort, rather than admit its own weakness, a guilty party or scapegoat has to be found. Defeat, by outsiders, leads to a search for hate objects among insiders:

> Those group members who must bear the burden of being the scapegoats through their sacrifice, cleanse the group of its own failings, and in this way re-establish its solidarity: the loyal members are reassured that the group as a whole has not failed, but only some 'traitors'; moreover, they can now reaffirm their righteousness by uniting in action against the 'traitors'.[243]

The inner enemy can be real, he or she can be a dissenter who has opposed certain aspects of group life. He or she, however, can also be 'invented', in order to bring about—through a common hostility towards him or her—the social solidarity which the group needs.

Conflict Binds Antagonists. Coser, along with Simmel, believes that conflict has a threefold function: '(1) Conflict initiates other types of *interaction* between antagonists, (2) it acts as a *stimulus for the establishing of new rules, norms and values* and (3) it *reaffirms dormant norms* and thus intensifies participation in social life.'[244] By definition, engaging in conflict means that a relationship between the parties has been established. Conflict results in a cross-fertilization of ideas, norms, values and cultures of previously unrelated societies. Conflict establishes relations where non existed before or have broken down. Hostile interaction is often the means to 'test' and 'get to know' the previously unknown.

During the course of the conflict between two parties, new rules and overall social rules are created. Coser sees it as a change in the meaning of conflict, but I will take a broader view: because of the interaction between groups, to include changes in values and norms, and even changes the initial interests.[245] Old rules and norms are modified

---

242. Cf. Coser, *The Functions of Conflict*, p. 106.
243. Coser, *The Functions of Conflict*, pp. 106-107.
244, Coser, *The Functions of Conflict*, pp. 121-28.
245. Cf. Coser, *The Functions of Conflict*, p. 124.

because of the interaction and the conflict. Mere contact between groups or individuals, does not necessarily lead to changes in values, but to my mind, interaction through conflict does. 'By bringing about new situations, which are partly or totally undefined by rules and norms, conflict acts as a stimulus for the establishment of new rules and norms.'[246]

Furthermore, conflict brings into the conscious awareness of the contenders and the community at large, norms and rules that were dormant before that particular conflict. It brings about the need for the application of rules that, had no conflict occurred, might have remained dormant and forgotten. It brings about new conditions, adjustments in norms and the re-evaluation of old norms. This has implications for our later assessment of the conflict between Jesus and the Pharisees and the conflict between the Matthean community (believers in Jesus) and the Jewish leadership. What changes in values and norms did the conflict of interests between these two groups bring about?

The Spiral of Conflict

I have chosen a broad definition of conflict to *include* both latent and manifest conflicts. Nevertheless, distinctions can be made as far as the development of conflict is concerned, as long as we keep in mind that one stage of conflict is no more, or no less *conflicting* than another. Because conflict can be viewed as a process as well, some differences in nuance in its development have to be noted.[247]

The model of Kriesberg is quite simple and convincing.[248] Conflicts are seen as moving through a series of stages. Not every conflict goes through all the stages, but each stage depends to a significant degree on an earlier stage.

> Nevertheless later stages affect what is analytically prior. This recursive quality occurs through feedback and anticipations of later stages. Finally, specific struggles never revert to prior conditions exactly as they were. One struggle generally leads to another in an on-going spiral of conflict.[249]

To Kriesberg the full cycle in a social conflict consists of five stages. First is the objective or underlying social conflict relationships. Secondly, the two or more parties start believing they have incompatible

246. Coser, *The Functions of Conflict*, p. 124.
247. Cf. Turner, *The Structure of Sociological Theory*, p. 188.
248. Kriesberg, *The Sociology of Social Conflicts*, pp. 18-19, 268-73.
249. Kriesberg, *The Sociology of Social Conflicts*, p. 269.

goals. Thirdly, there is the initial way in which the adversaries pursue their contradictory aims. Fourthly, the intensity and the scope of the struggle escalates and de-escalates and then finally, the conflict comes to some kind of end and there is an outcome. But this outcome at the same time holds the potential for the emergence of a new conflict.

Awareness. Firstly, there is the *objective or underlying conflict relationship*. We can call this stage the 'latent' phase of conflict.

This first stage implies that there exist a number of slumbering emotions, vague frustrations, aggression and grievances, which are present, but not that apparent or clear. Also from Turner's analysis of the stages of conflict (which he derives from Dahrendorf and Coser), it is clear that conflict in this phase, although present, remains vague.[250] In the social system of interdependent groups we find unequal distribution of the scarce and valuable resources available. But, why and how these inequalities are present is not clear; it must depend on the specific kind of society. In agrarian societies, as we have seen above, inequality is embedded in the system itself.

The Manifest Stage. The second stage in Kriesberg's model is the phase where two parties believe that they have incompatible goals and a social *conflict emerges*.[251] The conflict becomes manifest when adversaries define their goals which are then opposed by the other side. 'These aims [and interests] are based upon some collective identity and sense of grievance.'[252] Those in conflict become, or are made aware of their differences.[253]

The Conflict Mode Stage. A further stage of conflict, the third in Kriesberg's view, is the way in which the adversaries pursue their contradictory aims.[254] Kriesberg calls this phase the *conflict mode*.[255] Once the adversaries are in conflict, they select some way of contending with each other. Says Kriesberg: 'Three fundamental ways of

250. Turner, *The Structure of Sociological Theory*, pp. 188-96.
251. Kriesberg, *The Sociology of Social Conflicts*, pp. 61, 269.
252. Kriesberg, *The Sociology of Social Conflicts*, p. 269.
253. Turner, *The Structure of Sociological Theory*, pp. 189-90.
254. Kriesberg, *The Sociology of Social Conflicts*, pp. 107, 269-70.
255. Kriesberg, *The Sociology of Social Conflicts*, p. 272.

inducing the other side to yield what is desired were distinguished: coercion, persuasion, and reward.'[256]

Coercion involves trying to make the other side yield through feared or actual injury. Those that use this mode believe that the pain of not complying will be worse than that of complying. Coercion means punishment if there is no complying.[257]

By *persuasion*, the conflicting parties believe that the adversary should comply because that which is pursued (or sought) is consistent with his own long term or more general interests and values. The idea here is to appeal to more abstract principles, shared identities or previously neglected values and considerations. This is done by communication or by convincing the other side through deeds and demonstrations.[258]

Reward is also called 'positive sanction'. The idea is that one side offers the other a reward for compliance rather than a punishment for not complying.[259]

The 'Termination Mode' of Conflict. The next phase, as Kriesberg sees it, is that of the termination modes: the *escalation* or the *de-escalation* of conflict.[260]

Escalation means increasing the magnitudes of conflict behaviour either in scope or in the way in which the struggle is conducted.[261] Under the process of escalation, Kriesberg deals with *changes within a struggle unit* and *changes in the relation between adversaries.* Since the former has more to do with *intra*-group conflict (as opposed to *inter*-group conflict), I will only reflect on the latter. Changes in the relationship between adversaries with regard to the expectation of the issues in contention, the polarization of relations and third party involvement, is likely to allow the conflict to escalate.

There is always a change in the relationship between adversaries, also with the *de-escalation* of a conflict. *New ties and bonds emerge,* even while they are struggling against each other. Strangely enough,

256. Kriesberg, *The Sociology of Social Conflicts*, p. 270.
257. Cf. Kriesberg, *The Sociology of Social Conflicts*, p. 180.
258. Cf. Kriesberg, *The Sociology of Social Conflicts*, p. 107.
259. Cf. Kriesberg, *The Sociology of Social Conflicts*, pp. 108-109.
260. Kriesberg, *The Sociology of Social Conflicts*, p. 270.
261. Kriesberg, *The Sociology of Social Conflicts*, pp. 155-63.

mutual respect can evolve out of this contact and two parties can eventually reach an agreement and understanding.

As far as the *contraction of goals* is concerned, each side believes that its actions will stop or prevent the escalation of conflict behaviour by the other side. This, however, is seldom the case. Coercion hardly ever leads to the intimidation of people on the opposite side and their withdrawal of support from their leaders. Nevertheless, coercion *can* lead to de-escalation in two ways: one possibility is that coercion is sufficient to physically prevent the other side from continuing with conflict. The other side then loses its capacity to continue its conflict behaviour at the same level and must allow the conflict to de-escalate.[262] The other possibility is that one side loses its will to persist in the conflict. It doubts its abilities and questions the desirability of continuing. However it is brought about, says Kriesberg, if one side finds that the adversary's coercion has reduced its ability to pursue its goals, it is likely to contract the goals; the issues in contention are likely to become more limited.[263] The conflict de-escalates.

De-escalation comes before conflict termination. Under termination of conflict it is understood that some people agree that the conflict has ended. Turner only views the *increased intensity* (escalation) in his model.[264] Intensity involves emotional arousal, but it also denotes the channelling of emotional energies and willingness to sustain these energies in the pursuit of objective interests.

Every conflict has an end. The last stage is the *outcome* of conflict. There are four kinds of outcome: withdrawal, imposition of goals on the other side, compromise, and conversion.[265]

Conclusion

My intention was to develop a conflict theory, based on the works of two authorities: Dahrendorf and Coser. We have seen, from the critique of Dahrendorf, that structural functionalism does not adequately explain the phenomenon of conflict. It does not view conflict positively as part and parcel of human experience and society, therefore

---

262. Kriesberg, *The Sociology of Social Conflicts*, p. 167.
263. Kriesberg, *The Sociology of Social Conflicts*, p. 167.
264. Turner, *The Structure of Sociological Theory*, pp. 192-93.
265. Some of these outcomes can be combined (see Kriesberg, *The Sociology of Social Conflicts*, pp. 206-208 for more detailed information).

we turned to the conflict theory. The basic assumptions of conflict theory as summarized by Dahrendorf are:

(1)   Every society is at every point subject to processes of change; social change is ubiquitous.

(2)   Every society displays at every point dissensus and conflict; social conflict is ubiquitous.

(3)   Every element in a society renders a contribution to its disintegration and change.

(4)   Every society is based on the coercion of some of its members by others.[266]

After a lengthy discussion on whether to adopt a broad or narrow definition of conflict, I opted for the former, following especially Fink and Bieder. I defined conflict as follows:

> Conflict is the permanent presence of antagonism (conscious or unconscious), opposition and incompatibility between two or more persons or groups. This antagonism, opposition and incompatibility lies on the level of interests, goals, values and expectations, which are seen as the causes of conflict. Conflict may or may not escalate to the point of violent coercion.

As far as the causes of conflict are concerned, I have previously stated that, on a high level of abstraction, almost all conflicts can be reduced to having a basic cause; that is the *strive/drive for the maximizing of own interests*. Dahrendorf presents interests relationally in terms of class-interests, meaning that it is in the interests of the rulers to remain in power and in a position of authority. Their interest lies in keeping the status quo. However, it is in the interests of the subordinates to change, for they also want to obtain power and authority. Any particular conflict can be reduced to two groups: those who attack and those who defend. As soon as conflict emerges, it is between the two dominant groups only, although there can be more than two interest groups in one society. Dahrendorf presents us only with interests indicated as 'defending' or 'attacking'.

Lenski distinguishes between 'individual' and 'social' interests. He identifies a number of individual interests and ranks *survival* as the highest.[267] Then follow health, status and prestige, comfort, salvation

---

266. Dahrendorf, *Class and Class Conflict*, p. 162; see also *idem*, 'Towards a Theory of Social Conflict', p. 174; *idem*, *Gesellschaft und Freiheit*, p. 210.

267. This indeed corresponds with the two most basic needs as Maslow, cited by

and affection and finally the instrumental interests such as money, wealth and education.[268] To Lenski, all are subordinate to one basic need: survival. Survival, however, means not just staying alive. Humans have constant basic needs like food and housing. But they have always been able to produce a surplus of goods, which is an advantage they have over nature. For these essentials for survival to remain available and for mankind to have constant access to the surplus services and needs, there is a constant struggle for control of these commodities.[269] Consequently, the possession of power and authority is necessary to be able to control those goods and services that are scarce.

But, power and authority as such are not only interpreted in terms of survival. Dahrendorf places the emphasis on authority, that is a sociological relation of domination and subordination. Authority is legitimated power. To Lenski, power (and following on from power, privilege and prestige) is the second part of what he calls a 'curious dualism', next to needs (or survival). Humankind (and especially the elites of society) strive for power and authority to be able to determine the distribution of the surplus goods and resources in society. This causes an unequal division of power and authority in society, as well as an unequal distribution of scarce resources, and this leads to conflict. This brings us back to Dahrendorf's view: if there is a group that has access to the basic resources and the surpluses, and also has

Fisher has given, namely *physiological needs* (i.e. basic internal deficit conditions that must be satisfied to maintain bodily processes) and *safety needs* (i.e. needs that must be met to protect the individual from danger; Fisher, 'Needs Theory, Social Identity and an Eclectic Model of Conflict', p. 91). Galtung also gives a list of basic needs. The first two of his list more or less correspond with those of Maslow. They are: *security needs* (survival needs)—to avoid violence, and *welfare needs* (sufficiency needs)—to avoid misery (Galtung, 'International Development in Human Perspective', p. 309).

268. See also Fisher, 'Needs Theory, Social Identity and an Eclectic Model of Conflict', p. 91; Galtung, 'International Development in Human Perspective', p. 309.

269. This could correspond with the 'higher up' needs of *esteem* (i.e. the need to achieve, compete and mastery as well as motives for recognition, prestige and status), and *self-actualization* (i.e. the ultimate motivation, involving the need to fulfil one's unique potential; cf. Fisher, 'Needs Theory, Social Identity and an Eclectic Model of Conflict', p. 91). The two (as I see it) 'higher' needs Galtung identified are: *identity needs* (needs for closeness)—to avoid alienation, and *freedom needs* (freedom of choice, option)—to avoid repression (Galtung, 'International Development in Human Perspective', p. 309).

the power, privilege and prestige, there will be a constant struggle between this group wanting to *keep* it (authority) and those who in one way or another want to *obtain* it.

We have seen Lenski's definition of 'social interests'. Social interests are the ends towards which the co-ordinated efforts of the whole are directed. But these interests hardly ever represent the interests of the whole of society, rather, as he points out, they are those of the dominant group who present their interests as being those of the whole of society. Therefore, we cannot really speak of 'social interests', but, as Dahrendorf does, of 'class' or 'group' interests.

Almost all causes of conflict can be translated back to interests in some way or other, as we have seen above. This is how reality presents itself to us. But, interests have to be put into words, they have to be identified and expressed. The term group identity can be used, which in turn finds expression in goals. But if goals are hardly ever reached, or if expectations (expressed in goals) are not met, if people feel deprived or feel themselves to be treated unfairly then there is cause for grievance and conflict.

Values articulate the interests of individuals or groups. Mostly this articulation and codification is done by intellectuals in the service of the rulers. Or to put it another way, interests are presented in the form of values or ideologies which means that a conflict caused by different interests could also be said to be caused by different ideologies. Consequently it is the ideologies that seem to be incompatible because they serve different interests.

With regard to the units of conflict, along with Dahrendorf, we have identified the quasi-group as a potential interest group. They have latent interests but are not yet organized into a group. They act as the recruiting field for the interest groups that are groups in the strict sense of the word. They have a structured organization, programme, goal and personnel.

We have seen that in an agrarian society a huge gap existed between the upper classes, who had authority, and lower classes, who had virtually none. Thus, in an agrarian society, such as the Matthean community, there was an ever present potential for conflict. I will, however, go into this aspect in more detail in the following chapter.

There are certain functions of conflict that need to be stated. Conflict can contribute both to the disruption and to the maintenance of a system. In both cases changes are recognized. Dahrendorf, who focuses more on the violent disruption of a society, which in turn grows into a new system, does not really indicate what kind of changes are involved. Coser, while concentrating on the influence conflict has on maintaining a system, does give us some indication of the changes involved, especially the influence it has on the parties concerned.

Conflict has a number of functions, apart from the overall, generalized one of bringing about change. It brings about a change in relationships both within the group and in how it relates to external groups. To sum up: conflict has a group-binding function. Through conflict, boundaries are set, identity is created and a sense of belonging is achieved. Part of this process of identity is the constant search for an enemy, both in and outside the group. Furthermore, conflict can function as a safety-valve within a group. It can act as an indicator of the intensity of the relationship, for the more intense the conflict, the closer the relationship might be. But the reverse is also true: the closer the relationship, the more intense the conflict. Both love and hate, affection and antagonism, consensus and coercion are always dialectically present in any relationship, as well as in a society. Conflict causes greater intolerance within the group as outside pressure increases. This is particularly true of renegadism, for a heretic competes for the continued loyalty of the in-group. Renegadism threatens the unity of the group and can cause a split.

Challenges from both inside and outside the group function as a means of readjusting the inner values and identity. Conflict also has a changing effect. Extreme conflict, especially if the opponent is strong and influential, leads to contact which in turn inevitably changes both the conditions of the struggle and the reasons for the struggle, that is, causes a re-adjustment of values and ideologies. New norms and values are created, but old dormant ones are re-evaluated and even given new content and meaning. Conflict thus not only results in structural change, as Dahrendorf claims, but also, since conflict cannot leave a group untouched, acts as a stimulus to the readjustment and re-evaluation of values, and even leads to a change of these values to suit the newly developed interests. In this regard, conflict contributes to the breaking down of boundaries and not just to maintaining them.

Whether conflict contributes to a disequilibrium, namely, the breaking down of boundaries (Dahrendorf), or to an equilibrium, that is, the maintenance of boundaries (Coser), it does bring about change and subsequently almost always leads to *renewed* conflict. The fact that almost all conflict theorists agree that every society contains in itself the seeds of spiralling conflict (see Kriesberg and Turner), makes a synthesis between the views of Dahrendorf and Coser possible. Conflict is viewed positively in eventually contributing to the maintenance of a system (equilibrium), but as soon as a new equilibrium is reached, new interests develop, new parties evolve and a new disequilibrium then emerges. In this Dahrendorf is correct. Change brings about conflict and conflict brings about change in a never-ending spiral. The outcome of one conflict is at the same time the possible basis for another. This is what is called 'the spiral of conflict' (see the figure below).

Deduced from the above, I have presented a few categories which serve as the model with which I eventually wish to analyze the text of Matthew 8 and 9. Category one (1) was derived from the section on the causes of conflict. Categories two and three (2–3) from the sections on the causes and units of conflict. Categories four and five (4–5) were deduced from the sections on the functions and the spiral of conflict. These categories are:

(1)   What *interests* are involved (as prime causes of conflict)? Closely related to interests, are the categories of goals, values and expectations, but, as we have seen, they are all subordinate to the concept of interests.

(2)   The interests of the different groups involved are interpreted in terms of *survival*, and

(3)   especially in terms of their relationship to *power and authority*.

(4)   We have seen that the prime function of conflict is to bring about *change*.

(5)   The last category states that in any society conflict is *always potentially present*, even though the present conflict has been resolved. In fact, conflict of interests is *open-ended* in that conflict is an ever-ongoing, never-ending spiral.

The following spiral (taken from Kriesberg[270]) clearly illustrates this last point:

---

270. Kriesberg, *The Sociology of Social Conflicts*, p. 274.

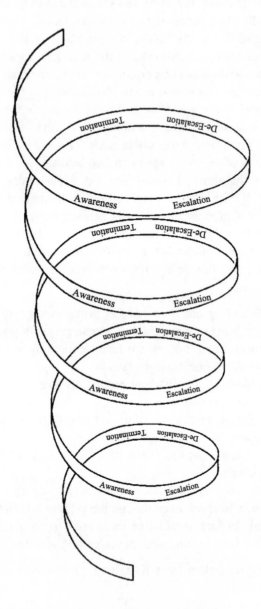

Figure 4. *The Spiral of Conflict*

Chapter 3

THE SOCIAL LOCATION OF THE MATTHEAN COMMUNITY[*]

Introduction

We have seen from the previous chapter that, generally speaking, *opposing interests* normally form the basis of most conflicts. This statement is based on the rather lengthy discussion on the causes of conflict, which served to establish a model/theory for the interpretation of Matthew 8 and 9. But this discussion functioned at a very high level of abstraction, or at a so-called 'macro-sociological level'. Matthew 8 and 9 will function at a 'micro-sociological level', as a case study to which our theory will be applied. The following chapter will act as a link between these two levels, in other words, to link the conflict theory (the macro-sociological level) to the text of Matthew 8 and 9 (the micro-sociological level). This chapter will function on a level which I call a 'meso-sociological' or 'in between level'. It refers to the social location of the Matthean community. Along with Rohrbaugh I take the term 'location' simply to mean a position in a social system shared by a

---

* I take note of the distinction Stanton makes between the '*community*' and the '*communities*' of Matthew (G.N. Stanton, *A Gospel for a New People*, pp. 50-51 and 'The Communities of Matthew', p. 379. Stanton asks (suggesting that there is more than one Matthean community), 'Is it not much more likely that Matthew, like Luke, envisaged that his Gospel would circulate widely? If so, then it is no surprise to find that his criticisms of his readers are severe but imprecise' (Stanton, *A Gospel for a New People*, p. 51). I take this as a likely possibility, especially because of the enlarged geographical location as suggested by Segal (Segal, 'Matthew's 'Jewish Voice'', pp. 26-29. I accept that there might have been more than one community or congregation to whom Matthew wrote his Gospel. This could explain the often different (even conflicting) themes present in the Gospel (cf. Stanton, *A Gospel for a New People*, p. 46). However, for the purposes of this study I will refer to the community of Matthew in the singular, accepting the possibility that it could also be more than one.

group of people.[1] 'Location' is an inclusive term. It deals with the social stratification and the consequent relations (and conflict) within and between different groups. The aim of this chapter will be to locate the community of the Gospel of Matthew in terms of its 'social stratification'. This is necessary to understand the background of the conflicting interests between the Pharisees and the Matthean community. I also wish to place the conflict in Matthew 8 and 9 in the broader debate of conflict in Matthew as a whole, in terms of whether Matthew wrote his Gospel in a so-called *intra muros* or *extra muros* situation.[2] Furthermore, I wish to establish the social location of the community and its conflict in terms of the debate of the so-called formative Judaism.[3] This is regarded as necessary in order to further explicate the *conflict of interests* in the broader context of the Gospel, and in particular in Matthew 8 and 9. For the basic outline of this chapter, I wish to acknowledge the work of Richard L. Rohrbaugh who made a similar study on the Gospel of Mark.[4]

Social Stratification in the Gospel of Matthew

Before I enter into a discussion on the social stratification in the Gospel of Matthew, I have to briefly define this concept. 'Social stratification', as a general rule is 'The division of a society into a number of strata, hierarchically arranged groupings.'[5] Lenski defines social stratification as follows: 'I equate social stratification *with the distribution process in human societies—the process by which scarce values are*

---

1.   Rohrbaugh, 'The Social Location of the Markan Audience', p. 394 n. 1.

2.   Cf. Carson, 'The Jewish Leaders in Matthew's Gospel, pp. 161-63; A.G. Van Aarde, 'ἠγέρθη ἀπὸ τῶν νεκρῶν (Mt. 28.7): A Textual Evidence on the Separation of Judaism and Christianity', *Neot* 23 (1989), pp. 219-33 (223-25); J.D.G. Dunn, *The Parting of the Ways: Between Christianity and Judaism and their Significance for the Character of Christianity* (London: SCM, 1991), pp. 141, 156; Stanton, *A Gospel for a New People*, pp. 113-45 and 'The Communities of Matthew', pp. 382, 390.

3.   Cf. Overman, *Matthew's Gospel and Formative Judaism*; Stanton, *A Gospel for a New People* and 'The Communities of Matthew', p. 380.

4.   Rohrbaugh, 'The Social Location of the Markan Audience' and R.L. Rohrbaugh, 'The Social Location of the Markan Community', unpublished article, 1993.

5.   C.G.A. Bryant, 'Social Stratification', in M. Mann, (ed.), *The Macmillan Student Encyclopedia of Sociology* (London: Macmillan, 1983), p. 366.

distributed' (his emphasis).[6] Social stratification has to do with the basic question of '*Who gets what and why?*'[7] or how large a share does one get of limited goods such as land, wealth, health, friendship and love, honour, respect and status, power and influence, security and safety?

The Urban Elite

The social stratification in the Gospel of Matthew must be viewed in terms of the stratification in advanced agrarian societies.[8] Saldarini says that during the Hellenistic and Roman periods Jews in Palestine lived in an agrarian society which itself was part of a large agrarian, bureaucratic and partly commercialized aristocratic empire.[9] Lenski regularly uses the Roman empire as a test case to illustrate the features of advanced agrarian societies.[10]

The top layer of agrarian society, according to Rohrbaugh, is the so-called *urban elite*.[11] It seems, however, that he does not differentiate between the two different classes, namely the *ruler* and *governing classes*, as Lenski does.[12] Moreover, it seems that Rohrbaugh also includes in this group the *priestly class*, which Lenski regards as separate.[13] As Rohrbaugh indicates, the upper level of the urban elite included the senior military officers and priestly families as well as the

6.   Lenski, *Power and Privilege*, p. x; see also T.F. Hoult, *Dictionary of Modern Sociology* (Totowa: Littlefield, Adams, 1969), p. 304.

7.   Lenski, *Power and Privilege*, p. 3.

8.   See the section on *The Units of Conflict* in Chapter 2 for a discussion on the concept 'advanced agrarian society'; see also Duling, 'Matthew's Plurisignificant "Son of David" in Social-science Perspective, p. 101; Van Aarde, 'Aspekte van die sosiale stratifikasie van die ontwikkelde agrariese samelewing in die eerste-eeuse Palistina', p. 528; E. Van Eck, 'Galilee and Jerusalem in Mark's Story of Jesus: A Narratological and Social Scientific Interpretation' (DD dissertation; Pretoria: University of Pretoria, 1993), pp. 226-30.

9.   Saldarini, *Pharisees, Scribes and Sadducees in Palestinian Society*, p. 35.

10.   Lenski, *Power and Privilege*, pp. 189-242.

11.   Rohrbaugh, 'The Social Location of the Markan Audience', p. 383.

12.   Lenski, *Power and Privilege*, p. 219, 243; see also Saldarini, *Pharisees, Scribes and Sadducees in Palestinian Society*, pp. 40-41.

13.   Rohrbaugh, 'The Social Location of the Markan Audience', p. 383. Part of the privileged elements in agrarian societies were the leaders of the organized religions, the *priestly classes*. This was a variable class (cf. Lenski, *Power and Privilege*, p. 256). Depending on the specific society, they had the support of the governing classes in return for some spiritual gratitude.

Herodians and other aristocratic families.[14] The reason why Rohrbaugh groups them all together seems to be because they '. . . lived in the heavily fortified central areas of the cities, usually enclosed in separate walls, hence they were physically and socially isolated from the rest of the society.'[15]

The rulers were the heads of empires or centralized states. They regarded themselves as the owners of all the land and they had far-reaching powers. They controlled all classes by means of taxation, harsh measures such as confiscation and, with regard to the governing classes, by the granting of land and political rights.[16] However, kings and emperors never ruled alone. A very small minority (rarely more than 1–2 per cent of the population) shared the responsibilities of government with them.[17] 'To be part of the *governing class* was to possess the right, acknowledged and supported by the supreme power in the land, to share in the economic surplus produced by the peasant masses and urban artisans.'[18] This was their reward for upholding and enforcing the authority of the regime and ruler. This reward entailed vast amounts of wealth and money so that, as Lenski remarks, '. . . it appears *that the governing classes of agrarian societies received at least a quarter of the national income. . . and that the governing class and rulers together usually received not less than half*' (his emphasis).[19] The control of the economic and political systems was often legitimized by the religious and educational bureaucracy, a role frequently fulfilled by the *priestly class*.[20]

Land and office were the main economic resources in agrarian societies, therefore there was an almost continuous struggle between the ruler and the governing class to gain control of these resources and to maximize their own rights and prerogatives. In these countless struggles

14. Rohrbaugh, 'The Social Location of the Markan Audience', p. 383.

15. Rohrbaugh, 'The Social Location of the Markan Audience', p. 383.

16. Cf. Saldarini, *Pharisees, Scribes and Sadducees in Palestinian Society*, p. 40.

17. Cf. Lenski *Power and Privilege*, p. 219; see also Saldarini, *Pharisees, Scribes and Sadducees in Palestinian Society*, p. 40; Rohrbaugh, 'The Social Location of the Markan Audience', p. 383; Van Aarde, 'Aspekte van die sosiale stratifikasie van die ontwikkelde agrariese samelewing in die eerste-eeuse Palistina', p. 532.

18. Lenski, *Power and Privilege*, p. 220.

19. Lenski, *Power and Privilege*, p. 220.

20. Cf. Rohrbaugh, 'The Social Location of the Markan Community', p. 12; see also the role of the intellectuals as I explained it in the previous chapter.

between the ruler and the governing class, the ruler often had to turn to the common people for support. The common people, however, hardly ever gained anything in return. Says Lenski:

> It is no great exaggeration to say that *the outcomes of all the countless struggles between rulers and their governing classes had almost no effect on the living conditions of the common people, except as these struggles sometimes led to violence and destroyed their very livelihood* (his emphasis).[21]

With regard to offices, Saldarini says that the members of the governing class had the right of self-aggrandizement through grants from the ruler and 'honest graft' in conduct of office.[22] As Saldarini continues,

> Offices were often sold and the incumbent was expected to make his fortune from his position. Land ownership, the major form of wealth, was secondary to political power because political power was used to acquire land and wealth, and the lack of political power could result in the loss of land and wealth through taxation and confiscation.[23]

The members of the urban elite in Matthew can be identified by means of the following list:[24]

Urban Elite Mentioned in Matthew[25]

Caesar 22.17, 21	The chief priests and the elders
Rulers of the gentiles 20.25	21.23; 26.3, 47; 27.1, 3, 12, 20;
High officials 20.25	28.11-12
Herod 2.1	Elders 15.2; 16.21; 21.23; 26.3, 47,
Magi 2.1-12	57; 27.1, 3, 12, 20, 41; 28.12
The rulers of Judah 2.6	The chief priests and the teachers of
Herod the tetrarch 14.1, 3	the law (scribes) 2.4; 20.18; 21.15
Archelaus 2.22	The elders, chief priests, and the
The ruler 9.18-26.[26]	teachers of the law (scribes) 16.21

21. Lenski, *Power and Privilege*, p. 241.

22. Saldarini, 'Political and Social Roles of the Pharisees and the Scribes in Galilee', p. 200.

23. Saldarini, 'Political and Social Roles of the Pharisees and the Scribes in Galilee', p. 200.

24. See also Duling, 'Matthew's Plurisignificant "Son of David" in Social-science Perspective', p. 103.

25. Terms used in these tables are all the translated terms taken from *The Holy Bible: New International Version* (Cape Town: Bible Society of South Africa, 1978).

26. The 'crowd' mentioned in 9.25 might be seen as the family of the ruler and thus in this context part of the elite.

King (often used as part of Jesus' parables) 10.18; 11.8; 18.23; 22.2; 25.34-46	27.41
	The chief priest and the whole Sanhedrin 26.59
Philip 14.3	The chief priests and the Pharisees
Antipas 14.1, 9	21.45; 27.62
Man going on a journey 25.14-15	Pontius Pilate 27.2, 13-26
The high priest Caiaphas 26.3, 57, 62-66	Governor 27.11,14; 28.14
	Owner/Landowner 13.27; 20.1, 11;
The chief priests 2.4; 16.21; 20.18;	21.33
21.15, 23, 45; 26.3, 14, 47, 51, 59;	Physician 9.12
27.1-9; 28.11	Wealthy/rich young man 19.16, 22;
John the Baptist 3.1-16 [27]	27.57

Here a comment must be made concerning *teachers of the law (scribes)* in the phrases 'the chief priests and the teachers of the law' and 'the elders, chief priests and the teachers of the law'. Contrary to Rohrbaugh, who places the scribes (in the Gospel of Mark) among the urban elite, I wish to place them (as far as Matthew is concerned) under the retainer class (see below).[28] This is supported by Saldarini.[29] In the prediction of the passion, the scribes are mentioned as Jesus' enemies in Jerusalem along with the 'elders, chief priests' (16.21), and along with the 'chief priests' (20.18). In this they have more of a political function.[30] The scribes also appear twice in the passion narratives as part of the *complete leadership* of Judaism (26.57, 59; 27.41). All these cases symbolize that Jesus was condemned and rejected by the complete leadership in Jerusalem. Therefore, strictly speaking, the scribes as pictured in the Gospel of Matthew are not really part of the urban elite. They have to be seen here in relation to the other groups mentioned in these phrases.

The Pharisees are mentioned in close relation to the chief priests (see

27.   There is no indication in the Gospel of Matthew as to where we should place John the Baptist. If we take the evidence from Lk. 1.5 that the father of John the Baptist was Zechariah, who belonged to the priestly order of Abijah, it could be suggested that John (and his father) belonged to the priestly class, thus to the upper layer of society. This is, however, inconclusive.

28.   Rohrbaugh, 'The Social Location of the Markan Audience', p. 384.

29.   Saldarini, *Pharisees, Scribes and Sadducees in Palestinian Society*, pp. 161, 172.

30.   Cf. Saldarini, *Pharisees, Scribes and Sadducees in Palestinian Society*, p. 161.

table above). Van Tilborg says that seen in the larger context of the Gospel, the expression 'the chief priests and the Pharisees' has to be identified with 'the chief priests and the elders of the people' (21.45/ 21.23) and the 'chief priests that met with the elders' (27.62/28.11-12).[31] Therefore, the Pharisees mentioned in the table above, are strictly speaking, not part of the urban elite for the same reasons as the scribes. Serving the interests of the rulers should be regarded as part of the retainers' political function.

Retainers
Besides the ruler and the governing classes, agrarian societies had a large stratified system of other classes. The rulers and the governing class normally employed or maintained a small army of officers and professional soldiers. Furthermore, officials and bureaucrats such as clerks and bailiffs, scholars, religious leaders, legal experts, lower lay aristocracy, household servants and personal retainers, all served in specialized capacities. They were the so-called *retainer class*. Their specific function, despite their specialized fields, was the same: service to the political elite. Normally they made up no more than 5 per cent of the society. They were taken from the common people but kept separate, some even shared in the economic surplus.[32]

Retainers Mentioned in Matthew

Pharisees 3.7; 9.11, 14, 34; 12.2, 14, 24, 38; 15.1, 12; 16.1-12; 19.3; 22.15, 34, 41; 23.2; 13-29	Tax collector(s) 5;46; 9.9, 10, 11; 10.3; 11.19; 17.24; 18.17; 21.31, 32[33]
	Teachers/scholars 23.24
Sadducees 3.7; 16.1-12; 22.23, 34	Attendants of Herod 14.2
Teachers of the law (scribes) 2.4; 5.20;	Herodians 22.16
7.29; 8.19; 9.3; 12.38; 13.52; 15.1;	Disciples of the Pharisees 22.16
17.10; 23.2-29	Those who arrested Jesus 26.57
Centurion 8.5, 8, 13; 27.54	Soldiers 27.27; 28.12
One of the rulers 9.18	Guards 26.58; 28.4, 11
Officer 5.25	
Foreman 20.8	

31. S. Van Tilborg, *The Jewish Leaders in Matthew* (Leiden: Brill, 1972), p. 5.
32. Cf. Lenski, *Power and Privilege*, p. 243.
33. Both the centurion and the tax collector(s) can also be regarded as part of the so-called unclean class in as far as the Jewish community was concerned. The gentile centurion and the tax collectors (as retainers of the Roman Empire) were both regarded as unclean (see below on the discussion of Mt. 8.5-13 and 9.9-13).

A few remarks are necessary regarding the Pharisees, Sadducees and scribes. Concerning the Pharisees in Mark, Rohrbaugh says that they were not the dominant group in the conflict with Jesus.[34] This, however, is not the case in Matthew. Matthew tends to expand the role of the Pharisees as the opponents of Jesus. They are the most constant opposition to Jesus.[35]

Matthew groups the Pharisees, Sadducees and scribes together as the leaders of the Jewish people. As Van Tilborg says: 'It seems evident that Mt did not wish to create any distinction between the various groups.'[36] To Hummel the scribes were qualified by the Pharisees in Matthew.[37] Saldarini views these groups as a coalition, all competing for power and influence in Jewish society.[38] To Matthew, the Pharisees and scribes were learned groups *par excellence*. Their agenda did not differ sharply.[39] It is possible that some of the members of these parties could have belonged to the upper ruling classes, but in general, they fit into the retainer class who served the interests of the governing classes. They shared in the life of the elite, but not in its direct power.[40] They did not have any independent wealth or power but were not entirely without power.[41] Therefore we could say that they had indirect

---

34. Rohrbaugh, 'The Social Location of the Markan Audience', p. 16.

35. Cf. Saldarini, *Pharisees, Scribes and Sadducees in Palestinian Society*, p. 167.

36. Van Tilborg, *The Jewish Leaders in Matthew*, p. 6; see also Hummel, *Die Auseinandersetzung zwischen Kirche und Judentum im Matthäusevangelium*, p. 15; Kingsbury, 'The Developing Conflict Between Jesus and the Jewish Leaders in Matthew's Gospel'; *Matthew as Story*, pp. 17-24, 115-18; see also the section on 'The Calling of Matthew: Matthew 9.9-13' in Chapter 4.

37. Hummel, *Die Auseinandersetzung zwischen Kirche und Judentum im Matthäusevangelium*, p. 18.

38. Saldarini, 'The Social Class of the Pharisees in Mark', p. 70. A coalition is defined by Malina '. . . as a collection of people within some larger, encapsulating structure consisting of distinct parties in temporary alliances for some limited purpose' (B.J. Malina, 'Patron and Client: The Analogy behind Synoptic Theology', *Foundations & Facets Forum* 4.1 [1988], pp. 2-32 [20]).

39. Cf. Saldarini, *Pharisees, Scribes and Sadducees in Palestinian Society*, p. 171.

40. Cf. Saldarini, *Pharisees, Scribes and Sadducees in Palestinian Society*, p. 42.

41. Cf. Saldarini, *Pharisees, Scribes and Sadducees in Palestinian Society*, p. 172.

political power. Furthermore, to Lenski, the retainers had an important function in supporting the ruling classes in their effort to *maintain* their essentially exploitive position in society.[42] To a great extent the Pharisees (especially) acted as an important middle group between the people and the '... upper echelons of society.'[43] Saldarini states that this group [retainers and therefore also possibly the Pharisees] often gained their political power when the governing classes ceased to be effective rulers and left matters in their hands.[44] This opens up the possibility that the Pharisees gained strong political influence within Judaism in the post-70 CE period and that the retainers, that is, the Pharisees and scribes in Matthew, strived for the influence of the people, which could have intensified their conflict with the Matthean community. Add to this the fact that although collectively the members of the retainer class were terribly important to their superiors, individually most of them were expendable.[45] Therefore they constantly sought to maximize their rights and privileges.[46] This intensified the competition among the members of this class and also meant that any challenge to their position, from whatever side, caused a threat.

The Urban Non-Elite
We now have to look at the underprivileged classes of advanced agrarian societies. We have already seen that they comprised the merchants,[47] the peasants, the artisans, the degraded, unclean and expendables. With regard to the *urban non-elite*, Rohrbaugh includes the merchants, artisans, day labourers and service workers of various kinds in this group.[48] As a whole the urban non-elite comprised approximately 8 per

42. Lenski, *Power and Privilege*, p. 246.
43. Saldarini, 'The Social Class of the Pharisees in Mark', p. 71; see also Lenski, *Power and Privilege*, p. 246.
44. Saldarini, 'Political and Social Roles of the Pharisees and the Scribes in Galilee', p. 201; following Lenski, *Power and Privilege*, pp. 243-48.
45. Cf. Lenski, *Power and Privilege*, p. 246.
46. Cf. Lenski, *Power and Privilege*, p. 247.
47. The *merchant class* is placed by Saldarini in the so-called *upper class*. I have argued before that I would rather regard them as part of the *lower classes* (Saldarini, *Pharisees, Scribes and Sadducees in Palestinian Society*, p. 313 and 'Political and Social Roles of the Pharisees and the Scribes in Galilee', p. 200).
48. Rohrbaugh, 'The Social Location of the Markan Audience', p. 386. The day labourers are difficult to place for they also can be viewed as part of the peasantry as Rohrbaugh also indicates later on in his article (Rohrbaugh, 'The Social Location of

cent of the society. The *merchants* were in many respects more successful than the rulers and the governing class in gaining a share in the economic surplus, but they had no power of their own. Their activities were difficult to control, for they were almost always away buying and selling. They were a mobile group, supplying the privileged classes with merchandise. Their basic resources were wit and cunning which they used to counter the violence of the political elite.[49]

The *artisan classes* were never large and there was always considerable overlap between them and the peasants from among whom they were normally recruited. Although they had some skills with which they could bargain, they often lived in the cities in worse conditions than the peasantry. They were poor and underprivileged, their living conditions were depressing and they often suffered bad health. They did not have any influence or power in society.[50] They were often members of guilds which provided some form of organization among this group.[51]

The Urban Non-Elite Mentioned in Matthew

Joseph 1.18 (see 13.55 where there is reference to Jesus as 'the carpenter's son')[52]	15.15; 16.16, 22, 23; 17.24-26; 18.21; 19.27; 26.33-37, 58, 69, 73, 75
Mary 1.18; 27.56	Peter, James and John the brother of
Jesus' mother and brothers (and sisters) 12.46; 13.55	James 17.1
Jesus (as Joseph's son)	James, son of Zebedee and his brother John 4.21
The city-dwellers 8.34; 11.20	The mother of Zebedee's sons 20.20
Merchant 13.45	The fishermen 13.48
Money changers 21.12	Mary, the mother of James and Joseph and the mother of Zebedee's sons 27.56
Simon Peter and Andrew (as fishermen) 4.18	
Peter (on his own) 14.28, 29;	

the Markan Community', p. 20). As for myself, I would also rather place them within the peasant class.

49.   Cf. Lenski, *Power and Privilege*, pp. 248-56.

50.   Cf. Lenski, *Power and Privilege*, pp. 278-9; see also Saldarini, *Pharisees, Scribes and Sadducees in Palestinian Society*, p. 43 n. 26.

51.   Cf. Lenski, *Power and Privilege*, p. 279.

52.   Joseph, Maria and Jesus can also be seen as part of the peasantry. In fact, Crossan, *The Historical Jesus*, devotes a whole study arguing that Jesus was a Mediterranean Jewish peasant. However, whether they were part of the peasantry or

The Degraded, Unclean and Expendable Classes

The degraded, unclean and expendable classes of any agrarian society lived outside the city walls.[53] They were '. . . beggars, low-status prostitutes, the poorest day labourers, tanners (forced to live outside the cities because of their odour) and even some merchants.'[54] They were forced outside the cities at night. As for the so-called *unclean and degraded classes*, they were regarded as being even lower and more inferior than the common people.[55] The tendency of the 'decent' people was to avoid the members of this class. 'Sometimes the degraded status of these groups reflected *inferior ethnic origins*. . . at other times the status *reflected obnoxious or offensive characteristics of the occupation of the group*' (my emphasis).[56] This explains why the centurion in 8.5-13, from another ethnic group, was regarded as unclean by the Jews, although he was, in fact, a member of the retainer class in his own ethnic group. The same is true of the tax collector in 9.9-13: although part of the retainer class, his collaboration with the foreign rulers (which was viewed as offensive) placed him in the unclean class as far as the Jews were concerned (see my discussion on these two pericopes below).

The so-called *expendables* were at the bottom of the class system of agrarian society. This was a small group comprising about 5–10 per cent of society, although their numbers grew after great national disasters.[57] There was neither place nor need for them in society. As Lenski says, 'These [the expendables] included a variety of types, ranging from petty criminals and outlaws to beggars and underemployed itinerant workers, and numbered all those forced to live solely by their wits or by charity.'[58] The existence of this class was inevitable in agrarian societies for the population growth often outnumbered the demand

the urban non-elites, the fact remains that they were part of the lowest classes of society.

53.   See the work of R.L. Rohrbaugh, 'The City in the Second Testament', *BTB* 21.1 (1991), pp. 67-75, on the living conditions in the ancient city. See also B.J. Malina and R.L. Rohrbaugh, *Social-science Commentary on the Synoptic Gospels* (Minneapolis: Fortress Press, 1992), p. 85.

54.   Rohrbaugh, 'The Social Location of the Markan Audience', p. 387.

55.   Cf. Lenski, *Power and Privilege*, pp. 280-81.

56.   Lenski, *Power and Privilege*, p. 280.

57.   Cf. Lenski, *Power and Privilege*, pp. 281-83; Saldarini, *Pharisees, Scribes and Sadducees in Palestinian Society*, p. 44.

58.   Cf. Lenski, *Power and Privilege*, p. 281.

for labour. There were thus more people than the dominant classes found profitable to employ.[59] The only prospect for those in this class was occasional work at planting and harvest time and receiving charity in between. Otherwise, illegal activity was the best they could hope for.[60]

Unclean, Degraded and Expendables Mentioned in Matthew[61]

The man with leprosy 8.2; 10.8; 11.5; 26.6	Dumb man 9.32; 15.30, 31
	The deaf 11.5
Peter's mother-in-law (in as far as she was a sick woman) 8.14	The Canaanite woman 15.22
	The man with the withered hand 12.10
A woman who had been subject to bleeding 9.20-22	The sick 4.23, 24; 8.16; 9.12; 9.35; 10.8; 14.14, 35
Demon-possessed 4.24; 8.16; 8.28-34; 12.22; 15.21-28	The demon-possessed daughter of the Canaanite woman 15.22
Paralytic 4.24; 8.6; 9.2, 6	The (abandoned) children 19.13[63]
Lame/crippled 11.5; 15.30-31; 18.8; 21.14	'The tax collectors and the prostitutes' 21.31, 32
Crippled 15.30, 31	The eunuch 19.12
The epileptic(s) 4.24; 17.15	The poor 5.3; 11.5; 19.21; 26.9, 11
'Sinners' 9.10,11; 26.45[62]	Barabbas 27.16, 21
The blind men 9.27, 28; 11.5; 12.22; 15.14, 30,31; 20.30; 21.14	Robbers/bandits 21.13; 27, 38, 44

The Rural Peasants

The burden of supporting the state and the privileged classes fell on the shoulders of the common people; the peasant farmers, who constituted the majority (approximately 75 per cent) of the population.[64] They were called the *peasant class*. They lived in the villages and rural areas and were engaged in 'primitive' industries like farming and

---

59. Cf. Lenski, *Power and Privilege*, pp. 281-82.

60. Cf. Lenski, *Power and Privilege*, pp. 282-83.

61. See also Duling, 'Matthew and Marginality', pp. 653-54.

62. See the work of E.P. Sanders, 'Jesus and the Sinners' *JSNT* 19 (1983), pp. 5-36.

63. See the work of A.G. Van Aarde, *God–With–Us: The Dominant Perspective in Matthew's Story, and Other Essays* (HTS Suppl. 5; Pretoria: Tydskrifafdeling van die Nederduitsch Hervormde Kerk, 1994), pp. 261-76.

64. Cf. Lenski, *Power and Privilege*, p. 266; Rohrbaugh, 'The Social Location of the Markan Audience', p. 388.

extracting raw materials.[65] They comprised the freeholders, tenants, day labourers and slaves. This group supplied the *tax-income* of the privileged, often provided the *corveé* or forced labour, and were frequently regarded as the mere property of the rulers who had the right to between 30 per cent and 70 per cent of their crops.[66] They hardly ever had more than the bare necessities of life and lived in very primitive conditions.[67] In extreme circumstances their condition was so oppressive that they had to flee their land. To compound the misery of their economic situation, the peasants were often subjected to cruel and inhuman treatment by their superiors, which was often regarded as quite 'natural' from the viewpoint of the political elite. At best the peasants were often referred to as 'without heart', or 'without understanding'. Because there was very little contact between the rulers and the peasants, the governing classes were hardly ever concerned about the harsh conditions under which the peasants were forced to live.

The peasants were highly ambivalent about their social status. On the one hand they accepted their position and the explanation for it provided by the dominant ideology, and on the other hand, their miserable physical conditions made survival a priority, although when this was assured the desire for a better life emerged. Says Lenski: 'In other words, like their superiors, they were motivated to maximize their rewards, in as far as their situation permitted it. Thus, struggles inevitably developed between the peasantry and their masters.'[68]

Peasants Mentioned in Matthew[69]

Jesus (the protagonist of the Gospel story)	13.27; 18.23-35; 20.27; 21.34, 36; 22.3-10; 24.45-50; 25.14-30
The disciples of John 9.14; 11.2, 7; 14.12	Slaves/son 8.6, 8; 12.18; 14.2; 21.15
	Tenants 21.35-41
People 3.5; 8.27; 22.10	Peter's mother-in-law 8.14

65.   Cf. Rohrbaugh, 'The Social Location of the Markan Audience', p. 388.

66.   Cf. Lenski, *Power and Privilege*, pp. 267-68; Saldarini, *Pharisees, Scribes and Sadducees in Palestinian Society*, p. 43.

67.   Cf. Lenski, *Power and Privilege*, pp. 270-71.

68.   Lenski, *Power and Privilege*, p. 273.

69.   See also Duling, 'Matthew's Plurisignificant "Son of David" in Social-science Perspective', p. 103.

The crowd/s 5.1; 7.28-29; 8.1, 18; 9.8, 33, 36; 12.46; 13.2, 36; 14.13-19; 15.10, 30-39 17.14; 19.2; 20.29, 31; 21.8-11, 46; 22.33; 23.1[70] Many (πολλοί) 12.15 The disciples of Jesus 8.21-25; 9.37; 10.1; 12.1, 49; 13.10, 36; 14.15-18; 15.2, 12, 23, 32, 33, 37; 16.5, 13, 20, 24; 17.6, 10, 14, 19, 24; 18.1; 19.10, 14,23,25; 20.17; 21.1-2, 6, 20; 23.1; 24.1, 3; 26.8, 19, 20, 36,40; 26.56; 27.64; 28.7, 8, 16 Slaves/servants 8.9; 10.24;	The 'twelve' apostles 10.2-4 Fishermen 13.48 Those who were in the boat 14.33 Day labourers 9.37, 38; 10.10; 20.1, 8,9 The servants of the highpriest 26.51 Simon, man from Cyrene 27.32[71] The bystanders at the cross 27.39, 47 Mary Magdalene (and the other Mary) 27.56; 28.1

This is only a general and incomplete picture of an agrarian society. The possibility of upward mobility in these societies was slim (although it did, of course, happen, especially when the individuals' wealth in some way or other increased). Downward mobility was more likely due to large population growth on the one hand and very few positions of privilege on the other. Social stratification was therefore very apparent and conflict an ever present possibility. As far as stratification is concerned, this makes Dahrendorf's model also applicable to agrarian societies.

Social Location of the Community of Matthew

The social location of the community of Matthew is closely related to the concept of stratification. This discussion of the stratification has

---

70.   The crowd is not described in detail by Matthew. This could mean that all sorts of people, including women, could have been part of it. Furthermore, even the bandits, eunuchs, slaves, tenant farmers, and other artisans and fishermen could have been part of this group (cf. Duling, 'Matthew and Marginality', p. 654).

71.   I suggest Simon, a man from Cyrene, to be part of the peasantry. There are no further details given in the text (Mt. 27.40) except that he is 'a man from Cyrene'. I could only imagine him to be one of the masses (the crowd), grabbed (forced) by the authorities to do the job (carry the cross of Jesus). I could hardly imagine a person with a higher status being forced to do the carrying. He might have been a Jew, thus the name 'Simon', but he might have been regarded as unclean, and thus disregarded in Jewish society because he was in contact with the gentiles in Cyrene (a Greek city on the north coast of Africa; cf. M.J. Mellink, 'Cyrene', in G.A. Buttrick (ed.), *The Interpreter's Dictionary of the Bible: An Illustrated Encyclopedia.* I. *A–D* (Nashville: Abingdon Press, 1962), p. 754. However, I would agree that this is but a suggestion. The evidence really is very scant.

given us important background information in terms of the interest groups involved in the to be investigated conflict. What I intend to do here is to view Matthew in its social and historical setting.[72] I wish to place the emphasis on more specific aspects, such as the place of origin and the possible social conflicts in and around the community of Matthew.

An Urban Environment?
The question posed here is whether Matthew is set in an urban environment. If so, which city/ies is/are involved? What are the implications of this (geographical) setting in relation to the above-mentioned stratification systems in agrarian societies?

A widely accepted consensus was that Antioch in Syria was the place of origin of the Gospel of Matthew.[73] One reason for this view is that Matthew addressed a congregation/community that existed in Antioch. Meier argues that because Antioch was predominantly Greek speaking, it provides a 'natural site' for a Gospel written in Greek.[74] This was the setting for the circumcision-free mission. There was also a large Jewish population which could explain the Jewish tone of the Gospel. As Meier says, 'As a whole... Matthew's Gospel reflects a meeting place and melting pot of Jewish and Gentile influences. Antioch is a perfect location for this encounter and clash.'[75]

Rodney Stark also assumes Antioch to be the place of origin of the Gospel of Matthew.[76] He argues that the community of Matthew was an urban community.[77] He was particularly interested in describing

72. Cf. L.M. White, 'Crisis Management and Boundary Maintenance, p. 211.

73. Cf. Luz, *Das Evangelium nach Matthäus I*, pp. 73-74 for a literature list and arguments to substantiate this view; see also J.E. Stambauch and D.L. Balch, *The New Testament in its Social Environment* (Library of Early Christianity; Philadelphia: Westminster Press, 1986), p. 145; W.A. Meeks, *The First Urban Christians: The World of the Apostle of Paul* (New Haven: Yale University Press, 1983), p. 38; Kingsbury, *Matthew as Story*, p. 155; Duling and Perrin, *The New Testament*, p. 333.

74. J.P. Meier, 'Antioch', in R.E. Brown and J.P. Meier (eds.), *Antioch and Rome: New Testament Cradles of Catholic Christianity* (London: Chapman, 1982), pp. 11-86 (22-27).

75. Meier, 'Antioch', p. 23.

76. Stark, 'Antioch as the Social Situation for Matthew's Gospel', pp. 189-210; see also Duling and Perrin, *The New Testament*, p. 333.

77. Stark, 'Antioch as the Social Situation for Matthew's Gospel', p. 189.

the physical realities of daily living in Antioch as a typical ancient city. In great detail Stark describes the daily life (in particular the lives of the non-elite).[78] They suffered from chronic misery, overpopulation, filth, diseases and plagues. As Stark sums up:

> Any accurate portrait of Antioch in New Testament times must describe a city filled with misery, danger, fear, despair, and hatred. Antioch was a city where the average family lived a squalid life in filth and cramped quarters, where at least half of the children died at birth or during infancy, and where most of the children who lived lost at least one parent before reaching maturity. The city was filled with hatred and fear rooted in intense ethnic antagonisms and exacerbated by a constant stream of strangers.[79]

In this setting, Christianity arose as a revitalization movement that greatly mitigated the chronic misery and disorder in the cities.[80] The phrase '*For God so loved the world*' came as a puzzling, new and even revolutionary idea. Even more revolutionary was the principle that the Christian love and charity (and mercy) extended beyond the boundaries of family and tribe.[81]

However, neither the arguments of Meier nor Stark are all that conclusive. Could all this (the above arguments in favour of Antioch) not be said about almost any ancient city with both a Hellenistic and a Jewish population? Why should it particularly be Antioch? Kingsbury correctly criticizes Stark saying, 'Indeed, Stark simply presupposes, without demonstrating on the basis of an analysis of the Matthean text, that Matthew's Gospel originated in an urban area in general and in Antioch in particular.'[82] Luz accepts the possibility of a Syrian environment (*Raum*) and consents to Antioch being 'not the worst hypothesis' (*nicht die schlechteste Hypothese*), but it is no more than a hypothesis.[83] Says Luz: 'The gospel of Matthew is not interested in his place of origin. It was doubtless a one of the major Syrian towns where Greek was the lingua franca.'[84]

---

78. Stark, 'Antioch as the Social Situation for Matthew's Gospel', pp. 191-98.
79. Stark, 'Antioch as the Social Situation for Matthew's Gospel', p. 198.
80. Stark, 'Antioch as the Social Situation for Matthew's Gospel', pp. 189, 198-205.
81. Cf. Stark, 'Antioch as the Social Situation for Matthew's Gospel', p. 199.
82. Kingsbury, 'Conclusion', p. 261.
83. Luz, *Das Evangelium nach Matthäus* I, pp. 73-4.
84. Luz, *Das Evangelium nach Matthäus* I, p. 75.

There is now a trend to challenge this former consensus that Antioch was the place of origin of the Gospel.[85]

Overman accepts a Galilean city as the place of origin, because if the struggle with formative Judaism is taken seriously, then a Palestinian provenance is virtually assured.[86] 'Both formative Judaism and its successor, rabbinic Judaism, were Palestinian in origin and provenance. Within Palestine, Galilee is attractive because of the central role it played in early rabbinic Judaism.'[87] Overman indeed realizes that this alone is not sufficient to locate Matthew in Galilee. He adds to his argument Matthew's '. . . unusual concentration on Galilee'.[88] The Pharisees who were Jesus' opponents were limited to Galilee. Therefore a Galilean city, either Tiberias or Sepphoris, is suggested by Overman as the most plausible location of the Matthean community.[89]

Criticism of Overman's view comes from Alan Segal.[90] He argues that both Galilee *and* Syria should be considered as a single geographical area, not necessarily from every perspective but '. . . at least from the point of view of the development of Jewish and Christian hostility'.[91] On this subject Segal continues,

> In the history of earliest Jewish Christianity, the relationship between Galilee and Syria is quite obvious. The Jewish Christian heartland, settled by Jewish Christian refugees from Jerusalem, *was an arc of settlement that included both the Galilee, Jesus' home, and Pella, the destination of the Jerusalem refugees, and then arched into Syria through Antioch and Edessa* (my emphasis).[92]

85. Cf. Overman, *Matthew's Gospel and Formative Judaism*, pp. 158-15; Segal, 'Matthew's Jewish Voice', pp. 19, 26-29; Kingsbury, 'Conclusion', pp. 263-64; A.J. Saldarini, 'Delegitimation of the Leaders in Matthew 23', *CBQ* 54 (1992), pp. 659-80 (661); Stanton, *A Gospel for a New People*, p. 86; *idem*, 'The Communities of Matthew', p. 380; Garland, *Reading Matthew*, p. 3. Against his own previous assumption, Kingsbury states that the Matthean community was situated in an urban environment, perhaps in Galilee or perhaps more towards the north in Syria but, in any case, *not necessarily Antioch* (cf. Kingsbury, *Matthew as Story*, p. 148 against 'Conclusion', p. 264).

86. Overman, *Matthew's Gospel and Formative Judaism*, p. 158.

87. Overman, *Matthew's Gospel and Formative Judaism*, p. 158.

88. Overman, *Matthew's Gospel and Formative Judaism*, p. 159.

89. Overman, *Matthew's Gospel and Formative Judaism*, p. 159.

90. Segal, 'Matthew's Jewish Voice', p. 27.

91. Segal, 'Matthew's Jewish Voice', p. 26; see also Harrington, *The Gospel of Matthew*, p. 10.

92. Segal, 'Matthew's Jewish Voice', p. 26.

Segal calls Overman's claims that Galilee should be the location of the Matthean community 'extremely cogent'.[93] However, he continues, '. . . we cannot exclude the idea that Pharisees wandered further than Galilee proper'. Segal uses Paul as an example of a Pharisee (according to the Christian tradition) who moved beyond Galilee. To further substantiate his view, Segal says,

> Josephus records that Queen Helena and Prince Izates were convinced by a stricter Jew (from Galilee) to undergo circumcision in far-flung Adiabene. The position of this stricter Jew is consistent with Pharisaism, though to be sure it could be called uniquely Pharisaic. *So the religious spectrum of lands outside of Judea can be more mixed than the scholars usually admit* (my emphasis).[94]

Furthermore Segal says, 'The itinerant nature of the disciples that Jesus commissioned in Matthew 10 and 28 *makes unnecessary a strict choice between Galilee or Syria*. These disciples were constantly travelling and were used to being refugees' (my emphasis).[95] Thus both those in support of Antioch and those in support of Galilee as the location of the community of Matthew are in a sense correct. 'Galilee and Antioch were merely two fixed points in a rather loosely confederated group of congregations, united by missionaries who were more or less constantly on the move at first.'[96] The conclusion Segal eventually comes to is:

> Thus, the Matthean community lived in precisely the area that Jesus, while preaching in Capernaum, had called the land of promise. Clearly, this enlarged Galilee, from which Syrian cities like Antioch and Edessa can be considered proselytized satellites, was the centre of Matthew's attention.
> Because of the way in which Christian apostles travelled, the Matthean community could have considered Galilee to include virtually everything from the present-day Galilee through to Antioch.[97]

We can accept the widely acclaimed consensus that Matthew originated in an urban environment, although, as we have seen, there is a difference in opinion as to which city or cities. This could also mean that Matthew addressed a mainly urban community, comprising predominantly of urban non-elite. It is unlike that there were many members

---

93.   Segal, 'Matthew's Jewish Voice', p. 27.
94.   Segal, 'Matthew's Jewish Voice', p. 27.
95.   Segal, 'Matthew's Jewish Voice', p. 27.
96.   Segal, 'Matthew's Jewish Voice', p. 27.
97.   Segal, 'Matthew's Jewish Voice', p. 29.

belonging to the community who were part of the governing and retainer classes, although this can not be ruled out entirely (see below for
a suggestion on how these groups could have participated in the
community). As Stanton notes, the conflict of Jesus and his followers
(as transparency of the Matthean community) with the Jewish leaders
is a central theme of Matthew's Gospel.[98]

The Composition of the Community. Although a predominantly urban
environment, the enlarged geographical location suggested by Segal
(see above) opens up the possibility that the community could also contain other non-elite classes like the rural peasants, the unclean and the
expendables. With regard to this, White says that the Matthean community clearly looked to the Galilean ministry of Jesus for its roots, but
that Lower Galilee represented a distant place. 'It would appear, then,
that the Matthean community looked to the mixed environment—mixed
both as Jew–Gentile population and *village–urban society*—of the Syro–
Phoenician region as a symbol of its own situation' (my emphasis).[99]
Furthermore there always existed a strong interdependence between
urban and rural environments in ancient societies.[100] The so-called 'spatial organization' of ancient cities may support the suggestion that the
Matthean community could have been made up of both rural peasants
and urban non-elites. Says Rohrbaugh: 'The elite. . . lived at the centre
near the temple and the palace, while the poor lived on the periphery.
Outcasts lived outside the city along with others whose presence in the
city during the day was necessary or tolerated (tanners, prostitutes,
beggars, traders), but who were unneeded and unwelcome at night.'[101]
I thus conclude that Matthew not only wished to *revitalize* the ancient
urban inhabitants, as Stark argues, but also other under-privileged
classes.[102] I regard it as possible that the community of Matthew comprised members in and around the city including urban non-elite and

---

98. Stanton, 'The Communities of Matthew', p. 382; see also U. Luz, 'Die
Jünger im Matthäusevangelium', *ZNW* 62 (1971), pp. 141-71 (152-54); *idem, Das
Evangelium nach Matthäus* I, p. 67; Van Aarde, *God–With–Us*, p. 83.

99. White, 'Crisis Management and Boundary Maintenance', p. 241.

100. Cf. D.R. Edwards, 'First Century Urban/Rural Relations in Lower Galilee:
Exploring the Archaeological and Literary Evidence', in D.J. Lull, SBLSP 1988
(Atlanta: Scholars Press) pp. 169-82 (169, 171, 176).

101. Rohrbaugh, 'The City in the Second Testament', p. 72.

102. Stark, 'Antioch as the Social Situation for Matthew's Gospel', p. 190.

rural peasantry. Thus the Matthean community predominantly consisted of non-elite. We have to take note of the remark of White:

> While none of the major free cities of Lower Galilee are ever mentioned,
> an urban location for the Matthean community in the outline regions is not
> precluded. *What is more at issue in Matthew is the growing tension felt by
> the community over the intrusion of Pharisaic authority into their region
> so that they were being marginalized* (my emphasis; see below for a defi-
> nition of marginality).[103]

This community was in opposition to the Jewish leaders who were
mainly drawn from the ruling and retainer classes.[104]

103. White, 'Crisis Management and Boundary Maintenance', p. 240.
104. The suggestion that the Matthean community consisted predominantly of the
urban non-elite and rural peasants must not be interpreted too rigidly as if to mean
that no members of the upper classes could have been part of that community. The
mere fact that Matthew eventually became a written document, which was to be read
(in public), indicates that, at least in as far as the author himself was concerned, he
would have been from the retainer class. He was probably a scribe, because he was
able to write (unless he was an educated slave—of which there is no evidence at all).
This view is confirmed by Duling (Duling, 'Matthew and Marginality', p. 662).
Thus Matthew would have identified himself with the fate and interests of this
community and he therefore dedicated his Gospel to them. Matthew is concerned
about those from the lower strata (cf. Duling, 'Matthew and Marginality', p. 663). I
imagine that there would also have been some members of the community from the
upper classes. How many and in what relation or capacity they stood towards the
community is difficult to estimate. At least there would have been a few that were
able to read the Gospel aloud, in and to the congregation. It is known that ancient
communication, including reading, was an oral, collective activity and not the
private, silent experience that we consider it to be. Reading silently was unusual, reading in solitude even more so (cf. P.J.J. Botha, 'Greco–Roman Literacy as Setting for
New Testament Writings', *Neot* 26.1 [1992], pp. 195-215 [207]). It is regarded as a
fact that the majority of the ancient population were illiterate. This in particular was
true of the lower levels of the society. At the level of artisans and farmers, the majority of the males were illiterate. At this social level literate women were also quite rare
(cf. W.V. Harris, *Ancient Literacy* [Cambridge, MA: Harvard University Press,
1989], pp. 10, 13, 231; Botha, 'Greco-Roman Literacy as Setting for New Testament Writings', p. 201). Literacy was synonymous with education which was the
privilege of the wealthier upper classes whose children, (and slaves in as much as
they needed this education for the benifit of their masters), were given the opportunity to be educated (cf. Botha, 'Greco-Roman Literacy as Setting for New Testament Writings', p. 203). How could the community ever understand the Gospel if
there were not at least a few members from the upper or retainer classes who could
read the Gospel to the congregation?

It is likely that the majority of the community would have been members of the lower classes (or, as Duling calls these lower classes, the *involuntary marginalized*).[105] However, there could have been members of the upper classes as well. In fact, Matthew could have been from the retainer class himself (see above). But, how can these observations be linked together? The article of Duling, 'Matthew and marginality', gives us valuable information in this regard.

The work of Gino Germani called *Marginality*, served as the basis for Duling's (1993) theory.[106] Along with Germani (1980), Duling states that at a descriptive level, '... one can observe certain phenomena typical of urban ecological environments: segregated shantytowns, squatter settlements, poor working conditions, low standard of living, *and the exclusion of such groups from the decision making process* that affects their lives' (my emphasis).[107] Germani's definition of marginality, is quoted by Duling as: '... the lack of participation [exercise of roles] of individuals and groups in those spheres in which, according to determined criteria, they might be expected to participate'.[108] By 'lack of participation' is meant the inability of persons to conform to expected social roles with respect to sex, age, civil life, occupation, and social life in relation to levels of status in a social system. 'These statuses are based on social norms, values, and expectations rooted in law and legitimated by custom.'[109] The marginal person no longer participates in the 'normative scheme', that is, '... the set of values and norms which define the categories (status), the legitimate, expected, or tolerated areas of participation and the assignment mechanisms of individuals to each category'.[110] Usual 'objective resources', both material and non-material—education, jobs, purchasing power, housing—are not unavailable to marginal persons. But, the 'personal conditions' needed to exercise their social roles are absent.[111] This is particularly true of the unclean, the degraded and the expendables in an advanced agrarian society. Duling calls this *involuntary marginality*. In short this means:

105. Duling, 'Matthew and Marginality', p. 644.
106. G. Germani, *Marginality* (New Brunswick: Transaction, 1980).
107. Duling, 'Matthew and Marginality', p. 664.
108. Duling, 'Matthew and Marginality', p. 645.
109. Duling, 'Matthew and Marginality', p. 645.
110. Germani quoted by Duling, 'Matthew and Marginality', p. 645.
111. Cf. Duling, 'Matthew and Marginality', p. 645.

> ... individuals and groups who for reasons of race, ethnicity, sex, 'underdevelopment', and the like are not able to participate in normative social statuses, roles, and offices and their obligations and duties. *They fail to share in both material and nonmaterial resources available to other members at the centre of society, and thus who experience themselves as personally alienated* (my emphasis).[112]

Voluntary marginality may be summarised as follows:

separation   →   liminality/marginality   →   reaggregation

In this approach, marginality is seen as part of ritual.[113] There is a common pattern in ritual.[114] 'Separation' removes individuals or groups from their accepted status or role in a social system—from the centre to the margin. In the transitional ('liminal') phase, the individuals or groups are in limbo. They are 'neither here nor there'. In the third phase, the initiate re-enters the social system as a neophyte, often with higher status. The second, or marginal, liminal phase is characterized by *communitas*, a status-less, role-less phase marked by spontaneity, concreteness, intense comradeship, and egalitarianism.[115] The principle of *communitas* can be further developed. There are three kinds of communitas, as Duling cites Turner:

> (1) *existential* or *spontaneous* communitas. . . (2) *normative* communitas, where, under the influence of time, the need to mobilize and organize resources, and the necessity for social control among the members of the group in pursuance of these goals, the existential communitas is organized into a perduring social system; and (3) *ideological* communitas, which is a label one can apply to a variety of utopian models of societies based on existential communitas.[116]

Spontaneous communitas stands apart from social structure. Normative communitas represents an emergent microsocial group *within* a macrosocial system. Ideological communitas presents communitas as *derived* vision. Christian history knows this as the *ecclesiola in ecclesia*.

---

112. Duling, 'Matthew and Marginality', p. 648.
113. Cf. Duling, 'Matthew and Marginality', pp. 646-48, which he derives from the work of Victor Turner, *The Ritual Process: Structure and Anti-structure* (Chicago: Aldine, 1969).
114. Cf. Duling, 'Matthew and Marginality', p. 646.
115. Cf. Duling, 'Matthew and Marginality', p. 646.
116. Duling, 'Matthew and Marginality', p. 647.

Normative communitas is on the way to structure. Ideological communitas is voluntary 'outsiderhood'. It is not socially imposed marginality, but *voluntarily chosen.*[117] Thus, as Duling summarizes,

> *voluntary marginality*: individuals or groups who consciously and by choice live outside the normative statuses, roles, and offices of society because they reject hierarchical social structures, though there will be attempts to perpetuate this spontaneity by social control or in conventicles within the normative social system. *Though freely chosen, they will eventually share in some of the same conditions as involuntary marginals* (my emphasis).[118]

The lower classes (strata) or involuntary marginals are seen as the interest group of the community of Matthew. Thus we regard the majority of the community as involuntary marginalized. But those in the community who could have been from the higher strata (or classes) of society, whose direct interests do not really lie in the community of the involuntary marginalized, could still identify with the community as *voluntary marginalized* and, through this, share in the identity of the community with the other marginalized. In this way it is also possible for the author of Matthew, as a 'marginal man', to identify with the community.[119] The *marginal man* is defined as '. . . individuals and groups who, because of birth, migration, conquest, and the like are "doomed" to live in two different, antagonistic cultures without fully belonging to either'.[120] The author identifies with the marginalized, and therefore, as a member of the retainer class, he stands between the two cultures.

This suggestion about the composition of the Matthean community also has implications regarding the identity of the community, which I now wish to address.

Early 'Christian'–Jewish Relationships

The aim in this section is to consider the developing conflict situation between the early 'Christian'–Matthean community and the Jewish community and leadership. The intention will be to provide a link between the concepts of 'conflict of interests', stratification due to the composition of the Matthean community and the debate on the Jewish–Christian

---

117. Cf. Duling, 'Matthew and Marginality', p. 647.
118. Duling, 'Matthew and Marginality', p. 648.
119. Cf. Duling, 'Matthew and Marginality', p. 662.
120. Duling, 'Matthew and Marginality', p. 648.

relation (conflict) of the first century.[121] This information is needed in

121. As a matter of clarity, this conflict must be viewed as a *first century* Jewish–Christian conflict, and more specifically in relation to the community of Matthew. This must not be confused with the question about the so-called 'anti-Semitism' of the New Testament writings of Paul and Matthew (cf. D. Patte, '"Love your Enemy"–"Woe to You, Scribes and Pharisees": The Need for a Semiotic Approach in New Testament Studies', in T.W. Jennings, Jr [ed.], *Text and Logos: The Humanistic Interpretation of the New Testament* [Atlanta: Scholars Press, 1990], pp. 81-96 [84-85]; see also Harrington, *The Gospel of Matthew*, p. 20; U. Luz, 'Der Antijudaismus im Matthäusevangelium als Historisches und Theologisches Problem: Eine Skizze', *EvTh* 53 [1993], pp. 310-27 [310] on the notion of 'Anti-Judaism' in Matthew's Gospel). Indeed, the 'anti-Jewish' statements in the New Testament may come across as very harsh and hurtful to modern-day Jews (cf. P.J. Hartin, 'The Pharisaic Roots of Jesus and the Early Church', *Neot* 21 [1987], pp. 113-24 [123]). Along with Patte I reject an anti-Semitic reading as unfounded and unwarranted (Patte, '"Love your Enemy"–"Woe to You, Scribes and Pharisees"', p. 84). He regards such an interpretaion as disturbing: 'Nothing in Matthew justifies pogroms and Holocaust!' (Patte, ' "Love your Enemy"–"Woe to You, Scribes and Pharisees"', p. 84). However, says Patte: 'The hermeneutical problem raised by the explicitly anti-Semitic interpretations of Matthew cannot be resolved by simply rejecting these interpretations (although they should be rejected). Through its numerous polemics against the Jews, Matthew seems to have the more insidious effect of conveying to its reader a latent anti-Semitism by promoting an anti-Jewish stance' ('"Love your Enemy"—"Woe to You, Scribes and Pharisees"', p. 84). Burnett argues that it is impossible to accept the norms that guide the reading of Matthew and produce an interpretation that is not anti-Jewish. He says, 'In narrative-critical terms the thesis stated positively is that the "implied author" of Matthew encourages readers *in every age* to read the narrative in an anti-Jewish way' (F.W. Burnett, 'Exposing the Anti-Jewish Ideology of Matthew's Implied Author: The Characterization of God as Father', *Semeia* 59 [1992], pp. 155-91 [156]; his emphasis). We cannot deny the anti-Jewish elements within Matthew. However, I accept the danger posed by Patte (see above). In order not to fall into the trap of legitimizing the Holocaust, referring to the anti-Semitic character of Matthew, I have to view the conflict in terms of the first century environment. Burnett argues for an ideological critical reading of Matthew in order to resist the manipulation of the implied author (Burnett, 'Exposing the Anti-Jewish Ideology of Matthew's Implied Author', pp. 174-78). I agree. However, I disagree with Burnett that it matters little whether or not the original historical situation of Matthew was part of formative Judaism (Burnett, 'Exposing the Anti-Jewish Ideology of Matthew's Implied Author', p. 155). I think that the only way to distance oneself from the anti-Jewish tone (in terms of modern-day anti-Semitism), is to view Matthew in its first century environment and to take the social location into account. A citation of Dunn could support this view: '. . . *the charge of anti-semitism or anti-Judaism against Matthew has either to be dismissed or to be so redefined <u>within its historical context</u> as to lose most of its potential as justification for the anti-semitism*

order to understand the eventual analysis of the test case: the text of Matthew 8 and 9.

Matthew in Terms of the Debate: Intra Muros or Extra Muros. Was the community of Matthew still within or did it stand outside first-century Judaism? The works of Carson,[122] Van Aarde[123] and Stanton[124] give us meaningful access to these issues. Carson argues that (at the time of his article in 1982) there has been a gradual consensus on two points as to the *Sitz im Leben* of Matthew's Gospel.[125] Firstly, that the Gospel was written about 85 CE. Secondly, that in Matthew's Church there is in some kind of dramatic tension with respect to Judaism and synagogue worship. However, '. . . the precise nature of that tension is *hotly disputed*' (my emphasis).[126] No consensus has yet been reached on the nature of the tension between Matthew's community and Judaism since Carson's article in 1982, as the work of Stanton indicates almost a decade later. Stanton is much more comprehensive in dealing with this issue.

Stanton first discusses a group of scholars, representing what he calls '*the traditional view*'.[127] According to this view, Matthew was the most 'Judaic' of all the four canonical Gospels. Matthew was, as Stanton summing up this point of view says, '. . . the first Gospel to be written; the evangelist was a disciple of Jesus who wrote in Hebrew or Aramaic for a Palestinian Jewish Christian community'.[128] But, once the Markan priority is accepted, the main arguments for this view collapse. Also, this view does not really account for the Gentile mission or the numerous passages in the Gospel that reflect tension amongst the Jews.[129]

There are also the scholars who see the Gospel of Matthew as representative of some sort of congregation that sees itself as still *within* the

---

of later centuries' (Dunn, The Parting of the Ways, p. 156; italics by Dunn; my emphasis). Furthermore, as in due course I will argue in more detail, the conflict must be seen as a conflict *within* first-century Judaism and more specifically as a conflict with the *leaders* as retainers of Judaism and not with the Jews as such.

122. Carson, 'The Jewish Leaders in Matthew's Gospel', pp. 161-63.
123. Van Aarde, 'ἠγέρθη ἀπὸ τῶν νεκρῶν (Mt 28:7)', pp. 223-25.
124. Stanton, *A Gospel for a New People*, pp. 113-42.
125. Carson, 'The Jewish Leaders in Matthew's Gospel', p. 161.
126. Carson, 'The Jewish Leaders in Matthew's Gospel', p. 161.
127. Stanton, *A Gospel for a New People*, pp. 114-18.
128. Stanton, *A Gospel for a New People*, p. 114.
129. Cf. Stanton, *A Gospel for a New People*, pp. 116-17.

context of Judaism: the struggle with Judaism has taken place *intra muros*.[130] The Gospel of Matthew came into being in an essentially Jewish–Christian community, where the edification of the church independent of Judaism was in progress. Matthew's community had not yet broken its links with Judaism and they were still attached to the Jews (see Stanton's summary of the views of Kilpatrick, Bornkamm, Hummel and Davies).[131] Of significant importance is the view of Davies, which Stanton reflects, that a reconstruction of Judaism took place at Jamnia following the fall of Jerusalem in 70 CE.[132] The so-called Jamnian period, 70–100 CE, is to be seen as a many sided response to the need for unity and adaptation to changed conditions.[133] Jamnian Judaism was confronting Christianity and as a response, Matthew, and in particular Matthew 5–7, may be seen as the Christian answer to Jamnia. Stanton, together with Stendahl, questions whether the Christian answer to Jamnia was as direct as Davies suggested.[134] Therefore Stanton argues with many scholars in accepting that Matthew should be linked in some way to the Judaism of the Jamnian period, but rejects the notion that the struggle of Matthew's community was with 'the synagogue across the street', thus *intra muros*. The conclusion Stanton comes to in rejecting the *intra muros* view, moving towards an *extra muros* point of view, is:

> This second view rightly stresses that in many ways Matthew's Gospel is thoroughly Jewish, and it rightly accepts that many of the changes which Matthew has made to Mark are related to the circumstances in which Matthew was written. But this approach fails to do justice to some of the most important features of Matthew's Gospel. In particular it ignores or underplays numerous passages (in most of which the evangelist's own hand is evident) which suggest that the Christian communities to whom Matthew is writing are defining themselves over against Judaism and are being encouraged to accept Gentiles freely.[135]

---

130. Cf. Carson, 'The Jewish Leaders in Matthew's Gospel', p. 161; see also Stanton, *A Gospel for a New People*, pp. 118-24.

131. Stanton, *A Gospel for a New People*, p. 120; see also Van Aarde, 'ἠγέρθη ἀπὸ τῶν νεκρῶν (Mt 28:7)', p. 223.

132. W.D. Davies, *The Setting of the Sermon on the Mount* (Cambridge: Cambridge University Press, 2nd edn, 1966), pp. 290, 332; Stanton, *A Gospel for a New People*, p. 121.

133. Cf. Stanton, *A Gospel for a New People*, p. 121.

134. Stanton, *A Gospel for a New People*, p. 122.

135. Stanton, *A Gospel for a New People*, pp. 123-24.

This brings us to a group of scholars who judge Matthew's Gospel to be representative of a form of Jewish-Christianity that has broken away from Judaism, but are still defining themselves in contrast to Judaism. The struggle is therefore *extra muros*.[136] Stanton himself prefers a 'mediating position' between the *intra muros* view, and the view that Matthew himself could have been a Gentile; in which case, his community would have no link with 'the synagogue across the street'.[137] Both these views are seen as too implausible. As Stanton says,

> I am convinced that Matthew's community has parted company with Judaism and that some Gentiles have been accepted. Nearly every pericope of the Gospel reflects rivalry between 'church' and 'synagogue'. Matthew's communities are *extra muros*, but they are still responding in various ways to local synagogues and they still hope that even if Israel has been rejected by God, individual Jews will be converted.[138]

This view that the separation of Matthew's community from Judaism was complete and that they had already totally withdrawn from the Jewish assembly is confirmed by a number of scholars.[139] Five arguments are presented in support of the *extra muros* view:

(1)   The Jewish religious leaders and groups—in particular the scribes and the Pharisees—are consistently seen in a negative light. They are always at odds with Jesus and his disciples, so a 'ruler of the synagogue' cannot be a 'man of faith', and a scribe cannot be a true disciple.[140]

(2)   Matthew explicitly associates scribes and Pharisees with synagogues. There is a wedge between Jesus and his disciples on the one hand, and the synagogue on the other hand.[141]

---

136. Cf. Carson, 'The Jewish Leaders in Matthew's Gospel', pp. 161-62; Stanton, *A Gospel for a New People*, pp. 123-31.

137. Stanton, *A Gospel for a New People*, p. 124.

138. Stanton, *A Gospel for a New People*, p. 124.

139. Apart from Moule, Stendahl and E. Schweizer whom Stanton (*A Gospel for a New People*, p. 124) mentions, see also B.R. Doyle, 'A Concern of the Evangelist: Pharisees in Matthew 12', *AusBR* 34 (1986), pp. 17-34 (18); Kingsbury, *Matthew as Story*, p. 155 and Saldarini, 'The Gospel of Matthew and Jewish–Christian Conflict', p. 41.

140. Cf. Stanton, *A Gospel for a New People*, p. 128.

141. Cf. Stanton, *A Gospel for a New People*, pp. 128-29.

(3)   'Over against συναγωγή stands the ἐκκλησία, founded by
       Jesus himself and promised divine protection (16.18).'[142] The
       structures of Matthew's communities are developing quite
       independently from the synagogue. As he continues: 'The
       ἐκκλησία founded by Jesus continues to have a firm com-
       mitment to torah, but it has accepted Gentiles and developed
       its own patterns of worship and of community life. Its self-
       understanding is quite distinct from that of the synagogue.'[143]

(4)   There are passages that speak about the 'transference' of the
       kingdom to a new people who will include the Gentiles. Says
       Stanton: 'At 8.5-13 Matthew links two Q traditions (Luke
       7.1-10 and 13.28-9) in order to state starkly that those born
       to the kingdom will be replaced by Gentiles (including the
       Roman centurion whose faith is commended) who sit with the
       faithful (Abraham, Isaac, and Jacob) at the banquet in the king-
       dom of heaven.'[144]

(5)   'At the climax of his story at 28:15 the evangelist addresses
       his readers directly and refers explicitly to the relationship
       between synagogue and church in his own day.'[145]

With these arguments, summarized above, Stanton substantiates the
extra muros view. To a great extent they are convincing. But there remains a question as to why the conflict between Jesus and the Pharisees
really was so intense, especially if they in any case had no contact any-
more? I will return to this later on, as I wish to present my own point
of view.

A fourth group of scholars wish to argue that Matthew was not
Jewish at all. According to this view, Matthew was intended *for Gentiles
who are not in dispute with the Jews*. In their summaries of this view,

---

142. Stanton, *A Gospel for a New People*, p. 129; see also Duling and Perrin,
The New Testament, p. 337.

143. Stanton, *A Gospel for a New People*, pp. 130-31.

144. Stanton, *A Gospel for a New People*, p. 131. I would rather not see, as
Stanton does, the Gentiles as *replacing* 'those born to the kingdom' (Israel, the Jews)
but rather as *extending* Israel to include the Gentiles (cf. A.G. Van Aarde, 'Die
"heiligheid" van die kerk teen die agtergrond van die breuk kerk-sinagoge', *In die
Skriflig* 24.3 [1990], pp. 251-63 [259]).

145. Stanton, *A Gospel for a New People*, p. 131.

Carson[146] and Stanton[147] state that the community was totally separated from Judaism and was neither attacking nor defending itself
against any strand of Judaism in the Jamnian period, 70–100 CE. However, and I agree with Stanton, this last view is not really convincing.[148] He presents a whole series of counter arguments, but his last
question is the most telling (in his criticism of Van Tilborg):

> Is Matthew's anti-Jewish polemic so strong that we are forced to conclude
> that the evangelist himself cannot have been a Jew? The strength of
> Matthew's anti-Pharisaism was one of the reasons why Clark concluded
> that Matthew was a Gentile. S. van Tilborg has also claimed that the
> simplest explanation of the strong anti-Jewish currents in the Gospel is
> that he himself was not a Jew.[149]

In response to the latter view, Stanton is to my mind correct in his
comment that ferocious conflict is often a hallmark of a close 'family-
like' relationship.[150] On this I wish to elaborate below.

What the above summary of Stanton indicates, is that there is no consensus as to what the nature of the tension between Jesus (or the community of Matthew) and the Jews really was.[151] Therefore, it seems

146. Carson, 'The Jewish Leaders in Matthew's Gospel', p. 162.

147. Stanton, *A Gospel for a New People*, pp. 131-39.

148. Stanton, *A Gospel for a New People*, p. 135.

149. Stanton, *A Gospel for a New People*, p. 138. See S. Van Tilborg, *The
Jewish Leaders in Matthew* (Leiden: Brill, 1972), p. 171. In a later study, it seems
that Van Tilborg abandoned his previous view that Matthew was a pagan document
(cf. Van Tilborg, *The Jewish Leaders in Matthew*, p. 171), in favour of the view that
Matthew was a Jewish–Christian community (cf. S. Van Tilborg, *The Sermon on the
Mount as an Ideological Intervention* [Assen: Van Gorcum, 1986], p. 10).

150. Stanton, *A Gospel for a New People*, p. 138.

151. Some of the scholars who 'dare' a personal view run the risk of contradicting themselves. This seems to be true of both Dunn, *The Parting of the Ways*,
pp. 141, 156 and Stanton, *A Gospel for a New People*, p. 169. Dunn at first chooses
an *extra muros* view: 'And although most agree that Matthew was a *Jewish* Christian,
the view is strongly maintained that so far as he was concerned the final breach between
church and synagogue had *already* happened' (Dunn, *The Parting of the Ways*,
p. 141). With a quotation of Stanton, Dunn substantiates his point of view: 'Matthew
sees himself and his community as *extra muros*, outside the walls of Jerusalem:
"Matthew's community has recently parted company with Judaism after a period of
prolonged hostility"'(Dunn, *The Parting of the Ways*, p. 141; see G.N. Stanton,
'The Gospel of Matthew and Judaism', *BJRL* 66 [1984], pp. 264-84 [278]). However, a few pages further on, Dunn states something totally different: 'In the debate
as to whether Matthew is writing *intra muros* or *extra muros*, therefore, the evidence

that a clear picture does not exist and it remains difficult to choose between either an *intra* or *extra muros* view. There is little to be said in favour of either the first or the fourth view. However, a decision between the second and third views is more difficult.[152] My own view is that I doubt that the separation between the community of Matthew and Judaism was complete when Matthew wrote his Gospel. We should see the tension as representing something in between an *intra* and *extra muros* situation. The community is still within Judaism and yet it is outside as well, or at least *on its way out.*

The community of Matthew was still *very close* to Pharisaic Judaism, a fact which can be confirmed by our conflict theory (see Chapter 2 above, the section entitled *The Functions of Social Conflict*). This could account for the intensity of the conflict. As we have seen, the closer the relationship, the more intense and passionate the conflict becomes.[153]

However, although still within Judaism and in heated conflict with the leaders, the community was at the same time on its way out. I see

on the whole seems to favour *the former* [thus *intra muros*, and therefore contrary to his previous view]. No doubt Matthew's opponents and the opponents of Matthew's community (the Pharisees and 'their scribes') regard them as 'outsiders', meaning outside the walls of (early rabbinic) Judaism. But Matthew still speaks as an 'insider' and is attempting to portray a Jesus who would be attractive to others who also considered themselves 'insiders'. In other words, once again we seem to find ourselves confronted with the situation where the narrowing channels of rabbinic Judaism and Christianity respectively were still in competition for the head waters flowing from the broad channels of second temple Judaism' (Dunn, *The Parting of the Ways*, p. 156). Even Stanton, although clearly choosing the *extra muros* notion, seems to confuse some terms, which might contradict (or then at least confuse) his own view. He argued in some detail that the Gospel was written to a cluster of Christian communities '. . . which have recently *parted* [thus completed] company painfully with Judaism' (Stanton, *A Gospel for a New People*, p. 169; my emphasis). But then in the next line he states, 'Many of the Gospel's most distinct features are related to the "*parting* [thus still continuing *process* of parting, it seems not yet completed] of the ways:". . . ' (Stanton, *A Gospel for a New People*, p. 169; my emphasis). In fact, elsewhere Stanton explicitly states, 'Matthew's anti-Jewish polemic. . . *is part of the process* by which Matthew distances himself and his communities from his Pharisaic rivals: the tensions are real, *not a matter of past history*' (Stanton, *A Gospel for a New People*, p. 139; my emphasis).

152. Stanton, *A Gospel for a New People*, p. 139.

153. Cf. Coser, *The Functions of Conflict*, pp. 69-71; see also Dunn, 'Pharisees, Sinners and Jesus', p. 275; Overman, *Matthew's Gospel and Formative Judaism*, p. 160; Stanton, *A Gospel for a New People*, p. 101.

this as part of a *process* not yet completed.[154] They are *intra muros* but on their way to becoming *extra muros*. They are in the *process of developing* their own identity, which could explain the numerous anti-Israel passages in the Gospel. Matthew especially had developed his own way of interpreting the law which was contrary to the Pharisaic interpretation.[155] As Segal says: 'Rather the Matthean rejection of Pharisaic Judaism reflects a *growing* social rift between them and the waxing rabbinic leadership' (my emphasis).[156] Therefore, although I can go along with Stanton's proposal for the setting of the community of Matthew, I would like to add my own comments.[157] As an explanation for the intensified anti-Israel polemics, Stanton states that the community had recently parted company with Judaism.[158] I would rather say that because they are still *parting* from the Jews, the polemic is real indeed. The evangelist is indeed coming to terms with the trauma of the painful, *still ongoing process of separation* from Judaism, and with the continuing threat of hostility and even persecution. Matthew's anti-Jewish polemic could be seen as part of the self-defining of the Christian group which is acutely aware of the possible rejection and hostility of its 'mother', Judaism (this is my rephrasing of Stanton's view). Rather than saying that the Matthean community was alienated from Judaism, I would suggest that they (the community) were still *in the process of distancing* themselves from Judaism.[159] This could even, to my mind, be supported by evidence from developments within the text of Matthew's Gospel itself. Matthew at first depicts Jesus as sending his disciples not to the Gentiles, but to the 'lost sheep of Israel' (cf. Mt. 10.5-6). He still has strong ties with the Jews and still wishes to remain part of them. However, gradually the Gospel develops, finally ending with an explicit sending out to 'make disciples of all nations' (cf. Mt. 28.19). At first the community was not really ready for an 'open society', that is open to the Gentiles. But because of the conflict with its own people, the Jews (or rather their leaders), it developed a new, more 'open' identity, and gradually turned to the Gentiles for support. But this does not

154. See also D. Hill, 'On the Use and Meaning of Hosea vi.6 in Matthew's Gospel', *NTS* 24.7 (1977), pp. 107-19 (117).
155. Cf. Segal, 'Matthew's Jewish Voice', p. 31.
156. Segal, 'Matthew's Jewish Voice', p. 32.
157. Stanton, *A Gospel for a New People*, p. 157.
158. Stanton, *A Gospel for a New People*, p. 156.
159. Cf. Stanton, *A Gospel for a New People*, p. 166.

necessarily mean that the community had broken all ties with Judaism. Does the expression 'all nations' exclude the Jews? Certainly not.[160] In this regard White distinguishes between the *nation* (or 'people', τὸ ἔθνος) and *the nations* (i.e. 'Gentiles', τὰ ἔθνη).[161] The final legitimizing of the Gentile mission is framed in Jewish terms of making disciples of 'all nations' (τὰ ἔθνη). Thus, says White, 'It is not as yet a self definition of the church as a "third race". At the very least, then, Matt 21.43 and 28.18-20 seem to reflect a sense of the church as grounded in the identity of *the nation* of Israel, though made up of a mixed population that also included disciples drawn from among the gentile *nations.*'[162]

The Matthean Community in Relationship to Formative Judaism. Because I see the developing tension between Matthew's community and the Jews as a *process* rather than as a completed separation, we surely have to take note of the debate with regard to the so-called *formative Judaism* (see the work of Neusner, who coined this term).[163] It is the work of Overman especially that explicitly relates the community of Matthew to *formative Judaism.* Overman views the formative Judaism as one of the most profound influences in the development of Matthew's community.[164] This group, like the community of Matthew, was involved in a process of social reconstruction and definition. They, like the Matthean community, were still involved in a process of *'becoming'.* Formative Judaism was one of several movements struggling to gain more influence and control in the period after 70 CE. Both were emerging movements involved in a process of self-definition. They had much in common. In fact, they overlap and appear to be similar. 'This is

160. Cf. Stanton, *A Gospel for a New People*, pp. 136-37; see also Van Aarde, *God–with–Us*, p. 81.

161. White, 'Crisis Management and Boundary Maintenance', pp. 224-25 n. 48.

162. White, 'Crisis Management and Boundary Maintenance', p. 225; see also Van Aarde, *God–with–Us*, p. 81, on the universal implications of the concept τὰ ἔθνη).

163. J. Neusner, *Formative Judaism: Religious, Historical and Literary Studies* (BJSt, 37; Chico, CA: Scholars Press, 1982). See also R.A. Horsley, 'What Has Galilee to Do with Jerusalem? Political Aspects of the Jesus Movement', *HTS* 52.1 (1996), pp. 88-104 (89).

164. Overman, *Matthew's Gospel and Formative Judaism*, p. 2.

because formative and Matthean Judaism share the same social setting and context.'[165]

There were four basic elements in the attempt at consolidation and legitimation in formative Judaism. These are presented as features of the society in which the Matthean community developed and are here briefly summarized. The first is the highly sectarian nature of Judaism in the first century. A 'sect', as a general rule, can be seen as a 'minority' group that split off from what is perceived to be the 'parent body'.[166] The second is the hostility towards the Jewish leadership.[167] Much of the hostility and highly-charged rhetoric coming from these sectarian communities was directed towards the Jewish leadership. This is seen as widespread and it is a view shared by Matthew.[168] A third feature is the central role played by the law.[169] 'The law as interpreted within these groups emerged in this period as the means by which the sectarian communities legitimated their position and asserted their status as God's true people, in contrast to their opponents.'[170] The fourth is that these sectarian communities saw themselves quite exclusively as the only true covenant people of God.[171] Because of these features, a need for consolidation emerged. As Overman says, 'A new religio-cultural synthesis was now required if Judaism was to survive. This synthesis and the process of its construction and emergence in the post-70 period are referred to as *formative Judaism*.'[172] It was a period and process of reconstruction, re-definition, re-organization, consolidation and finding a structure that would ensure the continuing existence of Judaism. It was a process in which Judaism after 70 CE became more and more 'normative', although it was still not fully 'normative'.[173] It was a long process that took several hundred years and

---

165. Overman, *Matthew's Gospel and Formative Judaism*, pp. 3-4.

166. Cf. Overman, *Matthew's Gospel and Formative Judaism*, pp. 3-4; see also S.J.D. Cohen, 'The Significance of Yavneh: Pharisees, Rabbis, and the End of Jewish Sectarianism', *HUCA* 55 (1984), pp. 27-53 (29); J.H. Elliott, 'Stages of the Jesus Movement: From Faction to Sect', unpublished article (1990), pp, 1-2; Stanton, *A Gospel for a New People*, p. 90.

167. Cf. Overman, *Matthew's Gospel and Formative Judaism*, p. 19.

168. Cf. Overman, *Matthew's Gospel and Formative Judaism*, pp. 23, 151.

169. Cf. Overman, *Matthew's Gospel and Formative Judaism*, p. 23.

170. Overman, *Matthew's Gospel and Formative Judaism*, p. 29.

171. Cf. Overman, *Matthew's Gospel and Formative Judaism*, p. 30.

172. Overman, *Matthew's Gospel and Formative Judaism*, p. 35.

173. Cf. R.A. Wild, 'The Encounter between Pharisaic and Christian Judaism:

this process was in all probability set in motion by the so-called council of Yavneh (Jamnia).[174] It was a process in which the Pharisees, as the main opponents of Matthew's Gospel, played a quite significant role.

Yavneh and its Symbolic Role. The so-called council of Yavneh is viewed by Overman as the most significant event in the institutional development of Judaism in the period after 70 CE.[175] He says, 'Yavneh has been viewed as a watershed in the history of Judaism in that it established the rabbis as the authoritative body and marked the emergence of rabbinic Judaism as the normative form of Judaism.'[176] The reason might be that there was devastation after the destruction of the temple in 70 CE and that some sort of consolidation among the Jews was needed. The temple lost its prime focal point of Jewish sectarianism after its destruction. 'For most Jews... sectarian self-definition ceased to make sense after 70. The holiness of the Jerusalem temple, the legitimacy of its priesthood, and the propriety of its rituals were no longer relevant issues.' To most of the sectarian movements the temple and its priesthood and institutions no longer existed as the 'parent body' against which they could protest.[177] 'A sect needs an evil reality against which to protest, rail and define itself.'[178] Therefore, Yavneh had as its aim the forging of some unified coalition within Judaism. It was an attempt to end Jewish sectarianism.[179] Whether this attempt was successful remains debatable. The mere existence of, for example, the community of Matthew makes us doubt this. Furthermore, what the *real* effect of Jamnia was remains an open case. That it had a strong symbolic meaning as a legendary symbol of the *beginning* of

---

Some Early Gospel Evidence', *NovT* 27.2 (1985), pp. 105-24 (123); H.C. Kee, 'The Transformation of the Synagogue after 70 CE: Its Import for Early Christianity', *NTS* 36 (1990), pp. 1-24 (15).

    174. Cf. Overman, *Matthew's Gospel and Formative Judaism*, p. 37.

    175. Overman, *Matthew's Gospel and Formative Judaism*, p. 38.

    176. Overman, *Matthew's Gospel and Formative Judaism*, p. 38; see also Duling and Perrin, *The New Testament*, p. 336, who see the conflict between Jesus and the leaders as a conflict with 'Yavneh-inspired Pharisaism'.

    177. Cohen, 'The Significance of Yavneh', p. 45.

    178. Cohen, 'The Significance of Yavneh', p. 46.

    179. Cf. Cohen, 'The Significance of Yavneh', p. 28; see also Harrington, *The Gospel of Matthew*, pp. 14-15.

the task of social reconstruction in the wake of the destruction of Jerusalem is probable.[180] I agree with Overman:

> For now the most we can say about Yavneh is that it symbolizes the beginning of the end of sectarianism, and the initial efforts at forging a new coalition to perpetuate and reshape Judaism in the wake of the tragedy of 70. At the level of myth the symbolic import of Yavneh, as retold by successive rabbis, confirms them as the carriers of authority and legitimates them as the institution which would provide for learning and atonement henceforth.[181]

It is likely that Matthew and his community knew of this symbolic meaning attached to Jamnia, but that they challenged its legitimacy, and that this more than anything else was at the bottom of the conflict with the Pharisees. They challenged the interests of this group (still from within the Jewish ranks—see above) which had tried to establish some unity among the Jews. Although there is no direct indication as to whether there was a link between the Jamnian rabbis and the Pharisees, it is likely to have been the case. The only reason Cohen sees for the rabbis not regarding themselves as Pharisees (or as their descendants), was because they were not interested in publicizing this fact, since they (the rabbis) kept a low profile in post-biblical history.[182] This, however is not really convincing. The assumption of Segal is more convincing and applicable:

> Matthew's hostility to the Pharisees appears to correspond to the period in which the Pharisees were *becoming* rabbis—that is, extending their ascribed authority more widely through Galilee and Syria. That is a rather important perception, which we cannot get from the rabbinic evidence at all. Nor do we know exactly how their respect among the people grew.[183] But it is

---

180. Cf. Overman, *Matthew's Gospel and Formative Judaism*, p. 41.

181. Overman, *Matthew's Gospel and Formative Judaism*, p. 43.

182. Cohen, 'The Significance of Yavneh', pp. 36-38.

183. Van Aarde explains the growing influence of the Pharisees. To him it was due to a pre-70 CE strategy, which they continued after 70 CE, to extend the concerns of ritual purity, usually associated only with the priests and the temple, into the day-to-day living of the ordinary Jews. The strict purity regulations pertaining to the temple, were extended to the bed and board of every observant Jew (A.G. Van Aarde, ' "The Most High God Does Live in Houses, but Not Houses Built by Men. . . ": The Relativity of the Metaphor "Temple" in Luke–Acts', *Neot* 25.1 [1991], pp. 51-64 [59]; *idem Kultuurhistoriese agtergrond van die Nuwe Testament: Die eerste-eeuse mediterreense sosiale konteks* [Pretoria: Kital, 1994], p. 111).

crucial for understanding Jewish history. The synagogue adopted rabbinic authority out of respect for the rabbis' piety and power; they appear to have spurned the Matthean version of Torah interpretation, based on Jesus' principles (emphasis mine).[184]

These remarks by Segal, along with Neusner's interpretation of Josephus's *Antiquities*, confirm the likelihood of a link between Jamnia and the Pharisees.[185] This also supports my suggestion that there was a conflict of interests, also in 'political' terms between Matthew's community and the Pharisees, as the authoritative group at Jamnia:

> In Palestine in the twenty years from AD 70 to 90, the Pharisees, who had survived the destruction of Jerusalem in 70, had established themselves as the *dominant group*. Led by Yohanan ben Zakkai, they had created a Jewish administration at the coastal town of Yavneh. This administration had assumed those powers of self-government left in Jewish hands by the Roman regime. By AD 90, the head of the Yavnean government, Gamaliel II, grandson of the Gamaliel mentioned as the Pharisee in the Temple council in Acts 5.34 and son of Simeon ben Gamaliel, who was alluded to in Josephus' *Life* as a leader of the Jerusalem government in AD 66, had negotiated with the Roman government for recognition as head of the Palestinian Jewry. *The basis for settlement was the Yavneans' agreement to oppose subversion of Roman rule in exchange for Roman support of the Yavneans' control over the Jews. . . The Yavnean authorities, called rabbis—whence 'rabbinic Judaism'—thus continued the Pharisaic political and foreign polities initiated at the end of Maccabean times. Now, however, the Pharisees met with no competition* (my emphasis).[186]

This brings me to the same logical assumption as Overman, namely that the Pharisees were well positioned for the events of 70 CE and after, especially within formative Judaism and in the conflict with the community of Matthew.[187] As Overman says, 'There is then a strong Pharisaic element in the synthesis of post-70 formative Judaism.'[188]

---

184. Segal, 'Matthew's Jewish Voice', p. 36.

185. Segal, 'Matthew's Jewish Voice', p. 36; see also Harrington, *The Gospel of Matthew*, pp. 14-15.

186. J. Neusner, 'Josephus' Pharisees: A Complete Repertoire', in L.H. Feldman and G. Hata (eds.), *Josephus, Judaism, and Christianity*, (Detroit: Wayne State University Press, 1987), pp. 274-92 (280); see also Saldarini, *Pharisees, Scribes and Sadducees in Palestinian Society*, pp. 114, 119; Pantle-Schieber, 'Anmerkungen zur Auseinandersetzung von ἐκκλησία und Judentum im Matthäusevangelium', p. 153.

187. Overman, *Matthew's Gospel and Formative Judaism*, p. 35.

188. Overman, *Matthew's Gospel and Formative Judaism*, p. 37.

The Pharisees as Part of the Retainer Class in the Period of Formative Judaism. In the period after 70 CE the Pharisees established themselves as a growing and rising power. As the Romans took over the destroyed country, they found the Pharisees relatively untouched by the revolt, probably because in the pre-70 period they had withdrawn from politics.[189] After 70 CE, however, their role changed remarkably. They had never been enthusiastic about the revolution and therefore managed to survive the devastation. The Pharisees were determined to assume political leadership and, as Wild says when citing Neusner: ' . . . to strike an agreement with the Romans: "The Pharisaic party would keep the country peaceful, and the Romans would leave internal matters in the hands of the party".'[190] The Pharisees were the ideal candidates to take over the role of retainers of the Roman Empire (the ruler and governing classes) in Galilee and beyond to Syria.[191] The role of the Pharisees as retainers is confirmed by Saldarini as he says, 'The Pharisees fit best into the retainer class as a religious group and a *political force which interacted with the governing class,* often influenced society and sometimes gained power' (my emphasis).[192] As such, they did not have direct political power, but nevertheless acted as a political interest group protecting the interests of the rulers and, by influencing people, they gained importance.[193] A quotation of Saldarini is again applicable here: 'Whatever influence they achieved, they usually achieved with the help of a powerful patron, and they entered into coalition with other groups among the upper classes in order to gain influence and move those who had power.'[194]

189. Cf. J. Neusner, *From Politics to Piety: The Emergence of Pharisaic Judaism* (Englewood Cliffs, NJ: Prentice–Hall, 1973); Wild, 'The Encounter between Pharisaic and Christian Judaism', p. 107; Segal, 'Matthew's Jewish Voice', p. 27.

190. Wild, 'The Encounter between Pharisaic and Christian Judaism', p. 108; Neusner, *From Politics to Piety*, pp. 146-47.

191. Cf. Segal, 'Matthew's Jewish Voice', p. 27; see the theory of Segal, as described above, on the arc of territory as setting for the community of Matthew (Segal, 'Matthew's Jewish Voice', p. 19).

192. Saldarini, *Pharisees, Scribes and Sadducees in Palestinian Society*, pp. 39-40; see also White, 'Crisis Management and Boundary Maintenance', p. 221.

193. Cf. Saldarini, *Pharisees, Scribes and Sadducees in Palestinian Society*, p. 106.

194. Saldarini, 'Political and Social Roles of the Pharisees and the Scribes in Galilee', p. 204.

In short, it is assumed that the Pharisees emerged as the dominant and leading faction within first-century Judaism, *acting as retainers of the Roman Empire.* This view is confirmed by Josephus.[195]

Nevertheless there exists considerable doubt as to whether the Pharisees really were the dominant group in formative Judaism, acting as the retainers of the Roman Empire. Neusner dismisses the claim that the Pharisees were politically active in pre-70 CE Palestinian Judaism.[196] He views the presumed political activity of the pre-70 CE Pharisees as mere post-70 propaganda. But this still leaves open the possibility that they could have been politically active as retainers *after* 70 CE, although this can also be viewed as mere Josephian propaganda, and thus, according to Neusner, unreliable.[197] Even if this view could have been confirmed with evidence from the Gospels, Culbertson dismisses it as 'subjective, incomplete and caricatured'.[198] Just the same, although I would agree that the evidence is slim and subjective, and presents itself as propaganda (and built on secondary sources) some element of truth could be present. It certainly matches the historical setting as White describes it.[199] White says that during the revolt, much of Galilee, especially the larger cities, capitulated very quickly, and the entire region was pacified by the end of 67 CE.[200] When the war ended in 70 CE, the provincial status of Judea was upgraded and it was placed under its own Roman *legatus*. In the north, much of the territory of Agrippa II was returned to him with additional territories in Syria as a reward for his loyalty. As White continues,

> On the death of Agrippa II (ca. 92–93) his domain reverted to the Province of Syria, thus producing the peculiar boundaries that existed down to the time of the Second Revolt. . . It also appears that a portion of the northern expansion of Galilee achieved under Agrippa I was ceded once again to Phoenicia (Syria). With this new provincial status, the political boundaries

195. Cf. E. Rivkin, *A Hidden Revolution: The Pharisees' Search for the Kingdom Within* (Nashville: Abingdon Press, 1978), pp. 31-75; Saldarini, *Pharisees, Scribes and Sadducees in Palestinian Society*, p. 133; Dunn, 'Pharisees, Sinners and Jesus', p. 269; Overman, *Matthew's Gospel and Formative Judaism*, p. 14.

196. Neusner, 'Josephus' Pharisees', p. 290.

197. Neusner, *Formative Judaism*, pp. 73-74; see also D.R. Schwartz, 'Josephus and Nicolaus on the Pharisees', *JSJ* 14.2 (1983), pp. 157-71 (170).

198. P. Culbertson, 'Changing Christian Images of the Pharisees', *ATR* 64.4 (1982), pp. 539-61 (549).

199. White, 'Crisis Management and Boundary Maintenance', pp. 236-37, 241.

200. White, 'Crisis Management and Boundary Maintenance', p. 236.

for the Jewish population of Galilee, the Transjordan and the Syro–Phoenician cities were once again subject to administrative change, while culturally there was a lively exchange.

It is in this era of administrative reorganization that one should look for keys to the crisis behind Matthew's Gospel, since the issues of taxation and political boundaries were changed sharply.[201]

White is convinced that the breakup of the kingdom of Agrippa II was a time of massive administrative changes:

> The loss of a 'Jewish' monarch in these regions meant there was now a greater vacuum for those Jewish (and Christian) communities living outside the borders of the homeland. It is also possible to see it as occasion for the expansion of new lines of religious [and political] authority associated with the consolidation of the rabbinic academy in the Yavnean period (from ca. 90–120 CE).[202]

The administrative vacuum created by the decline of the Jewish monarch, could, to my mind, have easily been filled by the Pharisees as retainers. What the criticism above makes us realize is that it is a mistake to generalize on the overall role of the Pharisees, for as Dunn makes us aware, the Pharisees were themselves divided.[203] Therefore I agree with White that the conflict between Matthew's community and the Pharisees was very much a local issue, rather than a conflict in general terms between the Jews and the Christians.[204]

Whereas it remains difficult to find much detail on the overall role of the Pharisees as retainers and thus on their administrative and political functions, as far as *Matthew is concerned*, these functions were perceived as very important in the local environment. Although it can be argued that the Pharisees may have had a minor political and administrative role, it seems that Matthew experienced this role as being major. This is the basis for Overman's argument.[205] The Pharisees, as part of the Jewish leadership, were constituted by formative Judaism, as the most powerful body in Matthew's world. Each of the synoptic gospels as well as the Gospel of John and Acts, contains incidents, conversations and confrontations involving the Pharisees. Matthew contains

201. White, 'Crisis Management and Boundary Maintenance', p. 326.
202. White, 'Crisis Management and Boundary Maintenance', p. 327.
203. Dunn, 'Pharisees, Sinners and Jesus', p. 269.
204. White, 'Crisis Management and Boundary Maintenance', p. 291.
205. Overman, *Matthew's Gospel and Formative Judaism*, p. 156.

the most data about this and is at the same time the most hostile.[206] Pharisaic Judaism was the dominant form of Judaism at the time of the First Gospel.[207] This rests on an assumption, very generally agreed upon, that the Gospel received its final form in the years following the destruction of Jerusalem, probably around 85–90 CE, the period of Jamnia and the effective assumption or imposition of Pharisaic Judaism as the norm.[208] The story of Matthew reflects the experience of Matthew's community who increasingly experienced this hostility.[209] This assumption can be made from the text of Matthew itself (as well as from my own study of Matthew 8 and 9 specifically). The Pharisees, as part of the leadership, were held responsible for the arrest, trial, execution and death of Jesus. A deliberate attempt is made by Matthew to blame them, at the same time exonerating Pilate by means of the stories of his wife's dream warning him to have no part in the trial (27.18-19), his symbolic washing of hands in public (27.62-66) and the story of the guards being bribed to report that Jesus' body had been stolen (28.11-15). Matthew reports the Jewish leaders as deliberately accepting responsibility for Jesus' death.[210] This confirms the emerging antagonism between the community and the Pharisees (Jewish leadership), who were considered by Matthew to be the dominant authoritative group creating constant opposition. They were active in the Jerusalem leadership challenging Jesus' authority as a religious and social leader by assaulting its sources (9.32-34; 12.22-30) and arguing with Jesus about divorce (19.3-9). They were attacked by Jesus in a series of parables in chs. 21–22; they plotted against Jesus in 21.45-46. It is the Pharisee's lawyer who asked the last hostile question at the trial (22.34-35) and they joined forces with the chief priest in asking for a guard for Jesus' tomb (27.62-65).[211]

Matthew's Pharisees were also in dispute with Jesus about the importance of food rules (9.6-13; 9.14-17) and they also were concerned

---

206. Cf. Rivkin, *A Hidden Revolution*, p. 79.

207. Cf. Pantle-Schieber, 'Anmerkungen zur Auseinanderzetzung von ἐκκλησία und Judentum', p. 153; see also T.L. Donaldson, 'The Law that "Hangs" (Mt 22:40): Rabbinic Formulation and Matthean Social World', in D.J. Lull (ed.), SBLSP 1990 (Atlanta: Scholars Press, 1990), pp. 14-33 (30).

208. Cf. Doyle, 'A Concern of the Evangelist', p. 18.

209. Cf. White, 'Crisis Management and Boundary Maintenance', p. 238.

210. Cf. Kee, 'The Transformation of the Synagogue after 70 CE', p. 22.

211. Cf. Saldarini, *Pharisees, Scribes and Sadducees in Palestinian Society*, pp. 167-68.

with the source of Jesus' power in the two miracle stories of the healing of a dumb demoniac (9.32-34; 12.22-30). The closer Jesus got to
his trial and crucifixion, the more hostile the Pharisees became, and
the 'closer' the relationship with their allies was, the more the political
and retaining role of the Pharisees increased. As Saldarini says,

> But, as Jesus enters Judea (ch. 19), the Pharisees explicitly test Jesus and
> *take a more aggressive stance towards him by plotting and making*
> *alliances with other.* . . The increased hostility of the chief priests [as part
> of the ruling classes] and the Pharisees is met, in chs. 21 and 22, with a
> series of parables attacking them for not believing in Jesus. . . While
> Jesus is in Jerusalem, the chief priests are the constant centre of political
> opposition to Jesus and the other groups of leaders are *allied* with them at
> different times (my emphasis).[212]

It therefore seems possible that the Pharisees filled the political and
administrative (retaining) vacuum left by the revolt of 66–70 CE. They
almost never had direct political power, but acted on behalf of the
rulers and governing classes, thus serving their interests. Their function
should have been to keep the country peaceful and consequently, according to our conflict theory, their task was to maintain the status
quo. We have already seen that the prime function of the retainers,
and thus of the Pharisees, was to serve the rulers. Their interests were
concerned with the upper layers of society. Thus, any perceived challenge to their function as retainers, opposition to their ideology, or
attempt to change the status quo could have led to serious conflict.
Whether the opposition to them was religious or political, it became a
source of conflict. Matthew indeed challenged the Pharisees, and thus
provoked their hostility. He represented, as the 'marginalized man', the
involuntary marginalized. He was voluntarily marginalized and as such
challenged the interests of the Pharisees (which were those of the upper
classes), and defied them to change their ideologies (see below). But
Matthew also served another interest group, with another growing identity, which further heightened the emerging conflict. To this I now turn.

Group Boundaries and Self-Definition
This section cannot be seen in isolation. In the previous section I dealt
primarily with the possible reasons why the Pharisees might have
perceived the community of Matthew as a threat. The leaders of the
Matthean community, in identifying with Jesus had, presumably like

212. Saldarini, *Pharisees, Scribes and Sadducees in Palestinian Society*, p. 169.

him, turned to the quasi-group, that is, the lowest classes with their suppressed interests (see above in Chapter 2 on *What are the units of conflict?* for a discussion of these concepts). In doing this, whether they had intended to form them into an interest group or not, it was likely that the leaders of the community would have been drawn into confrontation with the religious leaders who were seeking authority and privilege from the Roman occupiers of the time. This gesture would have threatened their endeavour to gain influence with Rome and to receive support from the common people who were the same quasi-group as the Matthean community. The Jewish leaders sought support in their efforts to gain power. The Matthean community, in following Jesus, supported the interests of the weak and the underprivileged, who were in an extremely bad situation in a typical agrarian society. Both were part of the Jewish community, but the Jewish 'establishment' tried to maintain its position of authority (both religiously and politically) and advance its position with the Roman authorities. The leaders of the Matthean community (and Jesus) took up the interests of the weak and gained influence amongst the weak and the poor, so strengthening their own position as well. They had to survive as an interest group of 'Jesus-believers' who supported the interests of the weak.

The Conflict from the Side of the Jewish Leaders. The Matthean community seems to have been the interest group that supported the interests of the 'Jesus-believers', and because Jesus set an example of turning to the marginalized, they were probably at the same time the interest group supporting the quasi-group: the lowest classes of the society. In fact, one could say, the community of Matthew seems to have been the interest group of the lower classes in society. This is how they could have seen their own identity. There was thus, amongst other things, a struggle for authority over the common people and the peasantry.[213] This involved the conflict becoming further intensified, for they wished to gain the control and support of the peasantry. The ruling classes, in their internal struggles, as Lenski says, often had to turn to the lower classes (the common people) '. . . as a counterforce with a well-entrenched and united nobility'.[214] Lenski uses examples from Aristotle's *Politics* and Plato's *The Republic* to illustrate the

213. See also Saldarini, 'The Gospel of Matthew and Jewish–Christian Conflict', p. 45.
214. Lenski, *Power and Privilege*, p. 241.

tendency of certain rulers to ally themselves with the common people in opposition to the governing classes.[215] Similarly, the Roman emperors often allied themselves with the urban masses in their struggle with the senatorial class. In the interest of the Roman Empire, it could have been of benefit to the rulers if the Pharisees had done the same. The Pharisees (the dominant group among the Jewish leaders in Matthew's view) had to recruit new members (or at least new supporters) to survive, because they had insufficient power as retainers to remain in power without the support of both the rulers (above) and the peasantry (below).[216] The community of Matthew also had to recruit new members, resulting in competition with the Pharisees and increasing conflict.

A few remarks should be made on the subject of recruiting new members (supporters). Stark says that the Jews themselves did not try to convert others on a large scale.[217] However, I do not want to rule out this possibility. I have already argued that both Pharisaic Judaism and the Matthean community are to be seen as *formative* groups. I can only imagine that new groups in the process of formation need new members (or at least support). Says Duling: 'Thus, like the Pharisees, the Matthew group is not simply a group, but moving towards a corporation.'[218] A corporate group is defined by Malina as '. . . a collection of people forming a corporate body with permanent existence, *recruited* on recognized principles' (my emphasis).[219] We may therefore assume that there was a policy of recruiting and that the two groups were likely to have 'shot among each other's doves'. The Jews, as far as Stark is concerned, were, despite the Gentile mission, still the major source of Christian converts until as late as the fourth century.[220] We have to realize, however, that recruiting was never the *source* (or cause) of conflict. It would have merely *intensified* the existing conflict.

215. Lenski, *Power and Privilege*, p. 241 n. 201.

216. See also Saldarini, 'The Gospel of Matthew and Jewish–Christian Conflict', p. 54.

217. R. Stark, 'Jewish Conversion and the Rise of Christianity: Rethinking the Received Wisdom', in K.H. Richards (ed.), SBLSP 1986 (Atlanta: Scholars Press, 1986), p. 314-29 (314).

218. Duling, 'Matthew's Plurisignificant "Son of David" in Social-science Perspective', p. 106.

219. Malina, 'Patron and Client', p. 29; see also Duling, 'Matthew's Plurisignificant "Son of David" in Social-science Perspective', pp. 104-105.

220. Stark, 'Jewish Conversion and the Rise of Christianity', pp. 314, 320.

But, 'it takes two to tango'. We also have to view the conflict from the side of the community of Matthew.

The Conflict from the Side of the Matthean Community. It was the Jewish leaders who emerged as the controlling body in Matthew's environment. The community's experience and perception as a minority group, that is, being the 'underdogs', grew. They constituted the minority in their competition with formative Judaism and felt persecuted. As Overman says,

> The strong emotions and the sweeping manner in which the Jewish leadership is attacked and rejected by Matthew suggest a current and hotly contested struggle which the Matthean community seems losing. Matthew's accusatory language and name-calling indicate the position of power the Jewish leadership holds as well as the status of the Matthean community as *minority or underdogs* in this struggle (my emphasis).[221]

Throughout his Gospel Matthew describes in real terms the threat from this dominant group (and the competition from them) beginning in chs. 8 and 9 (9.34), and culminating in ch. 23. These writings are the response of a community struggling to survive in the face of the conflict and competition they are experiencing. It is the response to a threat facing the community namely, formative Judaism which was developing and gaining the upper hand in the Matthean setting.[222] The conflict between the community of Matthew and formative Judaism, forced the community to redefine its own identity. 'In their competition with one another they were forced to develop and change.'[223] This new emerging (changing from the parent body) identity is confirmed by a previous observation that social conflict always results in change on a wide variety of levels, especially on an ideological level. The conflict caused the community to accept newly ascribed values and ideologies.

Because the community experienced themselves as being 'marginalized', they could easily identify themselves with the truly 'marginalized'. They could have become a group taking up the interests of the

221. Overman, *Matthew's Gospel and Formative Judaism*, p. 147, see also pp. 154, 160. This view is confirmed by Saldarini 'The Gospel of Matthew and Jewish–Christian conflict', pp. 49-50; White, 'Crisis Management and Boundary Maintenance', p. 241 and Stanton, *A Gospel for a New People*, p. 167.
222. See also White, 'Crisis Management and Boundary Maintenance', p. 241.
223. Overman, *Matthew's Gospel and Formative Judaism*, p. 161.

underprivileged in order to grow and survive. They still kept the Jewish values, in fact, as argued earlier, they still regarded themselves as Jews (as indeed they were). However, they developed their own fresh interpretation of these values, because in their community (as in any other community) there still remained an urge to legitimize their own position (see below). I agree with Saldarini that because of the conflict and the resultant differentiation, the members of Matthew's community found their core identity and their 'master status' in being believers-in-Jesus.[224] 'All other aspects of their Jewish life and world view are filtered through this central commitment which has alienated them from many fellow Jews and coloured all their activities and relationships.'[225] All symbols became subordinate to the central symbol of faith: the Christ. The supreme norm for the life well-pleasing to God was no longer the Torah, but Jesus.[226] However, because of a previously taken stance that the community was still living within Judaism, yet developing a new identity that was the beginning of the process of departing, I do not entirely agree with Saldarini when he says, 'In the next generation this "master status" would crystallize in a Christian identity and lead them to drop their Jewish identity. Thus Matthew's Gospel entered the mainstream of non-Jewish, second-century Christian church.'[227] This might be true of a generation after Matthew, but not yet in the time of Matthew. They were indeed at the beginning of the process of separation, but certainly, as yet, not part of the 'non-Jewish church'. Saldarini, however, seems to rectify his view in the same article, which comes closer to the view I have myself. He says that the late first-century Matthean community had such a close relationship with the Jewish community that it had probably been a reformist movement which became a sect in response to the rejection of its programme for the reform of Judaism.[228] Matthew is developing a new community,

224. Saldarini, 'The Gospel of Matthew and Jewish–Christian Conflict', p. 57. By way of explanation, Saldarini is also adopted: 'The concept "master status" denotes a primary trait of a person to which all others are subordinate. Though we all occupy multiple social positions, statuses, and roles, one may predominate. In a racially stratified society such as the USA, being black is a master status' (Saldarini, 'The Gospel of Matthew and Jewish–Christian Conflict', p. 57 n. 58).

225. Saldarini, 'The Gospel of Matthew and Jewish–Christian Conflict', p. 57.

226. Cf. Hare, *The Theme of Jewish Persecution*, p. 5.

227. Saldarini, 'The Gospel of Matthew and Jewish–Christian Conflict', p. 57.

228. Cf. Saldarini, 'The Gospel of Matthew and Jewish–Christian Conflict', p. 59; see also Stanton, *A Gospel for a New People*, pp. 93-94, 96, 166.

and moving towards a new community organization which Saldarini describes as:

> First, it is still residually reformist and millenarian/revolutionist. Second, it has de-emphasized the thaumaturgical. The final commission to the disciples is to preach, teach, and baptize (28.19-20), not exorcise and heal (contrast 10.7-8).[229] Third, Matthew's emphasis on bringing non-Jews into the community (28.19) and on the integrity of his own community . . . suggests that the community is *moving* towards a conversionist orientation that seeks to bring a mixed group of people into the community (21.43). For the author, that new community is still Jewish and will still adhere to the bulk of Jewish law and custom. The author still has a waning hope that the other Jews will join him. . . [The community] is *beginning* to create a new community withdrawn from Judaism and the empire as well (my emphasis).[230]

In their search for a new identity, they developed their own new set of values and ideologies to serve their own interests. Every community has the urge to legitimize its own existence by its own set of values and ideologies.[231] One way of legitimizing a movement's existence is by what Overman calls the 'traditionalising' of a new movement.[232] Being traditional makes a movement accepted and legitimate. The movement must be identified with a greater, more established and traditional authority.[233] Overman is correct in his view that the so-called fulfilment citations (Mt. 1.22; 2.5, 15, 17, 23; 3.3; 4.14; 8.17; 12.17; 13.14, 35; 21.4; 26.56; 27.9) are an attempt by Matthew to traditionalize his movement/community.[234] More than half of the fulfilment citations are related to the narratives of the birth of Jesus, by this giving credibility to the birth of Jesus and to the community as well. As Overman says: 'The life of

---

229. Although it seems true that Matthew de-emphasizes the thaumaturgical (at least as far as the acts of healing are concerned), I do not agree that he de-emphasized its meaning, namely, to take up the interests of those in need. This is not what Saldarini says, and one should be careful not to deduce this from his statement (Saldarini, 'The Gospel of Matthew and Jewish–Christian Conflict', p. 59).

230. Saldarini, 'The Gospel of Matthew and Jewish–Christian Conflict', pp. 59-60.

231. See Chapter 2 on *Goals*.

232. Overman, *Matthew's Gospel and Formative Judaism*, p. 62.

233. Cf. Overman, *Matthew's Gospel and Formative Judaism*, p. 63.

234. Overman, *Matthew's Gospel and Formative Judaism*, pp. 74-78.

the Matthean community is in continuity with the Scripture, promises, and traditions of the history of Israel.'[235]

Another way of legitimizing a movement, which was particularly important in the post 70 CE period, was to present the community and its leaders as the true interpreters of the law.[236] In this regard Overman says 'What is most characteristic about the Matthean conflict stories is that these stories portray Jesus as an accurate and true interpreter of the law... Matthew, through his reworking of these traditions, justifies his community's interpretation and application of the law over against the accusations offered by the opponents.'[237] Overman focuses on three conflict stories to support his view: (1) the Sabbath controversy (Mt. 12.1-8); (2) Mt. 15.1-20 on the issue of ritual purity; (3) the debate about the so-called love command (Mt. 22.34-40).[238] Since the next chapter concentrates on the conflict in the miracle stories, I will not go into this issue here.[239] Matthew emphasized the importance of the law and Jewish traditions, but rearranged and reassessed them. For example, on the issue of tithing, he affirms this practice, but puts the emphasis on 'the weightier matters of the law: justice and mercy and faith' (Mt. 23.23; see also Mt. 9.13).[240] New emphasis is also given to forgiveness (Mt. 9.2, 6; see my discussion below).

A last brief remark must be made regarding the boundaries of the community. The boundaries are more open and the membership requirements have been modified. This is confirmed by Mt. 9.10 (see below). I agree with Saldarini that though the community of Matthew is very Jewish in tradition, thought and practice, it has in principle opened its boundaries to non-Jews.[241] I differ from him when he says, 'He [Matthew] does not declare himself a new or true, *nor does he give his community a new name over against Israel*. That will be left to the next generation' (my emphasis).[242] What about the reference to the community as ἐκκλησία, referring to a more inclusive community,

235. Overman, *Matthew's Gospel and Formative Judaism*, p. 78.

236. Cf. Overman, *Matthew's Gospel and Formative Judaism*, pp. 68-71.

237. Overman, *Matthew's Gospel and Formative Judaism*, p. 79.

238. Overman, *Matthew's Gospel and Formative Judaism*, pp. 79-89.

239. See also Saldarini, 'The Gospel of Matthew and Jewish–Christian Conflict', pp. 41, 48, 49 on the issue of Matthew as 'true' interpreter of the law.

240. Cf. Overman, *Matthew's Gospel and Formative Judaism*, pp. 93, 95; Saldarini, 'The Gospel of Matthew and Jewish–Christian Conflict', pp. 49, 52.

241. Saldarini, 'The Gospel of Matthew and Jewish–Christian Conflict', p. 51.

242. Saldarini, 'The Gospel of Matthew and Jewish–Christian Conflict', p. 51.

in contrast to the term συναγωγή, which referred to the more exclusive Jewish community?[243] Could this not be a new 'name'? At the very least it is a new concept referring to the Matthean community in such a way.

Nevertheless, Saldarini continues, 'Rather, prompted by the inclusion of Gentiles and marginal groups such as poor, sick, and outcasts, and influences by biblical passages that are inclusive of these groups, Matthew constantly defends the Gentiles' right to faith in and salvation from Jesus.'[244] The Gospel of Matthew, through the conflict it was involved in, changed its values and ideologies so as to include the non-Jews and marginalized. Through this he created a new identity: that of a community continually taking up the interests of the outcasts, following the example of Jesus as their 'master status' (see the discussion of the text of Mt. 8 and 9).

Conclusion

I now have to tie up the loose ends. In a highly stratified society such as an advanced agrarian society (which the community of Matthew was part of), it is likely that different interest groups would exist. As part of the upper classes we find the urban elite (the rulers and the governing classes). They possessed and managed most of the resources (including authority). The retainers, also regarded as upper class, played a supportive role in relation to the rulers. Going down the social scale, the lower classes (or involuntary marginalized according to Duling)[245] comprised of the urban non-elite, the unclean and degraded class and the rural peasantry. They had little or none of the surplus or scarce resources, and least of all authority. This section gave us important background information in order to identify the different conflicting interest groups in agrarian societies.

The implications of the geographical setting in relationship to the social stratification in advanced agrarian societies, have been investigated. The widely acclaimed consensus that Antioch was the place of origin of Matthew's Gospel was challenged, as was the alternative claim

---

243. Cf. Van Aarde, 'Die "heiligheid" van die kerk teen die agtergrond van die breuk kerk-sinagoge', p. 262; see also Duling and Perrin, *The New Testament*, p. 337.

244. Saldarini, 'The Gospel of Matthew and Jewish–Christian Conflict', p. 51.

245. Duling, 'Matthew and Marginality', p. 644.

of Galilee as the (sole) place of origin. Following Segal, we see Galilee *and* Syria rather as the area of its origin, an arc of settlements from Galilee through Antioch and Edessa and into Syria.

It is generally accepted that Matthew originated in a predominantly urban environment and was directed towards a community of predominantly urban non-elite. But the enlarged geographical location suggested by Segal, opens up the possibility that the community could also have comprised other (enlarged) non-elite classes. This is confirmed by the concept of *involuntary marginality* of Duling. I suggest that the community was a mixed community of not only Jews and Gentiles, but also of urban non-elite *and* rural peasantry (including also the outcasts, degraded and the expendables). Matthew by his Gospel did not only 'revitalize' the urban non-elite in their miserable conditions but also the other marginalized. We have also seen that there could have been a few members from the upper classes present in the community (such as the author himself), without having their direct (class) interests reflected in it. They are classified as *voluntary marginalized*. They could identify with the involuntary marginalized because of the phenomenon of voluntary marginality. The implications here are that the leaders of the community (who in their own right could be seen as retainers) are encouraged by the author to opt for voluntary marginality also.

There is wide consensus that there was tension between the Matthean church and the synagogue but the nature of this tension is disputed. A choice has to be made between the traditional view, an *intra muros* community, or that of a totally Gentile one (*extra muros*). I preferred a view somewhere in between. The community was still part of Judaism, but was on its way out. It retained its close ties with Judaism, but was in the process of being alienated from it. This explains the intense and passionate conflict.

The major opponents depicted in the Gospel of Matthew were the Pharisees. They appeared to be the most dominant group in the post-70 CE period. Whether this was historically the case can be challenged, but as far as Matthew is concerned, there is no doubt. They were well established after the war and filled the administrative and political vacuum it left. They gained the power and authority, if not in the whole of Palestine, then at least in Galilee and Syro-Phoenicia, the area in which the Gospel of Matthew probably originated and 'operated' as well. The Pharisees were likely to have been the dominant group within formative Judaism that emerged at Jamnia. This *formative Judaism* had a most profound influence on the development of the community of Matthew. A deliberate attempt to reconcile and unify the different Jewish sects was set in motion by Jamnia, which became its symbol. Matthew ought to have known this, but he (or at least his community) challenged the legitimacy of Jamnia. It was not that the community did not want to be part of Judaism any more, they regarded themselves as still being part of Judaism, but that because of their own marginalized position, they found a new 'master status', that is, believing in Jesus (who became the symbol of their position). They thus inevitably differed from the 'parent body'.

From the viewpoint of the Jamnian academy and the Pharisees, as prime adversaries in Matthew 8 and 9, this could be seen as a challenge to traditional values. Any such challenge to the attempted unification could have resulted in conflict, as I suggest happened in the society in which Matthew originated. Following Jamnia, the Pharisees emerged as the retainers of the ruling Roman Empire and had to maintain the status quo in favour of the Roman rulers. No form of opposition could be tolerated and it would be met with serious counter measures and accusations. They could have been threatened in their role as retainers by the community of Matthew, because the latter challenged their authority. Evidence of this can be found in the whole Gospel, and in Matthew 8 and 9 particularly.

In order to survive, both the Synagogue and the community of Matthew had to recruit new members. This could have further intensified the conflict. It must be realized that the recruiting of members or support was not in itself a cause of conflict. It merely *intensified* the existing conflict. Some research still has to be done on this issue. The last word has not yet been spoken.

In a predominantly urban environment, Matthew's community was likely to recruit new members from the urban non-elite and the peasantry. In fact, it seems likely that his community acted on behalf of the 'marginalized'. They took on the interests of the 'underdogs' and acted as an interest group for the lower classes of the society. This was because, in their conflict with the Jewish leadership they themselves had experience of being the 'underdogs'. They seemed to have lost ground with the leaders and consequently among the Jews as well in the era of *formative Judaism*. Thus they were forced to rethink and re-formulate their values and ideologies to suit the new, changing situation. They still very strongly identified with traditional values but reinterpreted them, laying more emphasis on justice, mercy and for-giveness. Because these were also the values of the Pharisees, as we will later see, they challenged the leaders for not 'putting their money where their mouths were'. In this period of reassessment and rethinking they were, in fact, in a process of departing from Judaism and because of this they became more intense and the accusations became extremely crude.

I can thus explain the conflict of interests as follows. The Pharisees represented the interest group that manoevered to retain the status quo both in their own interests and in those of the ruler and governing classes with whom they were in coalition. They had the authority, and wished to keep it. The community of Matthew represented the interests of the lower classes, constantly threatened by the Jewish leaders. They bargained for *change* in terms of values, norms and for control over themselves. This was a cause for apparent and inevitable conflict. The Pharisees represented the upper classes, and the Matthean community the lower classes. The former had no authority, but claimed that they had. This is the reason their interests clashed.

All this is but a theory that still has to be tested. The critique of Kingsbury seems to be that the various suggestions as to what the community of Matthew looked like, have a slim textual base.[246] He says, 'A final matter to which biblical social historians will want to attend as they advance their reconstructions of Matthew's community has to do with *reading the text of Matthew's Gospel itself*' (my empha-sis).[247] This is what I will attempt to do in the following chapter. Matthew 8 and 9 will be carefully read as a test case for the theory developed above on the conflict between the leaders of Israel and Matthew's community.

---

246. Kingsbury, 'Conclusion', p. 268.
247. Kingsbury, 'Conclusion', p. 268.

Chapter 4

EXEGESIS OF MATTHEW 8 AND 9
IN THE LIGHT OF CONFLICT THEORY

A story is by definition a serial of logical and chronological connected events.[1]

The Plot

The Gospel of Matthew is a narrative text. All the necessary compo-
nents as Chatman describes them, namely: a story, a content or chain
of events (actions, happenings), existents (characters, items or settings)
and a discourse, that is the expressions, the means by which the content is communicated, are present.[2] Matthew 8 and 9, as part of the
Gospel as a whole, is also a narrative. As such it is a literary product
of a redactor–narrator. 'Using, among other things, transmitted tradition, editorially processed in a re-interpretative and creative manner,
evangelists each communicate their own theological ideas by means of
the narrative form, as story-tellers.'[3] Whether viewed as a literary
product, or as a narrative text, the plot must be determined.

In my endeavour to determine the plot of the text, I will use the
categories derived from the extended conflict theory presented at the

1. M. Bal, *De theorie van vertellen en verhalen: Inleiding in de narratologie*
(Muiderberg: Coutinho, 4th edn, 1986), p. 27.
2. S. Chatman, *Story and Discourse: Narrative Structure in Fiction and Film*
(Ithaca, NY: Cornell University Press, 1978), p. 19; see also H.J.B. Combrink,
'The Structure of the Gospel of Matthew as Narrative', *TynBul* 34 (1983), pp. 61-90
(63); Kingsbury, *Matthew as Story*, pp. 2-3; M.A. Powell, 'Towards a Narrative-
critical Understanding of Matthew', *Int* 46.4 (1992), pp. 341-46 (345).
3. A.G. Van Aarde, 'Narrative Criticism Applied to John 4:43-54', in P.J.
Hartin and J.H. Petzer (eds.), *Text and Interpretation: New Approaches in Criticism
of the New Testament* (Leiden: Brill, 1991), pp. 101-28 (107); see also Van Aarde,
God-with-Us, p. 89; Combrink, 'The Structure of the Gospel of Matthew as Narrative', p. 67.

end of Chapter 2. I will furthermore attempt to explicate these categories as they unfold in the text of Matthew 8 and 9. I will also take the
results of Chapter 3 into consideration.

The Plot of Matthew 8 and 9
As a short and useful definition of what a plot is, we can refer to
Matera, who uses the following definition in analysing the plot of the
Gospel as a whole:

> By way of summary, we can say that although literary critics nuance their
> approaches to the plot, they agree that it has something to do with *how
> discourse arranges events by time and causality in order to produce a
> particular effect or, emotional response* (my emphasis).[4]

It is important to note that both the temporal element and the aspect of
causality are included in the definition of the plot. Crane and Rimmon-
Kenan,[5] focus mainly on the temporal aspect in relation to the
characters, against Forster,[6] who strongly focuses on the aspect of
causality as well (see below for a further discussion). The plot requires
a time aspect inasmuch as it has a beginning, middle and end.[7]

In addition, any plot requires change and conflict. 'All plots depend
on tension and resolution.'[8] Crane identifies three levels of change:

---

4. F.J. Matera, 'The Plot of Matthew's Gospel', *CBQ* 49 (1987), pp. 233-53
(236); see also Chatman, *Story and Discourse*, p. 43; A.G. Van Aarde, 'Die
Vertellersperspektief-analise: 'n Literatuur-teoretiese Benadering in die Eksegese van
die Evangelies', *HTS* 38.4 (1982), pp. 58-82 (72); see also the definition of Abrams
as cited by R.A. Culpepper, *Anatomy of the Fourth Gospel: A Study in Literary
Design* (Philadelphia: Fortress Press, 1983), p. 80.
5. R.S. Crane, 'The Concept of Plot', in P. Stevick, (ed.), *The Theory of the
Novel* (New York: Free Press, 1967), pp. 141-45 (141); S. Rimmon-Kenan, *Narrative Fiction: Contemporary Poetics* (London: Methuen, 1983), p. 18.
6. E.M. Forster, 'The Plot', in R. Scholes (ed.), *Approaches to the Novel:
Materials for a Poetics* (San Francisco: Chandler, rev. edn, 1966), pp. 219-32 (221).
7. Cf. R. Scholes and R. Kellogg, *The Nature of Narrative* (New York:
Oxford University Press, 1966), p. 211; Chatman, *Story and Discourse*, p. 47; Van
Aarde, 'Die Vertellersperspektief-analise', p. 72; *idem*, 'Narrative Criticism Applied
to John 4:43-54', p. 102; Combrink, 'The Structure of the Gospel of Matthew as
Narrative', p. 74; Matera, 'The Plot of Matthew's Gospel', p. 235.
8. Scholes and Kellogg, *The Nature of Narrative*, p. 212; see also Combrink
'The Structure of the Gospel of Matthew as Narrative', p. 74.

There are, thus, plots of actions, plots of character, and plots of thought. In the first, the synthesizing principle is a complete change, gradual or sudden, in the situation of the protagonist, determined and effected by character and thought [thus change in action]. . . ; in the second, the principle is a complete process of change in the moral character of the protagonist, precipitated or moulded by action, and made manifest both in it and in thought and feeling [thus change in character]. . . ; in the third, the principle is a completed process of change in the thought of the protagonist and consequently in his feelings, conditioned and directed by character and action [thus change in thought].[9]

These views of Crane are useful but limited, for he confines the change in the plot to the *protagonist* of the story. I am convinced that these changes are also applicable to the other characters of a story, that is, the helpers, the beneficiaries and possibly even the antagonists.[10] Culpepper takes up the concept of change as part of the plot to apply it even further to include the reader of the text as well:

A plot requires a *change of some kind*, and its peculiar affective power is produced by hopes and fears, desires and expectations it imposes on the *reader* as it unfolds the change from beginning to end. By the end of the story, the reader has been led to a particular emotional or volitional response: catharsis, satisfaction, outrage, anxiety or belief.[11]

Therefore, since change is such a vital part of the plot, and also a vital concept in conflict theory, a link could be made between the two.[12] Moreover, all plots depend on tension and resolution.[13] Since change (as far as conflict theory is concerned) is caused by conflicting interests, I dare to state that the change in the plot should not only lead to a change in the values (or even actions, character and thought[14]) of the protagonist and other characters or readers but also lead to a *willingness by the implied reader (and hearer) to experience a change in*

9.   R.S. Crane, 'The Concept of Plot', in Scholes, *Approaches to the Novel*, p. 239; see also Crane, 'The Concept of Plot', p. 141; R.S. Crane, 'The Concept of Plot', in M.J. Hoffmann and P.D. Murphy (eds.), *Essentials of the Theory of Fiction* (Durham: Duke University Press, 1988), pp. 131-42 (135).

10.   Cf. C. Bremond, 'De Logica van de narratieve mogenlijkheden', in W.J.M. Bronswaer, D.W. Fokkema and E. Kunne-Ibsch (eds.), *Tekstboek algemene literatuurwetenschap* (Baarn: Ambo, 1977), pp. 183-207 (190).

11.   Culpepper, *Anatomy of the Fourth Gospel*, p. 81.

12.   Cf. Culpepper, *Anatomy of the Fourth Gospel*, p. 81.

13.   Scholes and Kellogg, *The Nature of Narrative*, pp. 212, 239.

14.   Cf. Crane, 'The Concept of Plot' (1967), p. 239.

interests (and viewpoint), to those represented by the point of view of the implied author.

Thus, in my analysis of the plot, I wish to concentrate both on 'time' and 'causality'.

The Sequence in Time

A plot, as we have seen, requires the temporal aspects of a beginning, middle and end but none of these confined to a specified length. It could be anything from one sentence to expanded paragraphs. I will analyze these distinctive parts as well as the *more expanded parts*, according to the examples of Matera, Kingsbury and Bauer[15] in their analysis of Matthew as a whole, and Van Aarde in his analysis of Jn 4.43-54.[16]

My division of Matthew 8 and 9, more or less corresponds with the overall organization of the text as Patte presents it to us.[17] I agree with him that this passage displays a well-balanced surface organization. He says, 'It [the text] involves three groups of three miracle stories each (the third group could be viewed as having four miracle stories), the groups being separated by transition materials which serve either as conclusions or introductions [ends or beginnings] to the three major units'.[18] I differ slightly from Patte, following Beare[19] and Luz,[20] in that I take Mt. 8.1 as an introductory sentence to the first major unit (the beginning), and I include 9.33b-35 as a summary of the third major unit (the end).[21] Following Scholes and Kellogg who say, 'Not only every episode or incident but every paragraph and every sentence has its beginning, middle, and end', I will also subdivide the

---

15.   Matera, 'The Plot of Matthew's Gospel'; Kingsbury, *Matthew as Story*; Kingsbury, 'The Plot of Matthew's Story', pp. 347-56; Bauer, *The Structure of Matthew's Gospel: A Study in Literary Design* (JSNTSup 31, BiLiSe, 15; Sheffield: Almond Press, 1988).

16.   Van Aarde, 'Narrative Criticism Applied to John 4:43-54'.

17.   Patte, *The Gospel according to Matthew*, pp. 110-11.

18.   Patte, *The Gospel according to Matthew*, p. 110.

19.   F.W. Beare, *The Gospel according to Matthew: A Commentary* (Oxford: Basil Blackwell, 1981), p. 204.

20.   Luz, *Das Evangelium nach Matthäus*, p. 9.

21.   See also D.E. Garland, *Reading Matthew: A Literary and Theological Commentary on the First Gospel* (Reading the New Testament Series; New York: Crossroad, 1993), p. 91.

relevant units into beginning, middle and end.[22] I will not, however, analyze the text right down to the smallest units of sentences, as Scholes and Kellogg suggested.

A large number of commentaries agree on the fact that there are three units, each containing three miracle stories.[23] Only in as far as the structure of the first set of miracle stories (Mt. 8.1-17) is concerned, is there a broad consensus. Where the miracle stories are concerned, there is a huge diversity of suggested structures. It seems that in this regard one has to make up one's own mind. The structure of Davies and Allison comes the closest to my own.[24] Where I distinguish between Mt. 8.16-17 and 8.18-22, Davies and Allison combine them as a summary statement. The same is true of 9.9-17, which I divide into 9.9-13 and 14-17, while Davies and Allison keep these two pericopes together.

As an overall structure, I suggest the following:

1. The beginning or first group of miracle stories: Matthew 8.1-17
Introduction: The crowd is following Jesus: Mt. 8.1
    1. The healing of the leper: Mt. 8.2-4
    2. The healing of the centurion's servant: Mt. 8.5-13
    3. The healing of Peter's mother-in-law: Mt. 8.14-15
Conclusion: Healings and exorcisms as fulfilment of the prophecy. Mt. 8.16-17
2. The middle or second group of miracle stories: Mt. 8.18–9.13
Introduction: Responses to the would-be-disciples: Mt. 8.18-22
    1. The stilling of the storm: Mt. 8.23-27
    2. The destruction of the demons in the country of the Gadarenes: Mt. 8.28–9.1
    3. The healing of the paralytic: Mt. 9.2-8
Conclusion: The calling of Matthew and the controversy with the Pharisees: Mt. 9.9-13

---

22.   Scholes and Kellogg, *The Nature of Narrative*, p. 239.

23.   Patte, *The Gospel according to Matthew*, pp. 110-11; Davies and Allison, *A Critical and Exegetical Commentary on the Gospel according to Saint Matthew*, I, p. 69; *idem, A Critical and Exegetical Commentary on the Gospel according to Saint Matthew*, II, p. 6; Garland, *Reading Matthew*, pp. 91-93; Hare, *Matthew*, p. 88.

24.   Davies and Allison, *A Critical and Exegetical Commentary on the Gospel according to Saint Matthew* I, p. 69; *idem, A Critical and Exegetical Commentary on the Gospel according to Saint Matthew* II, p. 6.

3. The end or third group of miracle stories: Mt. 9.14-35
Introduction: The controversy with the disciples of John: Mt. 9.14-17
  1. The raising of a dead girl and the healing of a woman: Mt. 9.18-26
  2. The healing of the two blind men: Mt. 9.27-31
  3. The healing of the dumb man: Mt. 9.32-33a
Conclusion: The reaction of the crowd and the Pharisees, and the compassion of Jesus: Mt. 9.33b-35

The Beginning of the Plot: Matthew 8.1-17
In 8.1 a narrative-text, identified by a sequence of events, begins, following on from the discourse-text (with only one episode: the Sermon of Jesus on the Mount). The discourse-text ends with the distinct closing formula: ἐγένετο ὅτε ἐτέλεσεν ὁ 'Ιησοῦς ('When Jesus had finished saying these things. . . '; Mt. 7.28). Matthew also uses this formula to close the other discourses in 11.1; 13.53; 19.1 and 26.1. In 8.18, a new sequence of events begins with the sentence: 'ιδὼν δὲ ὁ 'Ιησοῦς ὄχλον περὶ αὐτὸν ἐκέλευσεν ἀπελθεῖν εἰς τὸ πέραν ('When Jesus saw the crowd around him, he gave orders to cross to the other side of the lake'). Therefore, 8.1-17 clearly forms one major unit. This unit comprises an introductory episode (or event) in 8.1; three healing episodes: the cleansing of the leper (8.2-14), the healing of the centurion's servant (8.5-13) and the healing of the mother-in-law of Peter (8.14-15); and finally a summary episode (8.16-17).

At the beginning, the action is introduced, expectations are generated and some tension created.[25] At the start, anything is possible.[26] One could say that a sort of disequilibrium is effected; a conflict is to be resolved through the narrative. The narrative has an element of conflict, introduced or created at the beginning.

The Opening Scene: Matthew 8.1. Mt. 8.1: καταβάντος δὲ αὐτοῦ ἀπὸ τοῦ ὄρους ἠκολούθησαν αὐτῷ ὄχλοι πολλοί ('When he came down from the mountainside, large crowds followed him') acts as the opening scene of both 8.1-17 and the whole sequence of events of 8.1–9.38. This opening scene links the Sermon on the Mount and the miracle stories: Jesus came from the mount and a huge crowd was following him. Which crowd are we talking about? The same crowd as

25.   Cf. Van Aarde, 'Die vertellersperspektief-analise', p. 72 and 'Narrative Criticism Applied to John 4:43-54', p. 102.
26.   Cf. Goodman, cited by Matera, 'The Plot of Matthew's Gospel', p. 239.

in 7.28, that was amazed by his teachings (ἐξεπλήσσοντο οἱ ὄχλοι
ἐπὶ τῇ διδαχῇ αὐτοῦ).[27] Gundry correctly calls Mt. 7.28-29 the
bridge from the sermon to the following narrative.[28] Following on
from 7.28-29, the opening scene (episode) in 8.1 already suggests the
presence of conflict: Jesus is regarded as having *more* authority than
the scribes (cf. 7.29). The mere fact that the crowd accepts Jesus'
authority rather than that of the scribes, places the scribes in opposition to Jesus and vice versa. And now in 8.1, this same crowd not
only acknowledges Jesus' authority, but also follows him.[29] They
become the principle audience in several stories to follow (Mt. 8.18;
9.8; 9.23; 9.33; 9.36).[30] Whether they will follow him to the end, still
remains to be seen, but at this point they follow Jesus instead of the
Jewish leaders. It is true that the leaders have not yet been mentioned
in this opening scene. But, because the conflict between them and Jesus
(and the community of Matthew) is assumed, we also surmise at this
early stage, that this acknowledgment of Jesus' authority could intensify
the conflict. This undermines the authority that the Jewish leaders
presumably have and places Jesus in a situation of conflict with the
leaders. The crowd does not consist of just a few people, they are
described as ὄχλοι πολλοί (a huge crowd). Furthermore it threatens
the position of the leaders, who might lose their potential support. The
crowd, put in the terms of our theory of conflict, remains the quasi-
group, the recruiting ground for both the leaders and the community
of Matthew (see above in Chapter 3 on *The Conflict from the Side of
the Jewish leaders*). The role of the crowd in Matthew is that of potential followers of Jesus.[31] However, the same people are also potential

27.   'Where the term ὄχλοι occurs in the Gospel of Matthew, the context is
coloured by Jesus' loving concern for them' (Van Aarde, *God-with-Us*, p. 85). Jesus
reveals the same concern for the blind, lame, leprous, deaf and poor, and therefore
this phenomenon can strengthen the suggestion that we are here dealing with the same
crowd as in Mt. 7.28-29.

28.   R.H. Gundry, *Matthew: A Commentary on his Literary and Theological
Art* (Grand Rapids: Eerdmans, 1982), p. 136.

29.   See R.H. Smith, *Augsburg Commentary on the New Testament: Matthew*
(Minneapolis: Augsburg, 1989), p. 25.

30.   Cf. P.S. Minear, *Matthew: The Teacher's Gospel* (New York: Pilgrim Press,
1982), p. 61.

31.   Cf. A.G. Van Aarde, 'Immanuel as die geïnkarneerde tora: Funksionele
Jesusbenaminge in die Mattheusevangelie as vertelling', *HTS* 43.1 and 2 (1987),
pp. 242-77 (264).

followers of the Jewish leaders. The fact that they eventually choose against Jesus in the passion narratives, especially in Mt. 27.23 when they cry out that Jesus should be crucified, confirms that this potentiality existed at this early stage of the Gospel. Therefore, any perceived threat to authority, even though it is still no more than potential loss of support, causes and increases conflict.

This introductory episode raises the question: 'How would the leaders and the crowd eventually react to Jesus' actions?' Thus, right at the beginning there is conflict: the crowd, acknowledging Jesus' authority rather than that of the Jewish leaders and then following him in huge numbers, threatens the vested interests of the leaders, who also need the support of the same crowd. An expectation is created: something should happen. Right at the beginning conflicting interests are at stake; those of the leaders and those of Jesus. The crowd serves to explicate these interests, as they also have to make a choice regarding whose interests to further (or serve). Here they choose Jesus' interests, thus creating tension and conflict. But will it remain that way? This turns out not to be the case as—toward the end of the Gospel—they choose the side of the Jewish leaders (cf. Mt. 26.47; 27.20; 22-25, 39).

The already existing tension is further heightened by the three miracle episodes. These pericopes (8.2-4; 8.5-13; 8.14-15) have certain things in common:

(1) In all these pericopes, Jesus deals with the 'social outcasts' of the Jewish community. They are all 'ritually unclean'. They were all excluded from full participation in Israel's religion. The leper because of his illness, the centurion because he is a heathen (and his slave being a slave) and the mother-in-law of Peter because she was a woman and ill.[32]

(2) They all are cured because of Jesus' willingness to help (he just touches them or only has to speak a word).

(3) They are all re-introduced into the community, despite their social or physical background: the leper by showing himself

32. Cf. Minear, *Matthew*, p. 62; Kingsbury, *Matthew as Story*, p. 27; Hare, *Matthew*, p. 90. See B.J. Malina, *The New Testament World*, pp. 122-52 on clean and unclean in the Jewish community. See also M.J. Borg, *Als met nieuwe ogen: De historische Jezus en waar het op aan komt in het geloof van vandaag* (trans. P. Ros; Zoetermeer: Meinema, 1995), pp. 68-69; this work was originally published in 1994 as: *Meeting Jesus Again for the First Time: The Historical Jesus and the Heart of Contemporary Faith* (San Francisco: Harper).

to the priest, the centurion because of Jesus' willingness to take him into the community alongside (or instead of) the Jews (cf. 8.10-12) and the woman who is able to resume her duties (viewed in Jewish terms) and serve Jesus, now as a healthy woman.

One of the most important spatial indicators of Matthew 8 and 9, is found in 8.1: καταβάντος δὲ αὐτοῦ ἀπὸ τοῦ ὄρους ἠκολούθησαν αὐτῷ ὄχλοι πολλοί ('When he came down *from the mountainside*, large crowds followed him'; my emphasis).[33] Not only does this verse link the Sermon on the Mount to the Miracle stories, it also has a communicative function in the narrative, which is important for the understanding of the text. Mt. 8.1 is closely related to 5.1: 'ἰδὼν δέ τοὺς ὄχλους ἀνέβη εἰς τὸ ὄρος· (my emphasis). Clearly, before (and for) the Sermon on the Mount, Jesus went *up to/on to* or he ascended the mountain. This was an analogy to Moses, who ascended mount Sinai to meet God (Exod. 19.3, 12; 24.15, 18; 34.1-3).[34] The mountain (or a mountain) to Matthew had an important connotation: 'In Matthew, the mountain is a place of prayer (14.23), of healing (15.28), of revelation (17.1; 28.16), and of teaching (24.3)'.[35] It was a place of isolation (although the crowd were with him; cf. Mt. 7.28). It was a place specifically to meet God. The mountain in particular was a place of teaching and learning. But here, in Mt. 8.1, Jesus *descended* the mountain, moving away from the place of isolation, prayer and teaching. The period of isolation and teaching was over.[36] But where did Jesus go? In antithesis to the mountain as a place of isolation, he went back to the scene of Mt. 4.23, to Galilee, to the people, to the world, that is, to Capernaum and Gadara, to meet the people and 'real-life' resistance.

---

33. Events always happen somewhere (cf. Bal, *De theorie van vertellen en verhalen*, p. 52). But the setting or space in a narrative is not just meant to present the reader with some 'background' information. It certainly has a communicative value: 'Space is a fully communicative epic category that, on the level of the story, the narrative and the discourse, works together considerably to determine the communication and the form of the work' (L.S. Venter, 'Ruimte [Epiek]', in T.T. Cloete [ed.], *Literêre terme en teorië* [Pretoria: HAUM, 1992], pp. 453-55 [455]; see also E. Van Eck, 'Galilee and Jerusalem in Mark's Story of Jesus, pp. 134-51).

34. Cf. Luz, *Das Evangelium nach Matthäus*, I, p. 198 and *idem*, *Das Evangelium nach Matthäus*, II, p. 9.

35. Luz, *Das Evangelium nach Matthäus*, I, p. 197.

36. Cf. G. Maier, *Matthäus-Evangelium*. I. (EDITION C–Bibel-Kommentar, 1; Neuhausen-Stuttgart: Hänssler, 2nd edn, 1983), p. 253.

His teaching was intended to be carried out in the world, amongst the people. His healings and acts of mercy were to be presented to, and into the world and all that was in it. The spacial indicator, ἀπὸ τοῦ ὄρους, in antithesis to the mountain, determined the setting of the whole narrative. It was meant to make Jesus' healings and ministry highly *concrete and real.*

In order to see how the conflict is developed, I will now turn to each miracle story.

The Healing of the Leper: Matthew 8.2-4. In the first healing episode, the following elements show that conflict is apparent: (1) the leprosy of the leper; (2) the leper's falling down before Jesus in paying tribute to him; (3) his address of Jesus as κύριε (Lord); (4) Jesus' touching of the leper, thus his immediate willingness to help and (5) the command Jesus gives to the leper to appear before the priest (8.4).

Leprosy was regarded as a dangerous skin disease.[37] There were harmless skin diseases as well, but we have to assume that Matthew here has in mind the illness that is referred to in Leviticus 13.1-46. This illness, in Rabbinic tradition, was seen as almost as difficult to cure as it was impossible to raise people from the dead.[38] Not only for health and hygiene reasons were the lepers forced to live outside the community, but also for ritual reasons: they were regarded as unclean. Any touching, or even being in the presence of a leper, would mean a transfer of this uncleanness.[39] This forced them to live on the edge of

37. Note the distinction that is made between disease and illness in the anthropology. Sickness as in disease is seen as a biomedical malfunction afflicting an organism, and it is a pathological state affecting only the individual (cf. Pilch, 'The Health Care System in Matthew', p. 102; *idem,* 'Understanding Biblical Healing', p. 62; Malina and Rohrbaugh, *Social-Science Commentary on the Synoptic Gospels,* p. 71. Sickness as in illness, is a socially disvalued state in which many others beside the individual are involved. A whole social network has been disrupted and meaning lost. Illness is not (only) a biomedical matter, but rather a social one (cf. Pilch, 'The Health Care System in Matthew', p. 102, 'Understanding Biblical Healing', p. 63; Malina and Rohrbaugh, *Social-science Commentary on the Synoptic Gospels,* p. 71).

38. Cf. H.L. Strack and P. Billerbeck, *Exkurse zu einzelnen Stellen des Neuen Testaments: Abhandlung zur neutestamentlichen Theologie und Archäologie,* II (Kommentar zum Neuen Testament aus Talmud und Midrasch; Munich: Beck'sche Verlag, 4th edn, 1965), p. 745; Luz, *Das Evangelium nach Matthäus* II, p. 9.

39. Cf. Strack and Billerbeck, *Exkurse zu einzelnen Stellen des Neuen Testaments,* p. 751.

society. We could say that in an agrarian society, because of their illness, they were forced into the class of the expendables or the unclean and degraded class.[40] Nobody had any 'need' of them, in fact, according to Strack and Billerbeck they were, along with the poor, the blind and the childless, regarded as the 'living dead'.[41] We have here someone from the lowest stratum of society thereby creating the potential for conflict and tension.

The leper falls down before Jesus in a gesture acknowledging Jesus' authority (again above that of the Jewish leaders). Jesus is worthy of the homage paid to him. In doing this, the leper is ignoring the rules; he is turning his back on the the system which in any case does not recognize his needs. In his own interests (indeed) he knows who to call for help, he knows where to find acceptance.

In addressing Jesus as κύριε, which Luz calls a 'hoheitsvollen Anrede', the leper once again acknowledges Jesus' power to cure.[42] This is an honorific address, which can mean both 'sir' and 'Lord' (*kyrie*).[43] Jesus responds immediately by stretching out his hand and touching the leper. He is willing to become unclean himself on the behalf of or in the interests of the leper. Without first demanding repentance (for leprosy was seen as punishment of sin and therefore repentance was required before any cure could be expected[44]), Jesus cures the leper, once again breaking through the prescribed traditional rule/value and again creating tension and conflict with the leaders. He undermines their authority (or so they might interpret it that way) by challenging their values on behalf of the sick man.

What does Jesus communicate as he ignores the rules and touches the leper? He not only demonstrates his power over illness but also, in the gesture of touching and his words: θέλω, καθαρίσθητι ('I am willing, be clean!') communicates his willingness to act on behalf of the weak. Says Waagenvoort: 'The first purpose of the touching was to strengthen the people who were physically or mentally weaker.'[45] Jesus

40. Cf. Lenski, *Power and Privilege*, p. 281; see above.
41. Strack and Billerbeck, *Exkurse zu einzelnen Stellen des Neuen Testaments*, pp. 745, 751.
42. Luz, *Das Evangelium nach Matthäus* II, p. 9.
43. Cf. Harrington, *The Gospel of Matthew*, p. 113; see also my discussion of Mt. 8.18-22, where this address again surfaces.
44. Cf. Strack and Billerbeck, *Exkurse zu einzelnen Stellen des Neuen Testaments*, pp. 745, 750.
45. Cited by G. Theissen, *Urchristliche Wundergeschichten*, p. 71.

communicates his willingness to help unconditionally. He not only healed the leper but made him ritually acceptable as well.

However, Jesus commands the cured leper to go to the priest. He does not totally abandon the Jewish/Mosaic law. In fact, again, in his own interest the cured leper has to be seen by the priest in order to be taken back into the community. But Jesus' commanding of the leper to go to the priest can also be viewed as a challenge to the system: it was Jesus who commanded and *not* the leaders. Furthermore, they are challenged to recognize the weak and take them back into society. But it is not only that the priest affirms the healed state of the leper and therefore takes him back into society, but that willingly or unwillingly he has to acknowledge that it was *Jesus* who cured the leper and then commanded him to go to the priest. Jesus has been honoured, and this further strengthens the already present latent conflict. This raises a few questions: Will the religious establishment also pay tribute to Jesus? Will they also accept Jesus' authority? Will they also abandon their own ruling position on behalf of the weak? In a way, the priest, by proclaiming the cured leper clean, is already acting in the interests of this marginalized man. Will he and the other leaders accept this challenge? Here, at the beginning of the miracle stories these questions indicate that there is conflict that still has to be resolved. These questions remain open and are to be answered later on in the text.

The Healing of the Centurion's Servant: Matthew 8.5-13. The elements in the episode of the healing of the centurion's servant, which contribute to the building up of conflict are: (1) the position of the centurion (ἑκατόνταρχος), his own authority and his acknowledgement of Jesus' authority; (2) the position and condition of the slave (παῖς);[46] (3) the surprised reaction of Jesus, his recognition of the faith of the centurion and his strong verbal attack on 'Israel' in 8.11-12; (4) Jesus' immediate response in curing the slave.

---

46.   The Greek word παῖς can be translated both by 'servant' or 'boy'. Only in Jn 4.51 is there a reference to this word as 'son'. However, I agree with Newman and Stine that here the word is probably used to mean the Roman officer's orderly (B.M. Newman and P.C. Stine, *A Translator's Handbook on the Gospel of Matthew* [London: UBS, 1988], p. 234). Hence the translation of παῖς μου in Mt. 8.6 can either be 'my servant' or 'the man who serves me' (see also Gundry, *Matthew*, p. 142; Davies and Allison, *A Critical and Exegetical Commentary on the Gospel according to Saint Matthew*, II, p. 21; Harrington, *The Gospel of Matthew*, p. 113).

Although not a very high ranking officer in the Roman army (he was in charge over 100 men, the smallest unit in the Roman army[47]), the centurion nevertheless was himself a man of authority (cf. 8.9).[48] He was a career soldier and in his world, was experienced and highly regarded.[49] Being a career soldier, he was part of the so-called retainer class.[50] Therefore, his prime function was to serve the political elite of the time, which was the Roman Emperor. His most important tasks were to preserve the interests of the rulers and to maintain the status quo. Although there was no particular relationship (as far as the text is concerned) between the centurion and the Jewish leaders, in terms of social stratification they were on the same level.

Nevertheless, there was something strange in the behaviour of the centurion in that he acted in the interests of his paralysed slave. A slave in both the Jewish and Roman environment belonged to the lower classes (in an agrarian society that would be the peasant class) and was regarded as being the possession of his owner. Although not necessarily always treated badly, the owner was nevertheless not obliged to treat a slave well. Here we have an example of an owner who cared for his slave, and acted on behalf of the slave whose condition was very weak (cf. 8.6). This is clearly recognized by Jesus in his response (8.10). But the centurion, being a Roman officer and a Gentile, has placed himself in a difficult position. He *is* not only already unclean (being Gentile in a Jewish society), but in terms of Judaism because of his contact with the sick slave *becomes even more so*. Put another way: the centurion was already marginalized because he was Gentile. He then chooses to become voluntary marginalized by acting in the interests of the slave which further intensifies his own marginalized position. Through his own action the centurion now becomes part of the weak. And although he still has some authority, he becomes a person on the edge of society. This same man, in his position and condition, acknowledges Jesus' authority and like the leper addresses Jesus as

---

47. Cf. Harrington, *The Gospel of Matthew*, p. 113.

48. See also R.P. Martin, 'The Pericope of the Healing the "Centurion's" Servant/Son (Matt 7:5-13 par. Luke 7:1-10): Some Exegetical Notes', in R.A. Guelch, (ed.), *Unity and Diversity in New Testament Theology: Essays in Honor of George E. Ladd* (Grand Rapids: Eerdmans, 1978), pp. 14-22 (15); Hare, *Matthew*, p. 91.

49. Cf. Newman and Stine, *A Translator's Handbook on the Gospel of Matthew*, p. 233.

50. Cf. Lenski, *Power and Privilege*, p. 243; see Chapter 3 on *Social Stratification in the Gospel of Matthew*.

κύριε (all elements, as we have seen before, which create tension.[51]

Furthermore, the centurion, on the basis of his experience in the army, knows that Jesus only has to command and his slave will be cured. As the centurion experiences authority in the military sphere, Jesus in the same way experiences authority in the spiritual sphere. Just as the emperor or higher ranking officers give him authority over others so God gives Jesus authority over illness.[52] It is important to note that he acknowledges *Jesus* to be the one to command (and no one else), and this further contributes to the tension by implying that Jesus also has subordinates. He has God-given authority which once again threatens the authority of those in power.[53]

At first glance it would seem that the Gentile officer accepts the stratification system between the Jews and non-Jews by not wanting Jesus to come with him into his home. However in the centurion's own acknowledgment of Jesus' ability to cure over a distance,[54] Matthew relativizes the boundaries between Jews and non-Jews, that is, between clean and unclean. Jesus is able to command and cure beyond all borders. There are no limits to Jesus having authority and carrying out his ministry.[55] Jesus responds in astonishment, not only to the centurions request (cf. 8.10), but also to his faith and attitude. In this context, Jesus expresses his surprise not having found such faith even in Israel. Faith is indeed found in the Gentile centurion. The significance of the centurion, as Davies and Allison correctly see it, is that he foreshadows the successful evangelization of the nations (28.16-20).[56] The centurion is a paradigm of the believer in so far as he exhibits true faith. He trusts implicitly in Jesus' power and authority. Matthew contrasts the faith of the Gentile with the unbelief of 'the sons of the kingdom' (8.11).[57] This once again puts Jesus in confrontation with the Jews and their leaders. Matthew uses this man to illustrate something that is lacking in Israel. It certainly is not a good testimony for

51.   See also A. Sand, *Das Evangelium nach Matthäus: Übergesetzt und erklärt*, p. 179.

52.   Cf. Harrington, *The Gospel of Matthew*, p. 114; Hare, *Matthew*, p. 91.

53.   Cf. Beare, *The Gospel according to Matthew*, p. 208.

54.   See also Sanders and Davies, *Studying the Synoptic Gospels*, p. 166.

55.   See also Patte, *The Gospel according to Matthew*, p. 114.

56.   Davies and Allison, *A Critical and Exegetical Commentary on the Gospel according to Saint Matthew*, II, p. 19.

57.   Cf. Davies and Allison, *A Critical and Exegetical Commentary on the Gospel according to Saint Matthew*, II, p. 25.

Israel (and its leaders), and therefore contributes even further to the present conflict. The faith of the centurion is something beyond anything that has been encountered in Israel. His faith meant that he knew Jesus would help: as Luz says: 'Jesus did not find the degree of faith exhibited by this heathen in a single person in Israel! "Faith" means the unconditional trust in Jesus' power to help, that would not be refused.'[58] The centurion knew that Jesus would not only act on his behalf because he was a Gentile but also on behalf of his slave, who was needy. His faith was more than just believing in Jesus' ability to cure. He perceived Jesus as having the power to help the weak, and had the insight to act in the same way as Jesus.

The people of Israel never doubted their own salvation.[59] They believed themselves to be in a privileged position as God's chosen people. Jesus challenges this belief and therefore the vested or religious interests of Israel. To Jesus, Israel was no longer in an exclusive position of privilege: from the east to the west (8.11), thus from all over the world all will dine with Abraham, Isaac and Jacob (symbols of the Jewish history) 'in the kingdom of heaven'. Malina links the phrase 'kingdom of heaven' to the sociological model of 'patron and client'.[60] To Malina, the 'kingdom of heaven' means to enjoy the patronage of God, the heavenly Patron.[61] The kingdom of heaven is seen as a new state of affairs, it is not a 'kingdom or reign' as such, but rather a realm, community or 'house'.[62] Thus, according to Mt. 8.11, all the people 'from the east to the west' will enter the kingdom of heaven, that is, the new community or new 'house' of God. They will enjoy God's patronage along with 'Abraham, Isaac and Jacob', namely, the rest of Israel. They will enjoy '... actual possession of the Patron's land; comfort and satisfaction meted out by the Patron; ready availability of the Patron to realize his part of the dyadic relationship (= mercy); acclamation by the Patron of being a favoured recipient of patronage (= called sons of God); and recompense for maintaining the patron's honour (= your reward is great in heaven)'.[63] This is a metaphor saying that *all people*

58. Luz, *Das Evangelium nach Matthäus*, II, p. 15.
59. See also Gundry, *Matthew*, p. 145.
60. Malina, 'Patron and Client', p. 9.
61. Malina, 'Patron and Client', pp. 9-10.
62. Malina, 'Patron and Client', p. 10.
63. Malina, 'Patron and Client', p. 10.

are now God's people. *All* people could turn to the God of Israel.[64]

Jesus did not differ from the traditional belief that Israel was God's chosen people. He did, however, challenge the exclusive claims derived from the phrase about the sons of Abraham, Isaac and Jacob in 8.11. With the word ἀνακλιθήσονται (they will sit at the table), Matthew already prepares the scene for 9.10-13, where Jesus *dines* with people who are not Jews. Furthermore, the phrase in 8.11: λέγω δὲ ὑμῖν ὅτι πολλοὶ ἀπὸ ἀνατολῶν καὶ δυσῶν ἥξουσιν καὶ ἀνακλιθήσονται μετὰ 'Αβραὰμ καὶ 'Ισαὰκ καὶ 'Ιακὼβ ἐν τῇ βασιλείᾳ τῶν οὐρανῶν· ('I say to you that many will come from the east and the west, and will take their places at the feast with Abraham, Isaac and Jacob in the kingdom of heaven'), serves as an ideological legitimation of the interests of Jesus in choosing the interests of the Gentiles and other social outcasts. Later in the narrative he demonstrates this interest by physically dining with those 'outcasts' or 'sinners'.[65]

Jesus not only challenges the privileged position of Israel, he also heightens the conflict further by declaring them to be no longer in God's presence because of their lack of faith in Jesus and what he stands for. The sons of the kingdom (υἱοὶ τῆς βασιλείας; Israel were part of the kingdom of God), were to lose the kingdom, they were to be cast out into the darkness (εἰς τὸ σκότος τὸ ἐξώτερον), which is an idiomatic expression denoting that they were to be removed from the abode of the righteous.[66] Most Jews imagined this place of perdition to be dark, in spite of its fire.[67] Israel was thus to be excluded from the feast and this could only be unpleasant because of the 'weeping and gnashing of teeth'(cf. 8.12).[68] But *why* were they to be excluded? The answer already seems apparent but still remains to be elaborated upon in the middle part of the narrative (see below). Jesus' willingness to help is reflected not only in his sayings in 8.10-12, where he is prepared to accept the heathen into his community,

64. Cf. Luz, *Das Evangelium nach Matthäus*, II, p. 15.

65. See below; see also my discussion on the ideological legitimation in the section on *Personnel* in Chapter 2.

66. Cf. J.P. Louw and E.A. Nida, *Greek–English Lexicon of the New Testament Based on Semantic Domains*, I (New York: UBS, 1988), p. 7.

67. Cf. Davies and Allison, *A Critical and Exegetical Commentary on the Gospel according to Saint Matthew*, II, p. 30.

68. Cf. Luz, *Das Evangelium nach Matthäus*, II, p. 15; see also Gundry, *Matthew*, p. 146.

but also in his short and immediate response in 8.13. He heals the slave immediately (καὶ ἰάθη ὁ παῖς [αὐτοῦ] ἐν τῇ ὥρᾳ ἐκείνῃ). He is willing to help, immediately and unconditionally, just as in the case of the leper.

Jesus addressed 'those who follow him' (τοῖς ἀκολουθοῦσιν; 8.10). Who were they? They were still the crowd of 8.1. As Gundry says, 'Matthew omits τῷ ἀκολουθοῦντι αὐτῷ ὄχλῳ (so does Luke) and refers simply to τοῖς [supply ὄχλοις from v. 1] ἀκολουθοῦσιν. The plural contrasts with Luke's singular and derives from v. 1.'[69] Therefore the question remains open: How would they respond to Jesus' physical deeds? They reacted positively to his teachings, but how would they respond when Jesus' real interests surfaced through his actions?

The Healing of Peter's Mother-in-Law: Matthew 8.14-15. At first glance the episode of the healing of Peter's mother-in-law does not seem to have many elements of conflict in it. However, because certain themes recur: (1) the woman being ill, and thus unclean; (2) Jesus' touching her; (3) her service to Jesus, the same elements of conflict remain present.

The subordinate position of Peter's mother-in-law, which for women was 'normal' in her society, was even worse in her case because of her being ill and thus unclean. Nevertheless, Jesus touches her and this, as with the leper, shows his willingness to act in the interests of this sick woman. He is (neither) concerned with her social position, nor her physical situation. Her response to Jesus is one of service, an indication that she, like those in previous examples, also acknowledges his authority,[70] thus reinforcing the element of conflict as it has developed up to this point. In making Jesus the subject of the verses describing him seeing the woman prostrate with fever, Matthew concentrates the attention on Jesus and this time allows him take the initiative in the exercising of his authority (8.17).[71] Anyone who takes such an initiative, inevitably places himself in confrontation with those who themselves presume to have authority and wish to maintain the status quo, that is, their own privileged position.

There is no request from the woman for Jesus to cure her (in contrast to the other two stories). This could indicate that Jesus acts in her

69. Gundry, *Matthew*, p. 144.

70. Cf. Patte, *The Gospel according to Matthew*, p. 116.

71. Cf. Gundry, *Matthew*, p. 148.

interests, even without her asking. He knows what is best for her even before she asks it herself. He takes the initiative on her behalf, in her interests. There is no dialogue in this miracle (as there is in the other two stories). Jesus acts in silence. Nevertheless, the point is clear: without Jesus, there is no one who cares for her, with Jesus, someone cares and someone takes her part (this is what he communicated by the gesture of touching, just as when he touched the leper earlier).

The Summary Episode: Matthew 8.16-17. The first part of the narrative ends with a conclusion or summary episode in 8.16-17. The summary in 8.16 has a threefold function, as Luz states,

> Firstly, it makes it clear to the reader that the miracle stories that have been told so far are only three examples of healing out of many. That is why the evangelist uses the wording from 4.23 again. Secondly, he wants to emphasise the absolute power of Jesus. That is why here, but not in the parallel text in Mark, Jesus heals *all* the ill people, and why he heals them by his sovereign word as he already has in 8.13. And finally, Matthew can prepare the reader for the quotation in v.17 with it (his emphasis).[72]

The three miracle stories are just a few examples of the many instances in which Jesus acted in the interests of *all* the sick (καὶ πάντας τοὺς κακῶς ἔχοντας) and weak (cf. 8.16). Matthew deliberately wishes to avoid the implication that some might be excluded and not healed.[73] What is important to note, as far as conflict theory is concerned, is that 8.17: ὅπως πληρωθῇ τὸ ῥηθὲν διὰ Ἡσαΐου τοῦ προφήτου λέγοντος, αὐτὸς τὰς ἀσθενείας ἡμῶν ἔλαβεν καὶ τὰς νόσους ἐβάστασεν, ('This was to fulfill what was spoken through the prophet Isaiah: "He took up our infirmities and carried our diseases"') is the first *major* articulation (in the terms of Dahrendorf[74]) or codification of the interests Jesus (and Matthew) represents (see also the assumption above that values, ideologies and norms are *articulated interests*). The quotation from Isa. 53.4 is taken out of its original context and put into Matthew's story as ideology (or value) to legitimate Jesus' position. Jesus takes all weaknesses upon himself and carries all illnesses. Yet, these healings were not just a new trend he had, they were *legitimized* deeds. As Davies and Allison say, 'The Scripture prophesied that Jesus the Servant would heal others. His miracles are, therefore, *not*

---

72. Luz, *Das Evangelium nach Matthäus*, II, p. 19.
73. Cf. Gundry, *Matthew*, p. 149.
74. Dahrendorf, *Class and Class Conflict*, p. 186.

simply the sensational workings of an extraordinary man but rather the fulfilment of the Scriptures and the exhibition of God's almighty will' (my emphasis).[75] These deeds were made into a *superindividual right,* they were made *respectable* by being referred to as the fulfilment of the (legitimate) prophecies.[76] By means of this citation, Jesus is presented as acting legitimately because he was fulfilling the prophecies. This heightens the legitimacy of Jesus himself, but since this is also seen as an editorial passage,[77] written by the implied author, this citation also strengthens the legitimacy of the interests of the author and his community. Or, as Luz says, 'The quotation shows how Jesus as Israel's messiah healed his people with *authority.* For Matthew it is important that this corresponds to God's plan as foretold by the prophets' (my emphasis).[78] This in itself increases the conflict potential for Jesus, and by implication the community of Matthew is 'exalted' to compete with the Jewish leaders for legitimacy and authority. Furthermore, we have already seen in Chapter 3 (see the passage on *The Conflict from the Side of the Matthean Community*) that one way to legitimize a new movement is to 'traditionalize' its existence. One way of doing this is to take over widely acclaimed and legitimate scriptures, passages or traditions. This is what occurs in this summary and in particularly the citation in 8.17. The same is true of the quotations from Hos. 6.6 in Mt. 9.13.

The Middle of the Plot: Matthew 8.18–9.13
Matthew 8.18 starts a new episode in time and space (as seen in the words, ἐκέλευσεν ἀπελθεῖν εἰς τὸ πέραν, 'he gave orders to cross to the other side of the lake'). Therefore, the middle part begins here at 8.18 and in my view ends at 9.13, because of the frequent use of the theme ἀκολουθεῖν (to follow), which is also taken up in 9.9 in the episode of the calling of Matthew (cf. 9.9-13). Moreover, 9.14 starts a new episode, with new characters (the disciples of John) and a new issue: the question of fasting. Thus, the middle part of the plot comprises an introductory event (8.18-22); three miracle events: the calming of the storm (8.23-27), the healing of the Gadarene Demoniacs

75. Davies and Allison, *A Critical and Exegetical Commentary on the Gospel according to Saint Matthew,* II, p. 37.
76. Cf. Coser, *The Functions of Conflict,* p. 112; see also above.
77. Cf. Sanders and Davies, *Studying the Synoptic Gospels,* p. 166.
78. Luz, *Das Evangelium nach Matthäus,* II, p. 19.

(8.28–9.1) and the healing of the paralytic (9.2-8), and finally a summary episode, namely the calling of Matthew (9.9-13).

The expectations created at the beginning of the plot, are developed further in the middle part. The initial action evolves further;[79] things now become probable.[80] Moreover, the conflict unfolds as it surfaces. It becomes manifest as one of the reasons why Israel was no longer part of the kingdom of God. In this section the strongest legitimization of the conflict of interests is developed (cf. 9.13; see below).

The Introductory Episode: Matthew 8.18-22. In the following section, attention will be paid to the following elements of conflict: (1) the *authority* of Jesus to take the initiative; (2) the evolving conflict within the *inner circle* of Jesus; (3) conflict with the Gentiles.

The middle part of the narrative, begins with the introductory episode of the eager scribe and the reluctant disciple, who were to follow Jesus to the other side of the lake, that is to Gentile country. The first question is: Why did Jesus want to go to the other side? Why did Jesus seemingly want to avoid the crowd? An immediate answer is not given by the text, but one can be suggested as I proceed.

Jesus gives a command to go to the other side, but he does not address anyone in particular. But, if his command is not addressed to anyone, what then is the purpose of the verb 'to command' (κελεύειν)? Patte sees it as an open invitation to follow him to the other side.[81] Thus, Patte takes it as both a command *and* a call to discipleship, as does Kingsbury.[82] Jesus is both exercising his authority *and* inviting the people in the crowd to become his disciples. Kingsbury says, 'As for the question about the recipients of Jesus' command, if κελεύειν does not connote in Matthew a calling to discipleship, it becomes impossible to construe all those who make up the crowd about Jesus as receiving his command to cross the lake (8.18).'[83] This means that, whether we take κελεύειν as a command or open invitation (or both), Kingsbury's view on the scribe who approaches Jesus (8.19), cannot be entirely

---

79. Cf. Van Aarde, 'Die vertellersperspektief-analise', p. 72; *idem*, 'Narrative Criticism Applied to John 4:43-54', p. 102.

80. Cf. Goodman, cited by Matera, 'The Plot of Matthew's Gospel', p. 239.

81. Patte, *The Gospel according to Matthew*, p. 119.

82. Patte, *The Gospel according to Matthew*, p. 119; Kingsbury, *Matthew as Story*, pp. 46-47.

83. Kingsbury, *Matthew as Story*, p. 47.

correct. He says, 'As Jesus is about to cross the sea with his disciples (8.18), a scribe approaches him who would arrogate to himself the authority to become Jesus' disciple and hence to embark with him on the upcoming journey (8.19).'[84] By implication Kingsbury suggests that the scribe took the initiative and that Jesus therefore admonished him (and we could say conflict presents itself here). But, Jesus took the initiative and the scribe responded to it. To Harrington the fact that Jesus commanded (8.18) is an indication that it was he who took the initiative.[85] This, to my mind, indeed strengthens the argument that Jesus took control. Therefore, if we want to see an element of conflict in this episode (and there is an indication of it), we have to see it somewhat differently from Kingsbury. The initiative lies with Jesus and therefore there is conflict, and not the other way round, as it appears that Kingsbury suggests (although Kingsbury here does not primarily focus on conflict as such).

The introductory episode (8.18-22), and 8.18 in particular, acts as an opening scene, especially for 8.23-27, and 8.28–9.1 (the episodes of the storm at sea and the healing of the Gadarene demoniacs). In the words of Davies and Allison: 'Why has Matthew placed 8.18-22 precisely where it is? Probably because for him the tale of the stilling of the storm is a parable, *a symbolic illustration of what it means to "follow" Jesus. In other words, a story about discipleship is prefaced by teaching on discipleship*' (my emphasis).[86] Furthermore, it opens up two new levels of latent conflict (see my discussion on manifest and latent conflict in the section on a *Charter* in Chapter 3): within the inner circle of Jesus' disciples (as seen in the confrontation with the reluctant disciple in 8.21-22), and with the Gentiles in their own country (thus the command to go to the other side). Of course, the conflict with the Jewish leaders remains apparent, as will be illustrated in Jesus' response to the 'eager scribe' (8.19), and later in a more obvious way in the closing episode (9.13).

The fact that Jesus was in a position to command the people (or disciples) to go to the other side and the fact that he had the authority to do so suggests that further conflict would follow. In fact, Patte says that

84.   Kingsbury, *Matthew as Story*, p. 51.

85.   Harrington, *The Gospel of Matthew*, p. 119.

86.   Davies and Allison, *A Critical and Exegetical Commentary on the Gospel according to Saint Matthew*, II, p. 39; see also Patte, *The Gospel according to Matthew*, p. 118.

the reader should not be surprised to find Jesus giving orders: he is entitled to do so![87] He has authority, already acknowledged previously by the crowd and those he has healed. We could say that the conflict, already evident at the beginning, is here developed further in terms of the question on *how* to follow Jesus. We find an indication here of what true discipleship means: discipleship means 'solidarity' with Jesus and his cause, it means sharing in the fate of the 'son of man', namely, Jesus, who shares the interests of the weak and underprivileged (marginalized). Therefore, sharing with Jesus, also involves sharing in his 'solidarity' with the weak and thus taking upon oneself the burden or the interests of those in need. Put differently, the disciples should be prepared to become 'voluntarily marginalized' themselves. This is, of course, a view that could lead to conflict, which is illustrated by the responses Jesus gives to the scribes and the disciples. How is this view reached?

As we have seen, the scribe comes to Jesus, willing to follow Jesus wherever he goes. But immediately there are doubts about his intentions. He seems over-enthusiastic and appears to be have overestimated his own ability to follow Jesus to the end.[88] Would he, as part of the privileged religious establishment, really abandon his vested interests as part of that group? Would he really become 'voluntarily marginalized'? He is explicitly described as *'one* of the scribes' (εἷς γραμματεύς), thus still belonging to that group. In 7.29 it was already suggested that the scribes were opponents of Jesus (being part of the Jewish leadership). Says Gnilka: 'As a scribe, he belonged to a group against which Jesus had a hostile attitude'.[89] Already in the scribe's address to Jesus this phenomenon is illustrated and his intentions and understanding questioned. He calls upon Jesus as 'teacher' or 'rabbi' (διδάσκαλε). This is the 'wrong' address for a 'true' follower of Jesus.[90] The use of the title 'rabbi' indicates that this scribe was indeed

---

87.   Patte, T*he Gospel according to Matthew*, p. 119.

88.   Cf. Gnilka, *Das Matthäusevangelium*, p. 311.

89.   Gnilka, *Das Matthäusevangelium*, p. 310.

90.   Cf. Gundry, *Matthew*, p. 152; R.T. France, *Matthew* (TNTC; Leicester: Inter Varsity, 1985), p. 159; Gnilka, *Das Matthäusevangelium*, pp. 310-11; J.D. Kingsbury, 'On Following Jesus: The "Eager" Scribe and the "Reluctant" Disciple (Matthew 8.18-22)', *NTS* 34 (1988), pp. 45-59 (51); Harrington, *The Gospel of Matthew*, p. 119.

from outside the group of disciples.[91] Consider the following statement of Kingsbury:

> ... one can detect a basic distinction in the use made in Matthew of the vocative 'teacher' or 'rabbi' (διδάσκααλε, ῥαββί) and 'Lord' (κύριε). 'Teacher' and 'rabbi' are terms of human respect. 'Lord' is a title of majesty. Judas, opponents, and strangers never... call upon Jesus as 'κύριε', but regard him only as 'teacher' or 'rabbi' and consistently address him as such. Persons of faith and true disciples never address Jesus as 'teacher' or 'rabbi' but always call upon him as 'κύριε'. ... Persons of faith and true disciples call upon Jesus as 'κύριε' because they thereby are seen, not merely to pay him human respect due to a teacher, but to attribute to him *divine authority* (my emphasis).[92]

The scribe, as one of Jesus' opponents, is depicted by Matthew as unwilling to address him correctly as κύριε and thus unwilling to attribute to Jesus the authority—consequently we once again have conflict! This becomes more apparent in Jesus' response. Jesus replies with a saying about the homelessness of the son of man (8.20). Following Jesus means sharing in his insecurity.[93] This is clearly a metaphor for being marginalized. I take the notion of 'homelessness' in 8.20 metaphorically. 'When so viewed, it is made to signify, variously, "hardship", "poverty", "the renunciation of security", "suffering"....'[94] I take this to be a metaphoric expression because it can mean more than a literal lack of lodging. It can also mean rejection.[95] Both these literal and metaphorical conditions are, in broad terms, typical of the peasant class in an agrarian society. We can also link 'homelessness' with 'repudiation'.[96] Thus Kingsbury says, 'Jesus... turns the scribe away with a saying about homelessness that the reader knows alludes to the life of discipleship as essentially being one of sharing in the repudiation Jesus must endure (8.20).'[97] Discipleship means sharing repudiation and conflict because of sharing in the conditions of the underprivileged (being

91. Cf. Sand, *Das Evangelium nach Matthäus*, p. 185.

92. Kingsbury, 'On Following Jesus', p. 51; see also Davies and Allison, *A Critical and Exegetical Commentary on the Gospel according to Saint Matthew*, II, p. 41.

93. Cf. Patte, *The Gospel according to Matthew*, p. 119.

94. Kingsbury, 'On Following Jesus', p. 50.

95. Gundry, *Matthew*, p. 152; Hare, *Matthew*, p. 95.

96. Cf. Kingsbury, 'On Following Jesus', p. 50.

97. Kingsbury, 'On Following Jesus', p. 51.

in solidarity with them), and this the scribe probably would not be prepared to do. As Gnilka says,

> This scribe is led into the security of the house of a teacher and thereby into certainty, whereas Jesus' disciples are thrown into existential uncertainty. The word is an example of *an anti Rabbinic tendency*. Therefore, it is no accident that it is directed at a scribe (my emphasis).[98]

Therefore, the scribe most probably would not follow Jesus in showing 'solidarity' with the powerless. He most probably would not become 'voluntarily marginalized' and thus would never become a true disciple.

Matthew 8.21 introduces a new level of conflict: that within the inner circle of the disciples. The disciple mentioned in the verse, addresses Jesus as κύριε, in line with true disciples and persons of faith.[99] But Jesus' response indicates some lack of understanding on the part of the disciple. Would he really follow Jesus? Does he really view discipleship 'correctly'? Apparently not. The answer Jesus gives to his request for permission to bury his dead father, appears to be harsh indeed but in its harshness lies its effectiveness.[100] Jesus is not against family ties as such in giving this answer to the disciple in 8.22 (although this verse reveals a critical attitude towards it[101]). In fact, within the context of Matthew 8 and 9, he acknowledges these family ties when he heals Peter's mother-in-law (8.14) and the ruler's daughter ruler (9.18). What it does show, is that discipleship cannot tolerate split loyalty.[102] One must not love one's own family *more* than Jesus.[103] Even well meant religious laws, prescribed and upheld by the religious leaders, could subtract from the disciple's prime task of following Jesus in his choice of championing the interests of the underprivileged. Well meant, but misplaced 'compassion' (burying his own father) could divert a disciple from Jesus' cause.[104] True discipleship entails the harsh

---

98. Gnilka, *Das Matthäusevangelium*, p. 311.

99. Cf. Kingsbury, 'On Following Jesus', p. 51.

100. Cf. Kingsbury, 'On Following Jesus', pp. 54-56.

101. Cf. E.P. Sanders, *Jezus, mythe en werkelijkheid* (trans. L. Debroey; Nijkerk: Callenbach, 1996), pp. 155-56; originally published in 1993 as *The Historical Figure of Jesus* by Penguin.

102. See also Sand, *Das Evangelium nach Matthäus*, p. 185; Davies and Allison, *A Critical and Exegetical Commentary on the Gospel according to Saint Matthew* II, p. 55.

103. Cf. Luz, *Das Evangelium nach Matthäus*, II, p. 26.

104. Cf. Gnilka, *Das Matthäusevangelium*, p. 312.

command to follow and, as expressed by the following pericope, to almost immediately embark with him (into the boat and storm, that is, uncertainty, trouble and so on) with him.[105] Whether the disciples realized this remains to be seen, and thus a new level of conflict is revealed: new interests are at stake and have to be brought into line with those of Jesus.

But, how far could this 'homelessness', 'familylessness' or solidarity with the conditions of the underprivileged be stretched? In answer to this question, physical examples are presented to us by Matthew in the three following miracle stories.

The Stilling of the Storm: Matthew 8.23-27. The episode of the stilling of the storm is linked with the previous passage by the renewed use of ἀκολουθεῖν. What Jesus in the previous passage explained 'theoretically', becomes true in a physical sense. In the boat, at sea, in the storm, the disciples were in real need, they were physically without a home and separated from their families. During the storm at sea they were in a very insecure situation.[106] In fact, in the storm, the disciples were themselves the needy, who were subject to distress. If we take the 'storm' (σεισμός), the 'sea' (θαλάσσα), the 'waves' (κύματα), metaphorically, these elements symbolize deep distress on almost all levels, including repudiation, trials, conflict and tension (as 'homelessness' in the previous passage was metaphorically meant). They are symbols of death and destruction.[107]

As a spatial indicator, the sea connotes something that comes close to our definition of marginality.[108] Jesus and his disciples were on their way from their own country to a foreign one: Gadara. Thus, the sea also functions as a border between two places.[109] Jesus and the disciples were in transit, they were no longer in their own country and not yet in a foreign country. They were 'in between somewhere and nowhere'. They were 'neither here nor there'. This is typical of being

---

105. Cf. Kingsbury, 'On Following Jesus', p. 56.

106. Cf. Patte, *The Gospel according to Matthew*, p. 121.

107. Cf. Luz, *Das Evangelium nach Matthäus*, II, p. 27; see also Davies and Allison, *A Critical and Exegetical Commentary on the Gospel according to Saint Matthew* II, p. 69.

108. Cf. Duling, 'Matthew and Marginality', p. 645; see above in Chapter 3, the section on *The Composition of the Community*.

109. Cf. Bal, *De theorie van vertellen en verhalen*, p. 54.

marginalized. They were therefore in a very uncertain and unpredictable situation in which they could only rely on God and Jesus.

It now becomes clear that following Jesus was by no means a 'romantic trip', it was indeed costly, even dangerous,[110] or as Gnilka says, 'Following Jesus was dangerous. It led to storms and to clashes with devastating powers.'[111]

One would expect that the storm (as a metaphor for outside forces of destruction and distress) would bring about a stronger cohesion within the group of disciples (as Coser sees the function of conflict; see above). But this does not happen. Instead, the disciples tremble with fear and are screaming for help. In their deepest fear and *angst*, they failed to realize that Jesus was in control.[112] He was sleeping, not because he had no interest in them (as the disciples accused him in Mk 4.38), but as a symbolic act demonstrating that even the forces of nature were subordinate to him.[113] He had nowhere to lay down his head (8.20), but during the storm, he laid down his head! One could say, when there is a storm, he is in his element or, when people are in need he is at his best, he then 'sleeps well'. The disciples failed to realize this, therefore they called out in deep distress: κύριε, σῶσον, ἀπολλύμεθα ('Lord, save us! We're going to drown!'). But again, Jesus was not unwilling to help. In fact, he once more acts on behalf of those in need, this time his own disciples. He still shares their *angst* and he commands the storm, the wind, water and sea to calm down, but not before he has rebuked his disciples for their little faith (ὀλιγοπιστία) or, one could say, for their lack of insight.[114] They were weakened by their fear. They were too paralysed to act in their distress, they were unable to endure the distress around them.[115] The fear, horror and pain

---

110. Cf. C. Klein, 'Hope in the Middle of the Storm (Bible Study Matt 8:23-27)', *LWF.D* 14.35 (1984), pp. 35-38 (35); Sand, *Das Evangelium nach Matthäus*, p. 188.

111. Gnilka, *Das Matthäusevangelium*, p. 318.

112. Gnilka, *Das Matthäusevangelium*, p. 317.

113. Davies and Allison argue that it is possible that an ancient motif of a sleeping deity lies behind this story (Davies and Allison, *A Critical and Exegetical Commentary on the Gospel according to Saint Matthew*, II, p. 72). They say that there are many Ancient Near Eastern texts in which sleep is a symbol of supreme and unchallenged ability. Only the one that is in complete charge can sleep in peace. Thus Jesus' sleeping indicates not powerlessness but the fullness of absolute rule.

114. Cf. Gnilka, *Das Matthäusevangelium*, p. 317.

115. Cf. Luz, *Das Evangelium nach Matthäus*, II, p. 29.

threatened to overpower them. Metaphorically speaking, we could say that the distress in the 'stormy' world around them, weakened their ability to face it. With Jesus in their midst, they should have stood firm in their faith, as Gnilka says,

> The disciples were not reprimanded because they were frightened. Being scared is human, we all experience it. They were reprimanded because they were frightened even though Jesus was with them in the boat. *Faith is a strength which overcomes fear* (my emphasis).[116]

They should have been able to overcome anxiety with faith, and with Jesus in their midst they should, as disciples, have been able to overcome need. They ought to have had the power and the willingness to take on the problems of their world and to make the interests of the anxious, needy and underprivileged their own, as they had seen Jesus do in their own case. This episode illustrates to them how real and how existential need really is. They were the underprivileged (marginalized) themselves. On the one hand they were in deep distress, and on the other hand they were subject to Jesus' making their interests his own. This was the case on the 'real historical-Jesus' level. But later, in the context of the Matthean community, the disciples, the possible leaders, should have remembered their previous state and understood what it meant to be in such a hopeless and distressed situation. Thus they should have followed Jesus' example and done the same to others. This is the new disposition with which Jesus challenges the inner circle of disciples. They are exhorted to do the same to others as Jesus does to them. This indeed gives them a new identity and a new 'family', that is, loyalty to Jesus and his cause. This ought to lead to a change in inner values and to an understanding of and solidarity with the really marginalized. In other words, in this new context, the 'disciples', namely, the Matthean community, have to realize that the real-life disciples of Jesus were marginalized. They now also have to opt for 'voluntary marginality' in order to identify with the involuntary marginalized in their own community, although this could lead to more hardship and persecution as Jesus' followers. This is why the boat is used metaphorically as a symbol of the community of Jesus, facing all sorts of storms at sea.[117]

116. Gnilka, *Das Matthäusevangelium*, p. 318.
117. Cf. Schweizer, *The Good News according to Matthew*, p. 221.

There is, however, another element of conflict in this episode. Although not realizing that the very presence of Jesus meant security, the disciples still addressed him as κύριε, and, as in the previous episode, by doing this they acknowledged Jesus' authority. Although scared to death, they turned to Jesus and to no one else. What is more, in the reaction of the people to what happened, they acknowledged Jesus' *extended authority* to include control over the forces of nature. This was a kind of authority the Jewish leaders never pretended to have. But, because of it the people would follow Jesus. How then would they still support their traditional leaders? The people acknowledged the *Vollmacht* of Jesus, rather than that of the leaders. In the words of Davies and Allison: 'The disciples are amazed because they have witnessed a previously hidden ability. Jesus can command *even* the wind and the sea. Clearly one greater than Jonah is here.'[118]

The Destruction of the Demons in the Country of the Gadarenes: Matthew 8.28–9.1. This episode is a continuation of the previous one. It is especially linked to 8.18 as it occurs on the other side of the lake at the place towards which they were heading. Sand calls this episode 'another exorcism'.[119] The previous one was an 'exorcism' of the storm, this is an exorcism of demons. Therefore it has implications for the way discipleship is perceived. Furthermore, this episode is one of the most significant in as far as it entails conflict and it contains the clearest examples of conflicting *interests*: (1) The ongoing latent conflict with the Jewish leadership; (2) the manifest conflict with the possessed demons; (3) the herdsmen; (4) the city-dwellers.

The ongoing conflict with the Jewish leaders in this episode is a further development of the conflict on the subject of contact with the Gentiles (cf. 8.5-13). Matthew again takes up the theme of uncleanness, this time even more explicitly. It is, as Patte says, 'The theme of uncleanness (see 8.1-13) is found once again. Arriving in this country, Jesus is met by unclean persons (two demoniacs coming out of the tombs, 8.28); there is a herd of unclean animals, pigs (8.30). This is pagan country.'[120] The Jesus of Matthew's Gospel openly goes into

118. Davies and Allison, *A Critical and Exegetical Commentary on the Gospel according to Saint Matthew*, II, p. 76.

119. Sand, *Das Evangelium nach Matthäus*, p. 189.

120. Patte, *The Gospel according to Matthew*, p. 124; see also Gnilka, *Das Matthäusevangelium*, p. 321; Sanders and Davies, *Studying the Synoptic Gospels*,

pagan country. He purposely makes contact with demoniacs and exor-
cises the demons. This contact with the most unclean that there is, the
grave-dwellers (or maniacs[121]), could certainly not be approved of by
the Jewish leaders and would even be regarded as disgusting. It is this
physical contact that later in the middle section would lead to manifest
conflict on a more ideological level (cf. 9.13; see below). In this episode
we have (again) a demonstration of Jesus identifying himself with the
interests of the unclean class (of an agrarian society[122]), and liberating
them from their unclean state in order to be reintegrated into society.
Here we also have (as in the previous episode) an example of Jesus
exercising his extended authority, this time not only over nature but
also over demons. The Jewish leaders cannot claim to have this kind of
authority and once again this contributes to the tension between them.

The conflict with the demoniacs, herdsmen and city-dwellers is much
more manifest at this point of the narrative than the conflict with the
Jewish leaders. Matthew mentions *two* demoniacs in order to give
extra importance to what happened.[123] They met Jesus (ὑπήντησαν—
[ὑπαντάω]). But this verb can also mean: 'to oppose someone in a hostile sense'.[124] Thus, they opposed Jesus because he disturbed them in
their domain. Although outcasts of society themselves, living in graves
and feared by people because of their violent character, they were in
charge of the area in which they lived. They had some interest in keeping the status quo. They had some security in their misery and they
seemed to be in control of their lives. As expendables or unclean, they
probably had no other option than to be violent and fierce.[125] Jesus
wanted to remove them from this miserable position but they did not
want to have anything to do with him. They did not want him to take
up their case or interests. The demons had supernatural knowledge (as

---

p. 169; Harrington, *The Gospel of Matthew*, p. 120 and Hare, *Matthew*, p. 96 on
Gadara as pagan country.

121. Hawthorn diagnosis the demoniac as suffering from schizophrenia, with
some manic-depressive symptoms (T. Hawthorn, 'The Gerasene Demoniac: A Diagnosis. Mark v.1-20. Luke viii. 26-29. (Matthew viii. 28-34)', *ET* 66 [1954], pp. 79-
80; see also Beare, *The Gospel according to Matthew*, p. 218; Gnilka, *Das
Matthäusevangelium*, p. 321).

122. Cf. Lenski, *Power and Privilege*, p. 281.

123. See Gnilka, *Das Matthäusevangelium*, p. 321 on the issue of duplication in
Matthew.

124. Cf. BAGD, p. 845.

125. Cf. Lenski, *Power and Privilege*, p. 281; see above.

far as Matthew was concerned): they knew Jesus' true identity without being told.[126] They recognized that Jesus was the Son of God (υἱὸς τοῦ θεοῦ), but they did not acknowledge his authority. Note the absence of the address κύριε, which those who do acknowledge his authority normally employ. Jesus wanted to have them back in society, but in their own interests (in their eyes) they wished to retain the status quo. However, Jesus' authority was supreme and he exorcised the demons into the pigs which ran into the sea and drowned. The conflict was resolved by Jesus' supremacy. Note that the demons (in the pigs) drowned in the sea (θάλασσαν) which, as we have seen from the previous episode, was itself a symbol of destruction. Thus we can say that the demons (read: evil) went under in the sea (read: evil as well). Is this perhaps a good example of the premise that all systems, even 'evil systems', contain in themselves the impulses operating towards their own supersedence and change (even destruction), as Dahrendorf claims?[127]

As far as the herdsmen were concerned, there was an economic interest at stake: they lost their livestock. Amongst the pagans (Greek and Roman) pigs were valuable animals, they were even used as sacrificial animals.[128] Conflict with the herdsmen is quite obvious, for, in the interest of the demoniacs (and therefore against their own), they lost their animals. Small wonder they ran to the city in panic to tell the story and probably to look for support. To the herdsmen the disturbed status quo meant a loss of income!

Matthew uses the same word in 8.34 as in 8.28, ὑπάντησιν. Just as the demoniacs 'opposed' Jesus, the city-dwellers also 'came in opposition'. The reason why the city-dwellers asked Jesus to leave is not given anywhere in the text.[129] We only read that they ('the whole city'—πᾶσα ἡ πόλις) went out to meet with Jesus and requested him to leave their area. Clearly there is conflict. But why? We have to read it in combination with the conflict with the herdsmen. It is hard to imagine that *all* the city's inhabitants opposed Jesus. Probably only the city's representatives or perhaps their leaders met him. The city in an

126. Cf. Davies and Allison, *A Critical and Exegetical Commentary on the Gospel according to Saint Matthew*, II, p. 81.

127. Dahrendorf, *Class and Class Conflict*, p. 123.

128. Cf. Gnilka, *Das Matthäusevangelium*, p. 322; Luz, *Das Evangelium nach Matthäus* II, p. 32; Harrington, *The Gospel of Matthew*, p. 120.

129. See also Davies and Allison, *A Critical and Exegetical Commentary on the Gospel according to Saint Matthew*, II, p. 85.

agrarian community (and in the Roman Empire in particular) was the seat of the authorities who maintained order and enjoyed civil and political power. An important function of the urban centre was the collection and overseeing of revenues, taxes and tolls.[130] There was a reciprocal trade relationship between rural areas and urban areas.[131] Since this was the case, and since the herdsmen lost their economic assets when they lost their pigs, thus also losing a source of income for the city's revenues, I suspect that the conflict between Jesus and the city-dwellers was based on economic reasons. The city lost a source of income in the process. Furthermore, pagan agrarian societies, like those of the Jews, were highly stratified.[132] Therefore I suggest that here again there was a conflict of interests: Jesus, in taking up the interests of the expendables, (the demoniacs), threatens the vested interests of the pagan city. They experienced some security in the miserable situation of the demoniacs; a security (sense of control) that Jesus threatened.

The implications of this conflict for discipleship, are clear. Whereas moving to a pagan country induced conflict with Judaism, because of (amongst other things else) the Jewish purity laws, the seed of an ongoing conflict had already been sown in this new environment (situation), for here also in the pagan country there were stratified systems and conflicting interests. In whatever new situation the disciples, in following Jesus found themselves, they had to identify with the interests of the underprivileged anew. Jesus helped the demoniacs (and indirectly the pagans as well). However, moving to the Gentiles because of rejection by the Jews, did not mean a 'happy-ending',[133] instead an ongoing conflict was to be expected because of Jesus' stand. As soon as one's own (economic) interests are at stake, whether Jewish or Gentile, taking up the interests of the unclean or expendables, or becoming 'voluntarily marginalized', remains a challenging task!

The Healing of the Paralytic: Matthew 9.2-8. In this section we deal

---

130. Cf. Overman, 'Who Were the First Urban Christians?, p. 166; see also Saldarini, *Pharisees, Scribes and Sadducees*, pp. 45-46; Rohrbaugh, 'The City in the Second Testament', pp. 67-75, on the political and economical position of the ancient city; see above in ch. 3.

131. Cf. Edwards, 'First Century Urban/Rural Relations in Lower Galilee, pp. 176-77.

132. Cf. Lenski, *Power and Privilege*; see above.

133. Cf. Gnilka, *Das Matthäusevangelium*, p. 323.

with: (1) authority, (2) manifest conflict and (3) conflict on an ideological level.

Although 9.1 can be seen as part of the previous pericope, it does prepare the setting for the new episode: Jesus moved back from the pagan country to his own city. How would he be received in his own place? His reception, as we will see, entailed further conflict rather than warm acceptance! In fact, he was not accepted in his own city for the same reasons that he had been rejected in the pagan country. The basic assumption is that Jesus' conflict with the Gentiles was one of conflicting interests. The same assumption can be held concerning his conflict with the Jewish leaders.

The emphasis of the story in this passage lies on the discussion (controversy) between Jesus and the scribes. The important question is: By what authority (*Vollmacht*) may Jesus forgive sins?[134] The miracle itself acts as material or as a trigger for the discussion: 'So the miracle fades even further into the background in favour of the spoken word than is already the case in Mark'.[135] Because of the emphasis on the forgiveness of sin, the miracle itself is pushed into the background.[136] The same is true of the use of the concept 'faith' (πίστις). Although we find that Matthew takes up a previous theme ('faith' as in 8.10), the emphasis does not lie here.[137] 'Faith' (πίστις) here indicates that the paralytic had confidence in Jesus' ability to heal; he recognized Jesus' willingness and authority to help him; he was not so 'paralysed' by his condition that he was without hope (against the 'little faith' of the disciples in the storm; cf. 8.23-27). He can take courage: with Jesus the paralysed can walk away, but without him, he will remain in bed.[138] For the first time in the narrative of Matthew 8 and 9, we find that the conflict with the Jewish leaders which has been latent up to this point becomes manifest.[139] For the first time (the already present) conflict surfaces. For the first time it takes the form of a direct challenge both

134. Cf. Sand, *Das Gesetz und die Propheten*, p. 64; *idem, Das Evangelium nach Matthäus*, p. 192.

135. Gnilka, *Das Matthäusevangelium*, p. 325.

136. See Schweizer, *The Good News according to Matthew*, p. 224; France, *Matthew*, p. 165.

137. See also Davies and Allison, *A Critical and Exegetical Commentary on the Gospel according to Saint Matthew*, II, p. 88.

138. Cf. Patte, *The Gospel according to Matthew*, p. 125.

139. See also Davies and Allison, *A Critical and Exegetical Commentary on the Gospel according to Saint Matthew*, II, p. 86.

from the side of the Jewish leaders and from that of Jesus. What is more, the conflict is much more intensified because, as we shall see, it became manifest on an ideological level. What in itself is still a conflict of interests now manifests itself as an ideological conflict (see my section on *Values* in Chapter 2 for the difference in nuance between a conflict of interests and an ideological conflict).

Let us first look at the conflict from the side of the Jewish leaders (some of the scribes—τινες τῶν γραμματέων; this has to be read along with my section on *The Conflict from the Side of the Jewish Leaders* in Chapter 3). They accuse Jesus in strong terms of being 'blasphemous' (cf. 9.3). The scribes saw themselves as (prime) authorities on the interpretation of the law and tradition.[140] They regarded it as their privilege and duty to interpret the religious laws and according to their belief, it was only God who had the prerogative to forgive sin/evil. As Gnilka states, 'In their view, this was blasphemy: a person claiming a divine privilege.'[141] In other words, in terms of the chosen conflict theory, the scribes (or Jewish leaders, including the Pharisees in the Matthean perspective; see below), in sustaining their own interests and authority as religious leaders (and probably political leaders; see Chapter 3, the section on *The Pharisees as Part of the Retainer Class in the Period of Formative Judaism*), were themselves in a position of privilege and able to decide who could and who could not be forgiven.

But, the scribes legitimized their own position of privilege following the value or ideology that only God is able to forgive. Their own religious position was articulated or codified by the ideology (value) that only God had the ability to forgive.[142] In this way they made their own point of view a 'respectable' one, one that transcended the mere level of own interests. Their position was further strengthened by the sanction laid down by the accusation of 'blasphemy', as soon as their position was challenged or threatened. They safeguarded their own position by labelling Jesus 'blasphemous'.[143] In this way, they ruled out the necessity and possibility for themselves (and those who supported them and their view) to forgive (and thus to turn to) people, that is, the

140. Cf. Rivkin, *A Hidden Revolution*, pp. 105, 113-14, 159, 176, 183; see also the controversy in Mt. 23.2-3.

141. Gnilka, *Das Matthäusevangelium*, p. 326.

142. See Dahrendorf, *Class and Class Conflict*, p. 186 on the codification of interests by ideologies; see above.

143. See Malina and Neyrey, *Calling Jesus Names* on the labelling process.

sinners, or in this context, the small ones (or marginalized) in society.[144] It was, in their view, impossible to forgive each other, because 'only God can do so'. Jesus seriously challenged this position. Through this the conflict was intensified, because it manifested itself on an ideological level. When Jesus took up the interests of the leper, the centurion's slave and Peter's sick mother-in-law (all of whom were marginalized), the conflict was present but latent but as soon as Jesus challenged the ideology which supposedly legitimized their interests, the conflict became much more intense, and Jesus himself became more vulnerable. As Patte says, 'Jesus could have had the power to heal the paralytic without exposing himself [that much] to the scribes as he healed the *paralysed* servant of the centurion (8.6). But by mentioning forgiveness of sins, he made himself [much more] vulnerable (cf. 8.20).'[145]

Furthermore, the presuppositions of the scribes towards illness, were also challenged. Illness, in this case paralysis, was viewed as being the result of sin. Put differently, illness was regarded as a punishment of evil. Disease was generally traced back to sin.[146] But in this case, as Malina and Rohrbaugh see it, Jesus first addresses the illness (being unworthy and cast out of the social network) and forgives the paralytic his sins, and then addresses disease (thus heals his biomedical malfunction, namely being paralysed).[147] By forgiving the sins of the lame man, and then curing him (9.2), Jesus countered this generally accepted view on illness and in so doing, possibly undermined the power of the

---

144. I take the 'sinners' and the 'small ones' (marginalized) to be the same because of the common Jewish view in that time that being ill means having sinned and therefore being a sinner (see Gundry, *Matthew*, p. 163; France, *Matthew*, p. 165; Gnilka, *Das Matthäusevangelium*, p. 326). Furthermore, there is a direct connection between the two concepts as can be seen from the address of Jesus to the lame man. Jesus addresses him in terms of endearment (cf. Davies and Allison, *A Critical and Exegetical Commentary on the Gospel according to Saint Matthew* II, p. 88) as: τέκνον (son, or child = small one), and directly thereafter Jesus forgives him his sins. And as a final argument, I refer to Mt. 9.10, where the tax collectors (also seen as marginalized) and the sinners are mentioned in one phrase referring to the same kind of people. Narratively speaking, we can thus refer to the marginalized in a collective character as 'the sinners'.

145. Patte, *The Gospel according to Matthew*, p. 127.

146. Cf. France, *Matthew*, p. 165; Gnilka, *Das Matthäusevangelium*, p. 326.

147. Malina and Rohrbaugh, *Social-science Commentary on the Synoptic Gospels*, p. 81.

scribes. As the intellectuals of society, the scribes were, amongst other things, responsible for creating and maintaining values and perceptions. By challenging generally accepted ideas, he indirectly challenged the scribes' authority.

The reaction of the crowd as seen previously (7.29) once again intensifies this (now manifest) conflict. In response to the healing and especially to Jesus' controversy with the scribes, the crowd accepted Jesus' view, thus rejecting the authority of their religious leaders. Not only were they surprised (as in previous responses) but they were also filled with respect (ἐφοβήθησαν) and praised God (ἐδόξασαν τὸν θεόν) for the fact that through Jesus, it had become *possible and necessary* to forgive sin (τοῖς ἀνθρώποις; cf. 9.8). The crowd honoured Jesus. Honour is a limited good, if one person wins honour, someone else loses it.[148] In accepting Jesus' authority and in honouring him, the scribes' honour was forced to diminish. The crowd, in accepting Jesus' view, gave the scribes all the more reason to suspect him and label him blasphemous.

In this episode, Jesus for the first time in Matthew 8 and 9 directly challenges the scribes in the way he addresses them in 9.6. He wanted to cure the paralytic in order for *them* to see his authority (ἵνα δὲ εἰδῆτε ὅτι ἐξουσίαν ἔχει ὁ υἱὸς τοῦ ἀνθρώπου ἐπὶ τῆς γῆς ἀφιέναι ἁμαρτίας; 'But so that you may know that the Son of Man has authority on earth to forgive sins'). Here Jesus *himself* stands in conflict with the scribes. A contributing factor (or source of grievance) to conflict, as we have seen from Kriesberg,[149] is an inconsistency (dichotomy) between what is expected and what is attained. Jesus expects more from the Jewish leaders than what they have actually attained. They have not reached the goal of real forgiveness of people on earth at all and this Jesus challenges by his demonstration of the miracle. The authority to forgive which the scribes claim to come only from God and belonging to God, has to be passed on to the people on earth (to man) as well. Jesus himself had this extended authority to pass on the power to forgive; he also expected it from the leaders—but they had failed.

148. Cf. Malina and Rohrbaugh, *Social-science Commentary on the Synoptic Gospels*, p. 76.

149. Kriesberg, *The Sociology of Social Conflicts*, pp. 76-77; see Chapter 2, the section on *Changes in Attainment and Expectations*.

If we translate this to the community of Matthew, the community has to understand that God's forgiveness has to be realized and put into practice by the people.[150] It is especially Davies and Allison who correctly apply this passage to the situation after 70 CE.[151] They say it is known that with the temple (the centre of the sacrificial system designed to reconcile Israel with God and to assure forgiveness), in ruins, religious Jews had to think anew about atonement. At such a time it might have been opportune to preach that God, in Jesus, had dealt with sin once and for all. Davies and Allison proceed,

> However that may be, Matthew's most characteristic contribution to the theological idea of forgiveness is his emphasis upon its pre-conditions. *Divine forgiveness cannot be appropriated unless one forgives others* (5.21-26; 6.12, 14-15; 18.15-35). God's forgiveness demands man's forgiveness. Perhaps again we may think of the situation at the end of the first century. The rabbis at Jamnia, aware of the dangers of Jewish disunity, were much concerned with unifying the factions that survived the war. Similarly Matthew, in the face of an increasingly diverse and expanding Christian movement, in which Jewish. . . and Gentile Christians continued to grow apart, may have given much reflection to the need for tolerance and forgiveness (my emphasis).[152]

Jesus does not refer to the 'son of man' as a title here, it merely indicates 'man/mankind'.[153] In this context he is clearly referring to himself as 'man' thus identifying with human beings and as such bringing forgiveness to humankind. The reference to 'son of man' (υἱὸς τοῦ ἀνθρώπου) in 9.6, in relation to 'the people' (τοῖς ἀνθρώποις) in 9.8 indicates that forgiveness is a human affair and not restricted to heaven alone, thus also the words 'on earth' (ἐπὶ τῆς γῆς) in 9.6.[154] It

---

150. Cf. H. Greeven, 'Die Heilung des Gelähmten nach Matthäus', in J. Lange (ed.), *Das Matthäus-Evangelium* (WdF, 525; Darmstadt: Wissenschaftliche Buchgesellschaft, 1980), p. 205-22 (216); see also Luz 'Die Jünger im Matthäusevangelium', pp. 156, 161; Sand, *Das Evangelium nach Matthäus*, p. 195.

151. Davies and Allison, *A Critical and Exegetical Commentary on the Gospel according to Saint Matthew*, II, p. 89.

152. Davies and Allison, *A Critical and Exegetical Commentary on the Gospel according to Saint Matthew*, II, pp. 89-90.

153. Or as Hahn calls it: *einzelne Menschen* (F. Hahn, *Christologische Hoheitstitel: Ihre Geschichte im frühen Christentum* (Göttingen: Vandenhoeck & Ruprecht, 1974), p. 22; see also Sand, *Das Evangelium nach Matthäus*, p. 66; Harrington, *The Gospel of Matthew*, p. 122; Sanders, *Jezus, mythe en werkelijkheid*, pp. 295-96.

154. Cf. Beare, *The Gospel according to Matthew*, p. 223; Patte, *The Gospel*

is, in fact, because of the authority of Jesus that people, and of course
the disciples in particular, are expected to have an attitude of
forgiveness (in the context of the middle section).[155] Small wonder that
Gundry calls this pericope: 'Jesus' authority to forgive sins as model
of the disciples' authority to forgive sins'.[156] The scribes seemingly
refused to realize this, although it was in their own interests to do so
in order to attain some unity among their contemporaries.[157] Therefore
Jesus sharply attacked (labelled) them as having 'evil thoughts' (cf. 9.4).
One should be able to forgive sinners unconditionally.

The Calling of Matthew: Matthew 9.9-13. The episode of the calling of
Matthew (9.9-13) acts as the conclusion of the middle part. In this
episode I am concerned: (1) with manifest conflict, as in the episode of
the healing of the paralytic (9.2-12); (2) again with conflict on an ideological level. In the previous episode the conflict was with the scribes,
this time it is between Jesus and the Pharisees. Rivkin remarks that
Matthew (like Mark), joined these groups together referring to them
as being one and the same, namely, authoritative teachers of the law.[158]
However, this is too simplistic. In following Kingsbury, I will not
view them as 'one and the same', but rather regard them, in a literary
sense, as belonging to one of the group of narrative characters, the so-
called 'antagonists', under the term 'the Jewish leaders' or the 'religious
leaders'.[159] As Kingsbury says,

> The term 'leaders' is itself used in Matthew's story to refer to groups of
> persons who occupy positions of authority in Israel (15.14; 23.16, 24).
> Literary-critically, therefore, this term can also aptly be used to denote all

---

according to Matthew, p. 126; see also Gundry, *Matthew*, p. 164; Davies and Allison,
A Critical and Exegetical Commentary on the Gospel according to Saint Matthew II,
p. 96.

155. Cf. Gnilka, *Das Matthäusevangelium*, pp. 327-28.

156. Gundry, *Matthew*, p. 161.

157. See the above citation of Davies and Allison, *A Critical and Exegetical Commentary on the Gospel according to Saint Matthew*, II, p. 90.

158. Rivkin, *A Hidden Revolution*, p. 114.

159. Kingsbury, 'The Developing Conflict between Jesus and the Jewish leaders
in Matthew's Gospel, pp. 58-60; *Matthew as Story*, pp. 17-24, 115-18; see also S.
Van Tilborg, *The Jewish Leaders in Matthew*, p. 6; Smith, *Augsburg Commentary
on the New Testament: Matthew*, p.18; I am also referring to the section on *Retainers*
in Chapter 3.

such groups of persons. *Those who comprise the religious leaders are the Pharisees, the Sadducees, the chief priests, the elders, and the scribes* (my emphasis).[160]

These various groups of leaders are presented as a unified front against Jesus, although historically they were much more diverse.[161] But this presentation as a unified front is not only literary-critically understandable (as protagonist against antagonist), it is also likely in relation to conflict theory, as presented by Dahrendorf.[162] There are but two parties in any particular conflict; those who wish to maintain the status quo and those who press for change. Therefore, both from a literary-critical and conflict theoretical perspective, we are still dealing in this episode with the same initial conflict between Jesus and the 'leaders', although the (antagonistic) characters have seemingly changed from the scribes to the Pharisees.[163]

In the closing episode of the middle part, a few 'old' themes are taken up again, elaborated upon or brought to a conclusion. The theme of following Jesus (ἀκολουθέω) is finally concluded and interpreted in terms of the interests of Jesus. The verb ἀκολουθέω is used again

160. Kingsbury, *Matthew as Story*, p. 17.

161. Cf. Kingsbury, 'The Developing Conflict between Jesus and the Jewish Leaders', p. 58; *Matthew as Story*, p. 18; see also Van Tilborg, *The Jewish Leaders in Matthew*, p. 6.

162. Dahrendorf, *Class and Class Conflict*, p. 126; see the section on *Incompatible Interests* in Chapter 2.

163. Note that the Pharisees are here mentioned for the first time in the narrative of Matthew 8 and 9, and the scribes are not mentioned again in these two chapters. Matthew makes some distinctions between these groups, but I will not attend to this issue here (see Kingsbury, 'The Developing Conflict between Jesus and the Jewish Leaders', pp. 58-59 and *Matthew as Story*, pp. 17-19 on this issue). I will debate no further on whether the evidence Matthew used in his treatment of the Jewish leaders was uncritical or at least anachronistic (see Carson, 'The Jewish Leaders in Matthew's Gospel: A Reappraisal', pp. 161-74).

But, why does Matthew make a distinction at all? To Rivkin (*A Hidden Revolution*, p. 113), Matthew is likely to replace the scribes with the Pharisees when he has Jesus raise the question as to the lineage of the Christ (cf. Mt. 22.41-46). But this is not the case in Mt. 9.9-13. There is no question about Jesus' lineage here. I would rather suggest a view that stands in connection with the citation from Hosea 6.6: ἔλεος θέλω καὶ θυσίαν· in 9.13, which could be linked with the Pharisees, rather than with the scribes (see below). Suffice it to say here that the criticism Jesus had against the Pharisees in this particular pericope, can be extended to the whole group of Jewish leaders within the broader Matthean context.

in 9.19 and 9.27, but not as a theme as such. Again the ongoing conflict is intensified to an ideological level. In fact, the calling of Matthew,
the tax collector, was: (1) a demonstration in the extreme and (2) a
legitimization of Jesus' interests, for according the Pharisaic view and
the purity laws, a tax collector was just about the worst example of a
wicked person.

Concerning the demonstration, it is common knowledge that tax collectors were the most unpopular and undesirable types in society.[164]
As such, and in relation to the theme of fellowship, this episode demonstrates two aspects that have also been dealt with in previous episodes
of the middle section: (1) the *immediate* willingness to follow and the
loyal response of a disciple called by Jesus, here in the person of the
tax collector (see also 8.18-22 on how a would-be-follower should
react, with the practical examples and consequences in 8.23-7 and 8.28-
9.1), and (2) the *practical consequence of forgiveness of sin* (cf. 9.2-
8) in the calling of a sinner and the actual dining with sinners.

The tax collector responded immediately when Jesus called him. But
more significantly he exchanged his own vested economic interests for
those of Jesus. He left aside his daily occupation in order to follow
Jesus. Whether this tax collector was wealthy, is hard to say. Malina and
Rohrbaugh say that some tax collectors became rich but that many
clearly did not.[165]

More emphasis should be given to the practical consequences of the
forgiveness of sin, illustrated in the previous episode. The table fellowship of Jesus in this episode clearly indicates that Jesus' talking about
forgiveness in 9.2 was more than mere words.[166] We have already
seen that the ideological legitimization that only God could forgive sin
was dangerous in that it could mean that forgiveness on earth, between
people, was unnecessary and impossible. Here, in the person of a tax
collector, we have an example of someone who was regarded as being
impossible to forgive, even by God. The Pharisees were of the opinion
that tax collectors were unable to repent because they could not know

164. Cf. Malina and Rohrbaugh, *Social-science Commentary on the Synoptic
Gospels*, p. 82.

165. Malina and Rohrbaugh, *Social-science Commentary on the Synoptic Gospels*,
p. 82.

166. Cf. Davies and Allison, *A Critical and Exegetical Commentary on the
Gospel according to Saint Matthew*, II, pp. 100-101.

how many people they had deceived.[167] And because they could not repent, they could not be forgiven because repentance was a precondition for forgiveness. The tax collectors in Jewish society were a particularly degraded and despised group of people because they sold their services to the foreign oppressor to the detriment of their own people. They were literally engaged in robbery, for some of them helped their superiors to mulct the public, and no doubt, part of what they collected, stuck to their own fingers. They were regarded as robbers and frequently classed with prostitutes and sinners.[168] Small wonder that the Pharisees granted them no forgiveness.

In spite of this Jesus calls the tax collector *without the precondition of repentance* to become his disciple.[169] He chooses him, a sinner of the worst kind, and thus this episode is an illustration of to what extremes forgiveness, articulated in the previous episode, could be taken. This calling was a merciful act, similar to healing. It denotes removing of sinfulness and uncleanness.[170] But not only does Jesus forgive and call a supreme sinner to follow him, he even dines with him. He physically comes very close to the sinners (tax collectors, thus outcasts). To share a meal in the household was a sign of closeness and intimacy.

167. Cf. E. Lohse, *Umwelt des Neuen Testaments* (Göttingen: Vandenhoeck & Ruprecht, 3rd edn, 1977), p. 56.

168. Cf. B.J. Bamberger, 'Tax Collector', in G.A. Buttrick, (ed.), *The Interpreter's Dictionary of the Bible: An Illustrated Encyclopedia* (5 vols., Nashville: Abingdon Press, 1962), IV, p. 522; Gnilka, *Das Matthäusevangelium*, p. 331. Malina and Rohrbaugh explains the unfavourable position of the tax collectors as follows: 'The tax collectors. . . were for the most part employees of the chief tax collector and were often rootless persons unable to find other work' (Malina and Rohrbaugh, *Social-science Commentary on the Synoptic Gospels*, p. 82). Van Aarde explains their unfavourable position in following Malina as follows: 'In the first century Mediterranean society certain families and institutions were ascribed to be irretrievably shameful, like prostitutes and tax collectors. Holiness was associated with divine order, and exclusivistic particularism. Prostitutes [and tax collectors] transgress these boundaries and do not retain the politics of purity. They respect no lines of exclusiveness' (Van Aarde, *God-with-Us*, p. 262). Therefore they are collectively referred to as 'the sinners'.

169. This view is confirmed by Sanders ('Jesus and the Sinners', pp. 23-24). Jesus offended the leaders by including the 'tax collectors' and the 'sinners', while they were still sinners, and without first requiring repentance. Thus Jesus offered forgivenss before requiring reformation. Jesus offered unconditional forgiveness and this was against the accepted viewpoint of the leaders.

170. Cf. Patte, *The Gospel according to Matthew*, p. 129.

That is why these household settings (as spatial indicators) also show
and contribute to the serious conflict of interests between Jesus and the
Jewish leaders: the household (and dining with sinners) signified an inclusive community in contrast to the exclusive space of the Jewish
leaders' temple.[171]

171. This makes it necessary to mention something of the household, for the meal
took place in a house (cf. Mt. 9.10).

The household is an important setting, especially in relation to the conflict
with the Jewish leaders. One of the confrontations between Jesus and the Pharisees
was because of Jesus' sitting at table (which would have taken place in the setting of
the household) with tax collectors and sinners (9.10). The fact that Jesus went into
the household of Peter (8.14) and that he dined with sinners, indicated his willingness to enter into the close (but not closed) and private (yet not exclusive) sphere of
the sinners. The characteristic features of domestic life were rooted in the institution
of kinship: solidarity, loyalty, trust, mutuality of obligations, generosity, sharing and
the like (cf. J.H. Elliott, 'Temple versus Household in Luke–Acts: A Contrast in
Social Institutions', *HTS* 47.1 [1991], pp. 88-120 [103]). The household symbol-
ized hospitality, fellowship and mutual support. It was a place par excellence of an
inclusive fellowship and reciprocal service. It was the place (setting) for showing
mercy and performing merciful acts of loving kindness (cf. Elliott, 'Temple versus
Household in Luke–Acts', p. 106). Says Elliott: 'The private space of the house and
home was the scene where hospitality, generosity, friendship, deeds of mercy, acts
of mutual aid and comfort, familial love and fraternal support, unmeasured and
unlimited, welded bonds of intimacy and solidarity' (Elliott, 'Temple versus Household in Luke–Acts', p. 115; see also 'Household and Meals versus the Temple Purity
System: Patterns of Replication in Luke–Acts', *HTS* 47.2 [1991], pp. 386-99 [390]).

The same is true of codes about meals and food. They also symbolize social
identity, commitment and loyalty. As Elliott says: 'Dining scenes like domestic scenes,
or dining events within domestic settings, describe the social engagements of Jesus
and his followers, the inclusive scope of their association with the margined and the
outsiders and their practice of material aid and social support' (Elliott, 'Household
and Meals versus the Temple Purity System', p. 391; my emphasis). This stands in
contrast to the social setting of the temple to which the Jewish leaders were attached.
As Elliott states: 'Temple functionaries and other agencies of the Temple apparatus
appear guided by their own self-interests in presenting an exploitive regime in which
the mighty remain in their seats and nothing but disdain and neglect is shown to those
of low degree' (Elliott, 'Temple versus Household in Luke–Acts', p. 101; my emphasis). The temple was seen rather as a place of oppression of the poor and powerless,
of redistribution of resources according to the interests of the wielders of power, of
exclusive space and society according to purity (cf. Elliott, 'Temple versus Household in Luke–Acts', pp. 108-109), which indeed stands in sharp contrast to the
household setting.

Jesus was thus willing to identify himself notoriously with the unde-sirables.[172] It cannot be said better than in Patte's words:

> Calling sinners is presented as a merciful act which is opposed to calling righteous people and offering sacrifices or partaking in sacrifices. This opposition expresses that calling sinners involves more than saying a word to them: *it also involves being associated with sinners, indeed, eating with them, and consequently breaking the priestly laws of purity* according to which any meal is like a sacrificial meal, since sinners by definition do not follow these laws. . . *Mercy—calling sinners—demands from Jesus association with sinners, and thus sharing their uncleanness* (my emphasis).[173]

But, this calling (and thus the forgiving) of sinners and even more so the dining (and thus the associating) with sinners was a major cause of a conflict of interests: *Jesus here openly chooses the side of the disgraced,* and he legitimizes his position by the analogy of the physician (9.12) and the ideological challenge to the Pharisees (9.13).

Jesus' strongest ideological legitimization of his position, lies in his repudiation of the Pharisees: πορευθέντες δὲ μάθετε τί ἐστιν, ἔλεος θέλω καὶ οὐ θυσίαν· ('But go and learn what this means: "I desire mercy, not sacrifice"'; 9.13). Jesus here directly challenged the Pharisees in the second person plural (μάθετε), as he did with the scribes in the previous episode. What Jesus regarded as a merciful act: healing, forgiving, calling and dining with outcasts, the Pharisees regarded as disgraceful and unclean. They were careful not to be seen in the company of sinners because it would jeopardize their position of privilege.[174] But it was precisely at this point that Jesus challenged them so decidedly. Jesus 'caught' them out on their own value system. The value of acting mercifully, which Jesus did, was also a precept of the Pharisees, especially after the destruction of the second temple in 70 CE, for the Pharisees then emphasised a 'change of heart' (see the citation of Neusner below). I assume that Matthew (the Gospel) was written in approximately 80 CE.[175] Thus it was likely that Matthew (the author) knew the core value that was widely propagated by one of the leading Pharisees of the time, Rabbi Yohanan ben Zakkai, who was the founder of the assembly at Yavneh and the leader of the Jewish reconstruction

---

172. Cf. France, *Matthew*, p. 167.
173. Patte, *The Gospel according to Matthew*, p. 128.
174. Cf. Beare, *The Gospel according to Matthew*, p. 227.
175. Cf. Luz, *Das Evangelium nach Matthäus*, I, p. 76.

after 70 CE.[176] To Matthew, the Pharisees were the dominant group in the period of *formative Judaism*.[177] Therefore he knew and shared their values.

In an attempt to rebuild Judaism, because the temple was destroyed Rabbi Yohanan ben Zakkai wanted to place more emphasis on a change of heart than on sacrificial duties. As Neusner states when he cites Rabbi Yohanan ben Zakkai:

> The surviving Pharisees of Jerusalem, assembled at Yavneh by Yohanan ben Zakkai, offered another viewpoint: The old order endures. The Lord still is served, sin is expiated, and reconciliation is achieved through the new sacrifice, which is deeds of loving-kindness:
>
>> For we have another atonement, which is like sacrifice, and what is it? Deeds of loving-kindness, as it is said, *For I desire mercy and not sacrifice* (Hos. 6.6).[178]

What was needed after the destruction of the temple was a re-emphasis on mercy, an act of compassion and loving-kindness.[179] Neusner says: 'Yohanan thought that through *hesed* the Jews might make atonement, and that the sacrifices now demanded of them were love and mercy'.[180]

In following the theory of Luz, namely that the conflict between Jesus and the Jewish leaders was a transposition of the conflict between Matthew and the leaders after 70 CE, I assume that the author translated

---

176. Cohen argues that there is no historical evidence that the rabbis (after 70 CE), and thus Rabbi Yohanan ben Zakkai, referred to themselves as being Pharisees, or even descendants of the Pharisees (Cohen, 'The Significance of Yavneh, pp. 37-40). But this does not mean that it was impossible for them to be Pharisees. From the evidence of the New Testament and Josephus we can deduce that they were. Cohen concludes that the rabbis were latter-day Pharisees who had no desire to publicize their connection with the Pharisees (Cohen, 'The Significance of Yavneh', pp. 40-41). He says that the rabbis assembled at Yavneh were Pharisees or descendants of Pharisees, but they made little of their ancestry (Cohen, 'The Significance of Yavneh', p. 50). Thus we also accept the rabbis at Yavneh of which the author of the Gospel knew to be Pharisees.

177. See above in Chapter 3; see also D. Hill, 'On the Use and Meaning of Hosea vi.6 in Matthew's Gospel', p. 119.

178. Neusner, *From Politics to Piety*, p. 98; see also Hill, 'On the Use and Meaning of Hosea vi.6 in Matthew's Gospel', p. 108.

179. Cf. J. Neusner, *First-century Judaism in Crisis: Yohanan Ben Zakkai and the Renaissance of Torah* (New York: Ktav, rev. edn, 1982), pp. 168-69; Luz, *Das Evangelium nach Matthäus*, II, p. 44 n. 38.

180. Neusner, *First-century Judaism in Crisis*, p. 170.

the above-mentioned 70 CE core value of the Pharisees back to the contemporary Pharisees of Jesus.[181] This view is also supported by Neusner.[182] He argues that since we do not know much of the pre-70 CE Pharisees, because there are no sources left from that period, all the information we have of the Pharisees of that period comes from sources after 70 CE. He says, 'All of the several sources concerning the pre-70 Pharisaic Judaism were shaped in response to the crisis of 70 AD.'[183] This includes the Gospels of the New Testament as sources.

In the terms of the so-called *formative Judaism* (see Chapter 3 above), the community of Matthew and the Pharisees was part of the same kind of organization. The community, as I have argued before, was still part of Judaism. Therefore it is likely that it still shared some of the same values of Judaism. *Thus Jesus and the Pharisees shared the same ideological basis.* This made the position of the Pharisees extremely vulnerable, for Matthew (the author) assumed that they *did not live up to their own core values*, whereas Jesus did.[184] Matthew thus incorporated the widely accepted core value of the Yavnean Academy, and a quotation from the Scriptures, into his story of the calling of Matthew (the tax collector) as an illustration of the full and real consequences of this widely accepted principle. *Through this he articulated the position of Jesus, for in challenging the Pharisees on their own accepted values, Jesus (and the author) legitimized his own chosen interests, namely the interests of the disgraced.* Jesus here both sharply rebukes the Jewish leaders for not seeing the full consequences of their own ideological system *and* at the same time reinforces his own position ideologically.

A brief remark must to be made on the disciples in 9.11. The Pharisees directed their question to the disciples, and not to Jesus himself. Through this the disciples are willingly or unwillingly involved in the conflict between Jesus and the Jewish leaders. They are, as followers of Jesus, in this way forced to choose, they are also forced to make a choice of interests. The narrative, however, does not disclose

181. Luz, *Das Evangelium nach Matthäus* I, pp. 66-67, 70; Luz, 'Wundergeschichten von Mt 8-9', p. 158.

182. Neusner, *From Politics to Piety*, pp. 1-4.

183. Neusner, *From Politics to Piety*, p. 3; see also Sanders, *Jezus, mythe en werkelijkheid*, p. 64.

184. See Lenski, *Power and Privilege*, p. 181 on the vulnerability that ideologies can create; see Chapter 2.

what their eventual choice was. It only tells us, and this is sufficient here, that they had to make it. Thus this was yet another challenge to their loyalty, a repeat of an earlier theme in the context of the middle section of the narrative of Matthew 8 and 9.

The End of the Plot: Matthew 9.14-35

Luz views the three controversy scenes (9.2-17) as a whole, seeing the confrontation between Jesus and the disciples of John as the third part (the others being the controversies with the scribes and the Pharisees).[185] Nevertheless, I prefer to follow Patte believing that the third group of miracles starts at 9.14, with the controversy with the disciples of John as the introductory episode.[186] Thus a fairly symmetrical structure is retained, as was the case in the other two major sections. This episode is still linked to the two main sections, it being the third example of opposition to Jesus. The last section ends at 9.35, again following the symmetrical pattern of the other two main sections, for in Mt. 9.35 we find the third major ideological legitimization of Jesus' position, in fact, it is the clearest of the three (see 8.17 and 9.12-13—all of which form part of the concluding episodes of the major sections). Clearly 9.36 starts with a new discourse between Jesus and the disciples. This final section thus comprises an introduction (9.14-17); three (four?) miracle stories; the episode of the ruler's daughter and the woman who touched Jesus' garment (9.18-26), the healing of the blind men (9.27-31), and the healing of the dumb man (9.32-33a); and a quite extended concluding episode (9.33b-35).

According to Van Aarde, the plot is unravelled in the conclusion.[187] At the end everything worked out in the beginning and developed in the middle, is seen to be necessary.[188] The smouldering conflict must burst into flames and it does in 9.34. Indeed, as Luz says in regard to the concluding part:

185. Luz, *Das Evangelium nach Matthäus*, II, pp. 34-49; see also Beare, *The Gospel according to Matthew*, p. 224; Davies and Allison, *A Critical and Exegetical Commentary on the Gospel according to Saint Matthew*, II, p. 107.

186. Patte, *The Gospel according to Matthew*, p. 130.

187. Van Aarde, 'Die vertellersperspektief-analise', p. 72; *idem*, 'Narrative Criticism Applied to John 4:43-54', p. 102.

188. Cf. Goodman cited by Matera, 'The Plot of Matthew's Gospel', p. 239.

All the themes and most of the motifs in the previous section reappear in this final section. The theme of faith (9.22.28f.) takes up 8.10.13. The way the blind follow Jesus (9.27 cf. 19) reminds us of 8.18-27; 9.9. The scenery in this story (9.27) takes up that of 9.9f. Jesus' actions in the boat (8.25) correspond to the "sleeping" and "raising" of the girl (9.24). The title *kyrios* 9.28 picks up on the basic christological tenor of (8.2-25). The presence of the disciples (9.19) reminds us that 8.18-27; 9.8-15 are about the community. The crowd of people expresses again the fact that the evangelist is telling of Jesus' miracles in Israel (cf. in particular 8.1-17). The Pharisees' negative reaction 9.34 shows that Israel was divided over Jesus in 9.2-17. So the heading "Final miracle" [9.18-34] is not an embarrassing expression. The Pharisees' final no to Jesus is a significant result for the continuation (cf. 12.24!) of this part of the narrative.[189]

Introduction: The Controversy with the Disciples of John: Matthew 9.14-17. In this episode, a new group who were in confrontation with Jesus appears: the disciples of John. But although the group is new, the issues of the conflict remain the same. The disciples of John here (in contrast to Mt. 3.7-10) seem in fact to be part of the Jewish establishment. They *are apparently upholding* the interests and (old) values of the Pharisees rather than those of Jesus.[190] Gundry says that Matthew intends showing a progression from the scribes (9.1-8) to the Pharisees (9.9-13) to John's disciples (9.14-17).[191] As an introductory episode, it prepares the scene for 9.34, the outbreak of the conflict. But as part of the final section of the narrative, it forms a link with the previous episode in that both 9.11 and 9.14, broadly speaking, refer to ritual codes. Furthermore, the three analogies (that of the wedding guests [9.15], of the unshrunken patch on the old garment [9.16], and of the wine skins [9.17]), more or less finish what was said in the previous episodes. This pericope stresses two important points: the fact that the timing (and occasion) for ritual practices should be appropriate, and (because of Jesus' notion about the timing of the fasting) the total foreignness of Jesus' view and mission.

Jesus in his answer to the disciples of John on the question of fasting (9.14), is not against fasting as such,[192] or in a broader context: he is

---

189. Luz, *Das Evangelium nach Matthäus* II, pp. 49-50.

190. Cf. France, *Matthew*, p. 168; Luz, *Das Evangelium nach Matthäus* II, p. 47.

191. Gundry, *Matthew*, p. 169.

192. Cf. France, *Matthew*, p. 169; Patte, *The Gospel according to Matthew*, p. 130.

not against ritual prescriptions as such.[193] What his answer: 'How can the guests of the bridegroom mourn while he is with them?' (9.15) amounts to is that he was against a rigorous view of 'fasting purely for fasting's sake'. Jesus reveals a quite pragmatic attitude in his answer, using the analogy of the wedding guests. To him the ritual must suit the time and the occasion and vice versa. And while he was with his disciples, it was not a suitable time for mourning. Jesus refers to himself as the bridegroom and for that reason there should be joy on account of the things he has done. He had taken on the interests of the sinners and the disgraced. It was time for a feast. The disciples of John and the Pharisees had to realize that they (and the sinners) were still in the presence of the bridegroom. They were still in association with Jesus, who himself associated with tax collectors and sinners. Relating to 9.10, where he dines with sinners, here, in the analogy of the wedding, there is once again an association with sinners but this time at a wedding feast. The bridegroom brings mercy (9.13) and joy. This is not the time for weeping, but for mercy.[194]

The two analogies about the old and the new, indicate the total strangeness of Jesus' ministry. It is so radically new that it does not fit with the old. Not that what he does and teaches was not known: the Jewish leaders knew of mercy and forgiveness. The newness lies in the real consequences of his teachings and deeds. He breaks away from the old interpretations of what God desires. He brings forgiveness, healing and reinstallation into the community and mercy on earth (cf. 9.6). His attitude is different from the old one.[195] He sees the will of God as the manifestation of merciful acts. Old values (ideologies), ritual purity, forgiveness, mercy and fasting, must be adapted to new conditions and new interests; they are not there for their own sake (fasting for fasting's sake and mercy for mercy's sake), they must accommodate the interests of the underprivileged. This is how the link between the three sets of analogies is made. Furthermore, the newness lies in the *new time*,

193. See Davies and Allison, *A Critical and Exegetical Commentary on the Gospel according to Saint Matthew*, II, p. 115.

194. Cf. Patte, *The Gospel according to Matthew*, p. 130; see also Gundry Matthew, p. 169; Sand, *Das Evangelium nach Matthäus*, p. 199; Davies and Allison, *A Critical and Exegetical Commentary on the Gospel according to Saint Matthew*, II, pp. 107, 110; Harrington, *The Gospel of Matthew*, p. 129; Malina and Rohrbaugh, *Social-science Commentary on the Synoptic Gospels*, p. 83.

195. Patte, *The Gospel according to Matthew*, p. 131.

the time of doing;[196] the time of joy and mercy. Thus there is conflict between new interests and old values. These values do not have to be replaced but they need to be reinterpreted, or, to state it differently, dormant norms (forgiveness and mercy) have to be reaffirmed.[197] Matthew also emphasises in 9.17 that both old and new should be preserved. 'The emphasis is on discontinuity. But the importance of continuity is also voiced.'[198] As a result of the conflict with the Jewish leaders, these old values, which they pursued, had to be reinterpreted and they could not remain untouched. If there had been no conflict, these values might have been forgotten by the early Matthean community as well as by the Jewish leaders. Because of the conflict, even the readers' own interests have to be re-evaluated and changed to those of Jesus'. It can be said in the words of Harrington:

> The passage also provides an important perspective on how Matthew perceived the Christian movement with respect to Judaism. For him [Matthew] it was the way in which Judaism could be preserved (9:17). Its preservation could happen only if the program of 'mercy' was followed and not the program of '(Temple) sacrifice' (9.13).[199]

The Raising of the Ruler's Daughter and the Healing of a Woman: Matthew 9.18-26. In as far as the development of the conflict is concerned, not much that is new evolves from this episode which has much in common with the healing of the centurion's slave in 8.5-13. Only a few points will be dealt with: (1) the question of authority and stratification; (2) the survival of the woman; (3) the emerging of conflict with the crowd; (4) the potentially ongoing conflict.

Very little is said about the ruler who is one of the characters in this episode. We do not know from the Matthean version who he was or what position he occupied. He is only described as ἄρχων εἷς ('one of the rulers'; Mt. 9.18), which is a general term for an official or important person.[200] It would be difficult, from the scant evidence of this

196. Cf. Luz, *Das Evangelium nach Matthäus* II, p. 47.
197. Cf. Coser, *The Functions of Conflict*, p. 124 on the reaffirmation of norms as one of the functions of conflict; see above.
198. Davies and Allison, *A Critical and Exegetical Commentary on the Gospel according to Saint Matthew*, II, p. 112.
199. Harrington, *The Gospel of Matthew*, p. 129.
200. Cf. Schweizer, *The Good News according to Matthew*, p. 229; see also Luz, *Das Evangelium nach Matthäus*, II, p. 52; Davies and Allison, *A Critical and Exegetical Commentary on the Gospel according to Saint Matthew*, II, p. 125.

pericope, to place him in a specific class. Nevertheless, he would have been a person with authority, as the centurion in 8.5-13 was, belonging to the upper stratum of his society (whether as a ruler or as part of the retainer class). There is also no doubt that he would have been a Jew, for the flute players (musicians) were only employed in Jewish households as an intrinsic part of the Jewish mourning ritual (cf. 9.23).[201] It was this Jewish ruler (leader?), who bowed down in tribute to Jesus, thus acknowledging Jesus' authority and expressing his faith and confidence in Jesus' power. The fact that his daughter is described as being already dead, further emphasizes the absolute confidence the ruler had in Jesus. The faith of the ruler is magnified.[202] The bowing down in tribute could be seen as flouring the social customs (if we assume that Jesus belonged to the lower class, whether peasant or the artisan),[203] especially in that it was done by a Jew who held a position of authority. This could only have fanned the flames of the ongoing conflict between Jesus and the Jewish leaders.

But Jesus' authority not only extended over the lines of stratification, it also exceeded the borderline of life and death. His authority knows no limits, not even death.[204] His extended authority/power is even communicated by the fringe of his garment (cf. 9.20).[205] What both the raising of the dead girl and the healing of the woman demonstrates (or symbolizes), is that Jesus is interested in the lives of people. He is primarily interested in living people, no matter what their social status. This interest in the *lives* of people demonstrates why it was not the right time to mourn (cf. 9.15). The stretching out of his hand to the dead girl (as in 8.1-4), symbolizes his helping power (*helfende Macht*).[206] Without Jesus' help, the girl remains dead (both literally and figuratively).

201. See Schweizer, *The Good News according to Matthew*, p. 229; Davies and Allison, *A Critical and Exegetical Commentary on the Gospel according to Saint Matthew*, II, p. 131.

202. See Gundry, *Matthew*, p. 172; Davies and Allison, *A Critical and Exegetical Commentary on the Gospel according to Saint Matthew*, II, p. 124, 126-27; Hare, *Matthew*, p. 105.

203. Cf. Saldarini, *Pharisees, Scribes and Sadducees in Palestinian Society*, p. 44; see also the issue of stratification discussed in Chapter 3.

204. See Davies and Allison, *A Critical and Exegetical Commentary on the Gospel according to Saint Matthew*, II, p. 124.

205. See Patte, *The Gospel according to Matthew*, p. 132.

206. Cf. Luz, *Das Evangelium nach Matthäus*, II, p. 52.

The woman, in touching Jesus' garment in the hope of being cured, acts here on her own behalf. Hence pursuing one's own interests is not always only to be regarded as a negative attitude. The narrative clearly illustrates that without Jesus, she would have remained ill. Thus, for her own good and her own survival, she had to turn to Jesus and this is even regarded positively by Jesus. He saw this as an act of faith (cf. 9.22).[207] She had been in great distress for so many years. Being regarded as unclean, she had been forced to miss out on affection and contact, so vital for survival.[208] She revealed an unlimited trust in Jesus' power to help her and Jesus recognized this faith.[209] As Luz correctly says,

> The story becomes. . . a paradigm for Matthew's understanding of faith. *Faith is something active, a risk, unlimited trust in Jesus* (cf. 14.28f.). Jesus answers such risk taking and promises God's help (8.10.13; 9.29; 15.28). *From the point of view of the people faith is risked prayer*; God helps strengthen the unsure and weak human risk taking with his power (my emphasis).[210]

This πίστις of the woman, stands in sharp contrast with the ὀλιγοπιστία of the disciples in 8.26. Faith meant the correct understanding of Jesus' power and the courage and willingness to turn to Jesus in need. Jesus responded to people with this attitude (both the ruler and the woman) and he himself was prepared to become unclean on their behalf. The woman in touching Jesus made him ceremonially unclean (she was *haemorrhaging* due to a menstrual disorder; cf. Lev. 15.25-33), and Jesus' touching of the dead girl, made him unclean also.[211] By turning to Jesus the woman had the chance of a new life.

The crowd had so far supported Jesus' authority and power. Here (9.23) though for the first time, there is evidence of an emerging conflict between Jesus and the crowd. They troubled Jesus (τὸν ὄχλον

---

207. See also M. Hutter, 'Ein altorientalischer Bittgestus in Mt 9.20-22', *ZNW* 75 (1984), pp. 133-35 (135); Davies and Allison, *A Critical and Exegetical Commentary on the Gospel according to Saint Matthew*, II, p. 124.

208. Cf. Lenski, *Power and Privilege*, p. 38; see above.

209. Cf. Gnilka, *Das Matthäusevangelium*, p. 341.

210. Luz, *Das Evangelium nach Matthäus*, p. 53; see also V.K. Robbins, 'The Woman Who Touched Jesus' Garment: Socio-rhetorical Analysis of the Synoptic Accounts', *NTS* 33 (1987), pp. 502-15 (504).

211. Cf. France, *Matthew*, p. 170; see also Davies and Allison, *A Critical and Exegetical Commentary on the Gospel according to Saint Matthew* II, p. 128; Harrington, *The Gospel of Matthew*, p. 131; Hare, *Matthew*, p. 106.

θορυβούμενον). Although they subjected themselves to Jesus' command,[212] for the first time they doubted Jesus' power. At first they had acknowledged Jesus' authority, but in so doing had already sown the seed of more conflict. Here this becomes apparent and the initial question as to whether they will keep following (acknowledging) Jesus, becomes critical. For the first time there emerges some doubt as to the sincerity of their acknowledgment of Jesus' power. The question whether they will follow Jesus to the end is not (yet) answered, yet the seeds of rejection already lie just below the surface. Even acknowledgment contains with it the possibility of rejection, and thus the conflict will go on because of Jesus' choice of interests. Furthermore, because Jesus' message is delivered on earth (εἰς ὅλην τὴν γῆν) the potential for conflict remains ever present (see also below; 9.31).

Sand sees this pericope as drawing a parallel with the community of Matthew. It is connected with the death and resurrection of Jesus. Death is vindicated. Salvation has broken through. It is time to live.

The Healing of the Two Blind Men: Matthew 9.27-31. Luz calls this pericope 'very short and colourless', and we can agree with him.[213] There is little that is new at this point but two aspects of the conflict merit attention: (1) the acknowledgment of Jesus' authority receives a new dimension with the notion of Jesus as the son of David (υἱὸς Δαυίδ), which here features in a prominent role and prepares the way for the crowd's reaction in 9.33b; and (2) the seeds of disloyalty (and conflict) were already planted in the seemingly vigorous acknowledgment of Jesus' power by the two blind men.

For the first time in the narrative of Matthew 8 and 9 (but also in the Gospel as a whole) Jesus is portrayed as the healing messiah of Israel.[214] It is as if Matthew first had to substantiate his claim through the previous miracles and is here bringing it to its conclusion. He first describes Jesus' acts of healing and then goes on to connect them with the title *son of David*. Having now related the miracle stories, Matthew

212. Cf. Davies and Allison, *A Critical and Exegetical Commentary on the Gospel according to Saint Matthew*, II, p. 132.

213. Luz, *Das Evangelium nach Matthäus* II, p. 57; see also Davies and Allison, *A Critical and Exegetical Commentary on the Gospel according to Saint Matthew*, II, p. 133.

214. See D.C. Duling, 'The Therapeutic Son of David: An Element in Matthew's Christological Apologetic', *NTS* 24, (1978), pp. 392-410 (393).

can now present a corrective view of the messiah to that which was prevalent among the Jews and their leaders. There is no doubt that in this context the *son of David* refers to the *Messiah*. As Maier says,

> 'son of David' is the standard designation for messiah among the Pharisees, Sadducees and Zealots, that is to say, most of the Jewish parties . . . There is no more room for doubt, now that the term son of David has been used, that Jesus is being addressed here as messiah.[215]

The corrective view Matthew wanted to present is as Luz states,

> In contradistinction to the hope of Israel for a kingly messiah which Matthew takes up (chapter 1), this constitutes a correction: *in fact, Israel's messiah is the one who heals those of his people who are ill* (8.1-9.31) (my emphasis).[216]

Thus, the long expected messiah of Israel not only was part of the lineage of King David,[217] but with regard to the aspect of the newness of Jesus' ministry (9.16-17),[218] the son of David, or the messiah, also came primarily to heal. A *characteristic* of the messiah was to act mercifully.[219] His being identified as the son of David legitimized Jesus' position further. The blind men are made to acknowledge Jesus' legitimate position. An element of conflict lies in the fact that it was the *blind men* who showed this new perspective of Jesus' authority and not those who normally functioned in society as ideologists, that is, the intellectuals and the leaders of a particular society. In the words of Maier: 'It is Israel's poor, represented by the two wretched blind people, *who are first to dare* to address Jesus as messiah' (my emphasis).[220]

---

215. Maier, *Matthäus-Evangelium*, p. 314; see also W. Grundmann, *Das Evangelium nach Matthäus* (ThHK, I; Berlin: Evangelische Verlagsanstalt, 3rd edn, 1972), p. 277; Gnilka, *Das Matthäusevangelium*, p. 344; Sand, *Das Evangelium nach Matthäus*, p. 203; Patte, *The Gospel according to Matthew*, p. 133; Luz, *Das Evangelium nach Matthäus 2*, p. 58; Davies and Allison, *A Critical and Exegetical Commentary on the Gospel according to Saint Matthew*, II, p. 135.

216. Luz, *Das Evangelium nach Matthäus*, II, p. 60. I would, however, differ slightly here from Luz in that I do not see this corrective view as 'against' the kingly messiah, but rather as 'alongside' it. By this it can further support Jesus' position as the long expected messiah who was from the lineage of David.

217. Cf. Hahn, *Christologische Hoheitstitel*, pp. 273, 278; Gnilka, *Das Matthäusevangelium*, p. 344.

218. Cf. Patte, *The Gospel according to Matthew*, p. 133.

219. Cf. Gnilka, *Das Matthäusevangelium*, p. 345.

220. Maier, *Matthäus-Evangelium*, p. 314.

Therefore they address Jesus with ἐλέησον ἡμᾶς, υἱὸς Δαυίδ ('Have mercy on us, son of David!').

At this point a few remarks on Jesus as the son of David should be made. In order to give legitimacy to Jesus' position, Matthew takes up an old tradition. Not only was Jesus seen as a descendant of David (thus son of David; cf. Mt. 1.1), and therefore having the ascribed honour,[221] he was also essentially the therapeutic son of David.[222] Jesus heals as David's son. Davies and Allison,[223] drawing from the articles of Duling[224] and Chilton,[225] say that *ben Dāvid* is always used in the Old Testament with reference to Solomon, who was later renowned as a mighty healer, exorcist, and magician. Matthew knew the Jewish legends regarding Solomon's power and probably intended to present Jesus in the same light. In this way Jesus was not only descended from David, he was, like Solomon, a skilled healer.[226] This further justifies Jesus' position, and indirectly, the position of the Matthean community.

Another aspect to be addressed is the question of why Jesus so abruptly ordered the (healed) blind men to remain silent. Almost all the commentaries consulted regard this as a difficult question with no obvious answer.[227] This command to remain silent, as Gnilka says, has no christological implications, as it had in Mark.[228] But, what then was the reason? I would suggest that he (Jesus, as presented by Matthew) wished to illustrate something. This might not be all that convincing, but at least it is an attempt to explain such an order in terms of my conflict theory. I here take one of the categories of the theory of conflict.

---

221. Cf. Duling, 'Matthew's Plurisignificant "Son of David" in Social-science Perspective, p. 113; see also Van Aarde, 'Immanuel as die geïnkarneerde tora', p. 264; *idem, God-with-Us*, p. 64.

222. Cf. Duling, 'The Therapeutic Son of David', pp. 399, 410.

223. Davies and Allison, *A Critical and Exegetical Commentary on the Gospel according to Saint Matthew*, II, pp. 135-36.

224. D.C. Duling, 'Solomon, Exorcism, and the Son of David', *HTR* 68 (1975), pp. 235-52 (235).

225. B.D. Chilton, 'Jesus *Ben David*: Reflections on the *Davidsohnfrage*', *JSNT* 14 (1982), pp. 88-112 (97).

226. Cf. Davies and Allison, *A Critical and Exegetical Commentary on the Gospel according to Saint Matthew*, II, p. 136; see also Gundry, *Matthew*, p. 176.

227. Cf. Grundmann, *Das Evangelium nach Matthäus*, p. 278; Maier, *Matthäus-Evangelium*, p. 375; Gnilka, *Das Matthäusevangelium*, p. 345; Patte, *The Gospel according to Matthew*, p. 133; Luz, *Das Evangelium nach Matthäus 2*, p. 62.

228. Gnilka, *Das Matthäusevangelium*, p. 345.

Conflict is always open-ended (even never ending); the resolution of one conflict contains at the same time the seed for the next. Thus, Jesus' authority is acknowledged by the blind men, yet in their very loyalty lie the seeds of disloyalty and conflict. How does this happen?

The healing of the blind men, like that of the woman of the previous miracle, is a good example of faith. The blind men had the courage to act by calling on Jesus for help. Indeed through this Jesus recognized their faith. The blind men expressed their faith very strongly in the words: Ναί, κύριε ('Yes, Lord'). There is no doubt that they acknowledged and recognized Jesus' power and authority (like all the beneficiaries of Jesus' miracles). Indeed they had confidence in Jesus. Nevertheless, ironically, although they were able to physically see again, they remained spiritually blind.[229] Despite their strong recognition of Jesus, they disobeyed him and they did not respect Jesus' viewpoint. Their strong expression of loyalty, Ναί, κύριε ('Yes, Lord'), contained at the same time the seeds of disloyalty and disobedience. Jesus also had an authority that these men did not acknowledge, and they disobeyed him.[230] Therefore their report about Jesus, positive though it was, nevertheless failed to present him as he truly was. 'Despite their own words, *they do not perceive that the fundamental characteristic of his authority is that he is the manifestation of God's mercy. They do not [really] recognize the radical newness of God's manifestation in him*' (my emphasis).[231] Therefore simultaneously their loyalty was countered by disloyalty and blindness with regard to what Jesus stood for. Therefore they were also in confrontation with Jesus in spite of being marginalized themselves. To be cured of blindness means (metaphorically speaking) more than just being able to see again. It means being able to 'see' Jesus' real purpose. Jesus opened the eyes of those who believed, but believing does not end there: it means clearly recognizing Jesus' mercy, not only for one's own benefit but also for the sake of all the others in need. The disobedience of the cured blind men shows that even first-hand observation or experience of the supernatural does not necessarily guarantee faithful discipleship.[232]

Finally, as in the previous episode, Jesus' actions were broadcast

229. Cf. Maier, *Matthäus-Evangelium*, p. 315.

230. Cf. Patte, *The Gospel according to Matthew*, p. 134.

231. Patte, *The Gospel according to Matthew*, p. 134.

232. See also Davies and Allison, *A Critical and Exegetical Commentary on the Gospel according to Saint Matthew*, II, p, 138.

throughout all that region (ἐν ὅλη τῇ γῇ ἐκείνη; cf. 9.31; see also 9.26). Because Jesus' message, actions, and viewpoint are narrated everywhere, the possibility of conflict going on beyond the episode itself, is increased (as we also saw in the episode on the healing of the Gadarene demoniacs in 8.28–9.1). Wherever Jesus takes the interests of the marginalized even 'throughout all the earth', *conflict is likely to erupt, not only with his opponents, but also with his disciples* (8.21), *the* (at first acknowledging) *crowd* (9.23, 25) *and even the beneficiaries or marginalized* (9.31).

The Healing of a Dumb Man: Matthew 9.32-33a. This episode is linked to the previous episode by αὐτῶν δὲ ἐξερχομένων ('While they were going out. . . '; 9.32). In fact, blindness and dumbness are normally tied together.[233] Therefore, as with the previous miracle, dumbness can be viewed both physically and metaphorically: the dumb man, after being healed, not only is able to speak (about the great deeds of Jesus), but is now without sin (possessed by a devil), since the devil had been exorcised. This episode prepares the reader for the reaction of the crowd and the Pharisees. It serves to sharpen the memories, for in this small episode almost all the previous elements are present: Jesus' willingness to heal the sick, exorcising demons and thus taking away sin (demon possessedness was a sign of evil), and it leads to a clear understanding of the reaction.

The Closing Episode: Matthew 9.33b-35. This closing episode comprises three parts: the twofold reaction of the crowd (9.33b) and the Pharisees (9.34), and a summary remark in 9.35.

The crowd responded by being surprised (ἐθαύμασαν), they were amazed that what Jesus had accomplished could be possible in Israel (that is, amongst the Jews). What Jesus had done, had no parallel. As Maier says,

> Even according to the opinion of Jewish historians, Jesus was the greatest prophetic figure since around 450 BCE, that is since the time of Malachai, after whom Israel experienced a time without prophets. Jesus' sermons and mighty deeds were really without parallel.[234]

Their expectations (as reflected at the beginning of the story) have

---

233. Cf. Schweizer, *The Good News according to Matthew*, p. 231.
234. Maier, *Matthäus-Evangelium*, p. 317.

been met: Jesus really has more authority than anyone else in Israel. Their response in 9.33b is overwhelmingly positive.

But, despite this positive reaction, which surely must have further increased the conflict with the Pharisees (as it did in 9.34) because the crowd once again did not recognize the authority of their leaders but that of Jesus, there still remains some doubt regarding the crowd. The initial question as to whether or not they will follow Jesus (see above), is still not answered. Their being amazed, is still neither faith, fellowship (discipleship), nor an unconditional choice for the interests and position of Jesus. They are still sitting on the fence. In my discussion on the causality of the text, I will return to this aspect again. The reaction of the crowd has great propaganda value for the readers (the Matthean community), but the possibility for conflict between them and Jesus remains wide open. Their positive reaction simultaneously contains the possible seed of their (later) rejection (as we have already seen in 9.23, 25). The words of Luz sums it up: 'The crowd would not understand any more than their (the miracles) outward facade. *The deep dimension and the ability of Jesus' miracles to reach into one's life would remain hidden from them*' (my emphasis).[235]

With the reaction of the Pharisees as seen from Mt. 9.34: οἱ δὲ Φαρισαῖοι ἔλεγον, ἐν τῷ ἄρχοντι τῶν δαιμονίων ἐκβάλλει τὰ δαιμόνια ('But the Pharisees said, "It is by the prince of demons that he drives out demons"'), the narrative of Matthew 8 and 9 comes to a necessary and inevitable end.[236]

For the first time in the Gospel, the conflict, which was first latent, then manifest, comes to a head in a clear outburst of open enmity. Instead of the Pharisees rejoicing in what Jesus had done, they rejected him and everything he stood for. They chose against him because they could not reconcile their interests as leaders (upper class) with those of Jesus, who identified himself with the interests of the lower classes. And in order to legitimate their own position, they labelled Jesus as himself

---

235. Luz, *Das Evangelium nach Matthäus*, p. 63.

236. France (*Matthew*, p. 174) and Luz (*Das Evangelium nach Matthäus* II, p. 9) regard this as the climax of the narrative. I, however, regard the conflict as part of the whole and therefore there is no clear climax. Nevertheless, I will view 9.34 as an inevitable outcome, because everything leads to this point. I see it rather as the termination of the conflict in Matthew 8 and 9 (see also Chapter 5, the section on *The Ongoing Potential of Conflict*).

being possessed by the demon.[237] Like the accusations of blasphemy in 9.3, this sanction acted to strengthen their own position.

The whole narrative ends with 9.35 (following Beare and Luz[238]), which is an almost *verbatim* repetition of the words of 4.23. This 'inclusio', which is typical of Matthew's style,[239] brings together the two great intervening sections: the sermon on the mount and the miracle stories of Matthew 8 and 9. At the same time it concludes the description of what Jesus represented. It places Matthew 8 and 9 in the broader context of the Gospel as a whole and thus also serves to emphasize the place of the conflict of these two chapters within the Gospel. Furthermore, it links the threefold nature of his ministry: teaching, preaching and healing under one heading: that of mercy and pity with those in need. By this, Jesus' whole being, as presented in the sermon on the mount (in his teaching and preaching) and by his acts (in his healings), serves as an outstanding cause for the conflict with the Jewish leaders. This verse (9.35) serves as a last (and one of the strongest) ideological legitimizations (and re-affirmations) of Jesus' position, for it puts Jesus' view into a broader context.

Causality in the Text

I included the element of causality as part of the definition of a plot. Unlike Crane[240] and Rimmon-Kenan,[241] who only place emphasis on the temporal succession of the plot as a minimum requirement for a group of events to form a story, I argue that the logical succession of events also has to be addressed. In line with the almost legendary statement of Forster:

> We have defined a story as a narrative of events arranged in their time-sequence. A plot is also a narrative of events, the emphasis falling on causality. 'The king died and the queen died' is a story. 'The king died, and then the queen died of grief' is a plot. The time-sequence is preserved, but the sense of causality overshadows it.[242]

237. For more on 'labelling', see the work of Malina and Neyrey, *Calling Jesus Names*.

238. Beare, *The Gospel according to Matthew*, p. 237; Luz, *Das Evangelium nach Matthäus*, II, p. 64.

239. Cf. Luz, *Das Evangelium nach Matthäus*, I, pp. 21-22.

240. Crane, 'The Concept of Plot', p. 141.

241. Rimmon-Kenan, *Narrative Fiction*, p. 18.

242. Forster, 'The Plot', p. 201.

In a story we ask: '... and then?'; in a plot we ask 'why?'.[243] We agree
with Bremond who states: 'With the absence of integration within the
unit of an event, one cannot speak of a narrative; then there is only
chronology, the wording of a series of facts without cohesion'.[244]

I have already dealt with the temporal (chronological) aspect of the
plot of Matthew 8 and 9 in considerable detail (see above). I want now
to deal with the issue of causality on the basis of the sequential model
of Bremond, which quite logically links up with and explicates the last
category of our conflict theory, that is, that of the ever present potential of conflict in any society or situation (see above). Why, then, are the
events arranged the way they are?

I will begin with the following answer: the events (in Mt. 8 and 9)
are arranged in such a way as to create both improvement *and* deterioration in the relationships of the characters, that is both an equilibrium *and* a disequilibrium. They are arranged thus in order to create
conflicting interests (or conflict). Even an improvement is *at the same
time* a deterioration, for any improvement in the interests of one
group is *at the same time* a deterioration of the interests of another.
And that is why conflict is present in the text of Matthew 8 and 9.

The model Bremond constructed was indeed more logically than
temporally orientated.[245] Basic to each narrative is the *function* or
process of events.[246] Each process has three elementary stages: As
Bremond says,

a. A function that in the form of a to-be-followed procedure, or a
    to-be-foreseen event, unlocks the *possibility* of the process;
b. a function that in the form of an actual procedure or event,
    translates this virtuality into *reality*;
c. a function that in the form of an achieved result, concludes the
    process (my emphasis).[247]

These stages, however, do not necessarily have to follow each other:

243. Cf. Forster, 'The Plot', p. 221; see also M.A. Powell, *What is Narrative
Criticism?* (Minneapolis: Fortress Press, 1990), p. 40.
244. Bremond, 'De Logica van de Narratieve Mogenlijkheden', p. 186.
245. Bremond, 'De Logica van de Narratieve Mogenlijkheden', p. 183; see also
Bal, *De Theorie van Vertellen en Verhalen*, pp. 27-28; Rimmon-Kenan, *Narrative
Fiction*, p. 22; A.P. Brink, *Vertelkunde: 'n Inleiding tot die lees van verhalende
tekste* (Pretoria: Academica, 1987), p. 22.
246. Bremond, 'De Logica van de narratieve mogenlijkheden', p. 183.
247. Bremond, 'De Logica van de narratieve mogenlijkheden', p. 184.

they may or may not be actualized, and the process of actualization may or may not automatically lead to success. Bremond schematized this structure as:[248]

		The achieved result (for example: the success of the applied methods)
	Actualization (the process itself) (for example: methods followed to achieve the result)	The missed result (for example: the failure of the methods)
Virtuality (possibility) (for example: the to-be-achieved result)	The absence of actualization (for example: the will-lessness or obstruction to act)	

Placed in the context of Matthew 8 and 9 (along with the concepts of beginning, middle and end, as presented in the previous section), we could say that at the beginning, the expectations created and the purposes to be achieved (*virtuality*) are manifold: first and foremost (due to the nature of the miracle stories), the sick are to be cured and reintegrated into the community; secondly, the crowd, disciples, leaders and beneficiaries are all to be brought into line with Jesus' point of view (the interests and ideology of Jesus) and to acknowledge his authority as the son of David (that is, the messiah). Thirdly the latent conflict is shown eventually to develop into manifest conflict.

This process (with all its aspects) is indeed *actualized* by a variety of means: firstly by the stories of the healings themselves, secondly by the dialogues of Jesus (Mt. 8.3-4; 8.6-13; 8.18-22; 8.25-26; 8.28-32; 9.2-7; 9.14-17; 9.18-22; 9.27-30), thirdly by means of the calling and dining scene (Mt. 9.9-10) and fourthly by the scenes of controversy (Mt. 8.34; 9.3-7; 9.10-13; 9.14-15; 9.34) and the ideological legitimizations by the citations from the Scriptures as well as the summaries (Mt. 8.17; 9.13; [9.16-17]; 9.35).

Eventually, *only half the objectives are achieved*: the crowd acknowledges Jesus and the sick are cured. The disciples finally do go along with Jesus, but remain 'of little faith' and the beneficiaries are cured but a

---

248. Bremond, 'De Logica van de narratieve mogenlijkheden', p. 184; I shall use the translated terms of Rimmon-Kenan, *Narrative Fiction*, p. 22.

few remain in doubt (9.27-31). A few endeavours even *fail*, of which the persuasion of the leaders to accept Jesus' viewpoint stands out the most. Thus there are successes and also failures. This will become even more apparent as I proceed.

These elementary stages can all be combined into more complex ones:[249]

(1) Combination by enchainment: The outcome of one sequence amounts to the potential stage of the next. Or as Bremond says: '... the same event within the perspective of the same character, at the same time fulfills two distinct functions...'[250]

(2) Combination by embedding: different sequences could be inserted into one another.

(3) Combination by joining: *the same sequence of events have a dialectical outcome.*

The last combination (by joining) can be schematized as follows:[251]

To bring about harm vs To-be-committed crime
↓ ↓
Aggression-process vs The committing of the crime
↓ ↓
Inflicted harm vs The crime committed = fact asking for satisfaction

Bremond continues,

> The vs (versus) sign, that here combines the two series, indicates that one and the same event from the perspective of an actor 'A', fulfils a function 'a', and seen from the perspective of 'B', a function 'b'... The distinction comes... between the area of action of an aggressor and that of a law-enforcer, within whose perspective such aggression amounts to the committing of a crime.[252]

But to Bremond all sequences in a narrative cycle can be divided into two fundamental types: *improvement and/or deterioration.*[253] Rimmon-Kenan says that an improvement sequence begins with disequilibrium and finally establishes equilibrium.[254] This can be the end of the story,

249. Cf. Bremond, 'De Logica van de narratieve mogenlijkheden', pp. 184-86; we will use the translated terms of Rimmon-Kenan, *Narrative Fiction*, p. 23.

250. Bremond, 'De Logica van de narratieve mogenlijkheden', p. 185; see also Rimmon-Kenan, *Narrative Fiction*, p. 23.

251. Cf. Bremond, 'De Logica van de narratieve mogenlijkheden', p. 186.

252. Bremond, 'De Logica van de narratieve mogenlijkheden', p. 186.

253. Bremond, 'De Logica van de narratieve mogenlijkheden', p. 187.

254. Rimmon-Kenan, *Narrative Fiction*, p. 27.

but when it is not, the equilibrium is disturbed and a process of deterioration follows. These two important sequences can also be combined into the above-mentioned complex sequences of enchainment, embedding and joining. However, I am here only interested in the combination of *joining* the sequences of improvement and deterioration because it has useful and relevant possibilities for the analysis of the logical relation of the events, and the logical outcome of Matthew 8 and 9.

The simultaneous joining of events that lead both to improvement and deterioration is only possible if the results are simultaneously different for two different actors whose interests are opposite. As Bremond says,

> But this simultaneousness. . . possibly means that the event has consequences for two actors simultaneously; actors who have *interests that are in opposition*: the deterioration of the fate of the one coincides with the improvement in the fate of the other (my emphasis).[255]

The link with conflict theory should be quite obvious and apparent. A basic assumption of conflict theory, as we have seen before, is that the pursuit of self-interests is basic to virtually all conflicts. There are two basic interest groups: those who want to retain the status quo versus those who want to pursue change. Thus, for the first group, change means a deterioration, while for the second it means an improvement. But this also works in reverse as the maintenance of the status quo is an improvement for one group, but a deterioration for those who pursue change (see Chapter 2 above on *Incompatible Interests* as a cause of conflict). This simultaneous joining of events is schematized by Bremond as follows:

> Possible improvement vs Possible deterioration
> Process of improvement vs Process of deterioration
> Achieved improvement vs Actual deterioration[256]

Depending on the perspective of the actor in question, the other actors (or characters) are qualified as allies/benefactors, opponents and so on. The qualification becomes the opposite when one moves from one perspective to the other. Thus, depending on the perspective of the beneficiaries or the Jewish leaders, Jesus becomes the ally/benefactor or the opponent. These actors (characters) are not to be confused with the characters of the narrative as a whole, for it does not concentrate on

---

255. Bremond, 'De Logica van de narratieve mogenlijkheden', p. 189.
256. Cf. Bremond, 'De Logica van de narratieve mogenlijkheden', p. 189.

the perspective of the 'hero' or the perspective of the author.[257]

Bremond's concepts of allies/benefactors and opponents comes close to the notion of characterization.

> *Character* is a figurative motive in the story part of a narrative text which obtains its contours through *characterization*.

> *Characterization* is the process by which the character is created through an interplay between the story, narrative text and narrative process on the one hand, and by literary conventions, language and reading processes on the other.[258]

Characters are 'life-like', they plan, decide, choose, react and feel like real people[259] and yet they need not be real.[260] They are constructs of the implied author to fulfil a particular role in the story.[261] As indicated in the above quotation from Johl, and as seen from Powell,[262] characterization is linked to character in that characterization is the *process* through which the implied author provides the implied reader with what is necessary to reconstruct a character from the narrative.[263]

257. Cf. Bremond, 'De Logica van de narratieve mogenlijkheden', p. 189.

258. J.H. Johl, 'Karakter/Karakterisering', in Cloete, *Literêre terme en teorië*, pp. 199-202 (199).

259. Cf. Culpepper, *Anatomy of the Fourth Gospel*, p. 101.

260. Cf. Bal, *De Theorie van Vertellen en Verhalen*, p. 88.

261. Cf. Powell, *What is Narrative Criticism?*, p. 51.

262. Powell, *What is Narrative Criticism?*, p. 52.

263. How are the characters built up? What techniques are used to present the characters? What sources are there to get to know them? Bal identifies two major sources of information: explicit information and implicit information (Bal, *De theorie van vertellen en verhalen*, pp. 96-98; see also Brink, *Vertelkunde*, pp. 76-79; Johl, 'Karakter/Karakterisering', p. 201). This corresponds with what Chatman calls the technique of telling and showing (Chatman, *Story and Discourse*, pp. 32-33; see also M.H. Abrams, *A Glossary of Literary Terms* (Fort Worth: Harcourt Brace, 5th edn, 1988), p. 23; Powell, *What is Narrative Criticism?*, pp. 52-53; S. Van Tilborg, *Al lezend stemmen horen* (Nijmegen: Katholieke Universiteit Nijmegen, 1994), p. 4. Bal's distinction between the two sources is presented more systematically by Brink: explicit information (or the technique of telling) is given by what an external narrator tells the reader about the character, by what other characters tell and what a character tells about him/herself (Brink, *Vertelkunde*, pp. 76-79). Implicit information (or the technique of showing) is information that the reader has to deduce from the characters' actions, speech, thoughts and values (cf. Powell, *What is Narrative Criticism?*, p. 52; see also Abrams, *A Glossary of Literary Terms*, pp. 23-24). To Brink implicit information is deduced from the characters' relations to other characters and their movements (Brink, *Vertelkunde*, p. 78).

Changes in the Sequence of Events
The question is: 'What progress has been made during the narrative?'
or *'What has changed* in or has been changed by the sequence of events
in Matthew 8 and 9?' I have limited myself to the perspectives of the
beneficiaries, the crowd, the disciples and the Jewish leaders because
the situations and insights of these characters (as far as latent or manifest conflict is concerned) undergo the most change if viewed them
from the point of the narrative as a whole.[264]

The Beneficiaries. In answering the question above I will start with
the most obvious, from the perspective of those who were favoured
and whose situation was improved by the sequence of events (in
accordance with the model of Bremond[265]): that is the needy, those who
were in need of help and whose handicaps were to be removed. They
are the leper, the Gentile centurion, the slave, the women (Peter's sick
mother-in-law, the woman who is haemorrhaging and the daughter of
the ruler), the paralytic, the tax collector, the two blind men and the
man who was dumb. They all are grouped together as the beneficiaries

---

264. Jesus not only functions as the so called 'protagonist' in the narrative, but in
terms of the model of Bremond, he acts as the benefactor of the beneficiaries. He is
the patron, or the supporter (as Bal, *De theorie van vertellen en verhalen*, p. 36
calls it; see also Malina, 'Patron and Client, pp. 2-32 on patron and client relationships in the synoptic theology, which the model of Bremond complements).
Jesus is the one (the subject) who makes things happen to others. There is indeed a
change in as far as his relations to the opponents are concerned. As I have repeatedly
indicated, he stood in conflict with the leaders and this conflict changed from latent to
manifest conflict on the side of Jesus in his repudiation of the scribes in 9.4 and the
Pharisees in 9.12-13. And because he took on the interests of the beneficiaries, he
stood as part of a stratified group against the opponents, the leaders. This corresponds with what we have seen from Dahrendorf (*Class and Class Conflict*, p. 126;
see Chapter 2 above on *Incompatible Interests*) that there can be only two opposing
groups in any particular conflict. If there is more than one party (as is the case in this
narrative), the parties tend to group together or 'form coalitions' but end up as two
opposing (stratified) groups. Bremond says that the model he was working out does
not represent one viewpoint; that of the 'hero' or that of the storyteller (Bremond, 'De
Logica van de narratieve mogenlijkheden', p. 189). Therefore here I will not focus
on Jesus' perspective in terms of the model of Bremond. However at the end I will
make a few comments about his role as 'hero' or 'protagonist' of the narrative who is
opposed to the Pharisees.
265. Bremond, 'De Logica van de narratieve mogenlijkheden', p. 190.

of Jesus' ministry and healing. The narrative begins with a disequilibrium (or an obstacle) in that they, either because of their illness,
or their background, have been demoted to the lowest strata of society,
the expendable or the unclean classes. *Possible improvement* would be
upward mobility, at least from the unclean/expendable class to the peasant class (from which they were excluded, being religiously unclean).
Whether they would have been able to move even further upwards on
the stratification ladder in an agrarian society remains to be seen. But
at least they would (inevitably in as far as conflict theory is concerned) have pursued such a possibility in order to improve their miserable position. In this situation they found Jesus (as the messiah) to be
their benefactor.

The *process of improvement* starts with Jesus' mercy. The means of
the process of improvement are Jesus' miracles and his calling of and
dining with the sinners (we have already seen before that all these
'marginalized' people can be, narratively speaking, grouped under the
collective character of 'the sinners'). These are all acts of mercy,
through which Jesus cleanses the sinners, thus allowing them to become part of the community again. He is willing to take up their interests, which immediately improves their situation. For in doing this
Jesus not only acts as an ally but also sociologically speaking, as the
'ideological legitimizer' for their possible pursuit of a better position.

The implication of them they becoming 'sons of Abraham' (Mt.
8.11) and the use of the phrase 'their sins were forgiven' (Mt. 9.5), can
be indications of the *achieved improvement* in their condition. Their
physical, religious and social needs have been addressed by Jesus as
the son of David (that is, the messiah). Due to this radical intervention
of the benefactor, their position has been fundamentally changed.
They were now also able (at least to some degree) to move upwards
on the stratification ladder. They could once again be admitted into society and into the community of the believers.

How are they 'built up' as a collective character? The fact that they
acknowledged Jesus' true authority is deduced from the *explicit* fact that
some of them fell down on their knees (Mt. 8.2; 9.2; 9.18) and *implicitly* from their humble requests to be cured (Mt. 8.2; 8.8). Furthermore, their acknowledgement of Jesus' authority is deduced *implicitly*
from their movements (actions; cf. Mt. 8.15; 9.21; 9.27). They immediately responded to Jesus (Mt. 9.9) and it is *explicitly* stated by Jesus
that they believed, thus acknowledging him (Mt. 8.10; 9.29).

The Crowds and the Disciples.[266] Regarding the situation of the crowds
there seems to be a similar development, namely a process of improvement from the beginning to the end. What improves is their acknowledgement of Jesus and his authority. At first their following of Jesus
seems to be only a movement from point 'a' to 'b'.[267] The process that
seems to be an improvement starts when Jesus reaches out to those in
need, gives examples and defines the implications of fellowship, calls
his followers, and dines with the sinners. In short, the process by which
Jesus improves the situation of the beneficiaries, is the same process
by which the crowds have to decide whether or not they want to
acknowledge him. Seemingly they do exactly that. Thus there seems to
be an improvement—they praise Jesus in 9.8, and in 9.33 they react
positively to his ministry. Yet this reaction remains relatively 'neutral',
or even doubtful if we take Mt. 9.23-24 (they laughed at Jesus) into
consideration. They were 'amazed', but it is not said that they 'understood' (9.33b). Carter calls it an openness in contrast to the response
of the Pharisees.[268] The expectations have been met, but not overwhelmingly. This is confirmed by the further development of the
collective character of the crowd in the rest of the Gospel.[269] In the passion the crowds eventually rejected Jesus' narratives (cf. Mt. 27.15ff.).
I agree with Carter that some ambivalence surrounds the crowds.[270]
The possibility of their positive (and negative) response to the mission
is still open.[271] This also confirms the assumption that there remains a
potential element of conflict between Jesus and the crowds, which was
not yet resolved in Matthew 8 and 9. Carter summarizes the role of the
crowds in the story of Matthew as:

---

266. By placing the crowds and the disciples together here does not mean that I
regard them as having the same narrative function. In fact they display very distinct
roles and characteristics in the narrative (cf. W. Carter, 'The Crowds in Matthew's
Gospel', *CBQ* 55.1 [1993], pp. 54-67 [58, 60, 62]. However, they are placed together here to fit into the model of Bremond in that, at this point in the narrative of
Matthew as a whole, they are both 'open ended' and undecided in terms of the conflict between Jesus and the Jewish leaders.

267. Cf. P.S. Minear, 'The Disciples and the Crowds in the Gospel of Matthew',
ATR Supplement Series III (1974), pp. 28-44 (30); see also Carter, 'The Crowds in
Matthew's Gospel', p. 59.

268. Carter, 'The Crowds in Matthew's Gospel', p. 60.

269. See Carter, 'The Crowds in Matthew's Gospel', pp. 60-64.

270. Carter, 'The Crowds in Matthew's Gospel', p. 58.

271. Cf. Carter, 'The Crowds in Matthew's Gospel', p. 61.

They are recipients of Jesus' compassionate ministry, a ministry to be continued by disciples. At times the *crowds exhibit some perception that God is at work in a special way in Jesus, yet they lack both the faith and understanding* manifested by the disciples and the hostility displayed by the Jewish leaders. At the end of the story, the crowds in Jerusalem display lack of faith and understanding as they participate in Jesus' death (my emphasis).[272]

The actions of the disciples are not really described in this narrative, although a few deductions can be made. They acted as Jesus' helpers and as exemplary characters of what fellowship means (cf. 8.18-27), that is, following Jesus wherever he went, in storms and even into pagan country. In Matthew 8 and 9, the disciples still remain indecisive but there is change as far as they are concerned, taking the Gospel as a whole. Whereas at first they were only onlookers and *listeners* (at the beginning of the Sermon on the Mount), they became Jesus' *partners* in Matthew 8 and 9 (cf. Mt. 8.23-27) and after Matthew 8 and 9, they were commissioned as the leaders themselves (cf. Mt. 10.5-14).[273] However, from Jesus' remark in Mt. 8.22 as a response to the disciple's delay following him and the remark about their little faith (8.26), we learn that they (still) failed to maintain their trust in Jesus and even as partners they were still indecisive in the same way as the crowds were. *There was a slumbering potential for ongoing conflict* (see Chapter 5 below).

The Jewish Leaders. The situation of the Jewish leaders changed dramatically in terms of latent and manifest conflict. The *possibility of a deterioration* in the relationship with Jesus, who from their perspective is the opponent, is already present at the beginning because of the reaction of the crowds (7.29), who perhaps, in exclusively acknowledging Jesus' authority, may cause the leaders to lose their control and support. The *process of deterioration* involves the same events as the process of improvement of the beneficiaries' position. The fact of Jesus healing and mingling with sinners and tax collectors, so putting into practice their own dormant values which they do not apply, intensifies the already existing conflict. This process which, viewed from the perspective of the beneficiaries, is a process of improvement is, at the same

---

272. Carter, 'The Crowds in Matthew's Gospel', p. 64.
273. Cf. Luz, 'Wundergeschichten von Mt 8–9', pp. 153-54; see also Chapter 1 on the discussion of Luz's work.

time, a process of deterioration when seen through the eyes of the leaders. This process causes them to react extremely negatively as in the situation in 9.34: ἐν τῷ ἄρχοντι τῶν δαιμονίων ἐκβάλλει τὰ δαιμόνια ('It is by the prince of demons that he drives out demons').

Jesus' mercy led to the improvement in the situation of the sinners, to the positive, but not overwhelming, response of the crowd and the disciples and simultaneously led to the deterioration of the relationship between Jesus and the Pharisees (as representatives of to the collective character 'the Jewish leaders'). In other words, the narrative of Matthew 8 and 9 ends in both an improvement *and* a deterioration, in equilibrium *and* disequilibrium. The equilibrium already contains in itself the seeds of conflict (as we have also seen in the individual pericopes and events of the demoniacs in Mt. 8.28-34, the reaction of the crowd in Mt. 9.23 and the healing of the two blind men). Thus, the equilibrium is at the same time a disequilibrium, which, deduced from the dimension of causality, is once again a strong indication of the deep rift between Jesus and the Pharisees. Even the narrative analysis, in following the model of logical sequences of Bremond, indicates that the conflict goes much deeper than what appears on the surface. Depending on the view of the actor(s), that is, depending on his/their interests, the sequence of events can be regarded as an improvement and/or a deterioration. Once again, but now from a narrative point of view, this confirms our initial assumption that the underlying conflict between Jesus and the leaders is based upon a difference in interests.

Clearly the Jewish leaders are the antagonists in the narrative. But, how are they built up as characters? In 7.29 they are *explicitly* depicted as having no authority which, as we have seen before was the 'spark' for the conflict between themselves and Jesus. Jesus is explicitly regarded by them as being blasphemous (9.3) and being from the devil (9.34). But this is more a reflection on the leaders themselves as being rather unreliable in their own judgment.[274] Their being unreliable (therefore 'evil') can be *implicitly* deduced from the request of the scribe to follow Jesus in 8.18. The scribe's enthusiasm remains debatable (see above). Furthermore, the leaders seem to be afraid of directly confronting Jesus in taking on the 'small ones', the disciples, rather than Jesus himself. They could be regarded as cowards (9.11). Lastly, as I have indicated above, they are viewed as being inconsistent

---

274. Cf. Bal, *De theorie van vertellen en verhalen*, p. 97; Powell, *What is Narrative Criticism?*, p. 53.

regarding their own values: they do not 'practice what they preach' (9.12-13), therefore they are false, thus 'evil'.

Jesus: Characterization and Focalization. Although not really part of the model of Bremond, attention must be given to the 'protagonist' of the narrative: Jesus. And because the protagonist of a narrative acts as the 'vehicle' for the narrator's ideological perspective,[275] I will pay considerable attention to him.

Jesus heals without precondition and contrary to conventions and expectations. Indeed, his dynamic attitude and actions bring him into opposition with the Jewish leaders. He persuades the reader to follow his view and interests. He is reliable and worthy of trust in his evaluation of others (cf. Mt. 8.10b; 8.26; 9.4; 9.22).

Jesus' character is *explicitly* described in 7.29 as one who has authority (in contrast to the scribes; other explicit remarks about Jesus made by other characters [Mt. 9.3; 9.11; 9.34] are, as we have seen, viewed as unreliable and regarded as reflecting the leaders themselves). By 'authority' I have already said that I mean being in a position where one is able to command. Jesus' character, however, is built up more by *implicit* aspects.

We learn from Jesus' actions (stretching out his hand) and speeches that where ever there was need, he was willing to help. This can be deduced from the following instances: In Mt. 8.3 he repeated the words of the leper: θέλω, καθαρίσθητι· ('I am willing, be clean!'). In 8.7 Jesus went with the centurion without any questions. He said: ἐγὼ ἐλθὼν θεραπεύσω αὐτόν ('I will go and heal him'). In the storm at sea, although repudiating the disciples for their little faith, Jesus nevertheless calmed down the storm and the sea (Mt. 8.26). He willingly forgave the paralytic and as a demonstration of his forgiveness, he healed him (Mt. 9.2-8). He willingly went along with the ruler to raise his daughter (Mt. 9.19). Furthermore, Jesus is presented as one who cares and encourages, not only concretely by his healings, but also by his words. To the paralytic he said encouragingly in 9.2c: θάρσει, τέκνον· ἀφίενταί σου αἱ ἁμαρτίαι ('Take heart, son; your sins are forgiven'). He encouraged the woman who suffered from haemorrhages (Mt. 9.20-22), with the same expression: θάρσει, θύγατερ· ἡ πίστις σου σέσωκέν σε ('"Take heart, daughter", he said, "your faith has healed you"'; Mt. 9.22b). In the short story of the healing of

275. Cf. Van Aarde, 'Narrative Criticism applied to John 4:43-54', p. 125.

the mother-in-law of Peter (Mt. 8.14-15) and in that of the healing of the dumb man (Mt. 9.32-33a), Jesus just stretched out his hand and healed them unquestioningly. Jesus was eager and willing to help, in fact, that is why he started his ministry and why he eventually came into conflict with the leaders.

From the thoughts of Jesus (as presented to us by the implied author), we learn of his ability to look through those he met. His evaluations are to be seen as reliable and trustworthy (in fact he *was* trustworthy as being one with authority). He was able to know whether or not there was faith and insight. He acknowledged those who had faith (Mt. 8.10; 9.2; 9.22; 9.28), but repudiated those who had little or no faith (Mt. 8.25; 9.4).

Of Jesus' values we know the following. Jesus came with a radical viewpoint: to take up the interests of the 'marginalized' people in society. His mercy knew no limitation. He was open to all. His boundless mercy was strengthened by his unlimited authority. He had authority (the ability to control) over illnesses, nature, demons, human-beings and even death. His mercy, like his authority, exceeded all conventions, purity laws and social codes. Jesus, messiah, Son of David (Mt. 9.27), gave new substance and new content to the dormant value: ἔλεος. When the blind men in 9.27 begged Jesus: ἐλέησον ἡμᾶς, υἱὸς Δαυίδ ('Have mercy on us, son of David'), it was already clear that the ἔλεος that was asked for meant a concrete reaching out to the sinners and the needy. When the blind men 'believed' in Jesus, they in fact understood this new perspective of Jesus (although they did not listen to him and remained silent).

Closely related to character and yet separate, is the matter of *focalization*.[276] Bal says, 'When events are reconstructed, it always happens from a particular view. One chooses a certain point of view, one sets

---

276. See Van Aarde, 'Die vertellersperspektief-analise', p. 60; Rimmon-Kenan, *Narrative Fiction*, p. 138; Bal, *De theorie van vertellen en verhalen*, pp. 108-109; Brink, *Vertelkunde*, p. 138; Venter, 'Fokalisasie', pp. 133-34; Van Eck, 'Galilee and Jerusalem in Mark's Story of Jesus', p. 105 for a discussion of the different terms, i.e. focalization and/or point-of-view. I do not make this sharp distinction and use these terms inter-changeably. I agree with Brink: 'Essentially it is not the name we give to it, but the fact that we take note there of that focalization can have different "contents" within the text, varying from the simply sensorial to the internal' (Brink, *Vertelkunde*, p. 139.

up a particular viewpoint, one presents from a specific angle.'[277] A narrative always manifests an 'idea'. Powell calls this the *evaluative point of view*:

> This refers to the norms, values, and general worldview that the implied author establishes as operative for the story. To put it in another way, evaluative point of view may be defined as the standards of judgement by which readers are led to evaluate the events, characters, and settings that comprise the story.[278]

Out of all these aspects, that is, those of time, causality, character and space, which all act as vehicles of an 'idea' that comprises a fundamental principle, the narrative point of view or 'focalized object' is derived.[279]

This corresponds with the theoretical possibility, as Bal[280] and Brink[281] view it, that the one who narrates and the one who looks (views) may be the same and fall together. All the characters and events are evaluated in terms of the perspective of the protagonist. Bal presents the same view: 'The reader always views alongside the character and will in principle be inclined to accept the view that is presented to him via that character'.[282] The reader is in a way 'manipulated' to associate and identify with (or even differ from) the protagonist of the Gospel, and thus also in Matthew 8 and 9 with Jesus.[283] Jesus is the subject of the focalization (the *focalizator* as Bal calls it). He is the point from which everything else is seen.

What, then, is or are the focalized object(s)?[284] When we speak of the 'object', we not only have to think in visual terms. Rimmon-Kenan, along with Genette, broadens the purely visual sense of focalization to

---

277. Bal, *De theorie van vertellen en verhalen*, p. 108; see also J. Van Luxemburg, M. Bal and W.G. Weststeijn, *Inleiding in de literatuurwetenschap* (Muiderberg: Coutinho, 2nd edn, 1982), p. 138.

278. Powell, *What is Narrative Criticism?*, p. 23.

279. Cf. Van Luxemburg, Bal and Wetsteijn, *Inleiding in de literatuurwetenschap*, p. 138; Bal, *De theorie van vertellen en verhalen*, p. 108.

280. Bal, *De theorie van vertellen en verhalen*, p. 109.

281. Brink, *Vertelkunde*, p. 138.

282. Bal, *De theorie van vertellen en verhalen*, p. 110; see also Van Luxemburg, Bal and Weststeijn, *Inleiding in de literatuurwetenschap*, p. 139.

283. Cf. Van Aarde, 'Narrative Criticism applied to John 4:43-54', p. 126.

284. Cf. Bal, *De theorie van vertellen en verhalen*, p. 112.

include cognitive, emotive and (especially) ideological orientation.[285] I therefore want to reformulate the question as 'What does Jesus focalize?' or 'What is his (ideological) point of view?' To answer these questions, I use the model of Bal, in order to get a clear picture of the focalizator:

> For a complete characterization of a character one must look at:
> 1.   How does it focalize? What is the attitude?
> 2.   What does it focalize? On what does it direct itself?
> 3.   By whom is this character focalized and how is it done?.[286]

Let us return to the character Jesus. Firstly then, how does Jesus focalize? What is the attitude? I can be very brief: Jesus is presented as someone who is really willing to reach out to the sick. This is the aim of his whole ministry. He *wanted* to help, he wished for the same attitude from his followers. By this, he challenged the leaders, whose dormant values were also to help, but they did not do so (Mt. 9.13).

Secondly, on what does Jesus focalize? What does he focus on? The answer is also clear: he focuses on the interests of those in need. But he also focuses on the other characters: the disciples, the crowd and the Jewish leaders. They all have to understand what true fellowship involves and the antagonists are challenged to change their views in accordance with those of Jesus.

Thirdly, who focalizes him? How do the other characters see Jesus? The beneficiaries all acknowledged him as having unlimited authority and power to heal, save, forgive and even raise the dead. Even the demons (8.29) acknowledged him as the 'son of God', thus having the authority to cast them out. He is acknowledged as the 'son of David' from whom they could receive mercy. But as we have seen before, the focalization of the Jewish leaders was seen to be unreliable. Therefore their viewing him as 'blasphemous' (9.3) and as 'from the devil' (9.34) in fact actualizes Jesus' point of view. This is also true of the disciples' little faith and when the people laugh at him on account of his remark that the dead girl of the ruler was just sleeping (9.24b). These focalizations of the other characters highlight the radicalness and foreignness (newness) of Jesus' view. Indeed, the focalization of the other

---

285. Rimmon-Kenan, *Narrative Fiction*, p. 71.

286. Bal, *De theorie van vertellen en verhalen*, p. 145; see also Van Luxemburg, Bal and Weststeijn, *Inleiding in de literatuurwetenschap*, p. 112.

characters, whether positive or negative, narratively supports the credibility and reliability of the focalization of the protagonist: Jesus.

The answer to the question: 'What does Jesus focalize?', is that the
intended reader is supposed to be persuaded to adopt Jesus' attitude
and to be sympathetic to his viewpoint; that is, to become willing and
eager to help those in need, regardless of their social background,
religious status or stratified position. In fact, being a follower of Jesus
means to act like Jesus does. It involves believing him, that is to willingly come to him and take on his perspective. It is being encouraged
by his touching and caring hand. Following Jesus can mean loneliness,
homelessness and getting involved in his conflict of interests as well. It
means the possibility of being rejected by your own people as well as
foreigners because of the choice made for the interests of the marginalized: the peasants, the unclean and degraded, and the expendable
classes. It means possible conflict because of a radically different perspective: the willingness to forgive other people on earth and above
all, even becoming involved in conflict *through being merciful*. Thus
Jesus' point of view is the legitimization of the plight and the interests
of the lowest classes of society. Mercy means advancing the interests
of the marginalized; this is what Jesus focalized on and this is what he
wishes his followers (and readers) to do also. As Gnilka says: 'Jesus
wants to liberate people from dehumanising prejudices.'[287] The
viewpoint of Jesus also implies a new community, a new family and a
new identity.

Conclusion

I have indicated that the plot of a narrative consists of a temporal and
causal element. The aspects of both the chronology and the cohesion
of events have been attended to. We analyzed Matthew 8 and 9 in terms
of beginning (Mt. 8.1-17), middle (Mt. 8.18–9.13) and end (Mt. 9.14-
35).

At the beginning, tension is created because the crowd viewed Jesus
as having more authority than their leaders (Mt. 7.29; 8.1). Latent
conflict is present: a contrast between Israel and the Gentiles becomes
apparent (Mt. 8.10). The beneficiaries (marginalized) call on Jesus as
Kyrie, acknowledging Jesus' authority, as in the rest of these miracle
stories. At the beginning, we have the first example of somebody who

287. Gnilka, *Das Matthäusevangelium*, p. 333.

voluntarily becomes (even more) marginalized (Mt. 8.5-13). The Gentile centurion himself was marginalized in being Gentile in a Jewish society. But, although he would have been part of the retainer class, he nevertheless took upon himself the interests of his sick slave, and so doing further 'voluntarily' marginalized himself. In Mt. 8.1 Jesus comes down *from* the mountain, the holy place. He now enters the 'world', the profane. An expectation is created at the beginning, as to what Jesus will do on earth, that is, in the profane place? Will he act mercifully? The first ideological legitimization of his position we find in Mt. 8.11 and again in 8.17.

In the middle section, the plot and the expectations already created are developed. The attitude of Jesus in intervening on behalf of the marginalized becomes even more explicit and apparent. It is combined with paraenetic material (Mt. 8.18-22; 9.2-8; 9.9-13). Jesus indeed forgives sins (9.6) acts mercifully (in the different miracle stories) and legitimates his stance by the citation from Hos. 6.6 (cf. Mt. 9.13). He indeed acts mercifully in the profane place, on earth (Mt. 9.6, 8).

Two other areas of conflict opened up: the challenging of the status quo of the demoniacs, and more particularly the conflict in economic interests between Jesus and the herdsmen and the city-dwellers (Mt. 9.33, 34). Furthermore, the disciples (of the Matthean community) are challenged to show faith as the marginalized do. On the community level they are challenged to become marginalized themselves as the real life disciples of Jesus. They have to realize that to follow Jesus can be 'dangerous' (i.e. containing the possibility of conflict) as the stilling of the storm illustrates (Mt. 8.23-27). Mt. 9.2-8 shows that not only God is able to forgive, but that through Jesus this is also possible for people on earth. Jesus forgives and by doing this he addresses the *illness* of the paralysed so that he (the paralysed) can again be taken into the community. Jesus' forgiveness and his acts of mercy challenge the dormant values of the Jewish leaders because they do not meet their own stated values (or, of course, those of Jesus and the Matthean community). They also regarded mercy as an important value, because after 70 CE they placed the emphasis on internal piety. Jesus, and through Jesus as their model, the Matthean community challenged the Jewish leaders' own values (cf. Mt. 9.13). Mt. 9.13 acts as one of the most important ideological legitimizations of his own view.

At the end of the narrative, the conflict comes to a manifest outburst in the reaction of the Pharisees in Mt. 9.34. The tension created the beginning now prevails. The Pharisees reject Jesus' authority totally. Jesus' merciful deeds enable the community to rejoice. It is a new time, a time likened to a wedding feast (Mt. 9.15). Jesus' position and interests are again legitimized by taking up the tradition of Jesus as the healing (therapeutic) Son of David, and by repeating the same words as in Mt. 4.23 in 9.35. This part of the 'inclusio' acts as the end of the miracle stories in Matthew 8 and 9.

The causality of the text is illustrated by applying the narrative model of Bremond which confirms the basic assumption that all conflicts are essentially conflicts of interests. The essential questions are. 'What changes occur during the narrative?', and 'Which relationships have changed?' Following the model of Bremond, particularly his concept of 'combination by joining', it was stated that the outcome of an event, can at the same time be both a success and a failure. The process of mercy has in the miracle stories the potential for both success *and* failure, for the improvement *and* deterioration of relationships *and* conflict. In fact the same events can lead to an improvement in one group's position and, at the same time, the deterioration in that of another group, particularly in as far as conflict is concerned. The merciful deeds of Jesus resulted dialectically in an improvement in the situation of the beneficiaries and a (deepening) deterioration of the relationship between Jesus and the Jewish leaders, in that the original latent conflict now became a manifest outburst. The narrative has both a 'happy' and a 'tragic' end.

Jesus is depicted as the model of the community. He is the one to follow. He acts unexpectedly, helps willingly and encourages the marginalized. His mercy and authority exceeds all limits. His attitude is one of willingness to help. He focuses on the weak. He challenges everyone—the Jewish leaders, the crowds, and the disciples—to do the same, to become involved and in the process marginalize themselves. He is viewed as the reliable *Kyrios*, the Son of man and the Son of David (the Messiah).

It is possible to schematize the joint sequences of improvement and deterioration as a logical (causal) sequence in Matthew 8 and 9, linked to some of the concepts we derived from the social location of the Matthean community, as follows.

The beneficiaries (the marginalized in terms of the text and social stratification) to be helped.	= The crowds and disciples to acknowledge the authority (i.e.the ability and position to control and command) of Jesus.	vs Potential (latent) conflict.
↓	↓	↓
Jesus' mercy in the miracle stories, dialogues, callings, dining with sinners.	= Exemplary stories and the miracles.	vs Jesus' mercy in the miracle stories, controversial dialogues, calling, dining with sinners.
↓	↓	↓
Healed and taken up in the community, i.e. moved upwards over stratification levels, given a new identity.	= Positive, but reserved (ambivalent) reaction of the crowds. Indecisive position (still) of the disciples. Potentiality of new conflict.	vs Manifest conflict. Total rejection of Jesus. Threat to their stratified position as retainers. Threat to their position to achieve unity within Judaism. Threat to their acquired authority from the Roman rulers.

Chapter 5

TYING UP THE LOOSE ENDS

Introduction

No community can or will ever be perfect, that is without conflict. Conflict was, is and always will be present as a creative force to make a society or community lively and real. Even the 'ugly face' of society plays a creative role. The community of Matthew was, in no way a 'utopian community'. It was very much involved in conflict. This conflict and its *dynamics* were what we wished to investigate.

In tying up the loose ends, our findings will be summarized under the headings of the categories already identified, namely: conflicting interests, survival, power and authority, changes and the ongoing potential of conflict. We will attempt here to put the findings of chs. 2, 3 and 4 into these categories. The contents of this chapter are not new therefore, but here everything is brought together.

Conflicting Interests

At the basis of this study lies the assumption that all conflicts are essentially those conflicts of class/group interests. Furthermore, all human activities are driven and motivated by the strive/drive principle for the maximizing of own interests. There is always a person/group wishing to rule or dominate and a subordinate person/group. They each serve different interests, the former to retain the status quo, the latter to pursue change.

The focus of this study was on the conflict between Jesus and the Jewish leaders as it unfolded in the plot of Matthew 8 and 9. We see this as a reflection of the conflict between the community of Matthew and formative Judaism. Jesus acted as the role-model both of and for the Matthean community after 70 CE. The conflict between the community and the Jewish leadership of this time (possibly the Academy at

Jamnia) was projected backwards to the time of the 'historical Jesus' and his contemporary adversaries, the leaders (as a collective nar-ratological character representing the Pharisees and the scribes). The Jewish leaders, as we have seen, belonged to the *retainer class* of their society. The community of Matthew regarded themselves as *marginal-ized* within this society. As we have shown in ch. 3, they comprised predominantly involuntarily marginalized people, being part of the urban non-elites, peasantry, unclean and expendable classes.

The Pharisees served the interests of the Roman rulers and opted in political and religious terms to maintain the status quo, in order to remain in control. In fact, they were perceived by Matthew as the dominant group within formative Judaism. Jesus was seen by Matthew as exalted by God himself because he was seen not as only being from the genealogy of David, but also as the therapeutic son of David (cf. Mt. 1.1-17; 9.27). He was therefore in a position to challenge the Jew-ish leaders, although he himself was from the lowest strata of society. This is applied to the community of Matthew in that they looked upon themselves as marginalized, but exalted by God. Therefore they saw themselves as being in a position to challenge the Jewish leaders who inturn regarded the community's existence as a challenge to their own position as retainers of the authorities. The Jewish leaders could have felt this to be a threat to their privileged status which they fiercely pro-tected their status.

Furthermore, the Matthean community was in the process of leav-ing the sphere of influence of formative Judaism, but because it was still part of Judaism, the conflict presented itself as very 'radical and peculiar', to use the words of Grundmann.[1] Grundmann, however, did not give a satisfactory explanation as to *why* the conflict was as intense as it was. We now know that this was because the community was still part of Judaism, and therefore its members were looked upon as rene-gades. Being still part of Judaism, they were very close to the Jewish leaders and yet they challenged their authority. Within the circle of Judaism, the community of Matthew was seen as a heretic group. In very intimate groups a sort of 'heresy hunting' often evolves because the so-called heretics claim loyalty from the group/society that they are still part of. This gave cause for a more intensified conflict. The leaders were losing influence, which is confirmed by the crowds' ac-knowledgement of Jesus' authority (Mt. 7.29; 8.1; 9.8; see also below)

---

1. Grundmann, *Das Evangelium nach Matthäus* (2nd ed.), p. 281.

and the addressing of Jesus as *Kyrie* (Mt. 8.2; 8.8; 8.25; 9.28; see also 9.18).

There were attempts from the academy at Jamnia to unify and reconcile the divided Jewish community after the disaster of the Jewish war. There was a wide spread need for tolerance and internal purity. Therefore Hos. 6.6: 'I desire mercy, not sacrifice' was stressed by Rabbi Yohanan ben Zakkai (see our discussion of the pericope of the calling of Matthew: Mt. 9.9-13 in ch. 4). However, it seems that the Jewish leaders did not measure up to their own standards (dormant values) and were challenged by the community of Matthew (cf. Mt. 9.13, the challenge of Jesus, as a representation of the community). The leaders did not meet the expectations of Jesus (or the community of Matthew); they failed to live up to their dormant values and they failed to pursue the value of tolerance. This is seen as a further intensification of the existing conflict.

The position of the Matthean community is confirmed by the choice Jesus made in the miracle stories to take up the *interests of the marginalized*. In fact, the miracle stories of Matthew are seen as exemplary stories to legitimize the point of view and identity of the community. Jesus deliberately chose the interests of the marginalized, or the 'beneficiaries' (in terms of the model of Bremond; see above). Therefore the Matthean community could easily identify with Jesus and also identify with the involuntarily marginalized of which they themselves were part.

The interests of the community and those of Jesus were 'ideologically legitimized' in a number of verses in Matthew 8 and 9. By this we mean that the interests of a group are transposed to a 'supra-individual' level which transcends the individual. In this way the individual or group can have 'a good conscience' about their interests which also intensifies conflict. This can be done by a number of means of which the traditionalization of values is one. Thus, Jesus (and the community) legitimizes his (their) interests by traditionalising his (their) position in citing verses from the 'Old Testament' (Mt. 8.17; 9.13) and by linking up with traditional figures (Abraham, Isaac and Jacob— Mt. 8.11; son of David—Mt. 9.27). Another way is claiming to be the true interpreter of the law and the tradition. As such Jesus challenged the presuppositions of the leaders with regard to illness and forgiveness (Mt. 9.6). The scribes did not live up to the expectation of forgiving people on earth. In other words, the scribes failed to pass on

God's forgiveness to the people, whereas Jesus indeed did (Mt. 9.6; see also the parable of the unmerciful servant in Mt. 18.21-35). Jesus' final legitimization of his position in Matthew 8 and 9 was the specific redactional phrase in Mt. 9.34.

The Jewish leaders legitimized their own interests by using the technique of labelling Jesus as 'blasphemous' (Mt. 9.3) and 'being from the devil' (Mt. 9.34). Of course, the implied reader is made to realize that this labelling is unreliable, and therefore conversely actually legitimizes the position of the protagonist.

Survival

One of the highest priorities of a human being is to survive. This means that he/she should have an adequate supply of basic needs (food and resources). In order to be in control of these, it is also necessary to have control of the surpluses. These are often acquired through being in a position of privilege which also means having access to power and authority (see also below). Those who have the possession of the limited resources, are constantly threatened by the possibility of losing them. It can therefore be said that survival depends on having and keeping power, privilege and prestige in order to remain in a position to control these basic resources. There is a need to be honoured for this. There is a fear of losing it. Support is necessary as well as new members. If all this is challenged, conflict is surely intensified. Therefore the Matthean community posed a threat to the Jewish leaders.

We have a number of examples from the text. The first, on the level of basic needs, is the example of the woman suffering from haemorrhaging (Mt. 9.20). She knew that in order to survive she had to go to Jesus for support and comfort. This also applies to the Matthean community. Also, there were the herdsmen and the city-dwellers (Mt. 8.33, 34) whose basic needs were threatened by Jesus' taking up the interests of the expendable classes, that is the demoniacs. Their survival, both in terms of basic needs and authority (to control the economic resources), was threatened, and thus the conflict intensified.

Power and Authority

A distinction is made between power and authority (although they often go together). By power, a person *enforces* his/her will on others, notwithstanding the position he/she holds. Often power is the ability one has to control scarce and surplus resources. Authority is more of a *relational term*, related to the *position* the person occupies to exercise this power.[2] Power is related more to the *individual*, whereas authority derives from a *social position*. In all societies or groups, there will always be people who are in a position of domination and those subordinate to them. Those who dominate tend to be more conservative, in that they wish to retain the status quo. Those a position of subordination often tend to be more revolutionary in that they pursue change (as we have also seen from the notion of interests). It is thus important to determine one's position in terms of domination or subordination. This is also true of the relationship between Jesus and the Jewish leaders. Jesus and the community of Matthew are, in fact, in a position of subordination because of their social status in terms of stratification, and the Pharisees and scribes (Jewish leaders) are in one of domination because of their status as retainers. Both, however, *claim* to be in control, thus *claim* to be in a position of domination. The Pharisees wished to remain in control (status quo). Jesus and the community wished to gain control (to bring about change). There indeed seem to be some 'politics' behind the conflict between Jesus and the Jewish leaders.

The Jewish leaders wished to remain in a position of control. They also wanted to be honoured. In fact, honour (like authority) in the first century Mediterranean world was perceived as a scarce resource. We read in the text of Matthew 8 and 9 of a few instances in which the crowds preferred to accept the authority of Jesus and not that of their own leaders (Mt. 7.29; 8.1; 9.8). There are also a number of instances where people fell down in tribute to Jesus (accepting his authority). One such person was from the retainer class himself (Mt. 9.18) and addressed Jesus as *Kyrie*, which is seen as a *hoheitsvolle Anrede*, in Luz's words (cf. Mt. 8.2; 8.6, 8; 8.25; 9.28).[3] At the end of the narrative the reader is led to believe that Jesus indeed had *more* authority than the leaders, which fulfilled the expectation created at the beginning (Mt. 7.29–8.1). The authority Jesus claimed to have exceeded that of the leaders in another way as well. It was an authority the leaders could never claim to have: Jesus had authority over illness (Mt. 8.2-4; 8.5-13; 8.14-15; 9.2-8; 9.20-22; 9.27-31; 9.32), he had it over the

2. Cf. Dahrendorf, *Class and Class Conflict*, p. 166; see the in-depth discussion in Chapter 2.

3. Luz, *Das Evangelium nach Matthäus*, II, p. 9.

forces of nature (Mt. 8.23-27), over the demons (evil forces; cf. Mt. 8.28-9.1) and even over death (Mt. 9.18-26). Jesus furthermore had *Vollmacht* to forgive sins on earth, that is to re-interpret the law and the tradition (Mt. 9.6; 9.13) in such a way that he could forgive uncon- ditionally before repentance was even asked for. The community, in identifying with Jesus claimed this sort of authority for themselves although they, in fact, were marginalized and belonged to the lower classes. This brought them into confrontation with the leaders, for it posed a serious threat to the authority they claimed as the retainers in the interests of the Roman rulers. They would never allow anyone from the lower classes of society to dominate them.

The situation depicted above is confirmed by Chapter 3 on the 'Social Location of the Matthean Community'. The Jewish leaders of the Jam- nian Academy filled the political and religious vacuum left as result of the Jewish war. They tried to reunite and rebuild (formative) Judaism. But the Matthean community, although still part of Judaism (they shared the same values; Mt. 9.13), was on its way out, out of the sphere of influence of the leaders (they broke the purity rules; Mt. 8.2-4; 9.11). This once again posed a threat to the position of the Jewish leaders, and thus there was intense conflict. They had almost lost their position of domination as far as the Matthean community was concerned.

The community was threatened as well. They were in the minority and clearly, although they claimed to have more authority, belonged to the lowest classes. The Pharisees' influence stretched beyond the possi- ble recruiting field of the community. They were under threat of being absorbed and persecuted by the leaders. They perceived themselves as being in a struggle for survival because they were the underdogs. The fact that the crowd, later on in the Gospel (in the passion narratives), indeed acknowledged the authority of the leaders contrary to their ini- tial (seemingly half-hearted) choice of Jesus, might confirm this. Fur- thermore, the community of Matthew pursued its own identity (see also below). They questioned the legitimacy of Jamnia by challenging the dormant values (forgiveness and mercy). They saw the leaders as not 'practising what they preached' (Mt. 9.6; 9.13).

Changes Brought About

We have seen that conflict is the creative force of change. The change manifests itself at the level of the community's identity, particularly in terms of values and boundaries.

Jesus became the 'master status' of the community of Matthew. All Jewish symbols became subordinate and were reinterpreted in terms of this master status. As Jews, the Torah played a significant role for them. But as a reformist movement they placed more emphasis on the weightier value of forgiveness (Mt. 9.6; 9.13), which, as we have seen before, acted also as the ideological legitimization of the Matthean community and their interests.

An important result of conflict is the re-assessment of a group's boundaries. Because the Matthean community evolved as the interest group for the marginalized people, they 'opened' their borders to become a mixed society, comprising all classes and all kinds of people (Gentiles and Jews). There are a number of references in the text to confirm this. In Mt. 8.11 'many from the east and the west' are incorporated into the tradition of Israel (Abraham, Isaac and Jacob). A Gentile centurion comes to Jesus for help (Mt. 8.5-13). Jesus issues an open invitation to all classes (to a scribe as part of the retainer class) to follow him, as long as they are willing to take up his stand (Mt. 8.18-22; see also my discussion of this particular pericope in Chapter 4, in particular the notion of the invitation). Jesus enters into Gentile country (Mt. 8.28–9.1). He rejects the claim of the scribes that only God may forgive, which made it impossible on 'doctrinal' grounds for people to forgive each other (Mt. 9.2-8). Jesus not only calls the upright citizen to follow him, but also the despised and the outcast (Mt. 9.9). The 'tax collectors and sinners' as unfavoured people dined with Jesus which was a gesture of closeness and intimacy (Mt. 9.10). As part of formative Judaism, the eventual outcome of the conflict was that the community moved out of the sphere of Judaism. However, this was not completed in the time of Matthew (the author).

The Ongoing Potential of Conflict

I have identified a number of instances where conflict was present because of the difference in interests. These were not really part of the primary conflict between Jesus and the Jewish leaders or the plot as a whole, but we have seen that they had in them the potential for new conflict. Although one would narratologically speaking not expect any possible conflict between Jesus and the beneficiaries in the story, sociologically the potential is always present. We saw this from the episode of the healing of the demoniacs in that Jesus challenged the sphere of control (status quo) of the demoniacs (Mt. 8.28–9.1) in order to cure them. Furthermore he challenged the economic interests of the Gentile herdsmen and city-dwellers who in terms of their Gentile background would have been among the beneficiaries in the Gospel. There was also the potential rejection and disobedience (conflict?) by two other beneficiaries: the two blind men. They spread the news about their cure despite Jesus' command not to make it known (Mt. 9.27-31).

In this study I focused primarily on the conflict between Jesus and the Jewish leaders as a representation of the conflict between the Matthean community and their contemporary Jewish leaders. But what about the potential of inner-community conflict? There are those who regard the conflict in the Gospel of Matthew as being primarily a conflict within the Matthean community itself and *not* a conflict between the community and the 'synagogue across the street'.[4] But are these two views totally irreconcilable? I do not think they are, particularly if the theory of conflict is taken into consideration. This falls slightly outside the primary focus of this study and also outside the text on which we concentrated. In Matthew 8 and 9, as we have seen, the disciples do not yet feature very strongly, although there are some inferences in the plot about discipleship. For this reason I will only give a few basic guidelines here, which could and should be developed in studies to follow, either by myself or by others.

In terms of the so-called spiral of conflict, we have seen that in the outcome and resolution of one conflict lies the potential the next. Conflict evolves as a never-ending spiral. Furthermore, the positive outcome for one group may very well at the same time be seen as negative for another. Equilibrium for the one is disequilibrium for the other, or dialectically speaking equilibrium is at the same time a disequilibrium. This is supported sociologically by the conflict theories of Dahrendorf and narratologically by the causal theory of Bremond. We may therefore ask: Is the tragic and 'negative' way in which the conflict between Jesus and the Jewish leaders in Matthew 8 and 9 comes to an end (in terms of the negative response and total rejection; Mt. 9.34), and the tragic result of the conflict in the passion narratives (in terms of the crucifixion; Mt. 27.32-44) the end of the conflict? It

---

4.   Cf. Smith, *Augsburg Commentary on the New Testament: Matthew*, pp. 20-21; *idem*, 'Matthew's Message for Insiders: Charisma and Commandment in a First-century Community', *Int* 46.3 (1992), pp. 229-39 (231); see also the discussion on the *intra-muros* view in Chapter 3.

certainly cannot be, for the outcome of one conflict is at the same time the potential beginning of another. In our case this implies conflict within the community of Matthew itself. Sociologically speaking, we can imagine that this was also a very close-knit community because at they had a common enemy (the Jewish leaders). Therefore there could also have been intensified conflict as a result of this close contact. They could also have searched for heretics within their own ranks. This certainly is what Minear implies by his study on the false prophesy and hypocrisy in the Gospel of Matthew.[5] Within the community there were also members who were leaders in a position of domination and members in a position of subordination. Just as Jesus challenges the Jewish leaders to 'practice what they preach' and take up the interests of the marginalized (which they failed to do), he also challenges the disciples (and thus the leaders of the Matthean community) to do likewise. There remains in the community a need for tolerance, forgiveness and mercy, just as desperate as in formative Judaism.

Evidence of this potential conflict already comes to the surface in Mt. 8.21-22; 8.23-27. Although the narrative role of the protagonist as 'helper'[6] is developed very strongly in Matthew 8 and 9, the potential conflict is brought into the inner circle of disciples by Jesus repudiating the one disciple for first wanting to bury his father (Mt. 8.21), and other disciples for their 'little faith' (ὀλιγοπιστία; Mt. 8.26). We have seen that in the 'real life situation', the disciples were perceived to be marginalized themselves. In the context of the community they are, as the leaders (retainers) themselves, challenged to become 'voluntarily marginalized'. They must take care to remain faithful to the legacy of Jesus, in fostering the interests of the lowest classes in their own society and community. Will they really do this? We are led to doubt this by the repudiation of their 'little faith' which is a potential parallel to the opponents of Jesus.[7] To Kingsbury it is in the third part of the Gospel (Mt. 16.21–28.20) that the conflict Jesus experiences with disciples becomes more intense.[8] Kingsbury says: 'It has to do with the disciples' imperceptiveness, and at times resistance, to

5. P.S. Minear, 'False Prophesy and Hypocrisy in the Gospel of Matthew', in J. Gnilka (ed.), *Neues Testament und Kirche: Für Rudolph Schnackenburg* (Freiburg: Herder; 1974), pp. 76-93 (76).

6. Cf. Kingsbury, *Matthew as Story*, p.129.

7. Cf. Van Aarde, *God-with-Us*, p. 88.

8. Kingsbury, *Matthew as Story*, p. 130.

the notion that *servanthood is the essence of discipleship*' (my emphasis).[9] Influenced by Minear,[10] Garland says that the disciples as leaders in as far as Matthew 23 is concerned, are susceptible to the same spiritual cataracts that blinded the scribes and the Pharisees.[11] And as Van Aarde correctly indicates: 'To depict this darker side of the disciples, Matthew uses the same names for the disciples as those he has used elsewhere for the Jewish leaders. The most striking examples of this are the names ὑποκριταί (Mt. 7.5; 24.51) and ψευδοπροφηταί (Mt. 7:15, 22).'[12] Or as Minear says: 'Matthew speaks in 7.23 of the ἀνομία of the false Christian prophets and in 23.28 of the ἀνομία of Jewish scribes. *What was true of the one group was true of the other*' (my emphasis).[13]

If we take the so-called *spiral of conflict* into consideration the conflict in Matthew 8 and 9 went through the following phases: (1) The parties became *aware* of the latent conflict in that the crowd in Mt. 7.28–8.1 acknowledged that Jesus had more authority than their leaders. (2) The conflict *escalated* through the narrative in the different miracle stories. The conflict became manifest and open, especially in the narrative of the healing of the paralytic (Mt. 9.2-8), and in the narrative of the calling of Matthew (Mt. 9.9-13). The conflict was further intensified by the different ideological legitimations in Mt. 8.17; 9.13; 9.35. (3) Eventually the conflict *de-escalated* and (4) was *terminated* (these two phases fall together) in the resolution in Mt. 9.34, the reaction of the Pharisees. In this resolution, the potential of renewed conflict in the next chapter (Mt. 10) was already present in the inner circle of the disciples. In Mt. 10.1, 7-8, Jesus commissioned the disciples to preach and heal. The spiral had started all over again. This, however, falls beyond the focus of this work, but it opens a new possible field of study: what stages did the conflict in the whole Gospel go through? Kingsbury has done a narrative study on the development of the conflict in Matthew. A sociological study still remains to be done.

9.   Kingsbury, *Matthew as Story*, p. 130; see also p. 139.

10.   Minear, 'The Disciples and the Crowds in the Gospel of Matthew', p. 32.

11.   Garland, *The Intention of Matthew 23*, p. 38.

12.   Van Aarde, *Kultuurhistoriese agtergrond van die Nuwe Testament: Die eerste-eeuse mediterreense sosiale konteks*, pp. 88-89.

13.   Minear, 'False Prophesy and Hypocrisy in the Gospel of Matthew', p. 93; see also Van Aarde, *God-with-Us*, p. 89.

In compounding this, I dare to say that the resolution of the conflict between the Matthean community and the Jewish leaders is, at the same time, the beginning of an internal conflict between the implied author and the leaders of the community, in that the author challenges the community leaders to become voluntarily marginalized themselves, in line with the involuntarily marginalized composition of the rest of the community.

BIBLIOGRAPHY

Abrams, M.H., *A Glossary of Literary Terms* (Fort Worth: Harcourt Brace, 5th edn, 1988).

Achtemeier, P.J., 'Gospel Miracle Tradition and the Divine Man', *Int* 26 (1972), pp. 174-97.

Albricht, W.F. and C.S. Mann, *Matthew* (AB; Garden City, NY: Doubleday, 1971).

Angell, R.C., 'The Sociology of Human Conflict', in E.B. McNeil (ed.), *The Nature of Human Conflict* (Englewood Cliffs, NJ: Prentice–Hall, 1965), pp. 91-115.

Bal, M., *De theorie van vertellen en verhalen: Inleiding in de narratologie* (Muiderberg: Coutinho, 4th edn, 1986).

Balch, D.L. (ed.), *Social History of the Matthean Community: Cross-disciplinary Approaches* (Minneapolis: Fortress Press, 1991).

Bamberger, B.J., 'Tax Collector', in G.A. Buttrick (ed.), *The Interpreter's Dictionary of the Bible: An Illustrated Encyclopedia* (5 vols.; Nashville: Abingdon Press, 1962), IV, p. 522.

Bastin, M., 'Jesus Worked Miracles: Texts from Matthew 8', *LV* 39.2 (1984), pp. 131-39.

Bauer, D.R., *The Structure of Matthew's Gospel: A Study in Literary Design* (JSNTSup, 31, BiLiSe, 15; Sheffield: Almond Press, 1988).

—'The Major Characters of Matthew's Story', *Int* 46.4 (1992), pp. 357-67.

Beare, F.W., *The Gospel according to Matthew: A Commentary* (Oxford: Basil Blackwell, 1981).

Benkin, R.L., *Sociology: A Way of Seeing* (Belmont: Wadsworth, 1981).

Betz, H.D., 'The Early Christian Miracle Story: Some Observations on the Form Critical Problem', *Semeia* 11 (1978), pp. 69-81.

Bieder, K., 'Determinanten der interpersonellen Konfliktbewältigung' (DPhil dissertation; Hamburg: Universität Hamburg, 1988).

Blau, P.M., and J.E. Schwartz, *Crosscutting Social Circles: Testing a Macrostructural Theory of Intergroup Relations* (Orlando: Academic Press, 1984).

Boissevain, J., *Friends of Friends: Networks, Manipulators, and Coalitions* (New York: St Martin Press, 1974).

Borg, M.J., *Als met nieuwe ogen: De historische Jezus en waar het op aan komt in het geloof vandaag* (trans. P. Ros; Zoetermeer: Meinema, 1995).

Botha, J., 'Socio-historiese en sosiologiese interpretasie van die Nuwe Testament', *Koers* 54.4 (1989), pp. 480-508.

Botha, P.J.J., 'Greco–Roman Literacy as Setting for New Testament Writings', *Neot* 26.1 (1992), pp. 195-215.

Boskoff, A., *The Mosaic of Sociological Theory* (New York: Crowell, 1972).

Bremond, C., 'De Logica van de narratieve mogenlijkheden', in W.J.M. Bronswaer, D.W. Fokkema and E. Kunne-Ibsch (eds.), *Tekstboek algemene literatuurwetenschap* (Baarn: Ambo, 1977), pp. 183-207.

Brink, A.P., *Vertelkunde: 'n Inleiding tot die lees van verhalende tekste* (Pretoria: Academica, 1987).

Brown, C., *Miracles and the Critical Mind* (Grand Rapids: Eerdmans, 1984).

—'Synoptic Miracle Stories: A Jewish Religious and Social Setting', *Foundations & Facet Forum* 2.4 (1986), pp. 55-76.

Bryant, C.G.A., 'Social Stratification', in M. Mann (ed.), *The Macmillan Student Encyclopedia of Sociology* (London: Macmillan, 1983), p. 366.

Bultmann, R., *Glauben und Verstehen*, I (Tübingen: Mohr, 1958).

—'Zur Frage des Wunders', in Bultmann, *Glauben und Verstehen*, I, pp. 215-28.

—*Die Geschichte der synoptischen Tradition* (FRLANT, 29; Göttingen: Vandenhoech & Ruprecht, 7th edn, 1967).

Burger, C., 'Jesu Taten nach Matthäus 8 und 9', *ZTK* 70 (1973), pp. 272-87.

Burnett, F.W., 'Exposing the Anti-Jewish Ideology of Matthew's Implied Author: The Characterization of God as Father', *Semeia* 59 (1992), pp. 155-91.

Burton, J. (ed.), *Conflict: Human Needs Theory* (Houndmills: Macmillan, 1990).

Carney, T.F., *The Shape of the Past: Models and Antiquity* (Lawrence: Coronado Press, 1975).

Carson, D.A., 'The Jewish Leaders in Matthew's Gospel: A Reappraisal', *JETS* 25.2 (1982), pp. 161-74.

Carter, W., 'The Crowds in Matthew's Gospel', *CBQ* 55.1 (1993), pp. 54-67.

Chatman, S., *Story and Discourse: Narrative Structure in Fiction and Film* (Ithaca, NY: Cornell University Press, 1978).

Chilton, B.D., 'Jesus *Ben David*: Reflections on the *Davidsohnfrage*', *JSNT* 14 (1982), pp. 88-112.

Cloete, T.T. (ed.), *Literêre terme en teorië* (Pretoria: HAUM, 1992).

Cohen, S.J.D., 'The Significance of Yavneh: Pharisees, Rabbis, and the End of Jewish Sectarianism', *HUCA* 55 (1984), pp. 27-53.

Collins, R., *Conflict Sociology: Towards an Explanatory Science* (New York: Academic Press, 1975).

—*Three Sociological Traditions* (New York: Oxford University Press, 1985).

Collins, R., (ed.) *Three Sociological Traditions: Selected Readings* (New York: Oxford University Press, 1985).

Combrink, H.J.B., 'The Structure of the Gospel of Matthew as Narrative', *TynBul* 34 (1983), pp. 61-90.

—'Dissipelskap as die doen van God se wil in die wêreld', in J.H. Roberts *et al.*, *Teologie in konteks* (Halfway House: Orion, 1991), pp. 1-31.

—'Resente Matteusnavorsing in Suid-Afrika', *HTS* 50.1 and 2 (1994), pp. 169-93.

Coser, L.A., *The Functions of Conflict* (Glencoe: Free Press, 1956).

—'The Functions of Social Conflict', in A. Coser and B. Rosenberg (eds.), *Social Theory: A Book of Readings* (New York: Macmillan, 1957), pp. 232-36.

—'Social Conflict and the Theory of Social Change', *BrJ Social* 8 (1957), pp. 197-207.

—'Conflict: Social Aspects', in D.L. Sills (ed.), *International Encyclopedia of the Social Sciences* 3 (New York: Macmillan and Free Press, 1968), pp. 232-36.

Coser, L.A. and B. Rosenberg, (eds), *Social Theory: A Book of Readings* (New York: Macmillan, 1957).

Court, J.M., 'The Philosophy of the Synoptic Miracles' *JTS* 23.1 (1972), pp. 1-15.

Craffert, P.F., 'More on Models and Muddles in Social-scientific Interpretation of the New Testament: The *Sociological Fallacy* Reconsidered', *Neot* 26.1 (1992), pp. 217-39.

—Review of *Teologie in konteks* (*Halfway House: Orion*) by J.H. Roberts, W.S. Vorster, J.N. Vorster, and J.G. Van der Watt (eds.), *Religion & Theology* 1.1 (1994), pp. 105-108.

Craig, W.L., 'Colin Brown, Miracles and the Critical Mind: A Review Article', *JETS* 27.4 (1984), pp. 473-85.

Crane, R.S., 'The Concept of Plot', in R. Scholes (ed.), *Approaches to the Novel: Materials for a Poetics* (San Francisco: Chandler, rev. edn, 1966), pp. 233-43.

—'The Concept of Plot', in P. Stevick (ed.), *The Theory of the Novel* (New York: Free Press, 1967), pp. 141-45.

—'The Concept of Plot', in M.J. Hoffmann and P.O. Murphy (eds.), *Essentials of the Theory of Fiction* (Durham, NC: Duke University Press, 1988), pp. 131-42.

Crossan, J.D., *The Historical Jesus: The Life of a Mediterranean Jewish Peasant* (San Francisco: HarperCollins, 1991).

Culbertson, P., 'Changing Christian Images of the Pharisees', *ATR* 64.4 (1982), pp. 539-61.

Culpepper, R.A., *Anatomy of the Fourth Gospel: A Study in Literary Design* (Philadelphia: Fortress Press, 1983).

Dahrendorf, R., 'Towards a Theory of Social Conflict', *J Confl Res* 2.2 (1958), pp. 170-83.

—*Class and Class Conflict in Industrial Society* (Stanford: Stanford University Press, 1959).

—*Gesellschaft und Freiheit* (Munich: Piper, 1965).

—*Essays in the Theory of Society* (London: Routledge & Kegan Paul, 1968).

—'Out of Utopia', in R. Dahrendorf, *Essays in the Theory of Society* (London: Routledge & Kegan Paul, 1968), pp. 107-28.

—'In Praise of Thrasymachus', in *idem*, *Essays in the Theory of Society*, pp. 129-50.

—'On the Origins of Inequality Among Men', in *idem*, *Essays in the Theory of Society*, pp. 151-78.

—*Homo Sociologicus* (London: Routledge & Kegan Paul, 1968).

—*The Modern Social Conflict: An Essay on the Politics of Liberty* (London: Weidenfeld & Nicolson, 1988).

Davies, W.D., *The Setting of the Sermon on the Mount* (Cambridge: Cambridge University Press, 2nd edn, 1966).

Davies, W.D. and D.C. Allison, *A Critical and Exegetical Commentary on the Gospel according to Saint Matthew*. I. *Introduction and Commentary on Matthew I–VII* (Edinburgh: T. & T. Clark, 1988).

—*A Critical and Exegetical Commentary on the Gospel according to Saint Matthew*. II. *Commentary on Matthew VIII–XVIII* (Edinburgh: T. & T. Clark, 1991).

De Jager, H., and A.L. Mok, *Grondbeginselen der sociologie: Gezichtspunten en begrippen* (Leiden: Kroese, 1983).

Den Heyer, C.J., *Opnieuw: Wie is Jezus? Balans van 150 jaar onderzoek naar Jezus* (Zoetermeer: Meinema, 1996).

Dibelius, M., *Die Formgeschichte des Evangeliums* (Tübingen: Mohr, 6th edn, 1971).

Domeris, W.R., 'Social Scientific Study of Early Christian Churches: New Paradigms and Old Questions', in J. Mouton, A.G. Van Aarde and W.S. Vorster (eds.), *Paradigms and Progress in Theology* (HSRC Studies in Research Methodology, 5; Pretoria: HSRC, 1988), pp. 378-93.

Donaldson, T.L., 'The Law that "Hangs" (Mt. 22:40): Rabbinic Formulation and Matthean Social World', in D.J. Lull (ed.), SBLSP 1990 (Atlanta: Scholars Press, 1990), pp. 14-33.

Dormeyer, D., 'Analyse von Matthäus 8 und 9' (unpublished SNTS paper, 1991).

Doyle, B.R., 'A Concern of the Evangelist: Pharisees in Matthew 12', *AusBr* 34 (1986), pp. 17-34.

Druckman, D., B.J. Broome, and S.H. Korper, 'Value Differences and Conflict Resolution: Facilitation or Delinking?', *J Confl Res* 32.3 (1988), pp. 489-510.

Druckman, D., and K. Zechmeister, 'Conflict of Interest and Value Dissensus: Propositions in the Sociology of Conflict', *Human Relations* 26.4 (1973), pp. 449-66.

Duling, D.C., 'Solomon, Exorcism, and the Son of David', *HTR* 68 (1975), pp. 235-52.

—'The Therapeutic Son of David: An Element in Matthew's Christological Apologetic', *NTS* 24 (1978), pp. 392-410.

—'Matthew's Plurisignificant "Son of David" in Social-science Perspective: Kinship, Kingship, Magic, and Miracle', *BTB* 22.3 (1992), pp. 99-116.

—'Matthew and Marginality', in Lovering, SBLSP 1993 (Atlanta: Scholars Press), pp. 642-71.

Duling, D.C., and N. Perrin, *The New Testament: Proclamation and Parenesis, Myth and History* (Fort Worth: Harcourt Brace, 3rd edn, 1994).

Dunn, J.D.G., 'Pharisees, Sinners and Jesus', in J. Neusner *et al.*, *The Social World of Formative Christianity and Judaism: Essays in Tribute to Howard Clark Kee* (Philadelphia: Fortress Press, 1988), pp. 264-89.

—*The Parting of the Ways: Between Christianity and Judaism and their Significance for the Character of Christianity* (London: SCM, 1991).

Edwards, D.R., 'First Century Urban/Rural Relations in Lower Galilee: Exploring the Archaeological and Literary Evidence', in Lull, SBLSP 1988, pp. 169-82.

Elliott, J.H., 'Social-scientific Criticism of the New Testament: More on Methods and Models', *Semeia* 35 (1986), pp. 1-33.

—*A Home for the Homeless: A Social-scientific Criticism of 1 Peter: Its Situation and Strategy* (Minneapolis: Fortress Press, 1990).

—'Stages of the Jesus Movement: From Faction to Sect' (unpublished article, 1990).

—'Temple versus Household in Luke–Acts: A Contrast in Social Institutions', *HTS* 47.1 (1991), pp. 88-120.

—'Household and Meals versus the Temple Purity System: Patterns of Replication in Luke–Acts', *HTS* 47.2 (1991), pp. 386-99.

Engelbrecht, J., 'Wonders in die Nuwe Testament', *ThEv(SA)* 17.3 (1984), pp. 4-11.

—'Trends in Miracle Research', *Neot* 22 (1988), pp. 139-61.

Fiensy, D., *The Social History of Palestine in the Herodian Period: The Land is Mine* (Lewiston, NY: Edwin Mellen, 1991).

Fink, C.F., 'Some Conceptual Difficulties in the Theory of Social Conflict', *J Confl Res* 12.1 (1968), pp. 412-60.

Fisher, R.J., 'Needs Theory, Social Identity and an Eclectic Model of Conflict', in J. Burton (ed.), *Conflict: Human Needs Theory* (Houndmills: Macmillan, 1990), pp. 89-112.

Forster, E.M., 'The Plot', in Scholes, *Approaches to the Novel*, pp. 219-32.

—'Flat and Round Character', in Hoffmann and Murphy, *Essentials of the Theory of Fiction*, pp. 40-47.

France, R.T., *Matthew* (TNTC; Leicester: Inter Varsity, 1985).

Freyne, S., 'Query: Did Jesus Really Work Miracles?', *The Furrow* 26.5 (1975), pp. 283-86.

Funk, R.W., 'The Form of the New Testament Healing Miracle Story', *Semeia* 12 (1978), pp. 57-96.

Galtung, J., 'International Development in Human Perspective', in Burton, *Conflict*, pp. 301-35.

Garland, D.E., *The Intention of Matthew 23* (Leiden: Brill, 1979).

—*Reading Matthew: A Literary and Theological Commentary on the First Gospel* (Reading the New Testament Series; New York: Crossroad, 1993).

Geertz, C., 'From the Native's Point of View', in P. Rabinow and W.M. Sullivan (eds.), *Interpretive Social Science: A Reader* (Berkeley: University of California Press, 1979), pp. 225-41.

Gerhardsson, B., *The Mighty Acts of Jesus according to Matthew* (trans. R. Dewsnap; Lund: Gleerup, 1979).

Germani, G., *Marginality* (New Brunswick: Transaction, 1980).

Gnilka, J., *Das Matthäusevangelium*. I. *Kommentar zu Kap. 1,1–13,58* (HThK; Freiburg: Herder, 1986).

Goodblatt, D., 'The Place of the Pharisees in First Century Judaism: The State of the Debate', *JSJ* 20.1 (1989), pp. 12-30.

Gottwald, N.K. (ed.), *The Bible and Liberation: Political and Social Hermeneutics* (Maryknoll, NY: Orbis Books, 1983).

Greeven, H., 'Die Heilung des Gelähmten nach Matthäus', in J. Lange (ed.), *Das Matthäus-Evangelium* (WdF, 525; Darmstadt: Wissenschaftliche Buchgesellschaft, 1980), pp. 205-22.

Grundmann, W., *Das Evangelium nach Matthäus* (ThHK, I; Berlin: Evangelische Verlagsanstalt, 2nd edn, 1971).

—*Das Evangelium nach Matthäus* (ThHK, I; Berlin: Evangelische Verlagsanstalt, 3rd edn, 1972).

Gundry, R.H., *Matthew: A Commentary on his Literary and Theological Art* (Grand Rapids: Eerdmans, 1982).

Hahn, F., *Christologische Hoheitstitel: Ihre Geschichte im frühen Christentum* (Göttingen: Vandenhoeck & Ruprecht, 1974).

Haralambos, M., *Sociology: Themes and Perspectives* (Slough: University Tutorial Press, 1980).

Hare, D.R.A., *The Theme of Jewish Persecution of Christians in the Gospel according to St Matthew* (Cambridge: Cambridge University Press, 1967).

—*Matthew* (Interp.: A Bible Commentary for Teaching and Preaching; Louisville: John Knox, 1993).

Harrington, D.J., *The Gospel of Matthew* (Sacra Pagina, 1; Collegeville, MN: Liturgical Press, 1991).

Harris, O.G., 'The Social World of Early Christianity', *Lexington Theological Quarterly* 19.3 (1984), pp. 102-14.

Harris, W.V., *Ancient Literacy* (Cambridge, MA: Harvard University Press, 1989).

Hartin, P.J., 'The Pharisaic Roots of Jesus and the Early Church', *Neot* 21 (1987), pp. 113-24.

Hawthorn, T., 'The Gerasene Demoniac: A Diagnosis. Mark v.1-20. Luke viii. 26-29. (Matthew viii. 28-34)', *ET* 66 (1954), pp. 79-80.

Held, H.J., 'Matthew as Interpreter of the Miracle Stories', in G. Bornkamm, G. Barth and H.J. Held (eds.), *Tradition and Interpretation in Matthew* (trans. P. Scott; London: SCM, 1963), pp. 165-299.

Hengel, R. and M. Hengel, 'Die Heilung Jesu und medizinisches Denken', in A. Suhl (ed.), *Der Wunderbegriff im Neuen Testament* (Wdf, CCXCV; Darmstadt: Wissenschaftliche Buchgesellschaft, 1980), pp. 338-73.

Heyer, C.J. den, *Opniew: Wie is Jezus? Balans van 150 jaar onderzfoek naar Jezus* (Zoetermeer: Meinema, 1996).

Hill, D., 'On the Use and Meaning of Hosea vi.6 in Matthew's Gospel', *NTS* 24.7 (1977), pp. 107-19.

Hoffmann, M.J., and P.D. Murphy, (eds.), *Essentials of the Theory of Fiction* (Durham, NC: Duke University Press, 1988).

Holladay, C.H., *Theios Anér in Hellenistic Judaism: A Critique of the Use of this Category in New Testament Christology* (SBLDS, 40; Missoula, MT: Scholars Press, 1977).

Holmberg, B., *Sociology and the New Testament: An Appraisal* (Minneapolis: Fortress Press, 1990).

Honecker, M., *Das Recht des Menschen: Einführung in die evangelische Sozialethik* (Gütersloh: Gütersloher Verlagshaus, 1978).

Horsley, R.A., *Jesus and the Spiral of Violence: Popular Jewish Resistance in Roman Palestine* (San Francisco: Harper & Row, 1987).

—'What Has Galilee to Do with Jerusalem? Political Aspects of the Jesus Movement', *HTS* 52.1 (1996), pp. 88-104.

Hoult, T.F., *Dictionary of Modern Sociology* (Totowa: Littlefield, Adams, 1969).

Huber, W., and H.E. Tödt, *Menschenrechte: Perspektiven einer menschlichen Welt* (Munich: Chr Kaiser Verlag, 1988).

Hull, J.M., *Hellenistic Magic and the Synoptic Tradition* (London: SCM, 1974).

Hummel, R., *Die Auseinandersetzung zwischen Kirche und Judentum im Matthäusevangelium* (BEvTH, 33; Munich: Chr. Kaiser Verlag, 1966).

Hutter, M., 'Ein altorientalischer Bittgestus in Mt 9.20-22', *ZNW* 75 (1984), pp. 133-35.

Johl, J.H., 'Karakter/Karakterisering', in T.T. Cloete (ed.), *Literêre terme en teorië* (Pretoria: Haum, 1992), pp. 199-202.

Jordan, H., 'Was verstand das älteste Christentum unter Wunder?', in Suhl, *Der Wunderbegriff im Neuen Testament*, pp. 177-209.

Joubert, S.J., ''n Verruimende invalshoek tot die verlede? Die sosiaal-wetenskaplike benadering tot die Nuwe Testament', *HTS* 47.1 (1991), pp. 39-54.

—'Much Ado about Nothing? In Discussion with the Study of Evert-Jan Vledder: "Conflict in the Miracle Stories in Matthew 8 and 9: A Sociological and Exegetical Study"', *HTS* 51.1 (1995), pp. 245-53.

Judge, E.A., 'The Social Identity of the First Christians: A Question of Method in Religious History', *JRH* 11 (1980), pp. 201-17.

Kee, H.C., *Miracles in the Early Christian World: A Study in Socio-historical Method* (New Haven: Yale University Press, 1983).

—*Medicine, Miracle & Magic in New Testament Times* (Cambridge: Cambridge University Press, 1986).

—'The Transformation of the Synagogue after 70 CE: Its Import for Early Christianity', *NTS* 36 (1990), pp. 1-24.

Kingsbury, J.D., 'Observations on the "Miracle Chapter" of Matthew 8–9', *CBQ* 40 (1978), pp. 559-73.

—'The Developing Conflict between Jesus and the Jewish Leaders in Matthew's Gospel: A Literary-critical Study', *CBQ* 49 (1987), pp. 57-73.

—*Matthew as Story* (Philadelphia: Fortress Press, 2nd rev. edn, 1988).

—'On Following Jesus: The "Eager" Scribe and the "Reluctant" Disciple (Matthew 8.18-22)', *NTS* 34 (1988), pp. 45-59.

—'Conclusion: Analysis of a Conversation', in D.L. Balch (ed.), *Social History of the Matthean Community: Cross-disciplinary Approaches* (Minneapolis: Fortress Press, 1991), pp. 259-69.

—'The Plot of Matthew's Story', *Int* 46.4 (1992), pp. 347-56.

Klein, C., 'Hope in the Middle of the Storm (Bible Study Matt 8:23-27)', *LWF.D* 14.35 (1984), pp. 35-38.

Klostermann, E., *Das Matthäusevangelium* (HNT, 4; Tübingen: Mohr, 2nd edn, 1927).

Köster, H., 'One Jesus and Four Primitive Gospels' *HTR* 61 (1968), pp. 203-47.

—'Grundtypen und Kriterien frühchristlicher Glaubensbekenntnisse', in H. Köster and J.M. Robinson (eds.), *Entwicklungslinien durch die Welt des frühen Christentums* (Tübingen: Mohr, 1971).

Kriesberg, L., *The Sociology of Social Conflicts* (Englewood Cliffs, NJ: Prentice–Hall, 1973).

Lategan, B.C., 'Reading Matthew 8 and 9: A Response to Detlev Dormeyer' (unpublished SNTS paper, 1991).

Layendecker, L., 'Conflictsociologie', in L. Rademaker and H. Bergman (eds.), *Sociologische stromingen* (sl.: Het Spectrum, 1977).

Lehmann, K., 'Der hermeneutische Horison der historisch-kritischen Exegese', in J. Schreiner (ed.), *Einführung in die Methode der biblischen Exegese* (Würzburg: Echter, 1971), pp. 40-80.

Lenski, G.E., *Power and Privilege: A Theory of Social Stratification* (New York: McGraw–Hill, 1966).

—'A Theory of Inequality', in Collins, *Three Sociological Traditions: Selected Readings*, pp. 89-116.

Lenski, G.E., and J. Lenski, *Human Societies: Introduction to Macrosociology* (New York: McGraw–Hill, 1982).

Lohse, E., *Umwelt des Neuen Testaments* (Göttingen: Vandenhoeck & Ruprecht, 3rd edn, 1977).

Louw, J.P., 'The Structure of Mt 8:1-9:35', *Neot* 11 (1977), pp. 91-97.

Louw, J.P., and E.A. Nida, *Greek–English Lexicon of the New Testament Based on Semantic Domains,* I (New York: UBS, 1988).

Lovering, E.H. (ed.), SBLSP 1993 (Atlanta: Scholars Press, 1993).

Lull, D.L. (ed.), SBLSP 1988 (Atlanta: Scholars Press, 1988).

Luz, U., 'Die Jünger im Matthäusevangelium', *ZNW* 62 (1971), pp. 141-71.

—*Das Evangelium nach Matthäus. II. (Mt 1–7)* (EKK, I.1; Zürich: Benzinger Verlag, 1985).

—'Wundergeschichten von Mt 8–9', in G.F. Hawthorne and O. Betz (eds.), *Tradition and Interpretation in the New Testament: Essays in Honor of E. Earle Ellis for his 60th Birthday* (Grand Rapids: Eerdmans, 1987), pp. 149-65.

—*Das Evangelium nach Matthäus. I. (Mt 8–17)* (EKK, I.2; Zürich: Benzinger Verlag, 1990).

—'Der Antijudaismus im Matthäusevangelium als historisches und theologisches Problem: Eine Skizze', *EvTh* 53 (1993), pp. 310-27.

Mack, R., and R.C. Snyder, 'The Analysis of Social Conflict: Towards an Overview and Synthesis', *J Confl Res* 1.2 (1957), pp. 212-48.

Maier, G., *Matthäus-Evangelium*, I (Edition C–Bibel-Kommentar 1; Neuhausen-Stuttgart: Hänssler, 2nd edn, 1983).

Malina, B.J., *The New Testament World: Insights from Cultural Anthropology* (London: SCM, 1981).

—'The Social Sciences and Biblical Interpretation', in Gottwald, *The Bible and Liberation*, pp. 11-25.

—'Normative Dissonance and Christian Origins', *Semeia* 35 (1986), pp. 35-59.

—'Patron and Client: The Analogy behind Synoptic Theology', *Foundations & Facets Forum* 4.1 (1988), pp. 2-32.

—'A Conflict approach to Mark 7', *Foundations & Facets Forum* 4.3 (1988), pp. 3-30.

Malina, B.J., and J.H. Neyrey, *Calling Jesus Names: The Social Value of Labels in Matthew* (Sonoma, CA: Polebridge Press, 1988).

Malina, B.J., and R.L. Rohrbaugh, *Social-science Commentary on the Synoptic Gospels* (Minneapolis: Fortress Press, 1992).

Martin, R.P., 'The Pericope of the Healing the "Centurion's" Servant/Son (Matt 8:5-13 par. Luke 7:1-10): Some Exegetical Notes', in R.A. Guelch (ed.), *Unity and Diversity in New Testament Theology: Essays in Honor of George E. Ladd* (Grand Rapids: Eerdmans, 1978), pp. 14-22.

Marxsen, W., *Einleitung in das Neue Testament: Eine Einführung in ihre Probleme* (Gütersloh: Gütersloher Verlaghaus, 1964).

Matera, F.J., 'The Plot of Matthew's Gospel', *CBQ* 49 (1987), pp. 233-53.

McCaslin, K., *What the Bible Says about Miracles* (What the Bible Says Series; Joplin: College Press, 1988).

Meeks, W.A., *The First Urban Christians: The World of the Apostle of Paul* (New Haven: Yale University Press, 1983).

Meier, J.P., 'Antioch', in R.E. Brown and J.P. Meier (eds.), *Antioch and Rome: New Testament Cradles of Catholic Christianity* (London: Chapman, 1982), pp. 11-86.

Mellink, M.J., 'Cyrene', in G.A. Buttrick (ed.), *The Interpreter's Dictionary of the Bible: An Illustrated Encyclopedia* (5 vols.; Nashville: Abingdon Press, 1962), I, p. 754.

Ménégoz, E., 'Der biblische Wunderbegriff', in Suhl, *Der Wunderbegriff im Neuen Testament*, pp. 39-79.

Menoud, P-H., 'Die Bedeutung des Wunders nach dem Neuen Testament', in Suhl, *Der Wunderbegriff im Neuen Testament*, pp. 279-99.

Minear, P.S., 'The Disciples and the Crowds in the Gospel of Matthew', *ATR Supplement Series III* (1974), pp. 28-44.

—'False Prophesy and Hypocrisy in the Gospel of Matthew', in J. Gnilka (ed.), *Neues Testament und Kirche: Für Rudolph Schnackenburg* (Freiburg: Herder, 1974), pp. 76-93.

—*Matthew: The Teacher's Gospel* (New York: Pilgrim Press, 1982).

Moiser, J., 'The Structure of Matthew 8–9: A Suggestion', *ZNW* 76 (1985), pp. 117-18.

Mouton, J., A.G. Van Aarde, and W.S. Vorster, (eds.), *Paradigms and Progress in Theology* (HSRC Studies in Research Methodology, 5; Pretoria: HSRC, 1988).

Nader, L., and H.F. Todd, (eds.), *The Disputing Process: Law in Ten Societies* (New York: Columbia University Press, 1978).

Neusner, J., *From Politics to Piety: The Emergence of Pharisaic Judaism* (Englewood Cliffs, NJ: Prentice–Hall, 1973).

—*First-century Judaism in Crisis: Yohanan ben Zakkai and the Renaissance of Torah* (New York: Ktav, rev. edn, 1982).

—*Formative Judaism: Religious, Historical and Literary Studies* (BJSt 37; Chico: Scholars Press, 1982).

—'Josephus' Pharisees: A Complete Repertoire', in L.H. Feldman and G. Hata (eds.), *Josephus, Judaism, and Christianity* (Detroit: Wayne State University Press, 1987), pp. 274-92.

Neusner, J. *et al.*, *The Social World of Formative Christianity and Judaism: Essays in Tribute to Howard Clark Kee* (Philadelphia: Fortress Press, 1988).

Newman, B.M., and P.C. Stine, *A Translator's Handbook on the Gospel of Matthew* (London: UBS, 1988).

Osiek, C., 'The New Handmaid: The Bible and the Social Sciences', *TS* 50 (1989), pp. 260-78.

—'The Social Sciences and the Second Testament: Problems and Challenges', *BTB* 22.2 (1992), pp. 88-95.

Overman, J.A., 'Who Were the First Urban Christians? Urbanization in Galilee in the First Century', in Lull, SBLSP 1988, pp. 160-68.

—*Matthew's Gospel and Formative Judaism: The Social World of the Matthean Community* (Minneapolis: Fortress Press, 1990).

Pantle-Schieber, K., 'Anmerkungen zur Auseinandersetzung von ἐκκλησία und Judentum im Matthäusevangelium', *ZNW* 80 (1989), pp. 145-62.

Patte, D., *The Gospel according to Matthew: A Structural Commentary on Matthew's Faith* (Philadelphia: Fortress Press, 1987).

—' "Love Your Enemy"–"Woe to You, Scribes and Pharisees": The Need for a Semiotic Approach in New Testament Studies', in T.W. Jennings, Jr (ed.), *Text and Logos: The Humanistic Interpretation of the New Testament* (Atlanta: Scholars Press, 1990), pp. 81-96.

Petzke, G., 'Historizität und Bedeutsamkeit von Wunderberichten: Möglichkeiten und Grenzen des religionsgeschichtliche Vergleichs', in H.D. Betz and L. Schotroff (eds.), *Neues Testament und Christliche Existenz: Festschrift für H Braun* (Tübingen: Mohr, 1973), pp. 347-85.

Pfuhl, E.H., *The Deviance Process* (New York: Van Nostran, 1980).

Pilch, J.J., 'The Health Care System in Matthew: A Social Science Analysis', *BTB* 16.3 (1986), pp. 102-106.

—'Understanding Biblical Healing: Selecting the Appropriate Model', *BTB* 18.2 (1988), pp. 60-66.

—'Reading Matthew Anthropologically: Healing in Cultural Perspective', *Listening* 24 (1989), pp. 278-89.

—'Sickness and Healing in Luke–Acts', in J.N. Neyrey (ed.), *The Social World of Luke–Acts: Models for Interpretation* (Peabody, MA: Hendrickson, 1991), pp. 181-210.

—'Insights and Models for Understanding the Healing Activity of the Historical Jesus', in Lovering (ed.), SBLSP 1993, pp. 154-77.

Powell, J., 'Social Theory as Exegetical Tool', *Foundations & Facets Forum* 5.4 (1989), pp. 27-40.

Powell, M.A., *What is Narrative Criticism?* (Minneapolis: Fortress Press, 1990).

—'The Plot and Subplots of Matthew's Gospel', *NTS* 38 (1992), pp. 187-204.

—'Towards a Narrative-critical Understanding of Matthew', *Int* 46.4 (1992), pp. 341-46.

Praeder, S.M., 'Miracle Stories in Christian Antiquity: Some Narrative Elements', *Foundation & Facets Forum* 2.4 (1986), pp. 43-54.

Rimmon-Kenan, S., *Narrative Fiction: Contemporary Poetics* (London: Methuen, 1983).

Rivkin, E., *A Hidden Revolution: The Pharisees' Search for the Kingdom Within* (Nashville: Abingdon Press, 1978).

Rex, J., *Social Conflict: A Conceptual and Theoretical Analysis* (London: Longman, 1981).

Robbins, V.K., 'The Woman Who Touched Jesus' Garment: Socio-rhetorical Analysis of the Synoptic Accounts', *NTS* 33 (1987), pp. 502-15.

Rohrbaugh, R.L., 'Methodological Considerations in the Debate over the Social Class Status of Early Christians', *JAAR* 52.3 (1984), pp. 519-46.

—'Models and Muddles: Discussions of the Social Facet Seminar', *Foundation & Facet Forum* 3.2 (1987), pp. 23-33.

—'The City in the Second Testament', *BTB* 21.1 (1991), pp. 67-75.

—'Social Science and Literary Criticism: What is at Stake?', *HTS* 49.1 and 2 (1993), pp. 221-33.

—'The Social Location of the Markan Audience', *Int* 47.4 (1993), pp. 380-95.

—'The Social Location of the Markan Community' (unpublished article, 1993).

Rowland, C., 'Reading the New Testament Sociologically: An Introduction', *Theology* 88 (1985), pp. 358-64.

Saldarini, A.J., *Pharisees, Scribes and Sadducees in Palestinian Society: A Sociological Approach* (Wilmington, DE: Michael Glazier, 1988).

—'Political and Social Roles of the Pharisees and the Scribes in Galilee', in Lull (ed.), SBLSP 1988, pp. 200-209.

—'The Social Class of the Pharisees in Mark', in Neusner *et al.*, *The Social World of Formative Christianity and Judaism*, pp. 69-77.

–'The Gospel of Matthew and Jewish–Christian Conflict', in Balch, *Social History of the Matthean Community*, pp. 38-61.

—'Delegitimation of the Leaders in Matthew 23', *CBQ* 54 (1992), pp. 659-80.

Sand, A., *Das Gesetz und die Propheten: Untersuchungen zur Theologie des Evangelium nach Matthäus* (BU 11; Regensburg: Pustet, 1974).

—*Das Evangelium nach Matthäus: Übergesetzt und erklärt* (RNT; Regensburg: Pustet, 1986).

Sanders, E.P., 'Jesus and the Sinners', *JSNT* 19 (1983), pp. 5-36.

—*Jezus, mythe en werkelijkheid* (trans. L. Debroey; Nijkerk: Callenbach, 1996).

Sanders, E.P., and M. Davies, *Studying the Synoptic Gospels* (London: SCM, 1989).

Scheffler, E.H., 'Jesus from a Psychological Perspective', *Neot* 29.2 (1995), pp. 299-312.

Schmithals, W., *Wunder und Glauben: Eine Auslegung von Markus 4,35–6,6a* (Neukirchen: Neukirchener Verlag, 1970).

Schniewind, J., *Das Evangelium nach Matthäus: Übergesetzt und erklärt* (NTD 1, Vol. 2; Göttingen: Vandenhoeck & Ruprecht, 11th edn, 1964).

Scholes, R., (ed.) *Approaches to the Novel: Materials for a Poetics* (San Francisco: Chandler, rev. edn, 1966).

Scholes, R., and R. Kellogg, *The Nature of Narrative* (New York: Oxford University Press, 1966).

Schwartz, D.R., 'Josephus and Nicolaus on the Pharisees', *JSJ* 14.2 (1983), 157-71.

Schweizer, E., *The Good News according to Matthew* (trans. D.E. Green; Atlanta: John Knox, 1974).

—*Matthäus und seine Gemeinde* (SBS, 71; Stuttgart: KBW, 1975).

Scroggs, R., 'The Sociological Interpretation of the New Testament: The Present State of Research', in N.K. Gottwald (ed.), *The Bible and Liberation: Political and Social Hermeneutics* (Maryknoll, NY: Orbis Books, 1983), pp. 337-56.

Segal, A.F., 'Matthew's Jewish Voice', in Balch, *Social History of the Matthean Community*, pp. 3-37.

Simmel, G., *Conflict* (trans. K.H. Wolff; Glencoe: Free Press, 1955).

–'Conflict as Sociation', in Coser and Rosenberg, *Social Theory*, pp. 193-97.

Sites, P., 'Needs as Analogues of Emotions', in Burton, *Conflict*, pp. 7-33.

Smit, D.J., 'Die prediking van die wonderverhale in die evangelies', in C.W. Burger, B.A. Müller, and D.J. Smit (eds.), *Riglyne vir prediking oor die gelykenisse en wonderverhale* (Woord teen die Lig, II.2; Kaapstad: NG Kerk-Uitgewers, 1987), pp. 201-24.

Smith, M., *Jesus the Magician* (London: Gollancz, 1978).

Smith, R.H., *Augsburg Commentary on the New Testament: Matthew* (Minneapolis: Augsburg-Fortress, 1989).

—'Matthew's Message for Insiders: Charisma and Commandment in a First-century Community', *Int* 46.3 (1992), pp. 229-39.

Stanton, G.N., 'The Gospel of Matthew and Judaism', *BJRL* 66 (1984), pp. 264-84.

—*A Gospel for a New People: Studies in Matthew* (Edinburgh: T. & T. Clark, 1992).

—'The Communities of Matthew', *Int* 46.4 (1992), pp. 379-91.

Stambauch, J.E., and D.L. Balch, *The New Testament in its Social Environment* (Library of Early Christianity; Philadelphia: Westminster Press, 1986).

Stark, R., 'Jewish Conversion and the Rise of Christianity: Rethinking the Received Wisdom', in K.H. Richards (ed.), *SBLSP 1986* (Atlanta: Scholars Press, 1986), pp. 314-29.

—'Antioch as the Social Situation for Matthew's Gospel', in Balch, *Social History of the Matthean Community*, pp. 189-210.

Strack, H.L., and P. Billerbeck, *Exkurse zu einzelnen Stellen des Neuen Testaments: Abhandlung zur neutestamentlichen Theologie und Archäologie,* II (Kommentar zum Neuen Testament aus Talmud und Midrasch; Munich: Beck'sche Verlag, 4th edn, 1965).

Suhl, A. (ed.), *Der Wunderbegriff im Neuen Testament* (WdF, CCXCV; Darmstadt: Wissenschaftliche Buchgesellschaft, 1980).

—'Einleitung', in Suhl, *Der Wunderbegriff im Neuen Testament,* pp. 1-38.

—'Die Wunder Jesu: Ereignis und Überlieferung', in Suhl, *Der Wunderbegriff im Neuen Testament,* pp. 464-509.

Theissen, G., *Urchristliche Wundergeschichten: Ein Beitrag zur formgeschichtlichen Erforschung der synoptischen Evangelien* (StNT, 8; Gütersloh: Gütersloher Verlaghaus, 1974).

Thompson, W.G., 'Reflections on the Composition of Mt 8:1-9:34', *CBQ* 33 (1971), pp. 365-88.

Tiede, D.L., *The Charismatic Figure as Miracle Worker* (SBLDS, 1; Missoula, MT: Scholars Press, 1972).

Turner, J.H., 'From Utopia to Where? A Strategy for Reformulating the Dahrendorf Conflict Model', *Social Forc* 52 (1973), pp. 236-44.

—'A Strategy for the Reformulating of the Dialectical and Functional Theories of Conflict', *Social Forc* 53.3 (1975), pp. 433-44.

—*The Structure of Sociological Theory* (Homewood: Dorsey, rev. edn, 1978).

Turner, V., *The Ritual Process: Structure and Anti-structure* (Chicago: Aldine, 1969).

Valkenburgh, P., *Anatomie van het conflict: Een model theoretische benadering* (Alphen aan de Rijn: Samson, 1969).

Van Aarde, A.G., 'Die Vertellersperspektief-analise: 'n Literatuur-teoretiese benadering in die eksegese van die evangelies', *HTS* 38.4 (1982), pp. 58-82.

—'Immanuel as die geïnkarneerde Tora: Funksionele Jesusbenaminge in die Mattheusevangelie as Vertelling', *HTS* 43.1&2 (1987), pp. 242-77.

—'ἠγέρθη ἀπὸ τῶν νεκρῶν (Mt 28:7): A Textual Evidence on the Separation of Judaism and Christianity', *Neot* 23 (1989), pp. 219-33.

—'Die "heiligheid" van die kerk teen die agtergrond van die breuk kerk-sinagoge', *In die Skriflig* 24.3 (1990), pp. 251-63.

—'Narrative Criticism Applied to John 4:43-54', in P.J. Hartin and J.H. Petzer (eds.), *Text and Interpretation: New Approaches in Criticism of the New Testament* (Leiden: Brill, 1991), pp. 101-28.

—' "The Most High God Does Live in Houses, But Not Houses Built by Men . . . ": The Relativity of the Metaphor "Temple" in Luke–Acts', *Neot* 25.1 (1991), pp. 51-64.

—'A Silver Coin in the Mouth of a Fish (Matthew 17:24-27): A Miracle of Nature, Ecology, Economy and Politics of Holiness', *Neot* 27.1 (1993), pp. 1-25.

—'Aspekte van die sosiale stratifikasie van die ontwikkelde agrariese samelewing in die eerste-eeuse Palistina', *HTS* 49.3 (1993), pp. 515-45.

—*Kultuurhistoriese agtergrond van die Nuwe Testament: Die eerste-eeuse mediterreense sosiale konteks* (Pretoria: Kital, 1994).

—*God-with-Us: The Dominant Perspective in Matthew's Story, and Other Essays* (HTS Suppl., 5; Pretoria: Tydskrifafdeling van die Nederduitsch Hervormde Kerk, 1994).

Van de Beek, A., *Wonderen en wonderverhalen* (Nijkerk: Callenbach, 1991).

Van der Loos, H., *The Miracles of Jesus* (Leiden: Brill, 1968).

Van Doorn, J.A.A., 'Conflict in Formal Organizations', in A. De Reuck and J. Knight (eds.), *Conflict in Society* (CIBA Foundation; London: Churchill, 1966).

Van Eck, E., 'Galilee and Jerusalem in Mark's Story of Jesus: A Narratological and Social Scientific Interpretation', (DD dissertation; Pretoria: University of Pretoria, 1993).

Van Gennep, F.O., *De terugkeer van de verloren vader: Een theologisch essay over vaderschap en macht in cultuur en christendom* (Baarn: Ten Have, 1989).

Van Luxemburg, J., M. Bal, and W.G. Weststeijn, *Inleiding in de literatuurwetenschap* (Muiderberg: Coutinho, 2nd edn, 1982).

Van Parys, G., 'Functies van het sociaal conflict: Een poging tot herformulering en actualisering van enkele proposities van L.A. Coser', *Tijdschrift voor Sociale Wetenschappen* 25.4 (1980), pp. 377-98.

Van Staden, P., *Compassion—The Essence of Life: A Social-scientific Study of the Religious Symbolic Universe Reflected in the Ideology/Theology of Luke* (HTS Suppl., 4; Pretoria: Tydskrifafdeling van die Nederduitsch Hervormde Kerk, 1991).

Van Staden, P., and A.G. Van Aarde, 'Social Description or Social-scientific Interpretation? A Survey of Modern Scholarship', *HTS* 47.1 (1991), pp. 55-87.

Van Tilborg, S., *The Jewish Leaders in Matthew* (Leiden: Brill, 1972).

—*The Sermon on the Mount as an Ideological Intervention* (Assen: Van Gorcum, 1986).

—'Efese en het Johannesevangelie', *Schrift* 141 (1992), pp. 78-112.

—*Al lezend stemmen horen* (Nijmegen: Katholieke Universiteit Nijmegen, 1994).

Venter, L.S., 'Fokalisasie', in Cloete, *Literêre terme en teorië*, pp. 133-34.

—'Ruimte (Epiek)', in Cloete, *Literêre terme en teorië*, pp. 453-55.

Vledder, E.-J., 'Die rol van "historisiteit" in die kommunikasie van die wondervertelling: "n Evaluasie van twee eksegetiese benaderinge', *HTS* 40.2 (1984), pp. 71-119.

—'"n Kritiese evaluasie van Colin Brown se studie: "Miracles and the Critical Mind"', *HTS* 42.2 (1986), pp. 327-38.

—'Conflict in the Miracle Stories in Matthew 8 and 9: A Sociological and Exegetical Study' (DD dissertation; Pretoria: University of Pretoria, 1994).

Voelz, J.W., 'Response to Detlev Dormeyer: Analysis of Matthew 8 and 9' (unpublished SNTS paper, 1991).

Vorster, W.S., Towards a Post-critical Paradigm: Progress in New Testament Scholarship, in Mouton, Van Aarde and Vorster, *Paradigms and Progress in Theology*, pp. 31-48.

Wallace, R.A., and A. Wolf, *Contemporary Sociological Theory: Continuing the Classical Tradition* (Englewood Cliffs, NJ: Prentice–Hall, 3rd edn, 1991).

White, L.M., 'Crisis Management and Boundary Maintenance: The Social Location of the Matthean Community', in Balch, *Social History of the Matthean Community*, pp. 212-47.

Wild, R.A., 'The Encounter between Pharisaic and Christian Judaism: Some Early Gospel Evidence', *NovT* 27.2 (1985), pp. 105-24.

Wright, E.O., *Class Structure and Income Determination* (New York: Academic Press, 1979).

INDEXES

INDEX OF REFERENCES

OLD TESTAMENT

INDEX OF AUTHORS